The Last Ottoman Wars

The Last Ottoman Wars

THE HUMAN COST, 1877–1923

JEREMY SALT

THE UNIVERSITY OF UTAH PRESS
Salt Lake City

The Defiance House Man colophon is a registered trademark of
The University of Utah Press. It is based on a four-foot-tall Ancient
Puebloan pictograph (late PIII) near Glen Canyon, Utah.

CIP data for this titls is available from the Library of Congress at https://lccn.loc.gov/
2018060585.

Errata and further information on this and other titles available online at
UofUpress.com

Printed and bound in the United States of America.

Contents

Acknowledgments

I am grateful to the true Ottoman scholars, including students at my former university (Bilkent), whose intensive primary research has benefitted this more-general study of late Ottoman history. I thank them all for the documentary detail that is essential to historical research. I also wish to thank others who helped in various ways by providing rare books or pointing to sources, among them Nuri Yildirim and Fatma Sarıkaya. With the help of Uğur Belger of Izmir, Nuri put me on the trail to more information about Hasan Tahsin (Osman Nevres), who fired the first Turkish shot after Greek troops landed on the Izmir waterfront in 1919. Fatma provided a rare, neutral source on the great fire in Izmir: Fred K. Nielsen, *American-Turkish Claims Settlement Under the Agreement of December 24, 1923, and Supplemental Agreements Between the United States and Turkey. Opinions and Reports* (Washington: United States Government Printing Office, 1937). Atilla Oral joined in the search for a suitable cover illustration. I am grateful for his assistance.

Very many thanks are due to Mehmet Oğuzhan Tulun, who found and translated excerpts from four books on the war and its aftermath: Halil Ataman, *Harp ve Esaret: Doğu Cephesi'nden Sibiriya'ya* [War and Captivity: From the Eastern Front to Siberia] (Istanbul: Türkiye İş Bankası Kültür Yayınları, 2014); Sami Önal, *Tuğgeneral Ziya Yergök'un Anıları: Sarıkamış'tan Esarete (1915–1920)* [Brigadier General Ziya Yergök's Memoirs: From Sarikamiş to Captivity (1915–1920)] (Istanbul: Remzi Kitabevi, 2007); and Mehmet Törehan Serdar, *Istiklale Açilan Ilk Kapı: Bitlis (Işgali ve Kurtuluşu)* [The First Door Opening to Independence: Bitlis (Occupation and Liberation)] (Bitlis: Bitlis Valiliği Kültür Yayınları, 2017), as well as Gürsoy Solmaz, *Ikinci Kuşak Anılarında Erzurum ve Civarında Ermeni Zulmü* [Armenian Oppression in Erzurum and Its Surroundings

According to Second-Generation Memoirs], *Yeni Turkiye* 60 (2014):1–29. Oğuzhan was always ready with helpful advice, no matter how busy he happened to be. Very many thanks are also due to Erman Şahin, a fine young scholar, who read two chapters, made helpful suggestions (and one correction), and pointed me in the direction of further useful research material.

Professor Justin McCarthy, Distinguished University Scholar at the University of Louisville, not only helped to select the maps that appear in the book but prepared them for publication. I wish to thank him for his generous assistance.

Thanks are also due to the editorial staff of the University of Utah Press for seeing the manuscript through to publication, especially Dr. John Alley, Editor-in-Chief when I made my initial approach; Pat Hadley, Managing Editor; Thomas Krause, Acquisitions Editor; and Jeff Grathwohl, who edited the text with patience, care, and consideration. On the business side, the marketing and packaging of the book were handled by Hannah New, Marketing Manager, and Dianne Lee Van Dien, Marketing Assistant. Many thanks to both of them for their enthusiastic participation in this project.

Professor Ali Doğramacı, former Rector of Bilkent University and currently Chairman of the university's Board of Trustees, arranged a modest financial grant when I took leave without pay in 2009–2010 to begin research for the book. Ali was a mainstay of daily academic life at Bilkent for many years, an ebullient and cheery figure on campus, never forgetting names and always encouraging academic staff to follow through on their ideas. I am grateful for his friendship and his help.

Thanks also to the Turkish people, whose taxes were the ultimate source of the research grant, provided through the Ministry of Foreign Affairs, which, along with the grant arranged by Ali, helped me get through a fairly impecunious year of reading, taking notes, and writing in the Australian countryside.

The book now published is very different from the one I thought of writing in 2009. I had intended to write just on the First World War as experienced in the Ottoman Empire, concentrating on the human cost. However, it was not long before I realized that the war came toward the end of a fifty-year cycle of history, one part leading to the next and all fitting together, creating the necessary context for understanding what happened after war broke out in 1914. The cycle ends with the Turkish War of Independence (1919–1922). Sources were an early issue. As nearly

90 percent of the Ottoman civilian population was illiterate in 1914, diaries would not have been written. First-hand experiences were recorded when armies and government administrators were able to return to occupied regions. There are many such documents in the archives, but not until many decades later—when the generation that survived the war was well into its old age—were oral histories recorded.

While much has been written on the fate of Ottoman Christians, the Muslim majority disappeared into history as if it had never existed. Recent books have begun to bring these previously invisible Muslims back into the light of day, and my overriding hope with this book is that I have gathered sufficient information to convey the enormity of their suffering. For the Ottoman civilians, the war was a catastrophe on an epic scale.

Some chapters here will be regarded as "controversial" because they challenge the mainstream narrative on late-Ottoman history. They are not controversial to me, for they put back into history what should have been there in the first place. I have written only the truth as I see it. No historian can do more. Some of the history—especially in the Balkans—is a complex mélange of names and dates that had to be digested. I have tried to avoid mistakes and errors of fact, but if I have still made them—and no doubt I have—the responsibility is all mine.

Maps

AUSTRIA - HUNGARY

RUMANIA

• Belgrade

• Bucharest

Saray

SERBIA

Sofia

MONTE-
NEGRO

• Üsküdar

OTTOMAN
EMPIRE

Edirne

İstanbul

Selanik

Bursa

GREECE

İzmir

Athens

OTTOMAN RULE

AUTONOMOUS

1876

MAP 1. Ottoman territories in the Balkans before the Ottoman-Russian war of 1877–1878.

MAP 2. Ottoman territories in the Balkans after the 1877–1878 war. While Bosnia remained sovereign Ottoman territory, according to the Treaty of Berlin (1878) it was placed under the occupation and administration of Austria-Hungary.

MAP 3. The Balkans after the war of conquest launched by four Balkan states (Bulgaria, Serbia, Greece, and Montenegro) in 1912. While they eventually fought among themselves over the spoils of war, all remaining Ottoman territory in the Balkans—with the exception of eastern Thrace (Trakya)—had gone by the end of 1913.

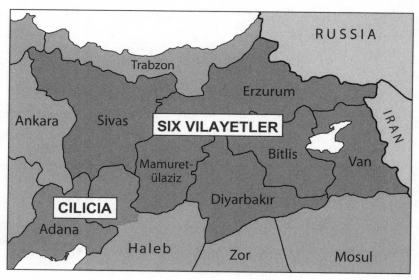

MAP 4. The six eastern *vilayetler* (sing. *vilayet*) that were at the center of European "reform" plans in the late nineteenth century.

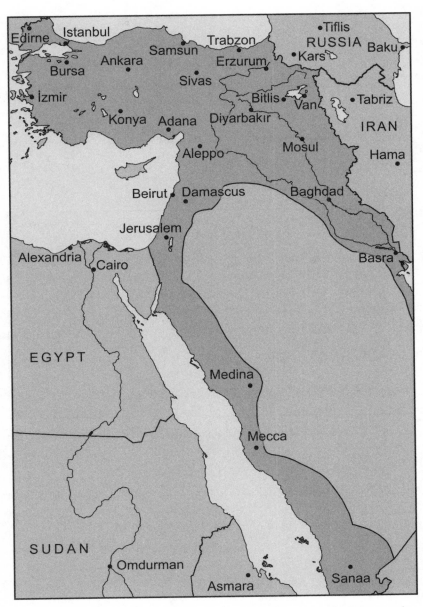

MAP 5. The Ottoman Empire in 1914. On the western Arabian Peninsula, Ottoman rule stretched as far south as Yemen until the collapse of the empire in 1918.

MAP 6. The borders of modern Turkey as ratified under the Treaty of Lausanne (1923).

Introduction

HOW SHOULD A WAR be studied, any war? How deep does the historian need to dig to discover the roots? What needs to be understood before even looking at what happened on the battlefield? How much needs to be known about government, finance, infrastructure, and social relations? Insofar as Britain, Germany, or France were concerned, the answers to many of these questions—as they relate to the First World War—would be taken for granted. Logistics are always an issue in war, but one need not ask whether these countries had a rail network or a developed road system because it would be known that they did. Russia and the Ottoman Empire fitted into different categories. Away from the cities, in the distant provinces, both were underdeveloped and closer to medieval than modern life, as measured by western European standards. Culturally, Russia was Christian but Orthodox, its rites even more florid to an English or German Protestant than those of the Catholic church. With its territories in the east stretching to the borders of China and down into Central Asia, it could accurately be called "half Asiatic," in the language of the time, but the expression was more pejorative than geographical. The jump from "half Asiatic" to "half barbarian" was a small one when war beckoned, and the threatening profile of the Russian "bear" needed to be magnified.

The Ottoman Empire was even more of an unknown. Indeed, what was frequently thought to be known was not known at all but was rather the product of centuries of religious and ethnic prejudice against Islam and "the Turk," fed constantly by the bad press arising from chronic Ottoman maladministration. Diplomats and consuls grappled with the causes in their dispatches, sometimes fairly, often not, but these accounts were far too complex and tedious in their detail to be summed up in any newspaper article and of interest anyway only to the small number of readers whose concern with Ottoman affairs went beyond the marginal. What did capture the imagination were the graphic and generally lurid accounts of the mistreatment of Christians in the Balkans at the hands of the "bashibozuks" (*başıbozuk,* "broken head," irregular soldiers) or the Kurds in eastern Anatolia. These reports were usually pieced together far from the scene weeks and sometimes even months later. They were often based on questionable sources, but this was the Ottoman Empire as it was generally understood in the run-up to the First World War.

Across this faltering empire, how did all the pieces fit together? Away from the battlefield, how did this war affect the lives—or end the lives— of the civilian population? While the social history of wars has caught up with the history of wars in Europe, this cannot be said of Turkey yet. The suffering of Ottoman Christians, especially the Armenians, has been the subject of many studies, but the immense losses suffered by Ottoman Muslims between 1877 and 1923 still have virtually no place in the "western" cultural mainstream, despite the epic nature of what they went through and often did not survive. Between 1877 and 1914, the Balkans were largely cleansed of their Muslim population, massacred or stampeded out of towns and villages by advancing armies in what we would now not hesitate to call ethnic cleansing. During the First World War and the fighting that continued afterwards, millions more Muslim civilians died in Anatolia, the Caucasus, and Iran or were turned into refugees. A central theme of this study will be to bring these invisible victims of war back into the picture. As long as they are outside the frame, how can any history of this period and these events be considered history?

In the last decades of its life, weakened by wars, uprisings, and chronic financial problems that affected society at all levels, the Ottoman government could only patch up problems that needed a permanent solution. Endlessly on the defensive, it was able through these repairs to defer but not prevent the final collapse in 1918. With the powers occupying Istanbul, the sultan was turned into a cooperative prisoner in his own palace, as strongly opposed to the nationalist "rebels," "outlaws," and "bandits" as his captors were until it became apparent that it was these "rebels" who had the support of the people and not the sultan.

One by one the Turkish nationalists defeated all their enemies. At this point the game was almost up. With only Britain left, David Lloyd George called on Commonwealth and Dominion governments to send troops back to the theater of war they had only recently left. However, his apparent readiness to take on "the Turks," rather than yield control of the straits, was never put to the test. France had already backed out of this entanglement, and now the various components of empire either said no to his request or made only token offers of help. Their unwillingness to go to war again on behalf of the British government and its imperial interests cleared the way for negotiations that ended with the recognition by the powers of the Turkish republic within its present borders.

This was a real peace compared to the "peace" in Paris, the consequences of which raise the question, "peace for whom?" Insofar as Germany was concerned, the punitive terms of Versailles set the stage for economic and social turmoil, the capture of power by the National Socialists, and eventually the Second World War. In the Ottoman Empire, the imposition of the mandates and the attempted imposition of the Treaty of Sèvres—the harsh Turkish parallel to Versailles—precipitated armed resistance in all territories that fell under allied occupation. The Turkish nationalists fought the French in what is now southeastern Turkey and after three years finally turned back an invasion that had brought a Greek army to within a day's march of Ankara.

In Article 22 of the League of Nations Covenant, the mandate system was described as a "sacred trust" of civilization. In Iraq, Syria, and Palestine, the phrase was sugar coating for an occupation pushed through with such force as was deemed necessary. The reality of the "sacred trust" was French tanks and the bodies of dead "rebels" put on display in the middle of Damascus, British planes bombing Kurdish villages in northern Iraq, British and colonial troops suppressing tribal uprisings in southern Iraq, and British troops and police killing thousands of Palestinians during the 1936–1939 uprising.

In western Turkey, a war launched by Greece in the name of fulfilling the Megali Idea turned a largely spontaneous struggle against occupation into a war of Turkish national resistance. Four days after the Greek landing at Izmir on May 15, 1919, Mustafa Kemal (given the surname of "Atatürk," "father of the Turks," in 1934 by the Grand National Assembly, the Turkish parliament) stepped ashore at the Black Sea port of Samsun and moved to the safety of the interior. At this transitional point between the collapse of the Ottoman Empire and the rise of the Turkish nation state, there was not yet a Turkish "people." However, the collective threat from Greece, Britain, and France was so great that ethnonational differences (especially between Kurds and Turks) had to take second place to a united national front. Ultimately, it was the Greek and Turkish peoples who paid the price for this war through death, large-scale destruction by the Greek army, and the population exchange of 1923.

In its declining years down to 1914 the enfeeblement of the Ottoman Empire went a stage further after each war it lost. The cost was not just lost territory and a twice-shattered army (after the 1877–1878 war with Russia and the Balkans war of 1912–1913) but the financial consequences, measured not just by the big things, i.e., the inability of the government to meet the interest on loans taken out on the European money market but the more mundane aspects of government: its inability to pay bills and the salaries of soldiers and civil servants (*memurlar*) on time, degrading its capacity to govern effectively and institute the reforms needed to pull the empire into a modern age characterized by industry, improved infrastructure, and centralized education and social welfare systems. Some parts of the empire had more of such things (the cities, Istanbul, Izmir, and Beirut, for example), but none had all of them, and in many parts of the empire they were absent altogether.

Maladministration and the inability of the government to defend the empire against aggression weakened it even in the eyes of the sultan's Muslim subjects. The earlier successes of Greek and Bulgarian nationalists encouraged Armenians and other Christians to follow them in the pursuit of autonomy and eventual independence. The hope (if not the expectation) of intervention by the powers was a critical element in their calculations. What is perhaps surprising is that an empire beset by so many lethal problems was able to remain standing for so long. Even right at the end it had sufficient strength to send a conquering army all the way to Baku.

The geography in this study ranges from the Balkans to eastern Anatolia and the Caucasus. The politics involves the interests of the Ottoman government, the European powers, and the Balkan monarchs for whom Ottoman weakness sharpened grandiose and irreconcilable irredentist claims. Their servants were quarrelling politicians and army officers who might not always be loyal, sometimes with lethal consequences. Ultranationalists, secret societies, and the church complicated politics still further. Every Balkan state had its backers among the European powers, whose endless jockeying for advantage created space for the scheming of their proteges. The inability of the Ottoman government to put its own house in order completed the mix, turning the Balkans into an arena of chronic political instability. Finally, the assassination of Archduke Franz Ferdinand in 1914 turned this house of straw into chaff.

Having just fought two more wars—after all the wars of the nineteenth century—in Libya (1911–1912) and against four Balkan states (1912–1913), the Ottoman Empire finally came off the fence in late 1914 and joined the war that ended in its destruction. In Ottoman domains, this was a modern war fought in a premodern setting. The rail networks, roads, communications systems, supply systems, arms factories, and industrialization of western Europe scarcely existed in Ottoman lands. Soldiers often had to walk long distances to the front. Diseases might kill them before they got there. In many of the war zones, there were no railways to carry supplies and ammunition to the front, so armies had to rely on wagons and draft animals.

These conditions affected the lives of civilians as well. In the eastern Anatolian provinces, the conveniences of life that people in Europe took for granted did not exist. Hospitals, clinics, and pharmacies were few and for all practical purposes inaccessible to people living in remote villages. The basics of sanitation and health care were scarcely understood and rarely applied in daily life, let alone even in hospitals. It is partly, if not largely, for these reasons that the death toll among soldiers from disease was higher than on the battlefield. As the army had some sort of integrated health system and civilians did not, the civilian death rate was probably proportionally higher. Only estimates can be made but the civilian deaths from all wartime causes probably hovers around 3 million.

Just as Justin McCarthy has published seminal studies on the fate of Muslims in the Balkans and Anatolia,[1] so Leila Tarazi Fawaz has focused on civilian life in Syria during the First World War.[2] In an even more recent study, Yiğit Akın has dealt with the misery of war on the home front, including the burdens carried by rural women in the absence of men.[3] All Ottoman civilians suffered terribly, irrespective of religious or ethnic background, and I follow as well as I can the consequences of the war in their daily lives. Disease, malnutrition, exposure, and internecine massacres were the prime causes of the death toll, with Allied blockades of the Mediterranean and Black Sea coasts destroying the import-export trade on which local cash economies were based and disrupting the transport of food and other daily necessities from one part of the empire to another.

Originally, I planned to write a book just on the First World War as experienced in and by the Ottoman Empire. However, I soon concluded that 1914–1918 would be more effectively discussed as part of fifty-year cycle of history, beginning with the Ottoman-Russian war of 1877–1878 and ending in 1922 after a Greek army invading Ottoman lands had been driven back to the Aegean coast. Resistance to this final attack—launched by Greece in 1919—soon turned into a war of national independence. By the time it ended the Ottoman Empire was gone and a Turkish Republic had emerged from the ruins. The trail I follow starts with the financial problems that affected every aspect of Ottoman life. It then moves to the nature of the land and the difficulties experienced by the people living on it before I turn to the crisis of 1877–1878 and its consequences.

The settlement of this conflict opened up the question of "reform" for the Armenian population of the eastern Anatolian provinces. Its strongest advocate was Britain, whose strategic interests lay in preventing Russia from capitalizing on Christian grievances in eastern Anatolia as it was thought to have just done in the Balkans. The "reforms" as proposed would have entailed provincial reorganization benefiting Armenians but excluding the Kurds, who, along with the sultan and ministers at the Bab i-Ali (Sublime Porte) government offices, reacted to these plans with the suspicion they undoubtedly deserved. The scene was thus set for conflict with the western European powers (particularly Britain), confrontation with Armenian revolutionary committees encouraged by European support, and a struggle between Armenians and Kurds over territory they both claimed that was to culminate in the violence of the First World War.

If quotes must be used around "reform," it is because European "reforms" for the Ottoman Empire were politically driven, ultimately, and were often inconsistent with the reforms the sultan and his ministers had in mind. "Reform" was also on the agenda in the Balkans, where four monarchs took advantage of political upheaval in Istanbul and the Italian invasion of Libya in 1911 to launch their own war against the Ottoman state in 1912. This counterpoint to the conflict of 1877–1878 largely completed the ethnic cleansing of Muslims from southeastern Europe: with Macedonia gone, all that remained was eastern Thrace and the small pockets of Muslims left in the victorious states. France and Britain had occupied Tunisia (1881) and Egypt (1882) before the European powers allowed Italy to join the imperial club by seizing Libya in 1911. A year later they sat back as four Balkan states embarked on a war of conquest against the Ottoman Empire: in the wash-up they allowed the aggressors to retain the spoils, which greatly enlarged Greece, in particular. These were the same powers that had repeatedly reaffirmed the commitment they had made in the settlement of the Crimean War (1853–1856) to maintain the territorial integrity of the Ottoman Empire. What really seemed to be on their minds was a share of the spoils when the empire finally collapsed. Could it be wondered that even by the 1880s the Ottoman government was turning toward Germany?

There is substantial evidence in support of this interpretation of history. Margaret MacMillan's reference to the British government having "propped up" the Ottoman government has to be questioned. The empire had certainly proved useful at times of crisis (most notably during the Crimean War) but otherwise Britain and other countries had kicked away the props whenever it suited individual or joint interests. Their central concern was that premature action by one power might suck all into a European war. Britain played this game of imperial chess more deftly than most, taking territory for itself when possible and allowing others to help themselves as long as they did not step on Britain's toes. If their annexations actively served British interests, all the better. Britain also meddled in the "Armenian question" without being prepared to pay for the "reforms" it was demanding or having a fallback plan when the sticks being turned in this wasp's nest upended it in the 1890s.

Under the heading of "battlefield sketches," some of the major military campaigns are covered in this study, but the bulk of the chapter on the "last Ottoman war" deals with the terrible consequences for the civilian population. Many narratives give the impression of a binary division between Muslim perpetrators of large-scale violence and Christian victims. In fact, there was no such division. Circumstances might change according to the fortunes of war, but Christians and Muslims alike were both perpetrators and innocent victims of such violence.

One would think that 1914–1918 was enough war for the time being but no sooner had it ended than the victors plunged into other wars: the small wars needed to impose their occupation on Arabs and Turks, the "war of intervention" against the Bolsheviks in the Caucasus, and the Greek invasion of western Turkey in 1919, strongly supported by Britain. Between 1918 and 1920, the victorious powers calculated that they could carve up the Middle East to suit themselves. In the short term, their calculations were borne out, thanks to their tools of diplomatic and economic persuasion ultimately backed by military power and the willingness to use it.

Even a book of this size can only skate across a broad surface. Categories that have been scarcely touched include the postwar fate of Ottoman civilians, the Armenians whose property had been stolen, the Muslims whose villages and homes had been destroyed, the orphans who had been placed in care, and the enormous flow of uprooted people. These themes are still far from having been fully explored, often generating more propaganda heat than historical light.

This study was written as an extended overview of late Ottoman history. While it is to be hoped that it will hold the attention of the specialist scholar, the primary intended audience is the general reader, outside Turkey, avid for history, knowing little of the Ottoman past beyond what is available in the mainstream, but open to challenges to what he or she might have read and believe to be true. I follow the historical trail only where it leads: interpretations are my own and finally, as always, responsibility for factual errors rests with the author.

Burhaniye, March 2019

A NOTE ON SPELLING AND NAMES

In the spelling of personal and place names, I have followed modern Turkish except where I am quoting directly from source. Thus, it is Abdülhamit rather than Abdulhamid, Zeytun rather than Zeitun or Zaytun, Istanbul rather than Constantinople, and Izmir rather than Smyrna. In the Caucasus and the Balkans, many cities underwent name changes as a result of war. I use the name by which the city was known, within the sovereign territory of which it was part, until the point of conquest and the subsequent name change: thus, Ottoman Selanik up to 1912 and Salonica following the capture of the city by Greece, and Tiflis until the reversion to Georgian Tbilisi after the collapse of the Russian empire. I have tried to be consistent, but the observant reader will no doubt pick up inconsistencies.

PART I

Late Ottoman Society

CHAPTER I

Cash-Flow Calamities

"ENDLESS MONEY FORMS THE SINEWS OF WAR." So wrote Cicero. More commonly, these days, his maxim is recycled just as "money is the sinews of war," from which we are invited to conclude that if there were no money, there could be no war. Unless we return to the days when humans killed each other with stones and sharpened sticks, this is undoubtedly true. Money is the staple diet of war. It pays not just for the weapons but food, medicine, fuel, clothing, transport, and the sustenance of the civilian population as well as the military. Money and the weapons it can buy will not always succeed in the face of human determination, but between rich and poor, money certainly gives the rich a powerful advantage.

At the same time, the cost of war can also bankrupt those on the winning side: Britain, broke and humiliatingly dependent on a former colony after the Second World War, is a prime example of the sour side of victory. The obverse of Cicero's observation is that money also forms the sinews of peace. "Good" government, social stability, and economic stability are all tied together by money. Thus, the unstable supply of money goes a long way toward explaining the severe problems experienced by the Ottoman Empire in the last cycle of its history.

By the end of the nineteenth century, the empire had fought many wars in its long life, but it was a long time since it had won one, partly because endless wars degrade the capacity to fight future ones. Peaking early, in the seventeenth century, the empire then had to struggle to hold its territory against the successive assaults of a dynamic and expanding Russia. Russia was an empire it could not defeat, however many wars it fought. In the nineteenth century, the loss of territory in the Caucasus, the Balkans, and around the shores of the Black Sea set the scene for further Russian triumphs. The loss of territory meant the loss of strategic position and the loss of population, crops, and tax revenue.

The territorial shrinking of the empire awakened consternation and alarm in Istanbul. Battlefield losses were only a symptom of a much deeper malaise. It was not just the military that needed reform but the entire system of government and the values on which it was based. This was how the reform movement unfolded in the nineteenth century, beginning with practical measures that led logically to an examination of the abstract values underpinning the strength of modern European societies. Ottoman Muslims would need to understand why modernizing reforms were being introduced, why, for example, it was necessary for Christians and Muslims to be equal before the same law and why, toward that end, *shari'a* (Turkish *şeriat*) law would have to be supplanted by secular codes imported from Europe. Effectively, the government was asking people to reframe the values and codes of behavior they had always taken for granted.

The general principle of equality before the law for all Ottoman subjects was expressed in two imperial decrees, the Hatt-i Şerif of 1839 and the Hatt-i Hümayun of 1856. While it may be true that the second decree was "essentially made in Europe and autochthonous in form alone,"[1] there is no doubt of the genuine push for reform by Ottoman statesmen. One problem was that while proceeding too slowly for European tastes, Ottoman reformers were moving too quickly for many of the sultan's subjects—especially imams, teachers, and judges still bound to traditional ways of thinking—who were in a position to influence the broader population.

Nowhere was this truer than in the question of the principles of religious equality affirmed by the sultan in 1856. He decreed that "every distinction or designation tending to make any class whatever of the subjects of my empire inferior to another class on account of their religion, language, or race shall be forever effaced." Furthermore, "As all forms of religion are and shall be freely professed in my dominions, no subject of my empire shall be hindered in the exercise of the religion that he professes." There were to be no distinctions in government employment, and mixed tribunals would be set up to deal with civil or criminal cases involving Muslims and Christians. How could these changes *not* be seen by conservative Muslims as a deadly challenge to the traditional order? Thus, while Christians celebrated, they mourned and, in some cases, vowed noncompliance.

In Europe, it was frequently argued that Ottoman reforms were a cloud of dust kicked up to give the impression that something was being done when in fact nothing was being done. The accusation was more representative of European bias than Ottoman reality. While reforms were introduced under European influence or pressure, the sultan and his ministers knew that reforms were badly needed (if not always the reforms envisaged by the European powers) and pursued them with persistence across decades.

The Muslim population of the empire was respectful of the sultan's position as *padişah* (a royal title of Persian origin) but it was mostly illiterate (and thus ill-equipped to understand the motives behind the reform movement), conservative, and deeply suspicious of the central government as represented in their towns and villages by officials, especially tax collectors and conscription agents.

The population of Anatolia was an ethnoreligious mosaic, overwhelmingly Muslim but with a substantial Christian population consisting mostly of Armenians and small Assyrian communities settled in the southeast. The ethnicities included Turks, Kurds, Circassians, Alevis, Laz (from the Black Sea coast), and nomadic Yörük tribal groups. In the Balkan territories, Muslim and Christian villages were interspersed. Nationalism eventually created a common Christian front against the Muslims, but among themselves the Christians were divided by deep doctrinal, territorial, and ethnic divisions centering on their self-perceived place in history.

"Ottomanism" was the ultimately failed attempt to bind the mosaic together by creating what had never existed before: an Ottoman sense of identity that would subsume all religious and ethnic differences.

MONEY AND SOCIAL ORDER

Throughout the nineteenth century, the Ottoman Empire suffered a chronic cash flow problem. The gyrations at the center as the government tried to make ends meet were felt in the daily lives of soldiers and civil servants who were underpaid, not paid on time, and sometimes not paid at all. In a society based on the payment of cash for goods, services and rent, the failure to pay could only breed resentment, corruption, mismanagement, and social decay the longer such a situation continued. The construction of palaces and the well-cushioned lives of sultans and *paşas* stood in stark contrast to those with scarcely enough to survive.

However, the central cause of the cash flow problem was not the profligacy of the ruling elites above what might be expected (sultans were no different from other monarchs in needing that extra palace to impress their royal peers) but the wars and loss of territory that emptied the treasury and shriveled the revenue base. As hard as it tried to reach financial *terra firma*, the Ottoman Empire was in the stumbling position of a man who takes one step forward only to be forced into taking one (or two) backwards. One crisis had scarcely subsided before the next appeared on the horizon, leaving the government continually struggling to catch its breath.

In his outstanding history of the Ottoman Bank, Edhem Eldem has penetrated the dark recesses of Ottoman finances. To the destructive long-term effects of war on the economic and therefore social stability of the Ottoman Empire must be added the effects of the Industrial Revolution and the steady absorption of the Ottoman economy into a world system dominated by the interests and needs of European governments.

The empire had more capacity to resist the encroaching European powers than any other Muslim territory but not enough to avoid a state of semidependency. As Professor Eldem has observed, "Ever since the 15th century, the Ottoman lands had enjoyed a relative prosperity linked to a considerable development of agriculture, trade, crafts production and finance,"[2] but with the Industrial Revolution the Ottoman economy "gave rise to a clear pattern of domination which gradually developed into a quasi-colonial situation of almost total dependence on western trade, finance, and capital."[3]

The Europeans were in the market for Egyptian sugar, tobacco, and cotton. In southeastern Anatolia, the magnet was the cotton of Çukurova; along the Black Sea, it was the coal of Zonguldak and the tobacco of the Bafra region. Mt. Lebanon produced raw silk, while the Syrian coastal seaboard was rich in citrus fruit (the famous Jaffa orange) and cereal crops down as far as Gaza (wheat and barley). Glassware and soap were produced on a smaller scale.

What left the empire as raw material would return as finished products, sheets, tablecloths, and farming or kitchen utensils. As these industrially manufactured items were often cheaper than the local product, the role of the artisan and therefore of his guild (*esnaf*) had to diminish. And as the guild was linked to the market, the mosque, and religious orders, a changing economic order meant a changing social order.

In Egypt, the sultan's Egyptian viceroy, Mehmet Ali (Arabic: Muhammad 'Ali), illiterate until middle age but clever, cunning, shrewd, ruthless when necessary, and possessed of great political skill, was determined to be master in his own house. This did not mean that he was hostile to foreigners, only that he would use them in his house but not allow them to run it. He employed Europeans to reorganize the Egyptian army and its medical services and even to run some of his small factories. European merchants flourished but only within the constraints he allowed. He would determine the country's development: from its resources alone, he would raise the capital needed to bring Egypt into the modern age as a fully independent state.

The growing, harvesting, and marketing of the most lucrative Egyptian primary products—sugar, cotton, and tobacco—were all controlled by his government. In a small-workshop way, Mehmet Ali began the process of industrialization as well. His intent was clear: sooner or later Egyptian and not European factories would be processing the bulk of that sugar, cotton, and tobacco. This could not be allowed by an industrializing Europe dependent on raw material from colonized lands far from its borders, and neither—for strategic reasons—could an independent Egypt be allowed to arise on the African coast of the Mediterranean Sea. Mehmet Ali's challenge to European domination drove the British Foreign Secretary, Lord Palmerston, into outbursts of splenetic rage: "For my part," he once wrote, "I hate Mehemet [*sic*] Ali, whom I consider as nothing but an ignorant barbarian, who by cunning and boldness and mother wit has been successful in rebellion."[4]

European political and commercial pressure finally met with success in the treaty of Balta Limanı (1838), signed at a time the sultan badly needed British support against Mehmet Ali. The treaty eliminated monopolies and opened up all Ottoman markets (not just the Egyptian) to British merchants, who were privileged with a 3 percent domestic transit duty compared to 8 percent for Ottoman subjects.[5] Over time, Mehmet Ali's attempts to establish "economic self-sufficiency and industrialization" withered on the vine. The poison chalice from which he was made to sip was "a permanent influx of foreign capital and foreign goods, which would indubitably deprive the country of any financial and economic independence."[6] In the long term, foreigners would run his house after all.

Politically, the treaty exacerbated the crisis that had been developing throughout the 1830s between Istanbul and Cairo. In June 1839, an Egyptian army led by Mehmet Ali's son Ibrahim moved north from Syria and defeated an Ottoman army at Nezib (now Nizip in Turkey's Gaziantep province). The Egyptian army could have continued toward Istanbul with little obstruction. Alarmed, Britain intervened in support of the sultan. Mehmet Ali was threatened and finally persuaded to withdraw from Syria on the promise of being confirmed as Egypt's hereditary ruler.

The confrontation with Mehmet Ali was only one of many crises marking the rule of Mahmud II (1808–1839). Barely escaping with his life even before he became sultan, he continued the program of administrative and military reforms begun by his overthrown and murdered predecessor, Selim III.[7] In 1826 he wiped out the janissaries, replacing them with a new standing army, initially called the Muallem Asakir-i Mansure-i Muhammadiye (Trained Triumphant Soldiers of Muhammad) but eventually known simply as the Asakir-i Mansure. Modelled on Selim III's *Nizam-i Cedid* (New Organization) army, by the 1830s the Asakir-i Mansure had grown to a force of about 120,000 men.[8] Recruitment was accompanied by training on the latest military lines (by European officers), new weaponry and new uniforms, and the application of reforms all the way down to provisioning and the creation of a better-educated officer class.[9]

At the same time, Mahmud II was determined to centralize power, a process that involved administrative reform, provincial reorganization, and the extension of the state's authority to all corners of the empire. Those who stood in the way (Serbian, Albanian, and Kurdish rebels for example) would be ruthlessly suppressed.[10] What the sultan had in mind stood at odds with the Ottoman tradition of government. As Şükrü Hanioğlu has observed, the Ottoman Empire was "an empire in the loose sense in which the term is used to refer to such medieval states as the Chinese under the T'ang dynasty." In the Ottoman state, the authority of the central government "rarely extended beyond the central provinces of Anatolia and then only weakly."[11] In the context of the modern European state, the empire was hardly a "state" at all.

RAISING REVENUE

The connections between war, uprisings, reform, and money are clear. A government as internally and externally harassed as the Ottoman government in the nineteenth century will be so busy defending itself it will scarcely be able to press ahead with reforms. Şevket Pamuk has estimated that government expenditures increased by 250 to 300 percent from the end of the eighteenth century to the late 1830s.[12] Mahmud II's achievements were striking but whether he was creating a new army or putting down rebellion, money remained the problem. It was not sitting somewhere waiting to be spent but would have to be raised.

In the period before the development of banks, loans from the Greek *sarraflar* or "financiers" of Galata were one source of revenue, but it was not long before the Ottoman government was looking at other options. One was to reduce the silver content in coinage. Such "debasement" of the main item of currency, the *kuruş* (subdivided into 120 *akçes*) would enable the government to increase the volume of money in circulation while holding down the cost of minting it.

The demand for money was highest at a time of war. It is no coincidence that the highest rate of coinage debasement in Ottoman history—the "Great Debasement" (1808–1834), as it is called in economic histories[13]—took place against a background of war with Russia (1806–1812 and 1828–1829), Iran (1820–1828), Egypt (the Syrian campaigns of 1831–1833), and internal uprisings that included the Greek revolt (1821–1827), the rebellion by Ali Paşa of Janina (Iannino) of 1820–1822, and the Wahhabi uprising in the Hijaz and central Arabia, put down by the Egyptians in a series of campaigns that ran from 1811 to 1818.[14]

With the exception of gold, metal coinage (copper and silver) was debased thirty times and lost 80 percent of its value over three decades.[15] In four years alone (1828–1832), the specie content of the *kuruş* was reduced by 79 percent. Pamuk observes that whereas in 1788 the exchange rate for one Venetian ducat was 5½ *kuruş* and for 1 pound sterling 11 *kuruş*, by 1844 the value had crashed to 50–52 *kuruş* for the ducat and 110 for the British pound. In just over half a century, the *kuruş* had lost 90 percent of its value against European currencies.[16]

This is not to be compared with the hyperinflation that afflicted Turkey in the 1990s, when salaries slumped and savings were cut in half as the inflation rate hovered around 100 percent annually, but today's Turks will surely be able to sympathize retrospectively with their nineteenth-century forebears. Across the sultan's domains, everyone was affected by the fall in value of the currency, from the shop owner to the small farmer, the merchant, the artisan, the bureaucrat, the soldier, the *qadi* in his court, the imam in the mosque, and the parents putting food on the table. Inflation severely affected the price of basic foodstuffs—rice, flour, cooking oil, chickpeas, mutton, honey, and olive oil—which increased 12–15 times over the fifty years from the late eighteenth century until the 1850s.[17]

In 1844, monetary reform led to the establishment of the *lira*, subdivided into 100 *kuruş*, as the main item of currency. By this time, the government had also introduced interest-bearing (8 percent) paper money known as the *kaime*.[18] As the *kaimeler* were initially hand written, they were relatively easy to forge, until printed with the sultan's seal (*tuğra*) from 1842, but they remained unnumbered. Merchants preferred gold, and as it was impossible to tell how many *kaimeler* had been put into circulation, they were widely distrusted, leading to their continual depreciation.

Following the war with Russia in 1828–1829, the sultan's Armenian *sarraf*, Artin Kazaz, arranged short-term loans from private European financiers to meet the cost of the war indemnity (originally set at 400 million *kuruş* at a time that the state's combined annual revenue amounted to about 200 million *kuruş*[19]). However, it was the cost of the Crimean War (1853–1856) that finally forced the Ottoman government into serious institutional foreign debt. The initial loan of £3 million that was issued in 1854 was augmented by a further £5 million in 1855, backed by the British and French governments on condition that the money would only be used for war costs. The government also rapidly increased the volume of *kaimeler* in circulation.

In 1856, the Ottoman Bank was established as a joint venture, with British interests holding 80,000 shares, French 50,000, and the Ottoman government 5,000. Reestablished as a state bank (the Imperial Ottoman Bank) in 1863 but still with French and British capital, it was given a monopoly to print bank notes that, unlike the *kaime*, could be immediately redeemed for gold. By this time, the bank was establishing branches across the empire and would be the first port of call when the government needed money, though its requests were not always granted.

With foreign loans, the empire was entering "a new phase of its history."[20] The Ottomans were well aware of the risk they were running. Damad Fethi Paşa once remarked, "If this state borrows five piastres[21] it will sink. For if once a loan is taken there will be no end to it. It [the state] will sink overwhelmed in debt."[22] However, the risk was one that had to be taken. Early in 1861, with a total domestic and foreign debt standing at £31 million and having taken out four foreign loans since the Crimean War, the Ottoman government and European money markets were plunged into crisis by the failure of a fifth loan. This had been set up by a French banker, Jules Mirès.

The terms the government was prepared to accept were proof enough of the desperation of its situation: the real return to the Ottoman treasury from a loan of 400 million francs would have been less than 165 million francs. The failure of the loan ruined Mirès, led to the collapse of the newly founded Banque de Turquie and shook the banks and financial houses of London, Marseilles, and Istanbul.[23]

In July, the British Foreign Secretary wrote that his government would consider itself a faithless friend of the Porte if it held out the prospect of a further loan: "It would be pouring water into a cask with a hole at the bottom."[24] But European governments were faced with a problem they would have to deal with one way or another. "What was at stake was more than just the financial market of Istanbul; it was the fragile equilibrium of the Eastern Question that could collapse altogether."[25] If it collapsed, so might the balance of power as represented in the Concert of Europe.

Accordingly, the British and French governments sent high-level financial advisors to Istanbul. The measures taken on the basis of their advice went some way toward calming the European and Istanbul money markets,[26] but the Ottoman people were still stuck with a debased coinage and paper money that lost purchasing power the longer they held it in their hands. By early December 1861, the *kaime* had lost so much of its value against gold in Istanbul that "merchants refused to accept it, business stood still, mobs formed [and] bakeries were sacked."[27]

The success of the Ottoman Bank in arranging a loan of £8 million in March 1862 enabled a forceful new Grand Vizier (Keçecizade Mehmet Fuad Paşa) to insist on the "retirement" (withdrawal) of the *kaime* in exchange for 40 percent of its value in cash and 60 percent in government bonds carrying a 5 percent interest rate. Foreign loans continued to accumulate, invariably on terms detrimental to the empire's long-term interests. By 1874, it had borrowed the equivalent of 238,773,272 lira (£217 million) but had received less than 127,120,220 lira "after the deduction of commissions."[28] In 1875, against annual revenue of 25.1 million lira (£22.8 million), the government was due to pay 30 million lira (£27.2 million) toward its foreign debt. In October, the Grand Vizier, Mahmud Nedim Paşa, announced that the debt would be paid off half in cash and half in 5 percent interest-bearing Treasury bonds. Effectively, the Ottoman government was announcing its insolvency.

A SLAVONIAN "CONSPIRACY"

In 1875, the Balkans were the setting for a crisis that was to end catastrophically for the empire yet again. Greece had set the standard for

ethnoreligious revolt, and in Bulgaria and Bosnia-Herzegovina signs of
trouble had been perceived long before. In June 1860, the British ambassador to the Porte, Sir Henry Bulwer, wrote of "a conspiracy among the
Slavonian race with the object of making a revolution in this Empire."
Chiefs had been selected and plans "more or less defined." Though not
formidable at present, "Its leaders imagine it may become so by exciting
the sympathies of the Great Western and Northern States."[29]

The crisis of 1875 was triggered in July by a peasant uprising instigated
by Balkan nationalists in Bosnia-Herzegovina. The nominal cause was
resistance to the demands of tax farmers, but attacks on Muslim villagers
exposed the insurrection's underlying ethnoreligious and protonational
nature. Intervention by Serbia and Montenegro ushered in a short war
with the Ottoman Empire before a second insurrection in Bulgaria in 1876
involving massacre and counter-massacre drew in the Russians. The newspaper reports from Januarius MacGahan of the massacre of Christians
at Batak inflamed and horrified European public opinion, with William
Gladstone taking the lead in demanding that "the Turks" be packed bag
and baggage out of the provinces that they had "desolated and profaned."[30]

These upheavals tipped the empire's finances over the edge. In early
October 1875, the government destroyed what was left of its financial
credibility on European money markets by defaulting on its loan agreement. This was followed by a default on the default when the government
made only one payment (in January 1876) under the terms agreed upon
with its creditors just a few months earlier. To meet an emergency now
worsened by war with Russia, breaking out in April 1877, the government
restored the *kaime,* repeating "the nightmare of its first experiment with
paper money."[31] Close to 2 million lira in *kaimeler* were put into circulation, which lost 90 percent of their value against gold before European
intervention and the introduction of monetary reforms in 1880, when the
kaime was again retired and a gold lira introduced.

To the costs of suppressing uprisings in the Balkans must be added
other commitments the government could not meet. "The salaries of civil
servants and the pay of the troops have been held up for more than a
year and there is terrible poverty both in Istanbul and the provinces," the
chief financial inspector of the Ottoman Bank, Octave Homberg, wrote
on April 3, 1876.[32] A few days later, he dealt with the effects of military
conscription: "The fresh levies of reservists are depopulating rural areas
at a time when the countryside is in most need of manpower, ruining the
agriculture that is the sole source of this nation's wealth."[33]

With no possibility of securing another foreign loan, the government put pressure on the bankers of Galata.

Asked for an advance of £2 million, the Imperial Ottoman Bank refused.[34] The Grand Vizier warned, "The officers and soldiers receive no pay yet they have to eat. If we do not supply them with provisions there is a risk of their committing acts of pillage."[35] An attempt in 1877 to raise money in Europe failed miserably. Of the £5 million offered in London only £3520 was taken up,[36] but by issuing a veritable snow storm of *kaimeler* the government managed to finance the conflict with Russia. Defeated in war, the Ottomans then had to bow to the wishes of the powers at the Congress of Berlin: with the lost territory went people and tax revenue, making it even harder for the empire to survive in the years to come.

Although reluctant to put control of its revenue in foreign hands, the government had to find some means of servicing its debts. Accordingly, in 1879 it leased the collection of tax revenue from six specified sources—liquor, fishing in the waters around Istanbul, silk production from four provinces, stamp duty, and the salt and tobacco monopolies—to a syndicate consisting of Galata bankers and the Imperial Ottoman Bank.

In the Sultan Abdülhamit's Decree of Muharrem 1881, even more extensive control over tax revenue was placed in foreign hands through the establishment of the Ottoman Public Debt Administration. Its board of seven members, representing French, Britain, German, Dutch, Italian, Austro-Hungarian, and Ottoman bondholders, reduced the Ottoman debt from £191 million to £96 million, interest payments from £62 million to £10 million, and interest service on the debt from £13.6 million to £2.7 million. In return, the Public Debt Administration was allocated the revenues granted in 1879 plus the annual tribute from Cyprus and the Balkans, accounting for about 20 percent of Ottoman state income. Now that he knew where he stood, the sultan could juggle finances elsewhere to try to make up for the shortfall and pay debts outstanding since the war. These included unpaid salaries and bills.

In northeastern Anatolia, villagers still held vouchers for the supply of goods to the army but were being told to pay their tax arrears before redeeming the vouchers. However, "The villagers neither wish to run the risk incurred in parting with their vouchers nor to expose themselves to the inevitable delay that must occur in the settlement of their claims if they have to carry them to Erzinjian [Erzincan], the headquarters of the 4th Army Corps."[37] On a journey westward from Sivas, a British consul reported,

Agricultural implements and other necessities of daily life were
being seized and sold by the tax collectors who did not even spare
the widows and orphans of soldiers who had laid down their lives
at Plevna, at Shipka or upon the mountains of Armenia [sic]. Not
more than one third of the men called up during the war have
returned to their homes and in nearly every village there are widows and orphans almost on the verge of starvation who are supported and helped by relations and friends not much better off
than themselves.[38]

Other causes of distress included the devaluation by half of the *beşlik*,[39]
a measure "which has given rise to serious disturbances in some of the
larger towns [and] has virtually ruined the peasantry of Anatolia, already
impoverished by the depreciation, first of *caimé*, then of copper." Small
groups of demobilized soldiers were begging their way home from village
to village "with nothing but the clothes on their backs and papers which
showed that they were from three to five years in arrear of pay."[40]

A severe winter, crop failure, drought, and a locust plague added to
the difficulties experienced by the rural population. Even in Ismid (Izmit),
close to the capital, people were dying within 10 miles of the railway ter-
minus. In Bursa, the *kaymakam* (a provincial subgovernor) had applied to
Istanbul for aid without receiving an answer. "In some places the peasants
are now living on one meal a day consisting of a soup of bran and water;
in others they are baking the vine stems and grinding them for flour; and
in others they are reduced to eating grass and herbs." The last harvest
in Izmit had failed because of the drought, while in Bursa it had failed
because of locusts *and* drought, with 450,000 cattle, sheep, and goats said
to have died in a severe winter.[41]

CHAPTER 2

A Difficult Land

THE FINANCIAL DIFFICULTIES sketched in the preceding pages return the narrative to the central problem of a government trying to govern without sufficient revenue to govern properly. The connections suggest themselves. A government that cannot pay civil servants and soldiers on time (and sometimes not at all) is failing at the most basic level. Unpaid or poorly paid civil servants are susceptible to bribery and soldiers to desertion. Yet here were governments with ambitious plans: an expanded bureaucracy and military, centralization, and the reform and reorganization of society at every level.

Where profits were to be made—through electrification and the development of railways, ports, harbors, and coal mines—foreign investors could be attracted, but there was no return on administrative reforms or the construction of roads that led nowhere from a commercial point of view. The bulk of investment took place in the west. In the view of a British consul, and everything known about the eastern Anatolian provinces confirms his judgment, Constantinople was "a whole century in advance of the provinces."[1] The Orient Express opened up rail travel to Istanbul and encouraged the construction of grand hotels that remain in operation to this day, including the Pera Palace and the Büyük Londra (Grand London). Istanbul and Izmir were the first to benefit from a conscious effort to modernize city life along European lines. Gradually, the towns and cities of the western Ottoman provinces acquired the conveniences of modern European life such as tramways and street lighting systems. By the 1870s, Istanbul was connected to Bulgaria and Greece by rail in one direction and to Konya in another. Izmir (Smyrna) was the hub of an embryonic developing rail system connecting the main towns of the western provinces.

In the eastern provinces, however, there was still virtually nothing in the way of modern infrastructure: few schools, doctors, hospitals, clinics, and pharmacies; no sealed roads, only dirt tracks that were frequently closed for long periods of time by bad weather. In 1878, a British consul wrote from Diyarbakir,

> In winter, Erzeroum and Diarbekir are, for all practical purposes of Consular control, as far apart (or rather much further) as London is from Constantinople. The road I came by has never been open at the season I travelled since the year following the Crimean War, and I should be very much surprised if a letter were to reach me by post from Erzeroum within three weeks of its departure. Last winter the post from here to Constantinople was delayed by impassable snow for fifteen days at a village only eighteen hours from Diarbekir, on the post road via Kharpoot and Samsoon, the same road by which I shall have to travel if I return to Erzeroum during the winter.[2]

As for the mail, a letter sent from the eastern provinces could take three to four weeks to reach Istanbul.[3]

There was a port at Trabzon, but there were no developed ports in the eastern Mediterranean despite the strategic importance and commercial potential of Mersin and Iskenderun. Produce was moved to and from Istanbul and the port cities of the Mediterranean, Aegean, and Black Sea coasts by caravans of oxcarts, camels, and mules. As there were few bridges, this mass of people, animals, and bags and bundles of produce generally had to be carried across rivers on rafts. These craft ranged in size from coracle to a large barge (kalak) with a wooden deck mounted on inflated animal skins (usually goat) that could carry tons of goods, men, and their animals at any one time.

Traveling from the interior to the coast might take many weeks. Overnight accommodation would most likely be one of the hanlar established in the towns, some of them centuries old. There, the animals would be tethered, and the produce unloaded in the courtyard before the merchant bunked down in a rough room.

Telegraph lines were laid in the middle of the nineteenth century, enabling the center to quickly learn what was happening on the periphery, but newspapers were few and far between. With illiteracy remaining at close to 90 percent until well into the twentieth century, most people could not read them anyway. What they knew (or thought they knew) was mostly based on hearsay, gossip, rumor, and travelers' tales. In the eastern provinces, the rugged terrain, towering mountains, steep valleys, and seemingly endless plains shriveled by the sun in summer, with snow meters deep cutting off villages for weeks if not months at a time in winter, hindered access and development even in the most propitious circumstances. At times of crisis, depending on the time of year, it could be impossible for the military to reach isolated regions.

As for railways, European capital was attracted to the Balkans and western Turkey but not to eastern Anatolia. Even in the Ottoman Balkans only 514 kilometers of rail line had been laid by 1866.[4]

Railway construction was not just a question of profit. Strategic considerations were of prime importance. In the early twentieth century, an Ottoman-German plan to build a railway from Berlin to Baghdad caused great alarm in London because of the perceived threat to British interests in the Gulf. Russia was also disturbed because of the close proximity of this line to Transcaucasia and northwest Persia.[5] It wanted to maintain the northeastern Anatolian plateau as a buffer against outside penetration seen to threaten its interests. In 1900, Russia persuaded the sultan not to grant foreign concessions for rail construction in this region, but by 1911 this agreement was collapsing under the pressure of Ottoman, French, and German commercial interests, so that all it could do was seek "compensation" for the "concessions" it could not avoid.

By 1914, sections of the Baghdad railway had reached the southeast, but with breaks, because tunneling through the Taurus mountains was still proceeding. At the war's end, the line had still not reached Baghdad, which the British had taken out of Ottoman hands in 1917.[6]

EPIDEMICS

Epidemic diseases and shortages of food added to the difficulties of peasant life. In 1873–1874, perhaps 40,000 square miles of Central Anatolia were ravaged by drought and then famine extending from summer through a heavy winter.[7] An estimated 150,000 people died, but even higher figures—up to 250,000—have been given. Having eaten their seed crops, starving people made their way to "Angora" and other towns as soon as the snows melted, dying in the streets from malnutrition and disease despite the relief efforts of the Ottoman government and foreign residents.

Mortality was especially high among children. The "Angora" correspondent of the *Levant Herald* reported that strong men were "whining and crying for a morsel of bread," and entire villages were depopulated. The mortality among sheep and goat herds in the region was "enormous," with mohair Angora goats reduced in number from 859,932 to 363,289 during the winter, and common goats and sheep from 1,086,734 to 186,399. Orphaned children died alone. So desperate were the people for food that in one village a camel that had died weeks before was dug up and eaten.[8] Corn seed could not be planted either because it had been eaten or because the snow was still lying too deeply on the ground. Even in better times, however, food supplies intermittently fell disastrously short, and people died from malnutrition.

The government established a relief committee, benefiting from donations from across the empire and replenishing stocks of food and farm animals in the devastated regions. Support also came from a famine relief commission operating through the British embassy, with contributions, large and small, from Britain and across Europe.

The calamity of 1873–1874 underlined the need for railway construction to proceed without delay, but that was only one of many suggestions made to prevent further disasters. The *Levant Herald* traced responsibility back to Mahmud II.

> It will seem strange to anyone unacquainted with Turkey, who reads these pages, that one year of scarcity should have resulted in such utter desolation. Strange, that there were no reserves of food in so rich a country; no middle class to render assistance during the few weeks which famine sufficed to make famine master of the country and to wreck its social organisation. To understand this, it is necessary to look back to the time of Sultan Mahmoud, the great reformer, who waged such ruthless war against the institutions of the country. Mahmoud, impressed by the tragedies which immediately preceded his reign and harassed by the insubordination of

the Derebeys, the feudal chiefs in the provinces, made it his study to destroy every power in the Empire and to reduce it to a central despotism.[9]

The "abrupt subversion" of the feudal system had dislocated the entire social system, with taxation and the inrush of foreign manufactured goods having a particularly savage effect on local economies. Gradually, between 1820 and the 1870s, "the manufacturing industry of Asia Minor faded away and a remnant which still exists, depends upon usurers and now does scarcely more than supply foreign markets with Oriental articles."[10] The fact of the famine only added to a mounting pile of foreign criticism for not introducing the reforms said to have been promised, and from some of the sultan's own disgruntled subjects for going too far with the reforms of the *tanzimat* era.[11] Bureaucratism, over-centralization, and the substitution of European codes of law for Ottoman were among the criticisms aimed at the reform process.

RESISTING CHANGE

The principle of equality before the law for all Ottoman subjects underpinned constitutional and administrative change. It was repugnant to many Muslims to the extent that the sultan's reform decree of 1856 caused "a rift between Muslims and Christians throughout Syria and Palestine."[12] Judges trained in shari'a law did not always like having to serve in the secularized *nizamiye* courts set up in the late 1870s. The *qadi* at Konya who refused to apply the new secular civil laws no doubt spoke for many others of his class.[13]

The task of persuading those entrusted with education, administration, and the judiciary to understand the need for reforms was likely to be more difficult in the east than the west. Comparatively, the western provinces were more developed at all levels, were closer to the capital, and thus were more susceptible to the demands and influence of the central government. In the eastern provinces, distance from the center and the authority of traditional powerholders were formidable obstacles in the way of change.

Nor did the abolition of tax farming in favor of direct taxation bring an end to corruption and the intimidation of the peasant population at

the hands of powerful landowners. The new provincial councils were
elected not by the people but by a small fraction of the people—the
land- and property-owning classes—and were manipulated by them in
their interests. The central government simply did not have the means to
eliminate such abuses. The capacity of the *vali* (the governor) to eliminate
them himself naturally depended on the force of his personality but was
equally contingent on the cooperation or noncooperation of the deeply
entrenched traditional forces around him.

Sultan Abdülhamit II's complaints that his orders were not obeyed by
provincial officials raises the question of how much authority he actually
had in remote regions far from Istanbul. His denial of political and press
freedoms seriously impinged on the lives of Ottoman liberals concentrated in the western cities of the empire but must have been meaningless
to the vast bulk of illiterate people living in the Anatolian hinterland,
if they had heard of them at all.

Increasingly, affairs of state were decided at the palace and not in the
government offices (the Bab-i Ali). The sultan kept his own counsel or
relied on the advice of a small circle of palace advisers, but the belief widely
held in European capitals that he controlled everything from the recesses
of Yildiz Palace has to be challenged. At times he scarcely controlled
even Istanbul. In the eastern provinces, as Arminius Vambéry remarked,
"Things have remained in the same condition as before the *tanzimat*, all
innovations have merely touched the outer surface."[14]

In the context of the wrongs suffered by Armenians at the hands of
"rapacious and disorderly Kurds," the sultan told Vambéry that he was
aware of the "gross neglect" of administrators in the eastern provinces,
but (and here he can be imagined throwing up his hands in despair) what
could he do? "My pashas have their own policy, they are utterly deficient
in patriotism and honesty."[15]

Is there an element here of the sultan shifting the blame to someone
else? His enemies would certainly say so, but the accusations of his critics
were often based on assumptions about his authority with little basis in
fact. "Absolutism" is a word commonly applied to his long reign. In fact,
while the suspension of the constitution in 1877 created political absolutism, absolute or absolutist rule over the entire empire in all its affairs
was another matter entirely. The Ottoman Empire during the reign of
Abdülhamit simply did not lend itself to this kind of government.

The sultan, when not being accused in Britain of being the Red Sultan
or Abdul the Assassin (or the Damned), was often caricatured as a spider

overlooking the imperial web from Yildiz Palace, the master of all he surveyed. Such propaganda served many purposes but was far from the truth.
The empire was a premodern, preindustrial state with almost nothing in
the way of the organization and technology that are the foundations of
modern authoritarian rule.[16] Even if the sultan did wish to create such a
state, its development would have taken decades. As it was, Abdülhamit
lacked both the money and the means to extend his authority to every
corner of the empire.

Sensibly, in these circumstances, he worked within the realm of what
was possible rather than pushing for changes the people would not accept
and he could not enforce. By the 1890s, European pressure and the loss of
Christian territories had pushed the sultan in the direction of what the
European press frequently referred to as "Pan Islam." The sultan's primary
focus, however, was on Muslim unity within the empire, not beyond its
borders. Historically, the eastern provinces had been the locus of numerous Kurdish rebellions. Force had been used to suppress them, but perhaps
cooperation (or cooptation) would be more effective, if the Kurdish tribal
chiefs could see advantages for themselves. This seems to have been the
sultan's approach. If he acknowledged the traditional claims of the tribal
chiefs, and they recognized his suzerainty, this symbiotic arrangement
could work well for both.

Accordingly, "loyal" Kurdish tribes were given special privileges, such
as tax and conscription exemption. Tribal schools (*mektebler-i aşiret*) were
also opened in Istanbul and the provinces for the children of tribal chiefs
(Arabs as well as Kurds) who in time might serve the government. The
Hamidiye tribal cavalry was established and given the Cossack-style uniforms that conferred status and authority (often abused) on its recruits.

Devolving a measure of officially-sanctioned authority to tribal chiefs
and *shuyukh* (sing. *shaykh*, modern Turkish *şeyh*) served the interests of
the government outside the towns, especially in remote regions where the
chiefs were far better suited to keep the peace than the sultan's governors.
This unwritten compact with the Kurds was effectively born of weakness
on the sultan's side and a shift in the balance of power on the Kurdish side,
away from the tribal chiefs in the direction of *shuyukh* more amenable to
the sultan's message of Muslim solidarity.

Abduülhamit's approach to provincial government was consistent
with the decentralized past up to the time of Mahmud II. His overriding
aim, of course, was centralization and consolidation of his own authority
but unlike Mahmud II he chose to win over the tribal chiefs rather than

break their heads. In the nineteenth century, Mahmud II seems to have been the exception to a general rule: as long as the sultan's authority was respected, governments in Istanbul had always been prepared to make flexible arrangements consistent with local conditions. This was demonstrated in the way they ruled the Hijaz (in cooperation with the *sharif* of Mecca), Mount Lebanon, the Balkans, and even the top of the Persian Gulf, where since the eighteenth century the shaykh of Kuwait had been nominally attached to the *vilayet* of Basra while, in practice, enjoying virtually full autonomy.

Such arrangements were not always respected by those holding delegated authority. Fakhr al-Din Ma'an II of Mount Lebanon (1572–1635) and Ali Paşa of Janina (1740–1822) paid with their lives for trying to break free of Ottoman control, and other rebels were to meet the same fate. Abdülhamit certainly seemed to think that governing with the backing of provincial notables, and giving something in return for what they were prepared to give was a more effective way of moving forward than working against them.

Apropos of the massacres of Armenians in 1895–1896, it was perhaps not so much that they showed Abdülhamit had "lost control" of his Muslim subjects in these regions[17] but rather that he never had such close control in the first place. The notion of centralized control over the lives of the inhabitants of these distant provinces does not square with what is known of the nature of the Ottoman state and the gross weaknesses of provincial administration even after attempts at reform.

"CORRUPT MACHINES"

The constitution of 1876 did not come out of a vacuum but was the culmination of a reform process begun before the time of Mahmud II. The participation of people at the level of notables and (to a degree) common folk was an essential part of these reforms. Already in the 1830s, inspectors and "commissions of improvement" (*meclis-i imariye*) were being dispatched from Istanbul to report on the state of provincial government. Advisory councils consisting of Muslims and non-Muslims were attached to governors, who were required to secure their approval of decisions taken.

After the broad principles announced in the reform edict of 1839 were reiterated and strengthened in the Hatt-i Hümayun of 1856, the government intervened to put further restrictions on the exercise of arbitrary authority in the provinces and in the administration of the Christian communities (*milletler*, sing. *millet*).

As Davison has observed, and there is abundant evidence to prove the point, the Greek and Armenian *milletler* in particular, "had become corrupt machines of business and politics manipulated for the advantage of the hierarchies."[18] It was the government and not the ecclesiastics that set in motion *millet* reforms that led to the establishment of lay assemblies invested with the power to elect both the patriarchs and the councils responsible for overseeing civil and church affairs.

Corruption and provincial maladministration were central themes in numerous dispatches filed by British consuls. Writing from Aleppo in 1860, Consul Skene drew a grim picture of a wealthy province being ruined by usury, speculation, and what seemed to be the downright theft of public money—at least going by the evidence of affluence among public servants born of poor families. Municipal institutions had been set up in a manner that was "not in harmony with the existing state of the country."[19]

The *derebeyleri* ("lords of the valley," sing. *derebey*)[20] might have been swept away, but the remedy had outweighed the evil: instead of one tyrant, "there are now many tyrants, each grasping his own advantage and all inferior to the Pasha in qualifications for government."[21] The *paşa* might be an improvement on the old feudal lord,[22] but the *ayan* (local notable)[23] remained a man of the same stamp as before the reforms so that "the better is thus controlled by the worse."[24]

The members of the *meclis* (advisory council), "cruel, venal and rapacious," understanding local conditions and dominating the local population, soon turned even "the most zealous pasha" into a mere instrument in their hands.[25] Skene's findings were echoed across the empire. In many cases, provincial reforms had not led to better government but worse: where an honest *vali* tried to do his best, his hands were likely to be tied by a corrupt council and lack of support from Istanbul.[26]

In 1864, the government introduced further reforms to provincial government aimed at greater efficiency and broader representation of the people.[27] The administrative structure began at the top with the *vilayet* (province) and extended downward through three subdivisions. The *sancak* was the largest subdivision of the *vilayet*; then followed the *kaza* of the *sancak*, and finally the *kariye* and *nahiye*, the smallest units of all, consisting in the *kariye* of town quarters with a minimum of fifty houses and in the *nahiye* of a commune of several hamlets. The heads of the three major divisions—the *vali* or governor of the province, the *mutasarrif* of the *sancak*, and the *kaymakam* of the *kaza*—were all appointed by the sultan. Beneath them stood the *muhtar,* the senior figure at the level of the *nahiye*, roughly comparable in status to a village mayor, elected by the people.

A "hierarchy"[28] of advisory councils (*idare meclisi)* operated at each of the three main levels of provincial administration. Each consisted of a mix of appointed officials and a small number of elected members. This administrative body was augmented with the *ihtiyar meclisi* (council of elders), responsible for the affairs of each religious community and, with the exception of the spiritual leaders who were automatically included, elected by Ottoman male subjects over the age of eighteen who paid at least fifty piasters a year in taxes.

The selection of candidates for election to councils at the three main levels ultimately boiled down to choices made by provincial officials. Even then, the government in Istanbul reserved the right to eliminate names from the lists it was given. An annual tax payment of at least 500 piasters[29] was clearly designed to restrict eligibility for the *idare meclisi* to the relatively wealthy middlemen through whom the central government could express its wishes and maintain its control. An elected *meclis-i umumi* (general assembly) was also created at the *vilayet* level but with insufficient authority to effect real change.[30]

A lot of horse trading must have taken place as lists of candidates were being drawn up, no doubt with straw men finding their way into lucrative positions on councils in return for agreeing to protect vested religious or commercial interests. The quality of appointed officials would naturally vary. Many governors sent to the east probably could not wait to return to Istanbul, Izmir, or Bursa. Even if well-intended and determined, a governor would soon run up against a range of obstacles, from dumb obstruction to passive resistance and noncooperation.

In the eastern provinces, outside the town and the governor's *konak* (mansion), tribal groups would inevitably resist infringements of what they regarded as traditional prerogatives. Old habits were going to die hard, with the reports of corruption and oppression that flowed toward the central government over the years indicating that among many local notables, officials, and tribal chiefs, those habits had not died at all.

Insofar as the representation of Christians was concerned, "The combination of Turkish officials in each *meclis,* plus the determining voice of officials in choosing the 'elected' members, meant that a Muslim majority was assured from *vilayet* down through to the *kaza* even in those Balkan regions where the Christian population was a great majority. For these reasons, the law of 1864 has been severely criticized."[31]

CONSULS AND GOVERNORS

The ubiquitous foreign (especially British) consuls often only had to push hard enough and persistently enough for the central government to withdraw a governor of whom they did not approve. The campaign launched against the *vali* of Aleppo in 1878–1879 over alleged mistreatment of Christians during his suppression of an uprising in and around the remote mountain town of Zeytun is a case in point. Zeytun was a troublesome spot. Its people refused to pay taxes and had a long history of rebellion. The *vali*, Kamil Paşa, did his best to defend himself, pointing out that his main accuser, Consul Henderson of Aleppo, had only recently arrived, "and not being clever enough or acquainted with the languages generally spoken" was entirely in the hands of his dragomen (interpreters) "who are not at all the right persons to employ." Therefore, "The information that the Embassy may get through him cannot be entirely relied upon."[32]

His point was an important one. The consuls often did not speak the local languages and had to rely heavily on their interpreters (invariably Christians and often Armenians), missionaries, or senior ecclesiastics for what they knew of local conditions. The Armenians of Zeytun were used to living relatively free of outside control and reacted badly to attempts by the authorities to pull them into line. Collisions with Kurds and the various agents of the government—tax collectors, police, *jandarma*, and soldiers—were frequent.

From the *vali*'s point of view, "Instead of being censured, he was entitled to the thanks of the Imperial Government for the vigorous and necessary measures which he had executed to suppress revolt and restore order."[33] Still, he was ultimately withdrawn, after months of complaints from Henderson to Istanbul, relayed through the British embassy to the Foreign Office and then from the Foreign Office back to the Ottoman government.

The financial, social, and economic disarray that was the subject matter of numerous dispatches from consuls and other observers was the background to the outbreak of one of the greatest crises to afflict the Ottoman Empire in its long history, the 1877–1878 war with Russia.

CHAPTER 3

Kurds and Armenians

IN THE SIX EASTERN PROVINCES that became a focal point of out-side attention in the late nineteenth century (Sivas, Erzurum, Mamuret el-Aziz, Van, Bitlis, and Diyarbakir) because of accusations of Kurdish and Ottoman state mistreatment of the Armenians, about 80 percent of the people were Muslim.[1] As the official censuses only classified the population on the basis of religion, "Muslim" would have included Turks, Kurds, Circassians, and other ethnic groups. The Ottoman Kurds were divided into two dominant language groups, Zaza and Kırmancı. Most Kurds were Sunni Muslim, but some were Alevi, and small numbers were Yazidi or even Jewish. At a secondary religious level, the influence of the Sufi Qadiriyya and Naqşbandi *tarikatlar* (ways) was significant, with tribal leaders often also *shuyukh* in one of the Sufi orders.

In these six provinces (*vilayet-i sitte*), the Kurds still followed a nomadic or seminomadic lifestyle, despite a growing tendency to settle in villages, migrating with their flocks of sheep and goats into the mountains during summer and returning to the valleys and plains for the winter. The tradi-tional Kurdish homeland overlapped the porous borders of three empires (Ottoman, Persian, and Russian).

The absorption of eastern Anatolia into the Ottoman state after the victory over the Persians in the battle of Çaldiran (1514) was followed by the establishment of a decentralized administrative system. In remote and often inaccessible regions, such an arrangement had benefits for the govern-ment as well as Kurdish tribal chiefs. Of the three administrative Kurdish divisions (*hükümet, yurtluk-ocaklik,* and *sancak*[2]), the *hükümets* enjoyed a wide remit of autonomy, relieved of cadastral surveys and taxes in return for the provision of military support in times of war. In this symbiotic relationship, the government would also support the hereditary leadership of the Kurdish tribal chiefs or *ağalar* (sing. *ağa*) and *beyler* (sing. *bey*). The balance for both sides was fine, but over the centuries the Ottoman system of loose control encouraged the growth of what were effectively autonomous emirates, within which confederacies would form dominated by one tribe.

The territory controlled by these Kurdish *mirs* (emirs or "princes") was vast. On a modern map, the territorial reach of the emirate of Botan included all of southeastern Anatolia up to Lake Van—what is now northern Iraq and northwestern Persia around Lake Urmia (Rizaye). Across the Ottoman-Persian border, the Kurdish hold on these territories became entangled in the rival claims of Tehran and Istanbul, watched closely from Moscow and European capitals.

The arrival of foreign Protestant missionaries early in the nineteenth century and the presence of foreign consuls brought the grievances of Christians living under Kurdish domination to the attention of the outside world. While their complaints generated outrage against the Kurds, generally depicted as wild and predatory, the central pillar of tribal authority was the ability of the tribal chief to protect everyone living within his domains, as well as to punish them when necessary. Generally speaking, it was not in his interests to mistreat his human flock. He relied on the Christians for taxation, labor, and the provision of fodder when the tribes came down from the mountains in winter and was unlikely to take action against Christians just because they were Christians.

Conflict usually arose over pasturage rights, alleged theft of stock, and the refusal of Christian villagers to pay taxes. These might be demanded as of traditional right or a "tax" might be no more than an arbitrary demand for money or goods, but religion itself was not generally the cause of conflict—even if that was the perception in Britain and other countries.

An enduring problem, prohibited by the Ottoman state but continuing in practice in the late nineteenth century, was *kışlak*, the winter quarter demanded by Kurds for themselves and their flocks as a right and provided by Armenians. Their reports of oppression at Kurdish hands are offset by the numerous accounts of social interaction, mutual assistance in times of want, and joint complaints to the government, indicating that reasons for conflict beyond petty quarrels must be sought in circumstances specific to the time. The central issues in the second half of the nineteenth century included foreign intervention on behalf of Armenian and Nestorian

Christians, Armenian uprisings in Kurdish regions, the growing Muslim distrust of Christians, the fear among Kurds that their land was being taken away from them, and the Kurdish seizure of land claimed by both.[3]

In the 1820s, the centralizing changes set in motion by Mahmud II had a profound effect on Kurdish society. New taxation and laws met with resentment. In Istanbul, it was clear that if the authority of the sultan's government was to be extended across the empire, the power of the *mirs* would have to be broken. The weakness of the central government in the provinces had greatly enhanced the powers not just of the *mirs* but the *ayan*.[4] However, while launching military campaigns against the *mirs* in eastern Anatolia, Mahmud II was facing a serious distraction arising from the Egyptian occupation of Syria.

In 1830, Mehmet Ali had sent his son Ibrahim to take Syria out of the sultan's hands, effectively taking the compensation the sultan had failed to give for services rendered in crushing the "Wahhabis" in the Hijaz and attempting to put down the Greek uprising in 1825. (Initially successful, the Ottoman-Egyptian campaign failed after joint Russian, British, and French naval intervention in 1827.) By 1839, the crisis created by successive defeats of Ottoman armies at the hands of an Egyptian army led to European intervention against Mehmet Ali. Mahmud II died on July 1, 1839, exactly a week after the victory of the Egyptian army at Nizip (June 24). The sultan's failure to stop the Egyptians was taken by the Kurds as "further proof that the Ottoman state had lost its stamina."[5]

Kurdish uprisings in the Dersim region (now Tunceli) were to follow. In 1875–1876, an Ottoman force sent to Dersim failed to suppress tribal rebels but still managed to establish governorates in several towns. Defeat in the 1877–1878 war with Russia strengthened the conviction among Kurdish notables that Ottoman power was in steep decline, feeding a specifically Kurdish protonational sentiment. Collisions between the Ottoman army and Kurdish forces were followed by the uprising led by Shaykh Ubaydullah across the Ottoman-Persian border in 1880 and the 1908 expedition to Dersim led by Ibrahim Paşa, the commander of the Fourth Army. Kurdish villages were destroyed, flocks were seized, and the people left "in a state of wretched poverty."[6]

During Mahmud II's campaigns, the eastern provinces were not quite as closed to outside scrutiny as before. This was largely due to the growth in the number of foreign consuls based in the east and the arrival of American missionaries founding churches and schools under the aegis of the American Board of Commissioners for Foreign Missions (ABCFM).

Changing circumstances that threatened Kurdish authority led to the war waged on the Nestorian Christians by Bedirhan, the *mir* of Botan. Partly, it seems to have been generated by Kurdish suspicion of the missionaries and their encouragement of the Nestorians (through their patriarch) to stand their ground against Kurdish "oppression." In an attack on the Nestorian Tiyari district in 1843, Bedirhan's tribal fighters killed thousands of men and carried off women and children, according to contemporary European accounts. Such reports, however, must be treated with caution, given the exaggeration that generally accompanied accounts of the mistreatment of Ottoman Christians.

A further large-scale assault was launched in 1846. The destruction and slaughter caused another wave of outrage in Europe with little apparent understanding of the deeper motives behind Bedirhan's actions. One was his opposition to recent measures taken in the name of centralization (the administrative partition of his tribal land between Diyarbakir and Mosul); the other was the Nestorian alliance with a rival of one of his tribal allies. In analyzing the reasons for his assault, while the Nestorians were no match for the fighting men he could muster, centralization was a direct, long-term threat to his authority from a government ready to break his resistance by force. In July 1847, Bedirhan surrendered and was exiled to Crete. It was a measure of how the government dealt with these issues that he was later able to return to Istanbul as a *paşa*.

By 1850, the power of the *mirs* had been decisively broken, but successful military campaigns needed to be followed by administrative measures to consolidate central authority. What the record shows is that older tendencies (corruption, inefficiency, and resistance to orders from the center) persisted, driving the sultan Abdülhamit (1876–1909) back toward older and more supple methods of dealing with the Kurds. The central government established a reformed provincial administration headed, however, by governors who frequently had neither the authority nor the resources to ensure that their wishes were obeyed. Outside the towns and cities, much real power still lay with *ağalar*, *beyler*, and *shuyukh* commanding respect on the basis of religion as well as tribal and family affiliations.

The emergence of Sufi religious leaders as political actors was scarcely confined to eastern Anatolia. In North Africa and the Caucasus, similar figures arose to meet the challenges of European invasion, occupation, and settlement. One of the best known was Imam Shamyl of Dagestan, a Naqşbandi, like the well-known Kurdish *shaykh*, Ubaydullah, from the Şemdinan family of Nehri. An extraordinary figure in Caucasian history, a warrior, man of learning, and skilled administrator, Shamyl inflicted crushing defeats on the Russians before his final surrender in 1859.

In Algeria, resistance to the French was led by Shaykh (alternatively, Emir) 'Abd al-Qadir ibn Muhi al-Din Mustafa al-Hasani al-Jaza'iri, a venerable figure in the Sufi Qadiriyya order, who met Shamyl when he went on *hajj* with his father to Mecca in 1825. Like Shamyl, 'Abd al-Qadir came from a long line of Sufi scholars. In the absence of any other central pillar of mobilization, these religious figures resisted occupation in the name of Islam. Religion gave their Sufi brethren the same mobilizing power in the eastern Anatolian provinces.

"HUMANITARIAN" PREJUDICE

The general situation facing the Ottoman Empire from the 1870s is critical to understanding the relationship between Sultan Abdülhamit and the Kurds. Abdülhamit acceded to the throne at a time of dynastic and state crisis: in the space of twelve months, one sultan committed suicide and a second was removed from the throne for reasons of mental instability. At the very moment of Abdülhamit's accession (August 31, 1876), the empire was facing one of the gravest crises in its history, perhaps *the* gravest, some might say.

Within eighteen months, the empire's armies had been defeated in yet another war with Russia and subjected to a humiliating treaty that stripped it of most of its territory in Europe. In 1882, having pledged to defend the empire against further aggression by Russia in the Cyprus Convention (June 1878), but leaving open the possibility of its own aggression, Britain invaded Egypt in the name of protecting the interests of European bondholders. In the coming years, the sultan had to deal with revolutionary uprisings in Macedonia and the eastern provinces, the annexation of the autonomous province of eastern Rumelia by Bulgaria, and war with Greece over Crete in 1897.

It has been asserted that in the nineteenth century "government-approved ethnic violence" was directed against groups "perceived to be in revolt or dangerous to the state": Greeks in the 1820s, Syrian Christians in the 1860s, Bulgarians in 1876, and the Zeytunli Armenians in 1862.[7] In fact, these revolts or uprisings were very real. In Istanbul, violent challenges to the government's authority were the issue on these occasions, not religion or ethnicity, but in the disturbed regions conflict was soon characterized by sectarian hatred. Greeks in the 1820s and Bulgarians in the 1870s killed many Muslims before government forces intervened and killed Christians. As for Syria in the 1860s, this was not a case of "government-approved massacre of dhimmis [non-Muslims]"[8] but of Maronite Christians and Druze fighting each other. The situation eventually degenerated into a general onslaught on Christians in Damascus, after which the Ottoman government imposed severe penalties on the Muslim ringleaders and the city collectively.

Ottoman authority on the Lebanese *jabal* had only been restored in 1840, following a decade of Egyptian occupation, and the state was still struggling to find a formula for stable government when these massacres occurred. They had deep roots in Druze-Maronite animosity, but ignoring the complexities and reflexively blaming the Ottoman government (or Islam) for all ills was a time-honored convenience of distant politicians and deeply prejudiced "humanitarians."

There is no evidence that the sultan hated Armenians or any other Christians. This personal reason given for massacres was fed by on-the-spot "experts" such as newspaper correspondent Edwin Pears, who had lived in Istanbul for decades and had nothing but contempt for the Ottoman government, the sultan, and Islam. If the sultan hated the Armenians—traditionally the *millet-i sadiqa* or "faithful community"—it was certainly strange that he allowed them to build his palaces, run his gunpowder factory, mint his money, look after his personal finances,[9] count his population,[10] run his ministries, and take high positions in his government.

Patrician members of the Armenian *amira* (aristocratic) class were part of the palace circle. Socioeconomic standing, not religion, was the dividing line between Christians and Muslims. The natural class friends and allies of wealthy and well-placed Christians were Muslims of similar standing, not their poor fellow-religionists (and certainly not the revolutionaries). Wealthy, educated, well-spoken, and urbane Armenians were a "natural intermediary" between the Ottoman Empire and the outside world.[11] No sultan had ever tampered with Armenian religious rights, and certainly Abdülhamit never did. Yalman even describes the Armenians as "the favorite and the spoiled children of the reform era."[12] Whatever the case, the reasons for the breakdown of the relationship between Muslims and Christians in the late Ottoman period are better sought in the circumstances of the time and not narrow, reductive, distorted, and bogus explanations focusing on the personality of one man.

Abdülhamit has been frequently (and loosely) called "paranoid."[13] In fact, many of the sultan's suspicions and fears were well-founded. He had good reasons for suspecting that the powers and their protégés were hovering over his empire waiting to swoop. Large chunks of Ottoman territory had already been swallowed by the time the sultan came to the throne. Much more was soon to follow in his Arab dominions (Tunisia in 1881 and Egypt in 1882) and in the Balkans.

The sultan had come to believe that the Europeans desired the "destruction of our state and would only be content once another *millet* had replaced the Osmanlı *millet* at Dersaadet [Istanbul]."[14] In general, Abdülhamit's reading of the situation he faced was not the product of delusions or paranoia. Behind their written and verbal commitments to the maintenance of the Ottoman Empire, European governments expected its collapse. They might not be willing its destruction, but they were certainly doing nothing to prevent it and were taking many actions that could only speed up the process.

Apart from the hovering powers, there were the revolutionary committees inside the sultan's empire, Macedonian, Armenian, and eventually Turkish, differing in their objectives but all seeking his overthrow. These threats were real and not the product of a paranoid imagination.

A THEOLOGICAL STATE?

Descriptions of the Ottoman Empire as an Islamic or "theological" state are not quite accurate.[15] The state was a legal hybrid, governed according to an interleaving of religious (*şeriat*) and secular (*kanun*) laws influenced by ancient Turkic traditions (*töre*). Like all European states, the central governing principle was the protection of the state. The empire was not a dogmatic state blindly following religion. Rather, like any European state, religion was used to justify whatever the state wanted to do at any particular time. Abdülhamit continued the modernizing and secularizing reforms of the *tanzimat* period, shifting the institutional and legal center of gravity ever further from Islam, so that by the time he was removed from the throne, little of it was left. With the exception of personal codes, Islamic law had almost totally been superseded by secular legislation based on European models.

Much attention was paid in London and Paris to "Pan Islam." Again, the nerve being twitched was self-interest. With hundreds of millions of

Muslims living under British and French rule, what might happen if the notion of Islamic solidarity caught on? In various territories, Muslims had rebelled against the European "yoke" (as Muslims might feel entitled to call it), but these small fires had never merged into one great fire.

In fact, while there were frequent calls to arms, while the sultan sought to strengthen the empire on the basis of Muslim solidarity, while he received envoys from distant Muslim lands, and while he supported their causes rhetorically and sometimes materially, there was no Pan-Islamic movement as such, organized in Istanbul or anywhere else. It was a specter in the European mind, but if it made European governments think twice about the effect of their policies on Muslims in the lands they had occupied it was valuable for that reason alone.

Educated and politically aware Muslims in and out of the Ottoman Empire were certainly agreed on the need to defend themselves and their religion against the common enemy—the encroaching European powers—but by no means were they united on how this should be done. They were respectful of the institution of the caliphate, but they also wanted constitutional government and the diminution of the powers of one man, whether sultan or shah. Whatever criticism might be made of the sultan's autocratic ways, he had at least succeeded in preserving the Ottoman Empire as a Muslim power, whereas the Qajar shah of Iran could claim neither religious authority nor popular support and had bartered away his country's putative independence through endless concessions to Britain and Russia.

"KURDISTAN" OR "ARMENIA"?

In the empire's eastern provinces, the rise of Shaykh Ubaydullah in 1879–1880 as the head of a protonational Kurdish movement[16] was stimulated by war, the disorder that followed, and British-sponsored "reforms" that Kurds regarded as threatening the very foundations of their society and their territorial rights.[17] It is ironic that the same Kurds who attract such sympathy now for their national cause in Europe and the United States were regarded in the late nineteenth century in the outside world as little more than predators of the Christians. Trying to maintain order, the sultan was extremely reluctant to interfere in the affairs of the Kurdish tribal chiefs, but sometimes the pressure from outside that followed the alleged mistreatment of Christians would be so great he had to take action.

The case of the Kurdish tribal leader Musa Bey is perhaps the leading example. Foreign governments—especially the British—had protested long and hard about complaints of abuse and oppression raised by Armenians and taken to the outside world by missionaries and consuls in their correspondence. Musa Bey had been implicated in an attack on two American missionaries in 1883, had abducted a young Armenian woman, and was accused of murdering two Armenians on separate occasions. The sultan was under European pressure to put him on trial.

This was easier said than done. Musa Bey might be a distant tribal chief, but he also came from a powerful family, could quickly raise a large body of armed men, and had strong connections in Istanbul. These complications notwithstanding, the sultan finally had to do something. Musa Bey was prosecuted in 1889, only to be acquitted of all charges, an outcome that caused as much outrage in Europe as the original accounts of his behavior.[18]

The trial was the unsatisfactory middle way Abdülhamit found between conflicting pressures. Nothing but a conviction and a long prison sentence, if not execution, would have satisfied Europe; nothing but an acquittal would have preserved peace among Kurds in the eastern provinces. A conviction and (even worse) a jail sentence could have caused turmoil in the east (already heading in that direction because of the "Armenian question"), in addition to which the sultan could not be seen as caving in to pressure from European governments, themselves under pressure from Armenian committees and their often well-placed supporters. These were the realities Abdülhamit had to balance against questions of innocence or guilt.

There were other occasions when tribal troublemakers were temporarily removed from the immediate scene but allowed to remain within the territory the central government called "Kürdistan." As the word of the tribal chief or the shaykh remained the most powerful influence in the daily lives of ordinary people outside the towns, the sultan was obliged to remain sensitive to tribal realities. Sorting out problems flexibly, quietly, and informally was far more his style than confrontation and the imposition of arbitrary standards.

Accordingly, following Kurdish attacks on villages, instructions were sent from Istanbul that "rigorous and repressive" punishment such as exile should not be imposed on the Kurdish chiefs. They should rather "be treated with leniency and only if they are persistent in their crimes" should legal procedures be applied. This response was directly tied to the activities of Armenian revolutionary committees whose intentions were well known. Thus, it was imperative "to avoid any act that would result in the loss of Muslim ascendancy in Kürdistan."[19]

The sultan and the Kurdish tribal chiefs were equally opposed to the European program of "reforms" for "Turkish Armenia" drawn up after the Congress of Berlin and forced upon the Ottoman state. In the view of the sultan and his ministers, as quoted by Aslıhan Gürbüzel, real reforms would consist of "the attainment of security [*ırz ve can ve malından emin olma*], education, and economical development of all classes of subjects [*sunuf-ı teba*]." This would be possible only when "the police forces are powerful in proportion to the importance of every district and the force is composed of honest individuals, when the judicial courts are regulated and schools are increased and when the means of commerce and prosperity are facilitated." Demands made under the heading of "reforms" (*isla-hat*) were "intrigues and privileges intended to lead to the establishment of Armenia—a name unheard of before—instead of Kürdistan."[20] This region had been called Kurdistan since ancient times and only recently had been called "Armenia" by the "malevolent" (*bedhahan*). Populated mostly by Muslims, said the sultan, Kürdistan "cannot be called Armenia."[21]

Many observers agreed with the sultan's reading of the situation. Armenians might live in particular towns or certain regions in substantial numbers, but nowhere did they constitute a majority. In 1881, a British ambassador tried to convince the Grand Vizier that "if the term Armenia was used, it was in a geographical rather than ethnic sense, and the Porte would labor under a mischievous misapprehension if it thought that either Europe or England were desirous of creating a hostile or aggressive Armenian imperium in the bosom of the Ottoman Empire."[22]

In fact, "Armenia" did not make sense, geographical, ethnic, or demographic, against the established facts on the ground. Moreover, events had moved a long way since 1881. It was the sultan's firm conviction by the 1890s that the establishment of some kind of separate Armenian presence in the eastern provinces, in the form of autonomy or a protectorate, was precisely what was intended behind the camouflage of "reforms." Certainly, it was what some British politicians and other public figures in the Gladstonian "humanitarian" camp would have wanted.

The Kurds were no less unsettled by the use of "Armenia." "What is this I hear," Shaykh Ubaydullah, venerated as a Naqşbandi Sufi guide as well as a Nehri tribal leader, remarked to an American missionary in 1880, "that the Armenians are going to have an independent state in Van and the Nestorians are going to hoist the British flag and declare themselves British subjects? I will never permit it even if I have to arm the women."[23]

Kurdish political self-awareness would therefore seem to have been stimulated not just by the development of nationalism elsewhere but by the growing weakness of the Ottoman Empire, the social turmoil that followed military defeat in 1878, and the perceived threat of the European powers (led by Britain) to remove land from the Kurds and place it under Armenian control.

Shaykh Ubaydullah, who had mobilized Kurdish horsemen to fight against the Russians in 1877–1878, subsequently believed that the central government, defeated and weakened by the war, was no longer capable of governing properly in the east. The war had been followed by social and economic turmoil, as returning soldiers and displaced groups of emigres from the Balkans roamed eastern Anatolia.

Having retained the arms given them during the war, and with Shaykh Ubaydullah promising protection and security to Christians as well as Muslims, Kurdish fighters defeated an Ottoman force before Shaykh Ubaydullah led a force estimated at 12,000 men into northwest Iran in 1880. This cross-border attempt to strengthen the Kurdish hold on territory and perhaps establish a central Kurdish authority in the region[24] alarmed the governments in Tehran and Istanbul and ended in the defeat of the Kurds by a Persian force and Shaykh Ubaydullah's capture and exile to Mecca. All of these developments can be seen as the first stirrings of Kurdish nationalism, underpinned by religious as well as tribal authority.

The Kurds deeply resented the slanders that were commonplace whenever the situation of Armenians and other Christians was being discussed outside the Ottoman Empire. H. F. B. Lynch, the chronicler of Armenian life in the east called them "parasites,"[25] and the words "predatory," "savage," "vagabonds," "a curse," and "depredations" were never far from the lips of their detractors.

These caricatures came from the pens or the lips of those whose marginalization and denigration of the Kurds was the obverse of their single-minded sympathy for Ottoman Christians. They were either not interested in or not capable of understanding the complexities of Kurdish society, "in which feudalism, tribalism, nomadism, urbanism, trade and commerce coexisted in conflict and unity."[26] Accusations of the theft of animals, plunder, murder, and mutilation filled the reports of the foreign consuls year after year. The Kurds were deeply affronted. Others, and Christians have to be included, committed crimes without accusing fingers being pointed at the entire group.

In a petition addressed to the central government in 1880, the tribes of Van acknowledged that because of nomadism they "could not benefit from education and modern industries,"[27] but that was no reason for passing such sweeping judgment on them. In this petition, the Kurds complained, "We are shown as oppressors while we are oppressed; although we are virtuous we are shown as sinners. Our misdemeanors are presented like crimes, our crimes like terrible murders. . . . The inappropriate behavior of one single person is ascribed to the wildness of the tribe."

Only recently, before a state commission was sent to Van to allocate famine relief, "A member of the [Armenian] patriarchate had said in anger: 'Do not help the Kurds, they are wild and disobedient. Let them perish because of hunger and at least in this way they will have the punishment they deserve.'" Yet Kurds paid millions of *akçes* in taxes and looked after themselves as well as others. Did they really deserve to be "discarded from humanity and from the divine law of civilization?"[28]

The commissioners had been travelling around Kurdistan for almost a year. In this period,

> Have they heard of any mass murders [*cinayet-i azime*] oppressing the sons of the country or plunderings on the part of the Kurds? Moreover, in which civilized country do troubles, murders [and] thefts not take place? Are crime and murder peculiar to Kürdistan? Who are those committing the worst acts like murder in X, Y, Z villages in the past three or four months? Who speak[s] against the union of Ottomans [*ittihad-i Osmani*] and confuse[s] minds with many malign and false rumors?[29]

With education, the petitioners insisted, the Kurds, looked down upon as savages, would produce many "elegant" intellectuals and "valuable protectors of the motherland."[30]

The disaggregation of responsibility for the disorder and turmoil that gripped the eastern provinces in the last quarter of the nineteenth century raises the question of Kurdish-Armenian relations and the reasons for their breakdown. The power of the Kurdish tribal chiefs was a double-edged sword, to be used to protect those who respected their prerogatives (including Christians) and to be used against those who did not. Kurdish life was underpinned by a deeply entrenched moral code governing individual behavior and collective responsibility, the understanding of which naturally differed according to the personality and vested interests of the *bey* or *ağa*. Honor, shame, and retribution were paramount, whether the Kurds were in conflict among themselves or with the outsider.

Armenian attacks on Kurds and other Muslims seemed deliberately intended to end in the reprisals that followed. Certainly, there could scarcely be any greater provocation to the Kurds than the murder of the son of a tribal chief and the violation of women during the Sasun uprising in 1894. British and American consular records are full of accounts from many parts of eastern Anatolia of mob attacks on Armenians in 1894–1896. On several occasions, large numbers of Kurds forced their way into towns to get at the Armenians. Laz, Circassians, and Turks were also involved, but the central role of the Kurds strengthens the argument that much more was involved in these years than a violent Muslim response to Armenian provocations.

Jelle Verheij has argued that Kurdish actions had all the characteristics of a Kurdish uprising, aimed at restoring the privileges weakened through Ottoman centralization and now further undermined by the apparent intention of the powers to create an Armenian state-in-being out of "Kurdistan." Thus, the dominant Armenian-western discourse, ruled by the idea that the massacres were organized by the Ottoman authorities (or the sultan himself), "does not reflect the complexity of the reality."[31]

Part of this reality was the relative weakness of government authority in the eastern provinces, as affirmed by the scathing remarks of virtually every passing European traveler. Corruption, nepotism, inefficiency, and sloth regularly featured in consular dispatches. The power the sultan supposedly had to control often chaotic situations but did not use because of his own malign purposes—in the view of some distant observers— is open to question. He had to tread carefully. He was frequently criticized for not sending the army against the Kurds, when doing so might have precipitated a Kurdish-Muslim uprising far more dangerous than the Armenian threat.

The sultan's establishment of the Kurdish Hamidiye cavalry in 1890 has been seen as an invitation to pillage. Yet confronted with Armenian uprisings and the infiltration of arms and men from over the Russian and Persian borders, the formation of a regional mounted force to police those borders and help suppress uprisings was a logical response. The Hamidiye were notoriously poorly-trained and ill-disciplined, however. When acting under the orders of their officers, they could be controlled, but when they were off duty there could be no official check on their activities.

In 1896, an attempt by Armenians to assassinate a Kurdish tribal chief in the province of Van touched off a round of bloody reprisals against Armenian villages. The arrival in Van township of the sultan's special representative (Saadettin Paşa) on a mission of inquiry was followed by a major outbreak of violence in June, when hundreds of Armenians barricaded themselves inside the Garden City quarter (as a later generation of rebels did in 1915). Fighting in the town ended when the militants were given a safe-conduct pass to the Persian border (many were reportedly killed on the way by Kurds) but continued in outlying districts, as Kurds laid waste to Armenian villages and killed their inhabitants. The flight of the survivors from districts with a substantial Armenian population "accelerated" the process of "Kurdification" in these districts.[32]

These conflicts underline the importance of the distinction that again has to be made between the behavior of the Hamidiye off-duty and their actions when under military command. Neither at Sasun in 1894 nor in the following years did the Hamidiye play a preponderant role in the military suppression of Armenian uprisings. When Kurds did take part in mob attacks and the massacre of Armenians, Verheij has written, "They were rarely under Ottoman command."[33]

Given the complexity of these events, responsibility clearly did not lie with the sultan alone or with his government. Rather, it was shared by all those involved, including Armenian revolutionaries inciting uprisings, and foreign governments whose interference only made the situation worse.

CHAPTER 4

The East in Flames

LIVING AMONG TURKS and Kurds in the eastern Anatolian provinces were Christians, predominantly Armenians but also Nestorian and Jacobite Assyrians and Chaldeans, as well as tiny Jewish communities. The Armenians were located in the same three empires as the Kurds. For the nationalists among them, the eastern provinces of the Ottoman Empire constituted not Kurdistan but "western Armenia," despite the small and scattered nature of Armenian communities between the Black Sea and Mediterranean coasts. They were most numerous in Van and Bitlis provinces. Across the Persian border, large numbers of Kurds and Armenians lived around Lake Urmia as the main numerical components in an ethnic mosaic that included even smaller Christian churches (such as the Chaldeans), Yazidis, and a sprinkling of Jewish communities.

The Assyrians of Hakkari in what is now southeastern Turkey were bound by the same tribal patterns of life and loyalty as the Kurds. However, whereas the Kurds were tied to the *shaykh*, the *ağa*, and the *bey*, the Assyrians gave their loyalty to the patriarch, the priests, and their tribal *muluk* (kings; sing. *malik*). Increasingly, the "plight" of all Ottoman Christians, especially after the signing of the Treaty of Paris (1856) ending the Crimean War, became enmeshed in the cogs of international politics.

The broad reform ideas broached by Layard during discussions with the sultan covering administrative reform and the development of railways and natural resources,[1] were not very different from what the sultan and his government already had in mind and were trying to achieve, but as noted, the "reforms" produced and refined in the wake of the Congress of

Berlin (1878) were entirely different. Their geographical focus was not the entire empire but only the six eastern Anatolian provinces. Their ethnoreligious focus was the Armenians, with the Kurds discussed only pejoratively.

The vaguely worded commitments set down in Article 61 of the Treaty of Berlin were the measuring stick by which the sultan was judged: "The Sublime Porte engages to carry into effect without further delay the improvements and reforms demanded by local requirements in the provinces inhabited by Armenians and to guarantee their security from Kurds and Circassians." Although the sultan had agreed to these "reforms," the years went by without them being introduced, opening the powers up to the accusation that they were not living up to their obligations to the Christians of the Ottoman Empire.

The debate over the situation of Ottoman Christians was strongly influenced by views that were deeply rooted in the historic Christian polemic against Islam. It was reflexively assumed by many, without the need to ask further questions, that Christians were "worse off" than the Muslims and that no Christians could possibly prosper under "Mohammedan rule." Criticism in Europe was deeply selective. Many Ottoman Christians were poor, many were exploited by feudal overlords, but so were Muslims and, unlike Christians, who could take their grievances to consuls and missionaries, the great mass of Muslims had no one, not even their own government, from whom they could seek redress. Christians (and Jews) were far more likely to prosper than Muslims, for the simple reason that banking, money-lending, and commerce were their monopolies.

In some important respects, the Muslims were far worse off: only they had to carry the weight of conscription—five years, as established in the regulations of 1839. Occasionally, Christians complained, but their insistence that they were prepared to serve in the army was disingenuous. The *bedel askeri* exemption tax was a small price to pay for escaping military service in remote and often unhealthy corners of the empire such as Yemen or the neighboring 'Asir region, from which the conscript might never return, given the high death rate from disease.

From Smyrna (Izmir), Consul Blunt, reporting in 1860 on the beneficial effects of the Hatt-i Hümayun, found that Christians lived on a footing of "perfect equality" with Muslims. Indeed, he wrote, "It may safely be asserted that the Christians are much better off than the Turks, for there is no drain upon the Christian population for troops and Christians pay the same taxes on their produce." The Muslim population seemed to be receding and the Christian population rapidly increasing. In Blunt's view, "The Turkish villager is, without a doubt, more frequently subject to oppression than the Christian."[2]

Consul Palgrave, reporting eight years later from Trabzon, after a visit to Erzurum, Kars, Ardahan, Amasya, Çorum, and Yözgat, places reported as "the strongholds of Turkish fanaticism," drew attention to the fact that while the Christians had channels of recourse through foreign governments and their consuls, the Muslims had no one.[3] In Aleppo, where Muslim-Christian relations had been deeply shaken by news of fighting between Druze and Maronites on Mount Lebanon and the subsequent massacre of Christians in Damascus, Consul Skene reported, "Religious tolerance is professed by the Government authorities in this province and there is no practical violation of the principle of any importance."[4] Christian churches had been built without the least opposition and the Christian population "has no great grievances to complain of."[5]

Between Muslims and Christians, the variables everywhere were great. The state of their relationship depended on time, place, and circumstances: the religious segmentation of society was typical of the Muslim order, but there was no basic demarcation with the Muslims on top and the Christians suffering below. Each religious community had specific grievances (in the case of the Christians, often directed against their own ecclesiastics), and both had grievances in common in an empire whose fatal weakness was that it lacked common loyalties that could transcend ethnoreligious differences and bind the people together. By the time the empire tried to cultivate the unifying sense of identity called "Ottomanism," it was too late. The national idea had already taken hold among Christians and was soon to grip the Muslim imagination as well.

GOSPEL TRUTHS

American Protestant missionaries had gone forth early in the nineteenth century, reinforcing the British missionaries who were already stationed in the Ottoman Empire and establishing "stations" across Anatolia and Syria. The Americans wrote as if they were engaged in a military campaign: the empire was territory to be penetrated and occupied, a citadel to be conquered and high ground to be seized. The language of conquest was physically symbolized in the founding of Robert College on a ridge of hills on the European side of the Bosporus. The principal targets of the missionaries were the eastern Christian churches, whose priests they regarded as corrupt and whose doctrines they believed to be in dire need of reform, bringing these churches to what the missionaries called a "higher form of Christianity" so they would serve as a good example for the Muslims.

The missionaries also proselytized among Muslims, convinced that all they were doing was passing on a message of truth. As the missionary Eli Smith told the annual meeting of the American Board of Commissioners for Foreign Missions (ABCFM) in 1832, they meant no insult when talking to Muslims but only wanted to prove "by sober and convincing argument . . . that he [Muhammad] is a false Prophet."[6]

Until the 1840s, apostates from Islam were still being executed. Even the appearance of a known convert could cause public disorder, but many of the missionaries remained blind to the consequences of their exhortations. They regarded the Hatt-i Hümayun as a door opening the way to the full expression of religious freedom, which they interpreted as their right to proselytize among Muslims as they saw fit. The Ottoman government's contrary view was that the *hatt* gave no license to people of one faith to undermine, insult, and cast doubt on the beliefs of people of another faith.

In Anatolia, the missionaries spread their gospel truths mainly among Armenians of the Armenian Apostolic Church (the Gregorians). In Syria, they focused on Mount Lebanon and the Maronites. The patriarchs of both churches anathematized them, with converts to Protestantism expelled from their local communities.

The Muslim majority in the empire was a mouth-watering target, but over the decades only the tiniest fraction of Muslims was converted to Christianity, not necessarily for lack of missionary zeal but because Muslims seemed impervious to their arguments. Missionary schools and colleges were appreciated for their standards of modern education but not without religious and nationalist suspicion of their motives.

Overt hostility to Islam and the Ottoman government was never far from the surface in missionary attitudes. The missionaries were a main conduit of information fed into the missionary and secular press in Britain and the United States. Their accusations at times of turmoil, often lurid and unsubstantiated, continually reinforced the historical image of the "terrible Turk." Their pious declarations of goodwill deceived neither the heads of the eastern churches nor the Ottoman government on whose goodwill the missionaries depended even while praying for its downfall. While some missionaries were aware that politics and religion were a combustible mix, others did not hesitate to step over the dividing line. "I do not share his gloomy apprehensions at all nor do any of the missionaries in Turkey," Dr. George Washburn wrote of his father-in-law, Cyrus Hamlin, the founding president of Robert College, who believed missionaries must stay out of politics if their institutions were to flourish.[7]

Funded by an American philanthropist, Christopher Rhinelander Robert, the college was established in the 1860s on a prime piece of land at Bebek, overlooking the Bosporus behind the Rumeli Hisar fortress built to prevent relief being sent to Constantinople during the Ottoman siege of the city in 1453. Robert died in 1878; the college is now Boğaziçi (Bosporus) University, the most prestigious in Turkey. Its original name has been perpetuated on the campus of what was the American College for Girls, now the Robert College coeducational secondary school at nearby Arnavutköy.

The difference of opinion between Hamlin and his son-in-law was caused by Dr. Washburn's support for Bulgarian nationalism. Under his administration, especially after the "Bulgarian atrocities" of 1876, the college had revealed itself, according to Keith Greenwood, as

> a purely Christian institution, a spokesman for Christian minorities in the empire and, if necessary, an intriguer in their behalf. Its director and two of its prominent professors were on the Ottoman government's list of political agitators.
>
> The government could have closed the college, arrested Paneretoff,[8] deported Washburn and Long [missionary teacher Albert Long] or taken any other course of action. That it did not was due to the fact that the long-dreaded Russo-Turkish war was about to break out and the Ottoman government was in desperate peril. It had no inclination to act against an institution which clearly had the support of an influential segment of British opinion. A much bigger game was afoot and the college in itself was not important enough.[9]

George Washburn had been in the Ottoman Empire for a long time but believed the sooner it was overthrown the better. Writing to Christopher Robert as Russia moved closer to war with the Ottoman Empire in 1877, he acknowledged that it was a critical time for the college,

> but I cannot for a minute believe that the progress of Christ's kingdom is dependent on the maintenance of the great anti-Christian

power of the false prophet. That power must go down and if God wills Russia to destroy, it will only be a repetition of what is recorded over and over again in the Old Testament when he used one heathen power to destroy another. Russia is not very Christian but it does not follow from this that she is not a proper instrument for God to use and punish and destroy this abominable Mohammedan despotism. She may do God's work in the east and prepare the way for his kingdom in the east though we do not like her. In the Turks as individuals I have a great interest, and I believe that Robert College has a great work to do for them, but there is no hope of reaching individual Turks as long as the Moslem power is unbroken.[10]

Dependent on the goodwill of the Ottoman government, yet sheltering Bulgarian nationalists, sympathetic to their struggle for independence, and even looking ahead to a successful war against the country in which he was living, it is no wonder that Dr. Washburn was regarded with great distrust by the sultan and his ministers, affecting their view of Robert College in general.

DEEPENING INTERVENTION

The exclusive missionary emphasis on the suffering of Christians and the awakening interest of foreign Christians in the affairs of Ottoman Christians softened the ground for deepening intrusions in Ottoman affairs by the powers. No doubt their humanitarian concern was genuine, but it still served as a mask for the completely unsentimental nature of their imperial interests, strategic and commercial. Public outrage in Britain and the U.S., fired up by the latest missionary or newspaper account of mistreatment of the Armenians, in particular, frequently ended in demands to put pressure on the sultan by sending warships to the Dardanelles or the eastern Mediterranean.

In the wake of the 1877–1878 Ottoman-Russian war, Britain was concerned that Russia would use the Armenians the same way it was believed to have used the Bulgarians in the Balkans: as an ethnoreligious stalking horse allowing it to entrench its strategic position, this time in eastern Anatolia, putting it close to vital British interests in the eastern Mediterranean and the Persian Gulf.

The Armenian "reform" project set in motion after the Congress of Berlin in 1878 involved detailed administrative changes in the eastern Ottoman provinces, from the appointment of *valiler* (provincial governors) down to an "ethnographical" separation of the different ethnoreligious groups at the smallest *nahiye* (commune) level. The British ambassador sought a division that would unite "as many homogeneous elements as possible, the Armenians, or when necessary the Armenians and the Osmanlis [Turks] being grouped together to the exclusion of the Kurds." [11] Nomads living in the mountains—mostly Kurds—who came down to plains inhabited by Christian villagers should not be included in the census and neither should they be allowed to settle temporarily in Christian villages. Once the region was demographically reorganized, it would be placed under the authority of a Christian governor.

In the view of the sultan and his ministers, what else could this be but the skeletal outline of a project for eventual Armenian autonomy. But apart from their visceral opposition to anything that smacked of further partition of Ottoman lands, the practical obstacles to this ambitious project were insuperable.

The Ottoman government was broke, and no offer of loans to fund these "reforms" was ever forthcoming from any of the powers demanding them. They were proposing European supervision over the courts, the prisons, the police, and the tax office when few of the inspectors who might be considered had any knowledge of the Ottoman language (a rich mixture of Turkish, Arabic, and Persian written in Arabic script and conforming to Turkish grammar). Practically, any attempt to separate the sultan's subjects on an ethnoreligious basis was certain to have explosive consequences on the ground. Ideologically, it would have sharpened differences at a time Abdülhamit was trying to create a common Ottoman sense of belonging.

While the idea of Armenian autonomy might have taken root in some minds, conditions on the ground were totally against it. The Armenians were scattered across the eastern provinces. They constituted less than 20 percent of the overall population, and there was not one cohesive territorial bloc that could serve as the core of an autonomous province. Armenians were most numerous in Van, but even there they constituted only about 30 percent of the population.

Kurds claimed most of the territory in which this "reform" program was to be enacted as theirs by traditional right, and they were far more numerous than the Armenians. [12] The gaps between what the powers were demanding, what was practicable, and what the sultan could be persuaded to accept were so great that there was no option over the years but for the "reform" project to be substantially modified.

THE "DISH OF LIBERTY"

An Armenian delegation led by a former patriarch went to the Congress of Berlin in 1878, hoping to dip into the "dish of liberty" along with the Serbs and the Bulgarians, only to find that while the Balkan Christians were holding iron spoons, theirs were paper, crumpling in their hands when their interests finally came up for consideration.[13] The loose references to "improvements and reforms" written into the Treaty of Berlin fell far short of their demands. Armenians wanted the autonomy other Christians had been given through European intervention. The Armenian patriarch told Layard that if Armenian demands were not met, "Armenia as a whole would within a short time rise against its ruler [the sultan] and annex itself to Russia," a measure that would "scarcely be consistent" with British interests.[14]

The Armenians had powerful international supporters. In Britain, Gladstone had long since taken up the cause of Christians living under Ottoman rule or in fact under Muslim rule anywhere. During the "Bulgarian atrocities" of the 1870s his voice was the most outraged in Europe. Calling for home rule in Ireland, yet ordering the invasion of Egypt in 1882, he was inevitably regarded as a moralizing hypocrite by his critics. Queen Victoria had to deal with him regularly when he was Prime Minister but couldn't stand him. Layard believed Gladstone had willfully turned the suffering of Bulgarian Christians to his own political advantage, writing that his "unscrupulous agitation" had turned public opinion in favor of Russian intervention, causing great embarrassment to the government.[15]

The ambassador held Gladstone largely responsible for the outbreak of war in 1877. As he wrote,

I remember being in the room of Mr. John Murray, the well-known publisher, when the first proof of Bulgarian Atrocities was brought to him.[16] It had not yet been published. I glanced over it and expressed my opinion that its publication would lead to the most serious consequences and eventually to war. I was then Minister at Madrid.[17] It may be asserted with confidence that they [Gladstone's tract and other publications] led to the war between Russia and Turkey which would not have taken place had the Russian Emperor and Government been convinced that England was resolutely determined to prevent it and I cannot but hold their authors responsible for the incalculable amount of misery and bloodshed which it produced, for the innumerable human beings who perished in it and who will still be its indirect victims."[18]

In a letter to Gladstone, Layard noted that those who had denounced the "Bulgarian atrocities" in 1876 had remained silent "during the infinitely greater outrages and cruelties committed by the Bulgarians upon the Musulmans."[19] Gladstone was offended but the charge was true. Not surprisingly, one of his first actions on being returned to office as Liberal Prime Minister in 1880, was to withdraw Layard in circumstances distressing, costly, and humiliating to the ambassador.

Relations between Britain and the Ottoman Empire rapidly deteriorated during the five years the Gladstone government was in power. It was hard to say which emotion in Gladstone was the strongest when it came to the Sultan Abdülhamit, loathing, contempt, revulsion, or hatred. A policy of threat and menace quickly replaced the personal relationship Layard had developed with the sultan.

Whether in power (1880–1885, a few months in 1886, and 1892–1894) or in opposition, Gladstone took a leading role in the attempt to create an Armenian agitation along the same lines as the campaign for the Bulgarians in the 1870s. Undoubtedly, he gained domestically from representing himself as the scourge of the sultan and the savior of Ottoman Christians. The cost was great damage to his country's standing in Istanbul. The warm relationship built on the joint struggle against Russia during the Crimean War was weakened at Berlin, and in the wake of the invasion of Egypt and continuing pressure and threats over the Armenian question, it turned cold. The sultan, feeling betrayed by Britain and personally affronted by Gladstone's hectoring, looked around for a more reliable friend and found it in Germany.

"PREPARING FOR REVOLT"

Of all the powers, Britain pursued the Armenian "reform" plan most doggedly. There was no safety net or plan B if plan A failed, which was eventually to be the case. Britain just pressed on, its eastern policy feeding off humanitarian concern and encouraging the aspirations of the Armenian national committees.

Small Armenian revolutionary groups, such as the Black Cross Party, the Armenagans, and the Defenders of the Motherland movement, had already taken up arms in the eastern provinces when the two organizations that were to dominate Armenian nationalist politics in the coming decades were established. The Hunchakian Revolutionary Movement was founded in Geneva in 1887, and the Dashnaktsutyun Armenian Revolutionary Federation in Tiflis (Tbilisi) in 1890. The leaders of both organizations were Russian Armenians who chose the remote and poorly administered eastern provinces of the Ottoman Empire—"western Armenia" in their understanding—as a more promising arena for revolutionary action than the Russian Caucasus.

The socialist programs of both movements were highly idealistic. The war against the Ottoman state was couched in universalist rhetoric calling for the destruction of all despotisms and the establishment of a democratic state guaranteeing individual rights and ensuring equality before the law for all citizens. Although the emphasis was on the liberation of "Armenia," the broad outlook was international and anti-imperialist, with the Hunchaks looking ahead to a time when other ethnonational groups, including Kurds, Azeris, and Ottoman Christians, would be emancipated and able to form "a general independent federation of Eastern nations" similar to the Swiss federation "once they are delivered from the Turkish yoke."[20]

In their 1891 proclamation of a "people's war" on the "Turkish" government, the Dashnaks declared, "The Armenian who yesterday begged on bended knee for assistance from Europe is now resolved to defend his rights, his property and his home and family with his own hands." These Armenians were resolved to be free or to die and were no longer imploring but were demanding "with gun in hand."[21]

Atamian has put forward two main reasons why, in the long run, the Dashnak federation proved more durable than the Hunchaks. One was the "rigidly" centralized nature of the Hunchak party compared to the decentralization of the Dashnaks, with the autonomy granted to the branches opened in many countries allowing flexibility in adapting to local conditions. Both parties stood on the same ground when it came to class consciousness, but while the Hunchaks put class interests above the national interest, the Dashnaks made a strategic choice, placing "the interests of the nation above all classes," and ensuring their domination of the national movement.[22]

Beyond the rhetoric, the practical problems in the way of "liberation" were so formidable that Armenian religious and secular leaders
seemed to have lost touch with reality. Initially, the Armenian patriarch,
Nerses Varbajedian, had called only for reforms supported by the British
government. Any attempt to turn part of the eastern provinces into an
autonomous Armenian province would be "out of the question," given
the preponderance of the Muslim population and the violence that would
inevitably ensue.[23] However, the patriarch was under pressure because
of sharp divisions in the Armenian community over how to proceed at
Berlin, resigning more than once and withdrawing his resignation on one
occasion only after an appeal by Layard.[24]

The Treaty of San Stefano (March 3, 1878) obliged the Ottoman government to introduce "improvements and reforms demanded by local
requirements in the provinces inhabited by the Armenians," the same
phrase adopted in the Treaty of Berlin (July 13, 1878). There had scarcely
been time for the Ottoman government to set any changes in motion,
even if it were so inclined, but with autonomy now "the order of the day"[25]
in the Armenian community, the patriarch changed tack. He now supported Armenian autonomy under the authority of a Christian governor,
arguing that the government's failure to redress Armenian grievances left
him no alternative. The autonomous region would include Sivas, Van, the
greater part of Diyarbakir, and the "ancient kingdom of Cilicia," extending
southwards from the Taurus mountains to the sea.[26]

The stimulus here was the autonomy granted to Bulgarian Christians at
the Congress of Berlin. A more precise model was the decentralized form
of government established on Mount Lebanon in 1861, the *mutasarrifiyya*,
maintained under the authority of a succession of Christian governors
until 1915. But whereas Mount Lebanon was a compact region in which
Maronite Christians formed the majority of the population, nowhere in
the sprawling eastern provinces of the Ottoman region were Armenians
in sufficient numbers to make such a project remotely feasible. Even the
most sympathetic European government was never going to be tempted
into trying to impose such a project on the Ottoman state. No matter how
many times Armenian revolutionary nationalists and their foreign supporters uttered the phrase "western Armenia," the reality on the ground
was that Armenians were a small minority.

While Ottoman censuses made no distinction between Muslims on
the basis of ethnicity, there is no doubt that the Kurds as one particular ethnoreligious group vastly outnumbered the Armenians. Apart from

what the sultan thought about the situation in the east, their tribal and religious leaders (often one and the same) were never going to surrender a land
they called Kurdistan and regarded as their own. The patriarch was clearly
aware of these realities but given prevailing Armenian public opinion he
may have felt there was no option but to support the call for autonomy.

Ideologically, and in the means they employed to attain their ends, the
Hunchaks and Dashnaks were strongly influenced by Russian revolutionary movements, especially Khozhdenie v Narod (Going to the People)
and Narodnaia Volya (People's Will). Terror was not terror but "self-
defense" to protect the people, to raise their spirit, inspire a revolutionary
disposition, and thus maintain the task at hand: "to shake the power of the
government" and create extreme fear in its ranks.[27] Civil servants, spies,
and Armenian "traitors"—those Armenian community leaders hostile to
the revolutionary committees, and often holding positions of government
authority—were all targets for assassination. The "wrecking and looting"
of state institutions were part of the program, along with the establishment of combat units and arming of the people.[28] The point of general
revolution would be reached when a foreign power attacked the Ottoman
Empire externally: at that point "the party shall revolt internally."[29]

Adherents of these organizations in cities and towns were heavily
concentrated in the artisan class (confectioners, shoemakers, tailors,
blacksmiths, etc.), with students and teachers also among them. Rural
communities could also be stirred into rebellion, often on the assurance
of forthcoming foreign support.

Revolutionary activities were not confined to the eastern Ottoman
provinces or the Russian Caucasus. Hunchaks and Dashnaks alike developed a network of subcommittees in the Balkans and many western
European cities, including Geneva, Zurich, Paris, Marseilles, and London,
where public sympathy for the Armenian national cause was continually
fed with horror reports of atrocities allegedly committed in the eastern
Ottoman provinces.

In London, keeping watch on the comings and goings of Hunchaks
and other "notorious Nihilists and Anarchists" from premises in the suburb of Acton, Sergeant Flood reported in 1895 on the arrival at Liver-
pool's Royal Albert Dock of printer's type and revolutionary literature in
French, Russian, Hebrew, and English, along with several thousand letters
from various parts of the world, "some written in very violent language."
According to his colleague, Chief Inspector Melville, the house of a well-
known Hunchak "is now a general rendezvous for Nihilists and that it is

the intention of the 'Hintchagist' party to start a revolution in Armenia early next spring and failing that the summer."[30]

Even before the Hunchaks took the lead in fomenting revolutionary agitation, there were warnings that Ottoman Armenians were "preparing for revolt" with the backing of the Tsar.[31] Russian Armenians were reported to be crossing the border with supplies of arms. In 1881, an American missionary at Van told of meeting two Russian Armenians who said they "had been sent here by their Committees in Tiflis to stir up the Armenians to revolt against the Turks, and they said there were 150,000 men in Russian territory ready to cross the frontier to give assistance. They said the Russian government had encouraged them, and had sold them arms for a quarter of the cost price." They had found the country people "much more ready to rise than the people of the city."[32]

In the Ottoman southeast, the mountain town of Zeytun seethed with discontent and hostility to government authorities. A visiting British military consul found that the Zeytunlis "do not improve on personal acquaintance. I find them to be a semi-barbarous and depraved community, little better than savages, and so ignorant, self-opinionated and conceited that it is impossible to do any good with them by argument and persuasion."

In his opinion, the Zeytunlis were deaf to anything a "Turk" might say. Evil-minded and inflammatory priests talked of justice when the real cause of their "violent language" was hatred of Muslims. The *kaymakam* (senior local administrator) lived in the military barracks outside the town, unable to make arrests for murder or robbery and confessing that "there is no government and that he is of no use."[33]

These were harsh words but the Zeytunlis had a long track record of bloody uprisings. They were a tough and hardy people, capable of fighting off large numbers of regular troops before escaping higher into the mountains. The region in which they lived was difficult to reach in good weather and was almost impenetrable from the outside in winter, the chosen season for some of their biggest challenges to authority.

There were numerous further warnings before the situation ended in a full-blown crisis. In 1891, Consul Hampson reported on a conversation with an Armenian in an "official" position, clearly with one of the revolutionary committees. The patience and endurance of the peasant population being exhausted, he told Hampson,

> They were determined to attract the attention of civilized nations by desperate means. On me asking what they hoped for, what they

expected as a result, he said that all they knew was that their situation was unbearable; that they realized the fact that any rising on their part could only mean the massacre of 20,000 or 30,000 of their number, but that nothing could be more hopeless than their present state, that they were determined to suffer anything in order to obtain some change and that, as the worst that could result, they hoped that Russia would be forced to interfere and occupy the country.[34]

They were buying arms from the Kurds, were better armed than generally realized, and believed that a large force of Armenians, amounting to 40,000–50,000 men according to some reports, and constantly augmented by fresh recruits, was standing ready on the border with Iran.

The numbers may have been exaggerated by a revolutionary talking up his case, but the fact of a developing insurgency was not to be doubted. Writing on December 23, 1893, Cyrus Hamlin concluded, "An Armenian revolutionary party is causing great evil and suffering to the missionary work and to the whole Christian population of certain parts of the Turkish Empire. It is a secret organization and is managed with a skill in deceit which is only known in the East." He wrote that an "eloquent defender" of the revolution had told him the aim of Hunchak bands was to commit atrocities against Turks and Kurds, enraging the Muslims, and provoking such bloody repression that Russia would intervene in the name of humanity "and take possession."[35]

In the next three years, the eastern provinces slid ever deeper into chaos. In August 1895, the British ambassador to St. Petersburg, Sir Frank Lascelles, referred to reports that "clearly proved the existence of a widespread revolutionary movement which was strongly supported by the Armenian committees abroad and more especially in England." Among the Armenians was "a large and active party who cared little for reforms or an improved Administration but sought to bring about a complete state of anarchy. No form of government, however ideally perfect, could ever satisfy this party, who aimed at the destruction of all authority and the general distribution of property."[36]

PITCHED BATTLES

Only a small number of revolutionaries were involved in the uprising in the Sasun, Kulp, and Talori regions of the Bitlis vilayet in the summer of 1894, but by playing on local grievances (centering on taxation and the usual complaints against the Kurds involving pastorage rights) and giving assurances of foreign support they were able to talk many credulous villagers into taking up arms. The region was an "ideal base" for the operations of the militants.[37] It was remote and populated by a mixture of Kurds and Armenians, both of whom were regarded by some observers not just as backwards but as "wild beasts," incapable of comprehending law and morality, and given to acts of brutality and villainy without any distinguishing line between them.[38]

Early in 1893, a provincial administrator arriving in Armenian villages at the head of a small police force to collect back taxes was attacked and driven off. At the same time, to prevent conflict between Armenians and Kurds, the central government had directed that Kurdish tribes be prevented from coming down from the mountains when winter fell and moving with their flocks into the Muş plain. In retrospect, this decision was seen as a mistake because the absence of the tribes allowed Armenian militants to mobilize.

In the summer of 1894, the refusal of Armenians to pay taxes, along with armed clashes with Kurds, precipitated a large-scale uprising. Called upon to suppress the rebels, the *muşir* (commander-in-chief) of the Fourth Army, Zeki Paşa, concentrated three battalions of troops (from Erzincan, Harput, and Erzurum) in the town of Muş. Getting them there took at least a week. The mountainous region of Talori was then a further fourteen hours' march. Compounding the logistical problems, clashes were being reported in districts four to six hours apart.

The reports from British and Ottoman sources about what happened remain basically irreconcilable. According to C. M. Hallward, the British Vice-Consul at Van, the trouble began when Armenians tried to retrieve cattle stolen by Kurds. After an "affray" in which two or three lives were lost,[39] Ottoman troops descended on the region between Talori and Kulp, and massacred women and children along with rebels who had surrendered before putting twenty-five villages to the torch. Several thousand people were said to have been killed in the most atrocious circumstances. Cattle and sheep were driven off, women were abducted, churches sacked and burnt, and priestly robes and sacred ornaments "publicly sold in the streets of Moush."[40]

In his response, Abdülhamit professed ignorance of the events described by Hallward, who "probably got his information from untrustworthy sources." The Armenians were inventing stories and, encouraged by British officials, were emboldened to proceed to acts of "open rebellion." The regional military commander, Zeki Paşa, had been instructed to report back, and if the information given to the British ambassador proved correct, "action will be taken accordingly."[41]

Consul Graves, in Erzurum, speculated that "there was reason to believe that the Bitlis government had secretly encouraged the Kurds to pick a quarrel and attack the Armenians in force but that the Talori men had made an obstinate defense and had killed large numbers of the aggressors." The motivation was said to be the desire of the authorities to destroy "the independence of the district."[42] Hallward's informants included the *mutasarrif* of Muş whom the Ottoman government believed, according to the British, was an unreliable source.[43] As Hallward himself admitted to his ambassador, Sir Philip Currie, "He cannot vouch for the accuracy of the information given him at Mush and as he cannot visit the scene of action I am unable at present to furnish your Lordship with a reliable account of what has taken place."[44]

Relying on what he was told at Muş, Hallward was unable to make an on-the-spot investigation because the Ottoman government feared the presence of foreign consuls would only further inflame the situation.[45] He had still not visited the region two weeks later, yet by this time Currie had convinced himself that his telegrams from Muş left little room to doubt the "substantial accuracy" of his reports.[46] Insurgents had been active the previous year, so that by May 1894 the regional military command was anticipating trouble again, while remaining confident of being able to suppress any uprising.

In the Ottoman version of what happened, a small group of militants led by "Murat" (Hamparsun), a graduate of the medical faculty of Istanbul University, had talked local Armenians into rising against the state, telling them that foreign forces would be coming to their assistance in balloons. In the Talori region, their propaganda had taken effect in villages named as Shinik, Shimal, Güligüzan, Ahpi, Hotek, Sinanin, Şeknih, Elifkard, Hozoz, Efek, Akchasir, and Talori while having no effect in another twenty-four.

Toward the end of July, insurgents left their villages and began joining with other groups coming from the plain of Muş and the districts of Kulp and Silvan. Their numbers were reported to have reached about 3,000. Many had only swords, daggers, axes, and flintlocks, but others had modern weapons. They mobilized on Mount Andok, overlooking the Talori valley.

In his summary of the ongoing action,[47] Zeki Paşa reported, "Their primary aim is to exterminate the Turks that appear on their way and subsequently attack Muş with the aim of extracting arms and equipment from the arsenal of the reserve militia and thus broaden the scope and sphere of the uprising."[48]

The rebels finally held back from attacking Muş because army reinforcements were approaching. Splitting into groups of several hundred, they then attacked Kurdish tribal encampments, murdering and stealing cattle. According to the Ottoman documents, they cut open the belly of the nephew of a Bekran tribal leader, stuffed gunpowder into it, and "burned him." In the village of Güligüzan, the insurgents were said to have raped women in three or four households before killing them. A number of men were forced to walk through the village wearing crosses. Others had their eyes plucked out.

Finally, the insurgents "reached a climactic point in their malignancy when they blasphemously denounced the Muslim religion and the state and shouted altogether, 'Long live our king Murat.'"[49] Village houses were destroyed, and in the aftermath "no visible evidence of the Muslim populace could ever be traced."[50]

The military campaign (late August–early September 1894) was waged on the basis of reconnaissance and intelligence received on the 1,200–1,400 armed men gathered on and around Mt. Andok. Military casualties were slight because the soldiers were firing from 700 meters (and had two field guns), while most of the weapons in Armenian hands had a range of only 200 to 300 meters.

Murat and ten of his companions were captured in a cave. Under interrogation, they were said to have revealed that the objective of the uprising was "to annihilate the Turks living in the area and then establish an independent state through the support and backing of England and other foreign states."[51] Relief was sent to the stricken area at the sultan's direction. Zeki Paşa reported that when the fighting ended, "The women, children, and the elderly who have been hiding in the mountains and caves gradually returned to their villages" and were given food and clothing according to Islamic and humanitarian principles.[52]

In London and other European capitals, it was claimed that there had been no Armenian rising but only an unprovoked attack by Ottoman troops and the Kurdish cavalry. Gladstone went on the warpath again, with the Duke of Argyll, Canon McColl, Canon Wilberforce, G. W. E. Russell (founder of the Forward Armenia movement), and titled ladies and lesser clerics all playing supporting roles. The Armenian death toll was exaggerated by Gladstone and his fellow "humanitarians," to the point that more Armenians were said to have been killed than were known to be living in the region. Zeki Paşa put the insurgent losses at 1,000, without distinguishing between dead and wounded.

An Ottoman commission of inquiry indicated that 228 armed men had been killed during the conflict—97 Armenians, 117 Kurds, and 14 soldiers. The authors of a detailed study estimate that 150 civilians "at most" had died as an indirect result of the fighting, bringing the total to 378. Three foreign consuls observing the proceedings disagreed. They put the total number of Armenian dead (other casualties not assessed) at 265, but in 1895 the British consul, H.S. Shipley, changed his mind and said the total could be as high as 900. Down to the present day, however, the figure of many thousand Armenians is still being repeated as fact.[53]

Called in because of a shortage of regular troops, the Hamidiye cavalry, along with Kurdish tribesmen, laid waste to villages across the region. Charges against them of massacre, rape, and pillage were justified, even if luridly exaggerated in the European press. As atrocities had also been committed by the insurgents, an element of revenge can be seen in the Hamidiye response, along with plunder "by impoverished tribesmen anxious to acquire the wealth and property of their neighbors."[54]

That the Ottoman government was aware of the underlying conditions that led up to this explosion in Bitlis is clear from a memorandum sent by the General Staff headquarters to the Prime Ministry some time after July, 1895.[55] It describes the general situation on the Muş plain as one of poverty and insecurity, with the people exploited by cruel tax collectors and "certain" violent *ağalar* and *beyler*. Local officials were doing nothing to prevent plunder and murder by Kurds, resulting in "no protection for the Armenians and no punishment for the Kurds." The behavior of *jandarma* toward civilians was described as "despotic." The prison in Muş, in the basement of the military barracks and packed mostly with Armenians, was in a "deplorable state." In one room without window or ventilation, a hundred prisoners had not even the space to sleep. Some of the prisoners had contracted typhus, without any separate quarters for the sick being provided until lately.

Given the insufficient evidence on which Armenians were being imprisoned, it was not surprising to the author of the memorandum that young Armenians would choose to take to the mountains and join the insurgents rather than risk imprisonment on the basis of false accusations.

The measures recommended to end these evils included tax relief, the settlement of debts owned by villages to "loan sharks" or the government Ziraat Bank, tighter control of the Hamidiye, and punishment of *beyler* and *ağalar* for their crimes.[56]

In the coming two years, reports of terrible atrocities in the eastern Ottoman provinces poured into Europe and the United States from missionary sources, British consuls, and newspaper correspondents writing reports far from the scene in Istanbul. Exaggerations, fabrications, and hysterical abuse of the sultan were all part of the "news" cycle.[57] Vice-Consul Fitzmaurice's graphic account of how Armenians were burnt alive in their church at Urfa in late December 1895, including the cries of the victims as the flames reached the upper galleries, caused horror and revulsion. The report was written as if he were an eyewitness, when in fact he did not visit the town until some two months later in the company of Ottoman commissioners of inquiry.[58] Newspapers published lurid articles based on the most dubious sources. Writing from Van, British Vice-Consul Devey singled out the London *Daily News* for publishing articles that had no basis in fact,[59] but newspapers of a supposedly better quality were equally at fault. "The gross mendacity exhibited by *The Times* and by leading papers in general is above all description," wrote Vambéry.[60]

THE "RACE FACTION"

Rioting in Istanbul at the end of September 1895—aimed at the Armenian patriarch as well as the Ottoman government—ended in the death of police and demonstrators while causing the near collapse of the stock market and shaking the Imperial Ottoman Bank to its foundations. The bank's English director had no doubt that the Armenian committees were deliberately trying to precipitate a financial crisis. "The agents of the Armenian committee have been going around the outlying districts endeavouring to frighten the holders of banknotes and encouraging them to change them into gold with as little delay as possible." A French financial inspector agreed: "The doings of certain Armenian agitators going from door to door creating panic caused the general distrust to extend even to the establishment of highest credit. Everyone, fearing a revolution, endeavoured to regain possession of funds in deposit with the local firms."[61]

Three days after the clashes in Istanbul, an attempt to assassinate a former governor of the eastern Black Sea province of Trabzon precipitated mob attacks on Armenians and their property. In the last two months of 1895, the biggest uprising of the period was launched in and around Zeytun,[62] where Hunchak revolutionaries had been stoking revolt since July, on the promise that British and French fleets would soon be arriving at Mersin and Iskenderun. By late October, small-scale but vicious encounters between Armenians and *jandarma* had culminated in a full-scale uprising, invariably described in Armenian sources ever since as "self-defense."

According to Ottoman documents,[63] the insurgents burnt down nearby villages and massacred their Muslim inhabitants. In the town itself, they stormed the military compound in late December, taking prisoner all 50 officers and 600 soldiers and later massacring most of them when they tried to escape. Weapons, ammunition, and other military supplies were seized, and the army barracks burnt. Sent to crush the uprising, an Ottoman force of about 18,000 faced an army of insurgents estimated by the Ottoman government between 12,000 and 14,000 men.[64] Armenian estimates of the number of insurgents range from a high of about 6,000 to Vahakn Dadrian's low of 1,500.[65]

Thousands of soldiers, insurgents, and civilians died before a ceasefire could be arranged through foreign mediation in early February. The sultan granted a general amnesty along with tax relief and agreed to the appointment of a Christian *kaymakam*. Under the terms of the agreement, the six instigators of the rebellion were given safe passage to Mersin, where they embarked for Marseilles at the Ottoman government's expense.

Inflamed by the reports of attacks on Muslims in other towns and villages and rumors of attacks being prepared in their own, Muslims reacted violently in the name of Islam and the sultan. The wave of violence that rolled across the eastern provinces in the autumn of 1895 immediately followed the sultan's acceptance of "reforms" that the powers had been trying to impose for years. The sultan chose to describe them merely as "changes to existing regulations" but still refused to publish them for more than a year because of the inflammatory effect he feared they would have on Muslim opinion. Despite the official silence, Muslims still heard reports, possibly very garbled, of what the sultan had conceded. Already resentful at European intervention on the side of the Armenians, incensed at the stories of Armenian attacks, and fearful that their land was about to be set aside as an Armenian province, Muslims across the east struck back at neighbors they now regarded as enemies.

Toward the end of August 1896, the Imperial Ottoman Bank head office in Istanbul was the target of a well-organized attack, when Armenian revolutionaries dressed as porters carried sacks into the bank filled not with silver for deposit but bombs and dynamite. Once inside, the Armenians barricaded the main entrance, took control of the roof, and placed bombs where necessary to blow the building up if the decision was taken. The entire staff of 140 was taken hostage, Sir Edgar Vincent, the bank's English director, alone managing to escape through a skylight. The Armenians demanded the release of prisoners and the enactment of reforms or the bank would be blown up in two days. As explained by their leader, Armen Garo, the seizure of the bank was one of seven attacks carried out across the city. Their aim was "to ruin Istanbul commercially and financially, causing the misery of the lower classes who would in turn revolt." Warned that many "if not thousands" of people were likely to suffer as a result, Garo replied, "The more victims there will be, the more it will serve our cause."[66]

Violence inside the bank resulted in the death of six staff, including four guards, one genuine porter (*hamal*), and a hapless office boy, Nicoli, "who had been standing at the window and whose body remained dangling from the cornice."[67] Bombs were thrown out the windows, leaving dead and wounded in the streets. In other locations, bombs were hurled at soldiers in Rue Pera, killing several, at a police station, and into a carriage, killing four women.

The sultan quickly offered a pardon and safe exit for the revolutionaries from the country, but as news of the attacks spread across the city mobs began to take revenge, clubbing and knifing Armenians to death in the old city, up and down the Bosporus, and around the shores of the Sea of Marmara. Theological students known as *softas* and street toughs were in the forefront of these attacks. Troops struggled to prevent them crossing the Galata Bridge from the old city to get at Armenians living and working in the financial district.

Negotiations involving the British, the chief dragoman of the Russian embassy, and the sultan himself ended the crisis. With Abdülhamit guaranteeing their safety, the Armenians were escorted to Sir Edgar's private yacht, *Gülnar*, before being transferred to the Messageries Maritimes steamer, *Gironde*, for passage to Marseilles. They left their revolvers and hundreds of rounds of ammunition on Sir Edgar's yacht and 45 bombs,

25 "dynamite cartridges," and 11.4 kilograms of dynamite inside the bank.[68] The extraordinary footnote to this episode was Armen Garo's subsequent return to Istanbul and his election to parliament after the constitutional coup of 1908 as the member from Erzurum under his real name, Karekin Pastermadjian.

The bank's directors told their Paris committee that the crisis had been solved "thanks to the active and efficient intervention of His Imperial Majesty."[69] However, although an end to the seizure of the bank had been successfully negotiated, attacks on Armenians continued in many parts of the city for several days, and Armenian militants maintained the tension with continuing bombings. The final death toll was put at thousands of Armenians but no more than several dozen Muslims.

Inevitably, because the sultan was always blamed after such upheavals, whispers quickly spread among diplomats and journalists that he was directly responsible, that he had orchestrated the onslaught on the Armenians, and that he even knew beforehand that the Dashnaks were going to seize the bank. This was all gossip, and there is no evidence for any of it.

From an Ottoman Muslim perspective, the bank had been seized and Armenians had killed people across the city, only for the sultan to give a free pass out of the country to some of the murderers. In these volatile circumstances, had the sultan also ordered Muslim troops or police to shoot at Muslim rioters, the blaze that started with the seizure of the bank might have turned into an inferno. From the sultan's perspective, letting the fire burn itself out might have seemed the best option. Salisbury, the British Prime Minister, by no means sympathetic to the Ottoman government, probably got closest to the truth when speaking of the violent upheaval in Istanbul, blaming "the race faction and the creed faction, driven to the highest point in their corruptest and most horrible form."[70]

If Salisbury was right, who had driven "the race faction and the creed faction" to this terrible point? While the sultan was uniformly held responsible in Europe and the U.S., he had warned the British not to impose "reforms" that he knew his people could neither understand nor accept. He foresaw trouble in the backward eastern provinces that he would be unable to prevent, but for which he knew he would be blamed. Whatever the sultan's responsibility, others clearly had theirs even if it suited them to sheet all the blame home to the palace. Britain had meddled ceaselessly in the affairs of Ottoman Christians, giving hope to Armenian revolutionary committees and ignoring all the danger signs as the situation in the eastern provinces rose to the boil. The committees themselves had done their best to provoke chaos through a campaign of sabotage, murder, and uprisings. They attracted world attention to their cause. Thousands of Armenians and a smaller number of Muslims died, but they still attained none of their political goals. This has to be regarded as a very bleak outcome.

Libaridian has written that although the revolutionaries knew their attacks would be met with harsh measures, "and that blood would flow, the argument that the parties invited repression and massacres in order to achieve Great Power intervention on their behalf is a false one."[71]

In fact, the provocation of European outrage was a critical element in Armenian strategies. The bloodier the suppression of uprisings (or could be represented in diplomatic, press, and missionary correspondence), the greater the public pressure on the powers to wring something out of the sultan and the closer they could be pushed toward direct action if he did not respond. The revolutionaries were too few and their domestic support base too small to have any hope of succeeding outside the nexus of external support built on outrage and the possibility of intervention. It was a gamble that ultimately failed. Tens of thousands of Armenians and a far smaller number of Muslims died in a wholescale collapse of communal order without the sultan being forced to grant Armenian "reforms" that would open the way to autonomy and eventual independence.

With diplomatic approaches failing, Gladstone demanded military intervention, claiming British obligations under treaty commitments. In fact, as Salisbury pointed out in 1896, there were no treaty commitments obliging the powers to take military action on behalf of the Armenians, neither in the Cyprus Convention or the Treaty of Berlin. There was only an article in the Berlin treaty under which the six signatories agreed "not to any outside person but to each other" that if the sultan introduced reforms, they would oversee their execution—"that is the whole." As for the use of force, nothing would have induced him "to an undertaking so desperate as that of compelling the sultan by force of arms to govern well a country which otherwise"—in Salisbury's view—"he was not disposed to govern well."[72]

PROBLEMS IN COMMON

By the 1890s, the strategic interests of the powers and therefore the relationships between them were entering a new phrase. Relations between Tsar Alexander III and Abdülhamit, both beleaguered monarchs with many problems in common, were now relatively cordial. The rapidly rising industrial and military power of Germany was beginning to cause alarm in London. The kaiser was hungry for colonial expansion in Africa and was also developing a warm relationship with the Ottoman sultan, out of which was to come the joint German-Ottoman plan to build a railway from Berlin to Baghdad and a perceived threat to British interests in the Persian Gulf. In the Far East, Japan's rising industrial and military strength was beginning to have the same effect in Moscow, alarmed by the potential threat to Russia's far eastern territories.

These pressures drove Britain and Russia toward the 1907 agreement dividing Persia into "spheres of influence" and resolving differences over Afghanistan and Tibet. As Britain was simultaneously moving toward an alliance with Japan (1902) as a means of blocking Russian expansion in the Far East, the amity of 1907 hardly meant that the "great game" was over. The phrase belongs to history, but in different forms and by different actors the game has been played down to the present day.

By 1900, imperial priorities were again being recalibrated. Long-term objectives in the Near East had not been forgotten, but for the time being Europe was exhausted—and to a degree bored—by the complexities of the "Eastern Question." The powers could do no more to redress the grievances of Ottoman Christians. They had done their best to lift the Ottoman Empire out of the ditch (as they would see it) only to be checkmated finally by their own rivalries. They could do no more. When opportunity beckoned elsewhere (notably Africa), why waste more time trying to revive a sick man who seemed beyond healing?

Having done so much to encourage Armenian national aspirations through pressure exerted on the sultan since 1878, Britain conceded by the late 1890s that there was no more it could do and walked away from the mess it had helped to create. For the time being, the Armenians would have to fend for themselves.

"DO YOU KNOW THIS GENTLEMAN?"

Between 1856 and 1896, no country lost more prestige in Istanbul than Britain, and in this period began the seeding of the Ottoman relationship with Germany. Abdülhamit liked to tell a story of how his father had called for him when he was a boy of six or seven. There are several versions of this episode, and this is one of them.

I found him in one of his apartments sitting on a sofa in intimate conversation with an elderly Christian gentleman. When my father noticed me, he called me to come nearer and kiss the hand of the stranger seated by his side. At this behest I burst out in tears for the idea of kissing the hand of a Giaour [non-Muslim] was to me in my experience absolutely revolting. My father, generally so sweet-tempered, became angry and said: "Do you know who this gentleman is? It is the English Ambassador, the best friend of my house and my country and the English, although not belonging to our faith, are our most faithful allies." Upon this I reverently kissed the old gentleman's hand. It was the Böyük Eltchi,[73] Lord Stratford Canning. My father's words were deeply engraved on my mind and so I grew up with the idea that the English were our best friends.[74]

How disillusioned he was to become as sultan. British ambassadors warned him, threatened him, and tried to intimidate him. They refused to help when he requested a small loan. Their government had invaded and occupied Egypt and never stopped badgering him about the Armenian question, even while doing nothing to restrain the activities of the Armenian committees in London.

Until 1876, Abdülhamit had led a protected palace life. He was a young man with no direct experience of politics suddenly subjected to one shock after another, beginning with the circumstances preceding his succession. This was "the year of the three sultans": Abdülaziz, deposed and later committing suicide (or being assassinated); Murad V, Abdülhamit's brother, ruling for a few months before being deposed on the grounds of mental instability; and finally, Abdülhamit himself. He immediately had to deal with a Balkan crisis followed by war and perhaps the most devastating defeat in Ottoman history.

The Russian advance on Istanbul and the sudden influx of a mass of refugees and armed men retreating from the front caused panic in the city and a sense that social order could collapse. The sultan "lost heart" and summoned Layard to tell him his life was in danger and that he and his family might have to take refuge on a British warship. Layard offered to make the embassy gunboat, the *Antelope*, available in case of need.[75]

The Treaty of San Stefano had been signed, and the sultan was waiting for the diplomats to gather in Berlin to decide his empire's fate when a Muslim political activist, 'Ali Suavi, led a large group of armed men to the gates of Çirağan Palace, the residence of Murat V, on the shores of the

Bosporus close to Dolmabahçe and Yildiz Palaces. Forcing their way in, they made their way to the inner apartments, where 'Ali Suavi tried to persuade the deposed sultan to buckle on his sword, leave the palace, and lead an uprising against his brother. In the chaos, 'Ali Suavi was killed. Murad took refuge in the harem until found and placed under the protection of his brother at Yildiz Palace.

In Layard's view, the affair had a deeply unsettling effect on Abdül-hamit, causing "a complete change in his character and disposition." He surmised that there was a "taint of insanity" in his constitution anyway, observable in his father, his uncle, and his grandfather, taking the form of "imbecility" in his brother Murad.[76] The sultan labored under delusions, believing that he was surrounded by conspirators, sacking faithful palace servants, and taking precautions against assassination by having guardhouses and military posts built around the palace grounds. On a subsequent occasion, "in a state of great mental excitement," the sultan told Layard he had positive information of an assassination plot "which was to be put into execution the following morning." He wanted the ambassador to take his wife and children into the protection of the embassy. In this disturbed state, he heard the distant sound of a trumpet and jumped up in fright, believing it was the signal for his assassination. Layard stayed with him until evening, when the nervous crisis seemed to have passed, but over days the ambassador received "almost hourly communications" from the sultan about the conspiracy and the threat to his life.[77]

Despite these reflections on the sultan's state of mind, Layard remained sympathetic. The ambassadors who followed him—appointed by Gladstone—were instructed to take a tough line. When the sultan was shown an advance copy of the speech George Goschen intended to make when he was received at the palace, he regarded it as so offensive that he returned it, warning that he would not receive the newly appointed ambassador if this was the speech he intended to make. The speech was purged of its most offensive phrases but still caused Abdülhamit great offence when it was made.[78]

To Layard it seemed "almost unmanly and even cowardly" to take advantage of the sultan's weak position by addressing him in language "which I would not use in addressing a more powerful and independent sovereign or even one of the smallest of European princes,"[79] but Gladstone was remorseless, writing that the sultan was a "consummate rogue who is pretending alarms he does not feel."[80] The task ahead of Lord Dufferin, Goschen's successor, was to "extort"[81] some beginning to the "reforms" demanded on the basis of the vague reference in the Treaty of Berlin.

THE "DEAR LITTLE MAN"

Under the pressure of the events of 1876–1878, it is understandable that the sultan seemed to have come close to a nervous breakdown. He was new to the job, which may have partly accounted for his reaction to the crises suddenly besetting him, but eventually he calmed down and settled into the duties of his office.

Contrary to the caricatures coming out of anti-Ottoman propaganda of the late nineteenth century, the sultan was known to be patient, forbearing in the face of criticism that must have pained him, timid and cautious, excitable when sensitive issues were being discussed, but "seldom becoming angry or abusive."[82] The heavy burdens of office undoubtedly had their effect on the "dear little man" who welcomed the Layards to Istanbul in 1877,[83] but they did not destroy him or turn him into the madman of European imagination. It was his unfortunate destiny to be one of the last sultans in the Ottoman line, called to defend the empire at a time its decline seemed irreversible.

Those who actually knew the sultan regarded him as intelligent, perceptive, and sensitive. He was abstemious, extremely hard-working, and given to simple pleasures down to the cigarettes he enjoyed with his coffee. He preferred *alafranga* music to Turkish (*alaturca*), occasionally inviting European singers to perform in the Yildiz Palace opera house for an audience of foreign guests. He enjoyed showing visitors his aviary and his stable of thoroughbred horses. He drew and sketched competently and took lessons in woodwork from a master craftsman, reputedly fashioning one of the chairs in a palace dining room set along with other items.[84] Reading was another pastime, especially the Sherlock Holmes novels of Arthur Conan Doyle. Lord Dufferin commented on his soft eyes, gentle manner, and low voice[85] and appeared reluctant to hector him.[86]

Despite (or perhaps because of) his many marriages, his attitude toward women was thoroughly modern. According to Layard, who saw him at the palace at least once a week, he was the first sultan to invite European women to his dinner table. He encouraged the education of girls and looked forward to the day "when Musulmans like Christians would have but one wife and when women in Mohammedan countries would no longer be kept in seclusion but would be permitted to mix freely with men and appear in society."[87]

A temporizer by nature, often irresolute, he preferred negotiated settlements, amnesties, and pardons to confrontation and executions—even for the most serious crimes. "There was always one last pardon," one of his Young Turk opponents once remarked. "The Sultan was not fundamentally a cruel man and much preferred banishment to execution even though the exiles usually worked against him."[88] There is a wealth of evidence to support this appraisal: the sultan's agreement to a mediated settlement at Zeytun despite a large-scale uprising in which many Ottoman soldiers had been killed, and the negotiated settlement that followed the seizure of the Ottoman Bank, are just two examples.

Massacres of civilians during the war with Russia appeared to deeply affect him. "He was frequently, he said, unable to sleep at night after receiving accounts of the shocking outrages they had perpetrated on the defenceless Mohammedan population and specially on the women and children and sometimes had wished that he were dead and had been spared the knowledge of the dreadful calamities that had befallen his country and people."[89] He reacted with the same shock and horror in the 1890s, when told by the U.S. Minister Plenipotentiary of atrocities allegedly committed against Armenians. The sultan regarded foreign newspaper reports as lies and declared, "Let me die before such things happen in my Empire."[90]

Even though he lost faith in the sultan, Layard continued to believe that the "accumulated misfortunes and troubles" Abdülhamit had experienced would have been sufficient to affect the mind "even of the strongest man."[91] Vambéry also became disillusioned, if far less sympathetically, writing that when the sultan "opened his heart to me" [I] saw "a dreary, horrible place."[92] In fact, the sultan had no reason to open his heart to the self-aggrandizing Vambéry, whose assertion, "I have absolutely nothing to do with the British government," was a lie: he filed confidential reports on Ottoman affairs and the views of the sultan in particular for the Foreign Office from 1889–1911.[93] The sultan probably knew this and used him as back channel for the representation of his views.

In his dealings with the powers, Abdülhamit would do what he could to satisfy them while trying to stop them from pushing him into doing what he knew he could not or should not do. He ordered the suppression of rebellions, but the claims that he or his government ordered the massacre of (implicitly innocent) Christian villagers or found such massacres acceptable were a fiction spread by missionaries and diplomats and maintained ever since by partisan "historians." If the sultan became increasingly distrustful and suspicious, it was at least partly because of the hard evidence before his eyes that his empire was being undermined from within and besieged from without. He was far from imagining all of it and had concluded from long experience that the powers were not be trusted. Their repeated assurances that they would uphold the territorial integrity of his empire turned out to be worthless in his eyes, and the experience was deeply embittering.

The tumultuous conditions of the time did not lend themselves to a smoothly enacted transition to a modern society. The sultan was committed to reform, but not the charter of "reforms" demanded by the powers. Neither would he allow a return to constitutional life, but if he was not a constitutional monarch neither was he a "dictator"[94] or a despot. The sultan clearly found it difficult knowing whom to trust, but was this because of his alleged paranoia or because he was surrounded by many people who were not really trustworthy, as some of his ministers believed? How many of his suspicions could be put down to paranoia (a careless phrase when used by historians without any training in psychiatry) and how many were grounded in reality?

Essentially, the sultan was a pragmatist who dealt with each problem as it arose and sought to avoid confrontation. When "Ottomanism" did not appear to be working because of the growing disaffection of Christian minorities, his default position was strength through Muslim solidarity, which, as a pious Muslim, if secular in his approach to modern life and his introduction of reforms, came to him naturally. Toward this end, the sultan devoted time and money to Muslim projects (most notably the Hijaz railway to Medina) and emphasized his role and responsibilities as the *khalifa*. Taken collectively, the destructive events of the last quarter of the nineteenth century created something of a siege mentality in Istanbul. Yet despite the bitterness and the immense loss of territory and Christian populations, the multiethnic Ottoman ideal remained a guiding imperative almost down to the First World War.

PART II

Balkan Crusades

CHAPTER 5

Ejecting the Muslims

THROUGHOUT THE NINETEENTH CENTURY, indeed down to the First World War and beyond, Ottoman governments had to find space for millions of Muslims pouring into Anatolia from the Balkans,[1] the Caucasus, and Crimea. Most came as refugees rather than "migrants" (*muhacirler*), the word often used to describe their status. However, a migrant makes a voluntary decision to live in another land and is accepted after an orderly process involving passports, work permits, and visas. The ejected Muslims of the Balkans, the Caucasus, and the northern and eastern shores of the Black Sea mostly fled in panic ahead of advancing armies or were actively driven out. The process began during the Serbian rebellion against Ottoman authority in 1804, resulting in the flight of tens of thousands of Muslims. Russia, Britain, and France ensured the success of the Greek struggle for independence in the 1820s. Thousands of Muslim civilians were killed and thousands more were driven out, ending "all Muslim settlement in southern Greece."[2]

The inability of the Ottoman Empire to defend itself fed the rise of ethnoreligious national movements everywhere and often ended in the loss of more territory. At the Congress of Berlin, the reallocation of conquered Ottoman land was followed by the cession of Ülgün to Montenegro in 1880; the cession of most of Thessaly and the southern Epirus to Greece in 1881; the annexation by Bulgaria of the autonomous Ottoman province of Eastern Rumelia in 1885; and in 1898 the loss of Crete, given autonomy under the rule of a Greek prince through the intervention of the powers, following a war that Greece had started and the Ottomans won on the battlefield but lost at the negotiating table.

The European powers presided over this piecemeal dismantling of the empire, even as they guaranteed its integrity. Britain added Cyprus to its strategic reach through a secret agreement with the sultan on June 4, 1878, a week before the opening of the Congress of Berlin. In 1882, its warships bombarded the Egyptian coastline at Alexandria and landed an army in the name of ending the disturbances the attack had caused. The khedive was largely autonomous by then, but Egypt was still an Ottoman possession, and this further violation of his sovereignty was the cause of bitter reflection by the sultan. Assurances given at Berlin that his empire's territorial integrity would henceforth be respected and protected seemed to be worthless.

From the attempt to overthrow the sultan, through the raid on the Çirağan Palace by 'Ali Suavi and his followers on May 30, 1878, to the raid on the government offices by a group of soldiers led by Enver Paşa on January 23, 1913, the continual leaching away of territory stirred religious and protonational anger across the empire. As Ebru Boyar has observed of one ethnonational group, the allocation of Ülgün (Albanian Ulkin, now Ulcinj) to Montenegro at the Congress of Berlin "represented a blow to Albanian faith in the Ottoman state."[3] But it was not just Albanians who were reaching the conclusion that the sultan was increasingly incapable of protecting his domains. Many ethnoreligious national movements had been picking up the same signals and acting on them.

Even before the war with Russia with 1877 (the "War of '93," or 1293, according to the Islamic calendar), the extent of territorial losses and the consequent effect on the lives of Ottoman Muslims was enormous. The massacres and ethnic cleansing of Muslims from conquered Ottoman domains throughout the nineteenth century and into the twentieth are rarely mentioned in "western" histories and have no place at all in a particular history of genocide, "from Sparta to Darfur."[4]

Analyzing Ottoman demographics since the 1830s, Kemal Karpat estimates that about 5 million Muslims from the Crimea, the Caucasus, and the Balkans had settled in Anatolia by 1908.[5] To these numbers have to be added the millions who died during the wars in these regions. The outflow of *muhaciler* continued long after the wars were over. Between 1880 and 1900, almost 240,000 Muslims migrated to Ottoman lands from Bulgaria alone.[6] The Ottoman territorial loss in four years (1878–1882) amounted to 232,000 square kilometers, with nearly all of what remained in southeastern Europe lost during the Balkan War (1912–1913).[7]

Around the Black Sea, the annexation of the Crimea in 1783 and a policy of "Russification" that included demographic transformation through the settlement of non-Muslims, led to the incremental migration of Tatars. During the Crimean War (1853–1856), the Russian state regarded the Tatars as an actual or potential fifth column.[8] The expulsion of "suspect" Tatars and oppressive state policies that are typical of the abuses of a colonized people everywhere led to the flight of hundreds of thousands of Crimean Tatars to Ottoman lands in just a few years.

In the Caucasus, the outflow of Circassians and other Muslim groups (such as Chechens and Abkhazians) followed the same sequence of Russian conquests and state policies centering on demographic transformation through the settlement of Christians.

Even after "peace" was restored, the continuing "migration" of Muslims could never be called voluntary. Without the duress of Russian occupation, Crimean and Caucasian Muslims would never have abandoned their traditional lands. The spirited resistance of the Imam Shamyl from the 1830s to the 1850s is evidence of how hard they fought to drive the Russians out.

As in the Crimea, by the early 1860s, "migration" of Circassians alone from the northern Caucasus into Ottoman lands had turned into a "mass exodus."[9] During this period, many Christians also left Ottoman lands to live under Christian rule. This two-way flow of "migrants" had a powerful effect on the demographic maps of both the Balkans and the Anatolian heartland of the Ottoman Empire, with long-lasting social, economic, and political implications.

UPRISINGS AND WAR

In the 1870s, Christian uprisings in Bosnia-Herzegovina and Bulgaria were suppressed with a ferocity that had European capitals in an uproar. The Balkan peasantry had long complained of unfair taxation. While such complaints were common across the empire irrespective of religious background, Europe was roused only by Christian grievances. On top of their common problems with Muslims, Christians also complained frequently of mistreatment at the hands of their own ecclesiastical authorities. Accusations of bribery and corruption were commonplace. In these troubled regions, a competent governor could effect great changes, as Midhat Paşa did in the 1860s, but within a decade, the combination of ethnoreligious nationalism, Pan Slavism, unredressed complaints against the Ottoman authorities, and revolutionary activism composed the combustible mix that exploded in the uprisings of 1875–1876 in Bosnia-Herzegovina and Bulgaria.

Balkan Christians were divided by deep religious, territorial, and historical rivalries (if not actual hatreds), but in their opposition to the Ottoman Muslim and government presence across the region they stood on common ground. In the 1860s, Prince Michael of Serbia had signed alliances with Rumania, Montenegro, and Bulgarian revolutionaries with the aim of ending Ottoman rule. In a separate agreement, Serbia agreed that Greece should have Thessaly and the Epirus, and Greece agreed that Serbia should have Bosnia-Herzegovina if these territories could be wrested from Ottoman hands.

A general revolt planned for 1868 foundered on a variety of rocks, not the least of which was the assassination on June 10 of Prince Michael. In the 1870s, uprisings in Bosnia-Herzegovina (July 1875) and Bulgaria (April–May 1876) led first to declarations of war on the Ottoman Empire by Serbia and Montenegro and then the likelihood of Russian intervention, threatening the balance of power in Europe unless the developing crisis was quickly resolved.[10] The uprisings were marked by the massacre of Muslim civilians.

In Bulgaria, villages were burnt, and the decapitated heads of Turks stuck on poles before the Ottoman *başıbozuk* irregular soldiers intervened. Hundreds of Muslims had probably been killed, but now thousands of Christian civilians were reported to have been massacred in the reprisals. Traveling through Bulgaria in late July–early August 1876, the London *Daily News* correspondent Januarius MacGahan, accompanied by Eugene Schuyler, the U.S. consul general for the Ottoman Empire, found evidence of savage massacres, with the most telling evidence coming from in and around the village of Batak. Inside the village school MacGahan reported seeing the bones and ashes of 200 (his estimate) women and children whom he said had been burnt alive. In the churchyard, he saw a wall of human remains covered with a thin layer of stones, while inside the church were the blackened remains of an "immense number of bodies." MacGahan estimated that seventy villages had been destroyed and 15,000 people killed in an onslaught lasting several days.[11] As he was writing several months later, he surely could not know exactly what had happened to these villagers, and neither could he be sure of anything like precise numbers, but, while there was reason to question the accuracy of his reports, there could be no doubt that fearful atrocities had been committed.

Europe was understandably outraged.[12] William Gladstone raised his voice to the heavens. In his sixpenny pamphlet, *Bulgarian Horrors and the Question of the East*, he declared that the question was not just one of "Mahometanism" but of the "peculiar character of a race," the Turks, who were "upon the whole, from the first black day when they entered Europe the one great antihuman specimen of humanity."[13] Gladstone's estimate of 60,000 Christian dead was ludicrous, but his tract further inflamed public opinion against the Turks, the Ottoman government, and Islam.

The crisis triggered intense bilateral and multilateral negotiations between the powers. In July, the Austrian-Hungarian emperor Franz Joseph and the Russian Tsar Alexander II, accompanied by their foreign ministers, met at Reichstadt (now Zakupy in the Czech Republic) to work out a common approach should there be war with the Ottoman Empire ending in a Russian victory. In their quid pro quo, parts of Bosnia-Herzegovina would go to Serbia and Montenegro, with Austria-Hungary retaining the rest. Russia would have its agreement to the reannexation of Bessarabia (Russian until 1856) along with territorial expansion in the Caucasus. Bulgaria would be given autonomy, but Austria-Hungary was assured there would be no large Slavic state. None of this was written down, which meant that when there was war and Russia triumphed, the two governments could not agree on what each thought had been agreed by the other.

On December 23, the powers (Russia, Britain, France, Austria-Hungary, Germany, and Italy) met in Istanbul to resolve the crisis. Their solution was to turn Bosnia-Herzegovina into an autonomous province except for the southern region. This would go to Montenegro along with the retention of Albanian territory it had conquered. In January, the Ottoman government announced its rejection of the powers' "irreducible minimum" on the grounds of the infringement of its sovereign rights. On January 15, Russia and Austria-Hungary signed the Budapest Convention, enabling the latter to annex Bosnia-Herzegovina in the event of war. The London Convention of March 31 was a last-ditch attempt to keep the peace, but as it basically reiterated terms already rejected by the Ottoman government, and rejected once again, it was doomed to fail from the start.

On April 24, 1877, Russia declared an "imperial war" that was at the same time "an anti-Ottoman crusade."[14] Hundreds of thousands of Muslim civilians in the path of advancing Russian armies and Bulgarian and Serbian armed bands (*çeteler*) were slaughtered or fled before their turn

came. Entire villages were devastated. Massacres and the most sadistic
atrocities, including crucifixion and burning villagers alive, were reported
from across the conquered territories. Counter-atrocities, if not on the
same scale, were reported to have been committed against Christian villagers by Circassian irregulars.

Towns and open fields on the way to Istanbul overflowed with Muslim
refugees. Many died on the road from starvation, exposure, or disease.
By January 1878, apart from the refugees who had reached Istanbul or elsewhere on the Anatolian mainland (some by train and some on steamers
chartered for the purpose by the Ottoman government), about 200,000
more were living in the greatest distress in and around Shumla (later
included in the new Bulgarian principality).[15]

Although Russia was eventually shamed into providing some relief,
the reduction of the Muslim population of Bulgaria (about 30 percent of
the total in 1877[16]) was clearly a war aim. Russia armed the Bulgarians,
did nothing to stop the massacres or the clearing of the Muslim population and issued no proclamation guaranteeing their safety until the war
was over and hundreds of thousands of people had already fled. It then
refused to allow many to return. A smaller but still substantial number of
Bulgarian Christians also left Ottoman lands. Many did not return.

On the basis of consular reports, Karpat estimates, "Some 300,000
Muslims (mostly Turks) were killed in the Danube province and eastern
Rumelia, and that of the approximately one million forced to flee from
their homes, only about a quarter returned after the war."[17] The scale of
the atrocities was so great that Queen Victoria was outraged and pressed
hard for the fleet to be sent to Istanbul,[18] a possibility anyway, once the
Russian army moved within striking distance of the city. Sympathy for
Balkan Christians was now superseded by the Russian threat to British
imperial interests.

EXTERMINATION

Already by July 1877, Layard was writing, "The proceedings of the Russians
and Bulgarians in Bulgaria and Roumelia have convinced the Mahom-
medan inhabitants and the Turkish Government that it is the deliberate
intention of Russia either to exterminate the Mussulman population by
the sword or to drive it out of the country."[19] Early in 1878, he wrote, ter-
rified Muslims were fleeing ahead of the Russian advance, accompanied

in many districts by Christians and Jews.[20] The atrocities committed included "wholesale murder and the violation of women and children."[21] In Layard's view, returning to motives, the Russians "were endeavouring to aid the Bulgarians in exterminating the Musulman population, or of driving it out of the occupied territories and to excite the Christian inhabitants of Macedonia to rise against the Turkish rule, in order to afford a fresh pretext for interference."[22]

The conquering forces included a Bulgarian legion of "Avengers" armed and trained by the Russians in Rumania. "Wherever they went they spread death and devastation among the unhappy Musulmans, sparing neither age nor sex.... These were the men whom the Emperor Alexander, when reviewing them previous to crossing the Danube, addressed as 'Patriots who were going to liberate the country and revenge the wrong and were engaged in a holy and religious work.'"[23]

Layard's findings are supported by mounds of documentary evidence. Massacre, rape, and expulsion were accompanied by the wholesale destruction of villages and the desecration of Muslim tombs, mosques, and cemeteries along with the destruction of libraries. The flames of burning villages could be seen for miles. West of Adrianople (present day Edirne) rich farmland was laid waste, "scarcely a village remaining unburnt, the inhabitants massacred or in flight, their crops, which this year have been unusually fine, in great part destroyed and the cattle gone."[24] Refugees were vulnerable to further attack on the road by Cossacks and Bulgarian bands. The documents tell of terrible suffering, of starving women and children bearing the wounds of sabers and lances packed into carts and railway carriages. A shocked Ellis Ashmead Bartlett wrote,

> Nothing in modern times has equaled, nothing has approached, the ruin, carnage and horrors inflicted upon a peaceful and innocent population by that Russian crusade. Before the war there were over two millions of Mussulman inhabitants in Bulgaria and Eastern Rumelia. There are now only some 550,000. The remainder perished by the sword or from cold and starvation during their flight, for the survivors were driven in helpless exile into Asia Minor.

The barbarities inflicted by Russians and Bulgarians on Muslims were "worse than any recorded since the fall of the Roman Empire or since the devastation of Europe by the Huns. Whole villages were destroyed with all their inhabitants, in many cases the Mussulmans, men, women and

children, being thrown back into the flames by the bayonets of their per-
secutors. In one case, 100,000 Mussulman refugees, encamped near Her-
manli, on the Maritza, were, in January 1878, driven by Skobeleff's cavalry
and artillery into the frozen Rhodope mountains. Not 5,000 survived."[25]

As Layard had done, Ashmead Bartlett singled out the Tunja valley,
famous for its roses, now infamous for the atrocities committed there by
Russian soldiers and Bulgarian volunteers. The reports tell of smoking
villages, murdered men, and violated women, with the fate of the Muslims
of Kezanlik "too horrible to narrate."[26]

Exploiting the chaos of war, the Greek government sent troops into
Thessaly and Epirus. In the wake of attacks on Muslim villages, the Ottoman government responded by sending Albanian and other irregulars into
the same regions, all regular soldiers having been sent to the Bulgarian
front. In Layard's words,

> Exasperated by the ravages and cruelties committed on the Mussul-
> man inhabitants by the Greek invaders, these undisciplined levies
> retaliated on the unoffending Christian population. The conse-
> quences were that these provinces were devastated and the most
> cruel and revolting outrages and massacres were committed by both
> sides. The Hellenic government was primarily responsible for this
> state of things. It had wantonly invaded its neighbour's territory and
> had excited those evil passions which found a vent in indiscriminate
> slaughter. The British government and other Powers remonstrated at
> Athens but in vain. They were met by the usual denials and excuses.[27]

Under pressure from the powers, Greece withdrew its forces from Thessaly
and the Epirus, even while continuing to encourage uprisings in both districts as well as on Crete. Atrocities by Ottoman forces were also reported
from Thrace as territory changed hands.

In Istanbul, where the sultan made arrangements to flee the city as the
Russian army drew closer, the situation was calamitous. Masses of starving
and often wounded men, women, and children were arriving daily, even
as thousands of others still fled before the Russian advance.

> In many districts the Christians and the Jews who were the spe-
> cial victims of Bulgarian cruelties are accompanying them. The
> towns and villages are deserted, the property of the inhabitants
> abandoned. Trains with from 8,000 to 18,000 of these wretched

fugitives have been arriving daily at Constantinople. Only open trucks can in most cases be provided for them. The weather has been intensely cold, the snow falling heavily. The poor creatures are packed together standing and then kept sometimes for more than 24 hours without food or shelter. As the trains arrive at the station the bodies of men, women and children frozen to death or who have succumbed to illness are dragged out of the wagons. Even the tops of the closed carriages are occupied by the women and children who in some instances, numbed by the cold, roll off and are killed.[28]

Colonel Blunt, a British officer with the Ottoman *jandarma*, reporting on the number of refugees he saw while traveling from Edirne to Çorlu, wrote that the trains consisted mostly of open cattle-trucks and luggage vans.[29] The vans were "crammed to excess, oftentimes containing as many as eighty and ninety women and children." Even the spaces between the vans were covered with people, who, in their anxiety to get away, placed planks over the buffers and coupling chains. Many of the refugees died from exposure to snow, frost, wind, and rain. Each morning, the dead would be collected and buried by scratching soil over their bodies. Many of the children who died were simply thrown from the train.

Mothers even killed their own children: "One day, not 100 yards from a train and in view of all, a woman took her two children, about five and three, and plunged a dagger into each of their hearts." Under interrogation she admitted committing the crime to prevent them having to experience the misery she had gone through, was still going through, and expected to face in the future.[30]

The country between Edirne and Istanbul, most of it occupied by the Russians, was a scene of "utter devastation and ruin. In the towns and villages, the mosques had been desecrated, defiled or destroyed, the Mussulman burying-ground violated and the tombstones removed and the Turkish houses sacked and generally burnt to the ground."[31] Women who remained were being raped by Cossacks. Victims of the Russians and their allies also included Greeks, robbed, mistreated, and in many cases killed.

In Istanbul, the refugees were housed in mosques and public buildings. A British committee formed by Baroness Burdett-Coutts cooperated with the Ottoman government and Muslim relief agencies in providing food, blankets, and medical help. Even Lady Layard pitched in. In April 1878, Layard received a report on the medical situation: "Typhoid, typhus, diarrhoea and the pneumonia are the prevailing diseases and the mortality amongst the refugees has been rated at from 300 to 500 *per diem*. Out of sixteen medical assistants sent by the Medical School to attend upon the sick refugees in the quarter of Stamboul, eight have died from typhoid contracted in the performance of their duties."[32]

Typhus had also broken out along the European and Asiatic shores of the Bosporus.[33] About 80,000 refugees were being housed in mosques, public buildings, and private homes, including 4,000 inside Aya Sofia, who were described as being "in the state of the greatest misery and for the most part prostrate and helpless from sickness."[34] Twenty-five to thirty people were dying every day from typhus or typhoid fever. The atmosphere inside the mosque was "absolutely poisonous and the condition of the place beyond description. The Turkish Government is only able to distribute food sufficient for the bare support of life to this vast crowd of starving human beings."[35]

On the outskirts of the city, where the Russian army was encamped at San Stefano (Yeşilköy), the Grand Duke Nicholas waited to enter in triumph. The main concern was how he should proceed. The sultan was prepared to receive him but blanched at the thought of Nicholas riding through the city with his generals to Yildiz Palace, on hills above the Bosporus. Various alternatives were suggested: horse or carriage to the palace by a back road; perhaps a tent pitched between the city and San Stefano instead of an audience at the palace; perhaps the sultan could send his yacht for the Grand Duke.

The Russians pressed their claims "with much harshness and persistence," but the sultan continued to stand his ground until a compromise was reached. The Grand Duke would not be received at Yildiz but at Dolmabahçe Palace, right on the water, so that no one but the sultan and his entourage would see him coming and going. Accordingly, Nicholas sailed down the Bosporus in the Tsar's own yacht, *Livadia,* on March 27 and was taken to the shore on a state barge. At Dolmabahçe, the problem of whether he should be met at the top or the bottom of the stairs was solved by the sultan meeting him at the bottom. The following day, the Grand Duke returned with his son for dinner. The sultan was not pleased with the attitude of the Grand Duke, which he described as "haughty and overbearing."[36]

In the meantime, refugees continued pouring into Istanbul. Of those Muslims who remained in the conquered Ottoman territories, many fled in the coming years rather than endure continuing official discrimination and brutality. Between 1876 and 1882 alone, some 600,000 Muslims left the Balkans. Demographic tabulations just for the Bulgarian Muslim population indicate that hundreds of thousands died in this period, while others never returned to their homes.[37]

"DISABUSE YOURSELVES"

The humanitarian catastrophe of the war was followed by the immense loss of Ottoman territory ratified at the Congress of Berlin (June 13–July 13, 1878). The war had thrown borders into the air once more, and the diplomats meeting in Berlin were going to sort them out. European interests were their overriding concern. "If you think the Congress has met for Turkey," Bismarck told Balkan and Ottoman delegates, "disabuse yourselves. San Stefano[38] would have remained unaltered if it had not touched certain European interests."[39] A Greek, Karatheodory Paşa, had been chosen as the head of the Ottoman delegation ahead of the negotiations. "We had very few men who cared to go to Berlin to face the decisions of this Congress and to give their signatures to this treaty of spoliation which we foresaw," the sultan told Henri de Blowitz, the celebrated correspondent of *The Times*. "Sacrifices were imposed upon me then from which I am still suffering."[40]

The claim that a Christian was sent to Berlin "to avoid the shame of a Muslim agreeing to a possibly dishonourable treaty" has been debunked by Roderic Davison.[41] Karatheodory Paşa was a high-level, thoroughly competent Foreign Ministry official chosen after considerations that did not include religious affiliation. The choice of a different person would have made no difference to the result.

The treaty was the public outcome of terms negotiated privately over the heads of the Ottoman delegation, which was treated rudely by Bismarck and put under continual pressure by Britain and Austria-Hungary to concede territory. The Ottoman government knew of secret British negotiations with Russia but was assured just ahead of the signing of the Cyprus convention (June 4) that Britain was still committed to maintaining Ottoman authority in its European provinces, "as well as in those of its Asian territory."

This was at least "skirting the truth,"[42] as Britain had already secretly conceded Kars, Ardahan, and Batum to Russia when Cyprus was handed to Britain in return for a pledge to use military force in defense of the

Ottoman Empire if Russia made any further attempts to capture its territory.

The treaty confirmed some of the provisions of San Stefano but introduced new elements. The overall package added up to independence for Serbia, Montenegro, and Rumania, with Montenegro allowed to retain the territory it had conquered in northern Albania, and Rumania gaining the northern Dobruca at the cost of having to concede southern Bessarabia to Russia. An autonomous Bulgaria was established, though much smaller than the principality created at San Stefano. Eastern Rumelia (southern Bulgaria) remained within Ottoman domains but with the stipulation that it must have a Christian governor approved by the powers. Bosnia-Herzegovina was subjected to dual authority, remaining part of the sovereign territory of one empire (Ottoman), but with Austria-Hungary allowed to "occupy and administer" the territory. Article 25 of the treaty also established joint Ottoman/Austrian-Hungarian administration of the adjacent subprovince (*sancak*) of Novipazar, which separated Serbia from Montenegro and was claimed by both. Under the treaty, Austria-Hungary had the right to establish a military garrison in the *sancak*.

Even before the diplomats gathered at Berlin, Albanian *beyler* had met in Kosovo (on June 10) and formed the Prizren League (Albanian League for the Defense of the Rights of the Albanian Nation). They marked out four Ottoman *vilayetler* (Manastir, Kosovo, Işkodra, and Janina) as the Albanian homeland, only for their claims to be so completely ignored at Berlin that their delegates "left quickly to save money."[43]

Albania refused to hand over territory allocated to Montenegro at Berlin, forming an army that successfully resisted this *diktat* of the powers for three years. They had drawn lines on the map to suit their collective interests, with the result that all Balkan delegates left the congress feeling half-fed or not fed at all. The strongest amongst them would wait for the right time to take what they wanted or what they calculated they could get with the support of one or another (or all) of the powers.

In southeastern Europe, only Macedonia was left under full Ottoman authority. Far from stabilizing the situation in the Balkans, the patchwork solutions of the Treaty of Berlin, while restoring European stability, failed to slake the territorial appetites of the Balkan states. Macedonia now became the central target of their irredentist territorial claims. In northeastern Anatolia, the districts of Kars, Batum, and Ardahan were ceded to Russia; in the eastern Mediterranean, Cyprus was gone even before the congress opened.

The loss of territory and a Christian population in the Balkans, plus the arrival over time of millions of Muslim refugees in the Ottoman Anatolian heartland, radically transformed the demographic structure of the empire. According to Karpat, "By 1880 the Anatolian population was already 80 percent Muslim and this percentage increased steadily thereafter."[44] Throughout this process of ethnoreligious imperial disintegration on one hand and ethnoreligious national consolidation on the other, the involvement of the powers was crucial. Neither the Greeks nor the Bulgarians would have achieved independence when they did without outside involvement, setting an example of dynamic internal-external interaction that other Christian groups quickly sought to emulate.

The Muslim refugees were resettled across the Ottoman Empire. There were far too many of them to be concentrated in any one area. Their legacy is to be found in the demographic makeup of every post-Ottoman state: Syria and Jordan have a substantial population of Circassian origin, while in Turkey itself the ethnic background of contemporary "Turks" bears the imprint of every Muslim group that found refuge in Anatolia from the nineteenth century onward. The Ottoman government tried to locate them where it thought they could adapt, where labor was needed, and where their skills (especially agricultural) might be useful in developing the country.

These uprooted humans included Circassians who had been settled in the Balkans after previous wars with Russia and were now, during and after the war with Russia in 1877–1878, shifted again. Many did not survive the transplant.[45] In Donald Quataert's assessment, "Most of the estimated 30,000 Nogay Tatars settled in the Arifye *kaza* of Adana after the Crimean War died from the heat while some 90 percent of the Balkan refugees settled nearly some fifty years later suffered the same fate."[46] The reduction of the Crimean Tatars reached its climax with the Soviet government's exile of the entire population to Siberia during the Second World War.

Friction between the local people and refugees "squatting" on their land was common. Many arrived with nothing but the clothes on their backs. In June 1879, a Christian delegation from Adapazarı waited on Layard at Therapia (Tarabya) to complain (on behalf of local Muslims as well) of the behavior of 40,000 Circassians sent to their region. They said they were living "almost in a state of siege" and handed the ambassador a list of robberies and murders allegedly committed by the refugees. Forwarding their grievances to the government, the embassy was told by Karatheodory Paşa that he was hardly surprised, as the Circassians, "having been hunted out of Europe and having been deprived of all they possessed, had been sent into Asia without any provisions having been made for their maintenance and support." Compelled to starve or steal, they would choose the latter.[47]

The war further poisoned relations between Muslims and Christians. According to Layard, Kurdish tribes "had taken advantage of the war to pillage the country and to rob and plunder its inhabitants, especially the Christians who were, it was reported, subjected to every manner of outrage. When Bayazid was retaken by these fanatics, they sacked the Christian quarter and committed the most horrible outrages on its inhabitants. When the Russian garrison of the fort of that place marched out of it with a flag of truce, prepared to surrender, they were massacred in cold blood." Promises were made to protect the Christians, but the Kurdish tribes were said to be "beyond the control of the Turkish authorities."[48]

Seeing that the Kurds had felt the full force of the Russian invasion and were themselves the victims of atrocities, such attacks were probably inevitable. Elsewhere, at Erzurum, some Armenians took advantage of the Russian occupation to mistreat Muslims. When the Russians withdrew, thousands of Armenian families living in the Alaşgirt Valley followed them back across the border.[49]

Not long after the war, fresh trouble broke out among the mountaineers of Zeytun. Lieutenant Chermside, making inquiries on the spot, reported that the town's chief characteristics were "destitution, squalor and abject misery. . . . I do not think I am exaggerating in stating my belief that it is the most unsuitable-looking town I have seen in Turkey."[50] The misery of war exacerbated long-standing grievances over taxation and inflamed relations between the Armenians and local Muslims, leading to an attack on tribal Yuruks by 200 Armenians headed by the "brigand chief" Babek and intervention by government troops. Some of Babek's followers were killed. The situation, as described in British consular reports, was extremely confused. There were complaints of harsh treatment of the townspeople by government officials mixed with references to the involvement of a *deli papaz* ("mad priest"), an Armenian bishop, "an ignorant illiterate man, of some force of character and bravery but wanting in temper and judgment."[51]

In the southeast, thousands of Kurds carrying the modern weapons they had been given to fight the Russians rose against local authorities in the town of Siirt. They were eventually suppressed by a military detachment sent from Muş, but reports of banditry, arson, and murder continued to flow in from across the region. The war, its continuing social impact across the empire, the carve-up at Berlin, and the insensitivity to Ottoman interests compounded the feeling within the Ottoman government and among Muslims everywhere that the powers were not to be trusted, whatever they said. The empire seemed alone, exposed and vulnerable in a predatory world.

CHAPTER 6

The Young Turks

IN MANY IMPORTANT WAYS, Ottoman government and society never recovered from the shock of the 1877–1878 war. One upheaval had followed another, with the reverberations continuing to the outbreak of the First World War. In 1906–1907, agents of the revolutionary CUP (the Committee of Union and Progress, or Ittihat ve Terakki Cemiyeti)—the "Young Turks"—harnessed public grievances to their revolutionary cause across the Black Sea and eastern provinces.

In January 1906, crowds demonstrating against the imposition of new taxes took over the telegraph office in Kastamonu and refused to disperse until the governor was dismissed.[1] The pattern was repeated in Erzurum, where the governor was replaced in April after the commander of the Fourth Army—the same Zeki Paşa who had crushed the Sasun uprising in 1894—failed or refused to obey government orders to intervene.[2] On both occasions, the protestors were a mix of Muslims and Christians.

Fresh demonstrations broke out in October, this time leading to street clashes in which protestors and *jandarma* were killed. The arrest of the mufti and others considered ringleaders of these disturbances only worsened the situation. The governor was besieged in his house before being captured and held prisoner in the central mosque. Both the police chief and his son were caught and beaten to death.[3] Zeki Paşa again refused to intervene and again the governor was replaced, but turmoil continued in Erzurum into the coming year. In March 1907, a CUP agent assassinated the military commander at Trabzon. The following month, the Russian and French consulates at Van were attacked by *jandarma* after being seen to side with the local people on the taxation question.[4]

At this stage, the CUP and Armenian revolutionaries had a common objective—the overthrow of Abdülhamit's "absolutist" regime—and were cooperating to achieve it. While the 1908 revolution would be initiated in the Balkans, public grievances resulting in violent demonstrations, assassinations, the discovery of arms and dynamite caches, and the arrest of CUP and Armenian revolutionaries had clearly created a receptive atmosphere across the empire for the historic change that would soon be coming. These events were watched closely by European governments and Balkan states already preparing for the war they would launch on the Ottoman Empire as soon as the time was right. Wars and the treaties that followed in the nineteenth century had given them a measure of independence or autonomy but not to anything like the full extent of their political and territorial claims. European sympathy and the active involvement of the powers encouraged them to keep asking for more and snip off Ottoman territory when the opportunity arose.

In 1880, the arrival of a European flotilla forced the Ottoman government and local Albanians to surrender Ulcinj to Montenegro, in line with a decision taken at the Congress of Berlin in 1878. The following year, again as the result of negotiations at Berlin, the sultan was compelled to cede Thessaly and parts of the Epirus to Greece. In 1885, Bulgaria annexed eastern Rumelia, and in 1898 Crete was taken away from the empire and placed under the administration of a Greek high commissioner. These were all the preliminaries to the attack on the Ottoman Empire by four Balkan states in 1912.

IMPERIAL CLUB

By the late nineteenth century, two recently unified powers—Italy and Germany—were knocking on the door of the imperial club. They were no more or less greedy than its founding members, but they wanted their share and were rapidly amassing the diplomatic and military power to pursue their claims. Of the two, Germany was regarded by Britain as the most threatening to its strategic and commercial interests. It was rapidly becoming an industrial dynamo capable of competing with Britain and France in world markets and having the same need of colonies for strategic reasons and their supply of raw material.

German armament factories were producing the best field guns in the world. Shipyards at Kiel and Hamburg were turning out a new generation of advanced warships that would enable Germany to challenge British naval supremacy. It was supplying weaponry and advisers to the Ottoman sultan who, irritated by British seizure of Egypt and interference in support of the Armenians, increasingly regarded Germany as a more trustworthy power.

The developing relationship between the two empires was underscored by the Kaiser Wilhelm's visit to Istanbul in 1898 and the use of German engineers under the command of Heinrich Meissner to build the Hijaz railway from Damascus to Medina. The simultaneous plan early in the twentieth century to connect Berlin to Baghdad by rail (the "Baghdad-bahn") generated concern bordering on panic in London, centering on the specter of a railway line carrying German troops to the top of the Persian Gulf.

Even by the 1880s, the alliances among the countries that would go to war in 1914 were rapidly taking shape. However, nothing lasts forever in diplomacy. Nothing is expected to last beyond the state's interests, and in the game of musical chairs played under the heading of "statecraft" prewar commitments were regularly made and unmade or broken by circumstances.

The Triple Alliance (Germany, Austria-Hungary, and Italy) collapsed in April 1915, when Italy switched sides, while the Triple Entente (Britain, France, and Russia), signed in 1907 and strengthened by supplementary agreements with other states, came to an end when the Bolshevik revolution removed one of the players. Weaker states hovered on the flanks of the stronger, wondering which bloc to join—if invited or pressured—and generally realizing that they would have to join one or another or risk being crushed in between.

Despite their imperialist engorgement of distant lands, France and Britain remained the philosophical and constitutional models for a rising generation of nationalists, even in colonized countries or countries under such imperial pressure that they could be called half-colonized.

After their constitutional revolution in 1905–1906, Iranian liberals looked to Britain for support, and the expectations were the same among the Young Turks. After all, the long period of "Hamidian absolutism" was over, and constitutional government had been restored. The sultan's subjects were now Ottoman citizens, with equal rights for all guaranteed before the law. Was not Britain the "mother of parliaments"? Was not

France the seat of the liberal values of the Enlightenment? Surely encouragement and support would come from both governments.

Like nationalists elsewhere, the Young Turks were to be disappointed. For Britain and France, constitutional government at home was one thing and constitutional government abroad a different matter altogether. In their colonies, their interests and the interests and aspirations of the people they occupied were irreconcilable. The occupied wanted the occupier to go home, the occupier was determined to stay, but anywhere their commercial and strategic interests were at stake, imperial European governments would try to break any party or association demanding national independence. What they sought were pliant figures who could have their constitutions but only if they were written in such a way as to safeguard the interests of the power looming over them. Similarly, they could have their independence as long as it was bogus: Egypt's "independence" as granted by Britain in 1922 falls squarely into this category.

The Young Turks had succeeded in 1908, overcoming a counterrevolution in 1909, but were too dangerously radical for British tastes. Britain was obliged to praise them for their restoration of constitutional government, but beneath this polite veneer lay hostility to their determination to be truly independent.

MACEDONIAN "REFORMS"

It was from Macedonia and largely because of Macedonia that army officers launched their bid to restore constitutional government in the Ottoman Empire. In October 1903, at Mürzsteg (Austria), Russia and Austria-Hungary agreed on a program of "reforms" for Macedonia. Overseen by representatives of the two powers but with Britain and France involved through the appointment of "advisors," the reforms would cover the administration, judicial processes, and policing. Christians would be recruited for the *jandarma*. In general, the program was directed toward redressing grievances that were keeping Macedonia in a state of turmoil.

Mürzsteg was beset by lethal problems from the start, beginning with the resistance by the sultan to this violation of his sovereignty. Further problems included obstruction by Ottoman officials; the general resentment by Muslims of what was seen as the privileging of Christians; the outright rejection of Mürzsteg by revolutionaries, with the dominant insurgent movement, the Internal Macedonian Revolutionary Organization (IMRO), at the top of the list; the lack of adequate funds for the whole scheme; and the failure to provide sufficient officials to oversee and monitor the program.

Furthermore, while committing to Mürzsteg, the powers undermined it by continuing to scheme against each other, or with each other, if that better suited the purpose. There was no common good except the European balance of power, which could not be allowed to fracture. Short of that, they continued their old jockeying for advantage. The sultan reluctantly agreed to the changes proposed at Mürzsteg. Civil administrators and Belgian, Norwegian, and Swedish gendarmerie instructors were brought into Macedonia, reforms were introduced, and amnesties declared, all to some good effect,[5] but the pace of change was too slow to bring calm to the province.

In 1908, the British king and the Russian tsar launched their own attempt to solve Macedonia's festering problems. On June 9, they met at Reval, on the Gulf of Finland, King Edward having sailed there on the royal yacht *Victoria and Albert*, stopping on the way at Kiel. As Tsar Nicholas II was the king's nephew and Empress Alexandra his niece, this was a family occasion as well as a grand imperial spectacle. Nicholas no doubt intended this parade of royal power to restore confidence in his family and his rule at a time both had been severely shaken by the 1905 revolution and the crushing military defeat Russia had suffered the same year at the hands of Japan. The brutal suppression of terrorist cells, with thousands executed or imprisoned, had been followed by reforms, turning Russia into a constitutional monarchy. However, with the Tsar refusing to let go the reins, and with thousands of government officials murdered in the space of a few years, the atmosphere remained turbulent.

Security in Reval was tight. The two monarchs hardly stepped ashore but hotels were still threatened with a 3,000-ruble fine unless they reported the presence of strangers within the hour. King Edward was received aboard the Tsar's royal yacht, the *Standart,* whose deck was crowded with admirals, other senior naval commanders and numerous members of the Russian royal family, from the Dowager Empress down to the heir to the throne, Alexei, then not quite four, and his older sisters, the grand duchesses Olga, Tatiana, Maria, and Anastasia.[6]

To mark the great occasion, the king conferred the status of admiral of the Royal Navy on the tsar, and the tsar returned the honor, insofar as it could be returned, seeing that Russia hardly had a fleet. Between the Japanese siege of Port Arthur (February 1904—January 1905) and the battle of the Tsushima straits (May 27–29, 1905), it had been almost destroyed. The only ship to escape Tsushima and reach Vladivostok, the cruiser *Almaz*, was lying at anchor only a short distance from where the king and the tsar paid their respects to each other.

In their talks, the two monarchs reaffirmed the importance of their 1907 agreement resolving differences over Iran, Afghanistan, and Tibet. Finally, they got around to discussing Macedonia. Britain had already submitted a revised plan for reform, and out of the royal discussions came agreement on the appointment by the powers of a governor-general for the province and the formation of a body of European military inspectors to assist him. The number of Ottoman troops would be reduced, with local revenue paying for the reforms, not the two governments proposing them.

As Andrew Mango has pointed out, the opposition of Austria-Hungary and Germany made it most unlikely that a Macedonian reform program put in motion by their imperial rivals would ever have been adopted,[7] but the news from Reval had explosive consequences in Macedonia, where army officers demanded the immediate restoration of the constitution to head off this latest imposition on Ottoman sovereignty.

A revolutionary mood spread across the province. Armed insurgent bands were formed under the leadership of CUP officers, with mutiny in the army spreading to Edirne and even the Aegean coast. Instructed to crush the rebels, Şemsi Paşa, the military commander in Kosovo, was assassinated before he could start.

The sultan wavered between the stick (arrests of mutinous soldiers) and the carrot (their release and the declaration of an amnesty), but on July 23 the CUP declared the restoration of the constitution in Manastir. This was followed by similar declarations in Serres, Drama, and other towns.[8] After taking advice from the Shaykh al-Islam that the demands the rebels were making were not contrary to Islam, Abdülhamit accepted the recommendation of his cabinet and restored constitutional government on July 24. Scenes of euphoria followed across the empire as Muslims and Christians embraced each other in a new sense of brotherhood that transcended sectarian loyalties. The shackles of absolutism had been broken, autocratic rule from the palace had been permanently ended, and a bright future seemed to beckon.

PRESERVING THE EMPIRE

The goal of the Young Turks was the preservation of a reformed Ottoman state, one based on independence, the principles of constitutional government, and equality before the law for all citizens irrespective of religion or ethnicity. Formed in the late 1880s as a secret society (the Committee of Ottoman Union) by students at the Ottoman Imperial Military Medical School, the Committee of Union and Progress (CUP), later the Party of Union and Progress, continued to operate secretively but effectively (especially inside the military) until 1908. The CUP then functioned openly, manipulating power from behind the scenes, until it seized government in the coup of 1913.[9]

After the restoration of the constitution, the CUP used its influence to purge the bureaucracy and drive monarchist ministers out of office. The cleanout extended to the inner palace. 'Izzet Paşa, a Syrian and one of the sultan's most influential advisers, fled to Geneva. Abu al-Huda al-Sayyadi, another Syrian, from Khan Shaikhun, a Sufi of the Rifa'i order and an adviser to the sultan since the 1880s, was arrested but later allowed to return to Syria.

The Young Turks were a somewhat eclectic group in which the CUP was to become the dominant element. Like all political movements, the Young Turks had their factions and internal power plays even from the beginning. A core issue was the structure of government once the constitution had been restored. Whereas the CUP stood for strong central authority, its more liberal opponents believed decentralization was more suitable to the Ottoman ethnoreligious melting pot. While both factions looked to Europe for understanding and support, neither shared the common European view that the empire was all but finished.[10] Through reforms and constitutional government, given time, they believed it could again take its place in the world.

The constitution would give Christians (and Jews, numerically very much smaller) as well as Muslims reasons to remain part of the body politic. As was the case in 1839 and 1856, the key word was equality, which, for the CUP, implied the abolition of the privileges Christians enjoyed under the protection of foreign powers through the "capitulations." Originally granted by the sultan as a privilege to European rulers, allowing them to intercede on behalf of Christians, the capitulations had long since been demanded by European governments as a right and extended to such extraterritorial privileges as their own courts and postal services. The capitulations provided Ottoman Christians with a powerful external voice against the central government, and an even stronger one if they had managed to acquire the citizenship of one of these powers.

Muslims might equally be the victims of mistreatment but had no such avenue of appeal. However, with the Young Turks anxious to win the support of the powers, the capitulations were not abolished until relations with Britain and France were irrevocably sundered by the outbreak of a general European war in 1914.

The stabilization of finances was a longer-term program that would eventually involve the replacement of the Christian merchant class with a Turkish bourgeoisie that did not then exist. Christians and Jews dominated trade and commerce, and many of the older families had acquired great wealth and standing at the palace.

Jewish community leaders were consistent in their support for the new constitutional regime. While the Armenian Revolutionary Federation was also in favor, elements within the Christian bourgeoisie soon had second thoughts. Enthusiasm waned as they "realised that Unionist aspirations were not compatible with their own traditional privileges and long-term interests."[11] The Greek patriarchate was a particular pole of resistance, objecting to plans for a common educational policy as well as the removal of non-Muslim *millet* privileges.[12] Given the choice between privilege and equality, some influential Christians clearly favored the former. As for the European powers, given the choice between supporting special rights that gave them leverage over the Ottoman government and supporting constitutional government based on the equal rights and obligations of all citizens, they too supported the former.

Not until late in the nineteenth century had Ottoman governments tried to create an "Ottoman" identity that would transcend other loyalties. In the traditional Ottoman order, as long as non-Muslims paid their taxes, obeyed the law, and acknowledged the sultan's sovereign power they were free to run their affairs as they wanted. Their autonomy can be regarded as one of the great triumphs of a tolerant Ottoman order but under the impact of ethnoreligious nationalism and European support for the territorial and political claims of Ottoman Christians, the government's failure to cultivate a common sense of Ottoman identity turned into an enormous liability.

Insofar as the substance of constitutional government was concerned, it was not just Christians with vested interests but Muslim sympathizers with the old order who felt threatened by policies that "undermined the position of all privileged classes regardless of race or religion."[13] The Muslim "old guard" was determined to preserve what was left of *shari'a* law, already deeply eroded by secularizing reforms. The political old guard, predominantly secularized Muslims, wanted reforms but without destroying the social and economic *status quo ante*. Its dominant figures, Kamil

Paşa and Ismail Kemal, looked instinctively toward England and regarded the Unionists (the CUP) with the same patronizing if not openly hostile manner that filled the dispatches coming from the British embassy.

The first elections since 1876 were held in November 1908, a few months after the restoration of constitutional government. The results were a mixed bag: of 281 deputies, 54 were "committed" Unionists, 147 were independents generally supportive of the CUP, and 74 represented the conservative Liberal Union (*ahrar firkası*).[14]

Out of necessity, because they were still hoping for British support, the Unionists supported the Liberal Unionist Kamil Paşa as Grand Vizier. Kamil, an Ottoman statesman of long experience, close to the British embassy and implacably hostile to the CUP, held office only until February 1909, when he was forced to resign after dismissing the ministers of war and navy without consulting parliament in what seemed to be an attempt to replace them with ministers close to the palace.

His resignation was soon followed by a counterrevolution instigated by the Muhammadan Union (Ittihad-i Muhammedi), founded on April 3. While its public face was the religious firebrand Derviş Vahdeti, the union was founded, according to Aykut Kansu, by the chief eunuch of the palace, the second eunuch, one of the sultan's sons, one of his nephews, and several others, including Derviş Vahdeti. In Kansu's view, the counterrevolution launched on April 13 was "a well-organized monarchist attempt to restore the old regime"[15] that must have had the sultan's seal of approval. Kemal Karpat, on the other hand, doubts that the palace was involved.[16] Vahdeti's followers included thousands of mutinous soldiers and *softas* (theological students). The Parliament was surrounded. Besieged and in an atmosphere of spreading chaos and murder, the government was forced to resign.

The army reacted immediately when news of the overthrow and the sultan's pardon of the mutineers reached Macedonia. Within a week an "operational army" (*hareket ordusu*), mobilized in Selanik (Salonica) and Edirne, had reached the outskirts of Istanbul under the command of Mahmud Şevket Paşa. Entering the city on April 24, it fought bloody battles with the counterrevolutionaries outside the government offices (the Bab-i 'Ali) and around the Taksim and Taşkişla army barracks.

Hundreds were killed on both sides. Yildiz Palace was surrounded as soldiers and civilian supporters of the counterrevolution fled the city. A "parliament in exile," hastily convened at Yeşilköy (San Stefano), voted to depose the sultan. The Shaykh al-Islam endorsed the decision with a *fatwa*, and Abdülhamit was packed off into exile in Selanik until allowed to return to Istanbul in 1912, just ahead of the Greek occupation of the city during the Balkan Wars. The sultan's brother, Mehmet Reşat, replaced him as Sultan Mehmet V. Derviş Vahdeti, other leading figures in the counterrevolution, and mutinous soldiers were soon executed.

"BOASTING AND PROVOCATION"

In the distant province of Adana, tension between Muslims and Christians had been building since the restoration of constitutional government. The Armenians in this southeastern Anatolian corner of the empire—Ottoman Çukurova but Cilicia for the Armenians and their European supporters—differed from the Armenians of the eastern provinces by speaking Ottoman Turkish as their first language. Many were adherents of the protestant Armenian Evangelical Church, formed in the 1840s after dissenting Armenians were expelled from the Gregorian mainstream. A further difference lay in the fact that while Armenians in the eastern provinces were scattered across the countryside, those in the southeast tended to be concentrated in towns and cities.[17]

The American missionaries who proselytized among them continued to play a significant role in their education. Like Armenians everywhere, the Armenians of the southeast took heart from the restoration of the constitution, but many still looked ahead to the day when they would have their own state. The Dashnaks and Hunchaks were active and urging rebellion. There was talk of the coming Armenian kingdom and, in the words of the British consul at Mersin (Major Charles Doughty-Wylie), "much vain boasting and wordy provocation" of the Muslims.[18] Armenians "intoxicated with the new wine of liberty often gave offence by wild and arrogant behavior."[19]

At the end of a play staged in Adana on March 29 in which an Armenian king, threatened with death by Timur (the fourteenth-century Turkic-Mongol conqueror Tamerlane), is visited by spirits who tell him his kingdom will be restored on the foundations of the unity of his people, Armenians in the audience, which included government officials, clapped and began shouting "Long live Armenia" and "Long live the Armenian kingdom."[20]

A fiery nationalist bishop, Musheg Seropian, played a key role in stirring up disorder. He traveled across the region urging people to arm themselves and is said to have personally smuggled arms into Adana.

At the same time, Ihsan Fikri, a prominent CUP figure and editor of the newspaper *Ittidal* (Moderation) had been publishing speculative articles about Armenian intentions that could only have alarmed Muslim readers.[21] Once the killing started, *Ittidal* held Armenians to account, claiming they had poured into Adana from other regions with the intention of changing the demographics ahead of demanding autonomy. In Der Matossian's view, the publication of such articles "were vital in shaping public opinion in Adana," including the belief among Muslims in an Armenian conspiracy.[22]

On April 9 a young Armenian carpenter, Hovhannes Yapuciyan, shot two other young men, both Muslims, before disappearing into the Armenian quarter of Adana and later leaving for Cyprus.[23] The issue between them was apparently not political but rivalry over a woman. The Muslim contender for her favors was killed and his friend seriously wounded.[24] Clearly, the killing was not a random event, as the men had been feuding for days, and the Armenian had taken the precaution of arming himself,[25] but the murder was the catalyst[26] for the unbridled violence that now engulfed the city of Adana and the region.

An angry mood among Muslims that the Armenians must be punished reached a crescendo with the funeral procession of the dead man on April 13. Bursts of gunfire and arson attacks throughout the city marked the general breakdown of order, as Muslims and Christians fought it out. In the coming days, Christian schools were burnt. Shops and houses in the Armenian quarter were ransacked and set on fire. On April 15, two American missionaries, Henry Maurer and Daniel Miner Rogers, were shot dead while trying to extinguish a blaze at the house of an elderly Turkish woman. Responsibility for the deaths would be contested, with the Ottoman Foreign Ministry claiming the missionaries had been caught in gunfire coming from nearby Armenian houses.[27]

From Adana, the flames of this fire spread to villages, towns, and cities across the province. According to a *New York Times* correspondent, James Creelman,

> News of the battle in Adana, the resistance of the Armenians and the killing of hundreds of Moslems ran everywhere on the Cilician plain, where the story of a proposed Armenian kingdom had been talked over for weeks. The whole country seemed to go mad. Villages were sacked, and in some cases the whole male population wiped out. Rough troops of horsemen swept from place to

place followed by hordes of running field hands with rifles, pistols, swords, daggers, and clubs. They shot the Christians in their houses, hacked them with their swords and scythes, beat their brains out, burned them alive. They trailed them through the wheat and barley fields with dogs and for days the hunting of men became a regular sport."[28]

Even though Creelman's lurid reports were written months after the event, so that he was dependent on what he was told and casting doubt on the veracity of his detail, the scale of the violence was undoubtedly terrible. Cattle, sheep, and goats were driven off into the mountains. Armenian women were carried off with them. The attackers were Turks, Arabs, Circassians, and Kurds. The destruction was massive. Photographs show the charred ruins of entire quarters of Adana, of Jesuit and Syriac churches and schools reduced to rubble as well as Armenian and refugee tents set up on the outskirts of the city. Like many others, Creelman blamed the "blatherskite" Armenian bishop whose inflammatory talk he believed had kindled this fire.

The Armenian death toll from this period of violence is generally put at about 20,000. Cemal Paşa, who replaced Cevat Bey as governor, put the death toll at 17,000 Armenians,[29] out of a total Armenian population in Adana province of about 50,000 within a general population of about 400,000.[30] "There was nothing to choose between the two sides as regards cruelties," Cemal wrote. "The Armenians never stopped attacking Turkish women and children, the Turks did the same, and the two infuriated races proved that there was no difference between them." Had Armenians been in the majority, Cemal had no doubt that "the Turks" (a term including Kurds and other Muslims) would have borne the brunt of the massacres.

In the aftermath, 130 Muslims and 95 Christians were arrested. Altogether, 47 people found guilty of murder or arson were hanged. They included members of some of the oldest families in Adana, the mufti of the *kaza* of Bahçe, Ismail Hakki, and his brother among them. The executions included 25 men hanged on one day, December 11, 1909.[31] Having escaped to Egypt, Bishop Seropian was sentenced to death in absentia. "If I had caught him I should have had him hanged opposite the mufti of Bagje [Bahçe]," Cemal wrote.[32]

Although Cemal was the governor, his estimate of the Armenian death seems considerably inflated. The government put the number of dead at 5,243 "non-Muslims" and 1,186 Muslims for a total of 6,429.[33] Armenian estimates ranged between 20,000 and "at least" 30,000.[34] Tetsuya Sahara questions the credibility even of the lower figures, set within the grossly inflated population estimates of the Armenian patriarchate, more than double the census figures. The government's final figures were based on detailed investigations across the province by four commissions of inquiry. Allowing for seasonal workers who may have been killed, the final total death toll would seem to stand somewhere between the official figure and 8,000.[35]

None of the single theories advanced to explain the tumult in Adana is ultimately satisfactory. Creelman, the *New York Times* reporter, put part of the blame on the "foreign education and foreign sympathy that inspired the Armenians to plan a Christian kingdom and nerved their oath-bound riflemen to kill hundreds of Moslems." He also believed that the "great massacre" was the outcome of "a deliberate plan carefully worked out by the Mohammedan League under the sanction of Abdul Hamid." However, although the Muhammadan Union may have been funded by the palace, there is no evidence that it or the sultan were responsible for the Adana violence.

The failure of officials, especially Cemal's predecessor as governor, to take charge of the situation seems to have been a key element in the total collapse of communal relations. Described in one account as "running about in dismay," the governor clearly panicked. According to missionary Trowbridge, "One man is responsible for the disorders here. This is the vali himself. He had the power to suppress lawlessness and massacre but deliberately refrained from doing so."[36] In his detailed analysis of these events, Tetsuya Sahara has dismissed all conspiracy theories advanced to explain what happened in Adana. In his view, the numerous elements that fed into the situation were all "an offshoot of the general disintegration process of late Ottoman society."[37]

STANDING ON PRINCIPLE

With most of "Turkey in Europe" already lost, the ambitions of Greece, Serbia, and Bulgaria came to rest on the remaining Ottoman territories of Albania, Macedonia, and Thrace. In Macedonia, the partisans of various ethnoreligious national movements—Bulgarian, Greek, and Serb—continued to kill each other as well as Ottoman soldiers and officials. Historical "Christian grievances," compounded by the failure, inability, or refusal of the government in Istanbul to institute the "reforms" demanded by the European powers were the levers—repeatedly pulled—that weakened the sultan's hold on his remaining Balkan domains. The Serbian and Greek eastern orthodox churches and the Bulgarian exarchate served as religious conduits for conflicting claims to "lost" territories. The cement holding mutual hostilities in check was the implacable hostility of all Balkan nationalists toward the Ottoman presence.

Political turmoil in Istanbul following the restoration of constitutional government in 1908 was an opportunity Balkan states did not hesitate to grasp. On October 5, Bulgaria declared its independence, with Ferdinand's installation as Tsar of the Bulgars immediately recognized by the powers. The next day, Austria-Hungary openly violated the Treaty of Berlin by annexing Bosnia-Herzegovina. On Crete, thousands of demonstrators also seized the moment, marching through Canea on October 7 to demand union with Greece. *Enosis* was proclaimed in the evening by the Cretan assembly. "There was much firing of guns and revolvers together with plenty of cheering but perfect order prevailed," the *New York Times* reported on October 8, claiming that "Mussulmans mingled with Christians freely and unmolested."

Britain raised its voice against the annexation of Bosnia-Herzegovina. A "cruel blow had been struck at the budding hopes of better things in Turkey," wrote the foreign secretary, in addition to which "we felt that the arbitrary alteration of a European Treaty by one Power without the consent of the other parties which were party to it struck at the root of all good international order. We therefore took a very firm stand on principle and said that, though our interests were not involved, we would not recognise Austria's action, and the changes she had made till all the other Powers which were parties to the treaty were ready to do so."[38] Thus, the "principle" angering Britain was not the violation of the sovereign rights of the Ottoman government. Neither was it Austria-Hungary's violation of the Treaty of Berlin. As stated by the British foreign secretary, the principle was the "alteration" of a treaty without the consent of the other European signatories. Had they all agreed beforehand, presumably there would have been no protest.

By way of compensation, Austria-Hungary handed the *sancak* of Novipazar (*yenipazarı sancağı*) back to the Ottoman Empire. As any diplomat would have expected, Serbia, regarding Novipazar as its own by historic right, was furious. It wanted territorial compensation and threatened to take the *sancak* by force, whatever the cost: "Either we must make of Serbia a huge cemetery or we must create Greater Serbia."[39] Narodna Obrana (People's Defense), formed in the wake of the annexation, took on the task of preparing the people for war.

In such an event, Russia's position would have been crucial, but in clandestine negotiations with Austria-Hungary Russia appeared ready to trade the interests of the Serbs for Austria-Hungary's "understanding" of its position on the straits. Russia sought the free passage of "not more than three warships at once" through the straits in peacetime, with the same right granted to other states bordering the Black Sea.[40] Whatever had transpired in discussions between the Russian Foreign Minister, Alexander Izvolsky, and his Austro-Hungarian counterpart, Alois von Aerhenthal, such a proposal would need the support of the other powers.

In London, the British foreign secretary did not actually say "no" but made it clear that the moment for such a proposal was "inopportune."[41] At this point, the Russian initiative lapsed. Izvolsky argued that that he had promised nothing in advance, in which case he surely would not have been so angry. He berated the Austrian foreign minister as being "tortuous and insincere and always wishing to compromise the person with whom he was dealing."[42]

While this episode ended in diplomatic humiliation for Russia and a weakening of its position in the Balkans, the Serbian threat of war and the greater threat of a Balkan conflict ending in general European crisis were both taken very seriously. For the British Foreign Secretary, writing much later, there was an "ominous parallel" between the events of 1908–1909 and the crisis of 1914. On both occasions, Austria-Hungary acted without apparently consulting Germany first, yet both times Germany rose to its defense. Russia, however, when challenged to stand with its Serbian protégés, "preferred humiliation" in 1909 only to face war in 1914.[43]

The powers adjusted to the new facts on the ground by post facto amending Article 25 of the Treaty of Berlin, allowing the annexation of Bosnia-Herzegovina. The Ottoman government was paid a trifle—2.5 million Turkish pounds—by way of compensation. Its territorial consolation only lasted until the attack by the Balkan states in 1912, after which Novipazar passed into Serbian and Montenegrin hands.[44]

Unrest in the Balkans—the heartland of the Ottoman empire—was now a dagger aimed at its heart. Since 1878, the government's inability to defend what was left of its territorial integrity had encouraged even Muslims to break away. Its cession of Ülgün to Montenegro in 1880 under the pressure of a naval demonstration by five powers (Britain, France,

Germany, Russia, and Austria-Hungary) off the Adriatic coast "represented a blow to Albanian faith in the Ottoman state" and furthered the case of Albanian nationalism.[45]

In 1881, resistance by the Prizren League in Kosovo and Üsküb (Skopje) was soon suppressed by an Ottoman expeditionary force. A second uprising followed in March 1910. On November 28, 1912, with Ottoman armies suffering crippling defeats on all fronts after the attack by the Balkan states, Albanian delegates meeting at Vlore declared their country's independence.

"SPHERES OF INFLUENCE"

In the early twentieth century, the rivalry of the powers continued to affect the destinies of lands far from their shores. The Great Game was still being played, and no territory and no ruler, king, prince, emir, sultan, shah, emperor, khedive, or maharaja could escape entanglement in the grand schemes and stratagems of the European powers. First and foremost, the "game" had been played by Britain and Russia, but now newcomers were entering the field. Their territories finally united in national states, Germany and Italy were looking for their share of the spoils in Africa and indeed anywhere there might be an opening. In the Pacific, Germany had already reached Papua New Guinea, which it held as a protectorate from 1884 until driven out by Australian forces in 1914.

At the same time that the Balkan states were preparing for war, a new threat to the integrity of the Ottoman Empire was arising on the other side of the Adriatic as the result of Italy's imperial and colonial ambitions. Italy had begun laying the foundations of an African colonial empire in the 1880s, but in challenging Emperor Menelik of Ethiopia, a charismatic figure of ancient lineage venerated by his people, it picked the wrong man and the wrong country. Not only were the Ethiopians fiercely independent but the emperor could send more than 100,000 men into battle. The Italians were fighting far from home on unfamiliar and difficult terrain. The heat alone was severely debilitating, while the clear technical superiority of the colonial army was insufficient to offset Ethiopian numbers.

In Sudan, the annihilation of the Hicks expedition by the followers of the Mahdi in 1883 had taught the British a bitter lesson. Now in Ethiopia it was Italy's turn to experience humiliation at the hands of a "native" army. On March 1, 1896, the emperor sent tens of thousands of soldiers—estimates run from about 70,000 to 120,000—against an Italian force of about 18,000 at Adwa. The Italians were routed, with more than 6,000 men killed and thousands taken prisoner.

This crushing defeat forced Italy to recognize Ethiopian independence. It continued to develop its colony in Eritrea, while waiting for a chance to establish a foothold on the North African coast. Following the French occupation of Tunis in 1881 (foiling Italy's designs on the same territory) and Egypt in 1882, only Libya was left as a point of entry.

Italy's view of itself—as expressed by the foreign minister—was that of a new nation that "had come late into the field of spheres of influence in countries bordering on the Mediterranean. He likened her to [an] unexpected guest at dinner for whom space must perforce be made."[46] In fact, Italy's drive for a place in the colonial sun had been tacitly accepted by the senior European powers: the table had been set and a chair was quickly found for the unexpected guest. Already by 1900, Italy and France had signed a secret agreement acknowledging each other's prior "right" to Libya (Italy) and Morocco (France). In the Anglo-French convention of April 1904, Britain had also acknowledged the French claim to Morocco, as long as France acknowledged Spanish interests in the same territory.

In 1902, very far from North Africa and the Ottoman lands, Britain had signed a treaty with Japan aimed at checking Russia and safeguarding the respective interests of both signatories in China and Korea. The outbreak of war between Russia and Japan in 1904 ended in the defeat of Russia and the destruction of both its Pacific and Baltic fleets. Shocked reaction across Europe at the victory of a small Asian country over a European power was mixed with admiration for Japan's mastery of modern warfare. "Yes, we used to be a nation of artists," a Japanese living in England is said to have mused. "Our art was really very good; you called us barbarians then. Now our art is not so good as it was, but we have learnt how to kill, and you say we are civilized."[47]

In 1905, at the height of the war with Russia, Japan's treaty with Britain was renewed but revised. In Article VI, Britain declared its "strict neutrality" unless other powers joined the war, in which case it would come to Japan's assistance. Irritated, the tsar responded favorably to the kaiser's suggestion "for Germany, Russia and France to come to an understanding for the purpose of putting an end to British and Japanese arrogance and insolence. Are you disposed to sketch out the main lines of such an agreement and let me see them?" The kaiser sent them off immediately but backed off when the tsar wanted to see what France thought of the idea. Informing France, the kaiser believed, would be dangerous because England was "her friend and perhaps her secret ally. The result would be an immediate attack from England and Japan in Europe as well as in Asia. Her [Britain's] immense naval superiority would soon enable her to overcome my little fleet and Germany would be temporarily paralysed. Any preliminary warning to France would lead to a catastrophe."[48] Within three years, however, Russia had settled its differences with Britain and was building a strategic alliance with both Britain and France.

Like the Ottoman Empire, Iran had fallen into political turmoil since its own constitutional revolution in 1905–1906 and was not well placed to resist further impositions by the powers. The Anglo-Russian convention of August 31, 1907, dividing Iran into "spheres of interest" meant that "the part of Persia by which India could be approached was made secure from Russian penetration," while "that part of Persia by which Russia could be approached was secured from British penetration."[49] This included northwest Persia from where Russia was able to launch attacks on the Ottoman Empire when war finally came. In the lead-up to the agreement, Grey thought that if Asian questions were settled favorably, then "the Russians will not have trouble with us about the entrance to the Black Sea."[50] In 1908, the discovery of oil at Masjid al-Sulayman turned control of Iran into a future *sine qua non* of British foreign policy.

AFRICAN "COMPENSATION"

Through these shifts in foreign policy, the growing threat for France, Britain, and Russia as the nineteenth century gave way to the twentieth remained Germany and its readiness to flex its muscles in pursuit of strategic, colonial, and commercial interests. In 1892–1893, Russia and France had signed a commitment to defend each other in the case of a German attack or an attack involving Germany.

In 1906, Britain produced a naval trump card with the production of a battleship (HMS *Dreadnought*) that rendered all others obsolete. Germany responded by building its own dreadnoughts. War was already being seen as inevitable. The First Lord of the British Admiralty, Admiral John (Jacky) Fisher accurately predicted that it would break out in 1914, but one could have broken out at any time.

One point of possible breakdown was the Franco-German crisis over Morocco where France had been expanding its influence since the late nineteenth century. In February 1905, a German cruiser paid a courtesy call to Tangier, and on March 31 the kaiser himself stepped onto the docks. A ride through the streets followed, according to a German envoy, "amid the indescribable joy of the natives and the European population."[51]

So far so good, but in an address to the sultan, Wilhelm remarked that "he looked upon the sultan as the ruler of a free and independent empire subject to no foreign control." In conversation with the French agent, the Kaiser insisted on free trade and complete equality of rights with other countries. When he said he would like to treat with the sultan directly, the French agent "became pale . . . he was about to respond but was curtly dismissed" and withdrew with lowered head.[52]

In the wake of the kaiser's blunt remarks, Germany and France prepared for war. Germany made it clear that it was too strong to allow itself to be bullied by a combination of other powers but backed down when most of the representatives of thirteen governments summoned to Algeciras (Spain) the following January to settle the crisis supported the French claim of prior right in Morocco.

Along with Britain, France, and Spain, Germany was given shared control over Moroccan finances, but only France and Spain had supervisory rights over the local police in the six nominated port cities. The outcome of the conference was a signal to Germany that if it did go to war, it would have all the major European governments against it with the single exception of Austria-Hungary. Italy upheld the secret commitment it had made to France in the agreement of 1900, despite its membership in the Triple Alliance with Germany and Austria-Hungary. According to this understanding, France would have a free hand in Morocco and Italy a free hand in Libya. Even the U.S. supported the French claim to a privileged position in Morocco.

In 1911, Morocco was the centerpiece of a second Franco-German crisis. Tension between the two powers had continued ever since the patchwork settlement of the last crisis. Germany was accused by France of fomenting rebellion upcountry and, through the German agent in Casablanca, Karl Ficke, inciting Germans to desert from the Foreign Legion. An unstable situation reached boiling point when rebels besieged the sultan ('Abd al-Hafiz) in the royal palace at Fas (Fez) in March. Despite German warnings, France occupied Fas in May and Meknes in June. Protecting its own interests, Spain seized Qasr al-Kabir and al-Araish, a port town near Tangier.

In response to these violations of the Algeciras agreement, the kaiser decided in late June to send the gunboat *Panther* to Morocco. It arrived off the Atlantic port of Agadir on July 1. Germany stated that its presence was necessary to protect the lives of German nationals, claiming that "natives" had attacked one on a farm. Germany denied having any territorial designs on Morocco: talk that it was after a naval base was a "hallucination,"[53] but it did seek "compensation." France was behaving "as if neither Germany nor a treaty existed."[54] Now France had to make choices: either it stuck to the letter of the Algeciras agreement, or it would have to compensate Germany through territorial "adjustments."

The compensation of which the German foreign minister and ambassadors spoke turned out to be a large slab of French Equatorial Africa (Gabon and the Middle Congo). If France was prepared to hand it over, then Germany would recognize what would effectively be a full French "protectorate" over Morocco.

Again, war seemed possible. France sounded out Britain on whether it would come to its aid if Germany attacked and received signals that it would. Britain would not fight so that France could keep Morocco, but it would fight to prevent Germany destroying the Anglo-French entente. In a Mansion House speech on July 4, David Lloyd-George (Chancellor of the Exchequer) said Britain would make great sacrifices to preserve peace, but if treated "as if she were of no account in the Cabinet of nations, then I say emphatically that peace at that price would be a humiliation intolerable for a great country like ours to endure."

Ultimately, as it turned out, no one was prepared to go to war over Morocco. On November 4, the crisis was settled in the Treaty of Fez, establishing a French protectorate over Morocco. Germany accepted the protectorate and in return was given about 275,000 square kilometers of territory in French Equatorial Africa, centering on the *moyen* Congo (middle Congo), to add to its West African colonial territory of Kamerun.

Watching this imperial haggling over territory only sharpened Italy's colonial appetite. It was looking for its own "compensation" and knew what it wanted: the uncolonized gap between Tunisia and Egypt, Ottoman Libya, where the ruins of Leptis Magna stood as testimony to this part of North Africa's place in the Roman Empire.

CHAPTER 7

Italy Invades Libya

WITH EUROPEAN GOVERNMENTS occupying virtually all of Africa, Italy wanted its share. This was perfectly understandable among the senior members of the imperial club. Their problem was not the Italian drive for colonies as such but how Italy's territorial ambitions could be accommodated without damaging their individual and collective interests.

By the late nineteenth century, Italy had already established a substantial colonial presence in Somalia and Eritrea. At Berlin in 1878, Britain had informally accepted France's claim to Tunisia in return for French understanding of its acquisition of Cyprus, signaling at the same time support for Italy's claim to Libya.

Italy still protested when France occupied Tunisia in 1881, but compensation followed in 1902 when Italy and France signed a secret convention that gave France a "right" of intervention in Morocco and Italy the same "right" in Ottoman Libya. Accordingly, Italy expected French support when it launched its campaign to occupy Libya.

Divided administratively into three provinces, Tripolitania (Ottoman Trablus Garp), Fezzan, and Cyrenaica, Libya had been governed by the Ottomans since the sixteenth century, mostly directly. Military garrisons (*ocaklar* or "hearths") were maintained along the coast where the Ottoman presence could be more strongly maintained.

In Cyrenaica, constituting the eastern half of the country, authority among the tribes away from the coastal towns largely rested in the hands of the hereditary tribal leaders of the Sanusi Sufi order. Fezzan to the southwest was vast, largely desert, sparsely populated, and thinly garrisoned.

The fact that this was all sovereign Ottoman territory mattered little to the powers, which indulged Italy: it could have Libya as long as it did not tread on their toes.

A mood of national pride and thwarted entitlement driven by government propaganda and commercial-colonial interests in Rome propelled the country toward a landing in Tripoli where thousands of Italians lived and the Banco di Roma had assiduously consolidated the Italian presence, giving Italy the pretext of safeguarding national interests should the day ever come when it decided to invade.

In 1911, anticipating an Italian landing, the Ottoman government sent a warship to Tripoli. Its arrival on September 25 boosted the morale of the local people while antagonizing the Italian government still further. On September 28, Italy demanded that it be allowed to send troops to Tripoli to end the disorder created through official Ottoman "negligence" and protect the Italian community. These were fabrications: there was no disorder, and no Christians were being threatened.

The next day, with the government in Istanbul having rejected an Italian offer it could not accept (occupation behind the façade of Ottoman sovereignty), Italy declared war, setting loose "the first stone in what for the next decade would turn into the avalanche which would overwhelm the Ottoman Empire."[1]

Within hours, Italian warships had destroyed one Turkish torpedo boat in the Ionian Sea and destroyed two more lying at anchor in Prevesa harbor. In the coming months, the Italian naval campaign would include the shelling of Ottoman targets in the Aegean, the eastern Mediterranean, and the Red Sea. European governments—Russia, Britain, France, Belgium, Spain, Portugal, and Serbia—quickly declared their neutrality, effectively giving Italy a free hand. In some quarters, there was outrage at Italy's act of "brigandage."[2] The British government, however, accepted Italy's justification for the invasion, the foreign secretary arguing that "any action Italy took to defend her interests had been brought by the Turks upon themselves."[3]

There was some concern at the possibility of unrest being stirred up among Muslims in British-occupied territories (notably Egypt and India) but tacit support for Italy overrode these considerations. It was considered "exceedingly foolish that we should displease a country [Italy], with whom we have always been on most friendly terms and whose friendship to us is of great value, in order to keep well with Turkey, who has been a source of great annoyance to us and whose Government is one of the worst that can well be imagined."[4]

A "WORK OF ART"

The Ottoman-Sanusi forces consisted of about 12,000 infantry, cavalry, and *chasseurs* at the time the Italians landed but never exceeded 25,000 men even at the height of the war. Some modern weapons (artillery and howitzers) had been acquired, but otherwise the heavy weaponry consisted of old-fashioned cannon with none of the firepower or range of the Italian naval guns and land artillery. The Ottoman contingent consisted of several thousand soldiers and officers sent as "volunteers" by the government in Istanbul. Including Enver and Mustafa Kemal, they sailed under cover to Alexandria and crossed Egypt's western desert into Cyrenaica.

Italian warships were standing off the coast of Tripoli when surrender was demanded on September 30. On October 3, having received no reply, the Italian ships bombarded the city from thousands of yards offshore. The shore batteries responded without having the range to actually reach the Italian flotilla. The forts on the coast at Alexandria had put up the same futile resistance to the British fleet when it bombarded Alexandria in 1882. The Italian shelling hit the lighthouse and damaged the governor's palace. Fires raged in the residential areas, leading to calls from foreign residents for Italian troops to land and restore the order that had just been destroyed, again repeating the pattern of the British landing at Alexandria. Two Ottoman naval vessels, the warship *Derne* and a gunboat, were scuttled on the orders of their commanders rather surrender to the Italians.

An advance force of ground troops disembarked on October 5, with tens of thousands more soldiers soon on their way in scores of transports sent from Naples and Palermo. Troops had already been landed at Tobruk when Tripoli was occupied, and in the coming weeks all major towns along the coast to Benghazi were shelled before being captured. The Ottoman force in Tripoli—about 3,000 men—had withdrawn to hills a few miles south of the city before the Italians landed. Somewhat inland, Ottoman-Sanusi forces prevented the Italians from ever penetrating the interior.

Italian battlefield losses were severe almost from the beginning. On October 23, an Italian contingent of several hundred *bersaglieri* was overwhelmed by resistance fighters at Shar al-Shatt (Italian Sciara Sciat), an oasis village on the outskirts of Tripoli. The Italians were clearly caught off guard. More than 480 soldiers and 21 officers were killed, an estimated 290 of them allegedly after being captured and tortured.

Press accounts of mutilation, including castration, and men being crucified set the scene for the outraged retaliation of Italian troops at the nearby Mechiya oasis settlement between October 24 and 26 when they were reported to have slaughtered thousands of civilians in their homes, on the streets, and in mosques. Resistance continued, with Mustafa Kemal leading a successful attack on an Italian outpost on November 22 that forced the *bersaglieri* to retreat to Tobruk. By this time, on November 5, Italy had annexed its new African colony.

Already by December, the initial Italian expeditionary force of 40,000 had swelled to more than 100,000. The army was well equipped at every level.[5] The *bersaglieri* cut a dashing sight in their white uniforms, down to their white spats, with a cockade of feathers falling to the right side of their white helmets. Motorized transport included cars and ambulances fitted with double rear tires for easier travel across the sand when troops moved away from the coast. Aircraft (Farmans, Blériots, Nieuports, and Etrich Taubes) and dirigibles were used in war for the first time, the dirigibles for aerial reconnaissance and the planes for bombing raids as well as reconnaissance.

Navy lieutenant Cipelli devised a hand grenade that could be thrown from an aircraft before he was killed when one exploded in his hands. Lieutenant Guilio Gavotti threw several from the cockpit of his Etrich Taube monoplane, becoming the first man in history to bomb the enemy from the air, before the Italian pilots decided that the grenades were too dangerous and did little damage anyway: instead, they dropped leaflets in Arabic calling for surrender.

The application of raw force and especially the use of airpower delighted the Futurist poet Filippo Tomasso Emilio Marinettti, a "Levantine" born in Alexandria and corresponding from Libya for a French newspaper. As art could be "nothing but violence, cruelty and injustice,"[6] what else could the invasion be but a work of art? The past was past: only the future counted. Marinetti delighted in speed, in the power of the machine, of the aircraft and the full-chested locomotive rushing invincibly across the landscape.[7] Similarly enraptured by the triumph of the machine, Gabriele D'Annunzio, later to become the poet revolutionary of Italian fascism, dedicated his *Canzone della Diana* to Lieutenant Gavotti.

As the war moved further from the quick and brilliant victory promised by the Italian government, the costs mounted. Military expenditure accounted for nearly half the Italian state budget for 1912–1913, which was probably an underestimate.[8] With Libya's oil wealth not yet discovered and with no other tangible economic returns, the war came eventually to be regarded as a thoroughly "negative page" in Italy's military history.⁹

From time to time, the Italian forces were able to inflict heavy defeats on Ottoman-Sanusi forces (notably in the battle around Zanzur oasis on June 8, 1912), but control of the interior remained frustratingly out of reach. Even before the end of 1911, Rome had decided to harass the Ottomans elsewhere. On November 19 and 20, along the eastern Red Sea coast, warships shelled the Yemeni port of al-Hudayda and the nearby quarantine station. Attacks on Aqaba and the Ottoman garrison at al-Qunfidha followed in January, with al-Hudayda also put under blockade.

On February 24, an Italian flotilla arrived off Beirut and demanded the surrender of an Ottoman destroyer and a coastal defense vessel lying at anchor. The ships not being handed over, the coastal vessel was destroyed with a torpedo from the *Garibaldi*, killing 8 officers and 55 men. The warship was sunk in later shelling. Bombardment of the town killed 66 civilians, wounded several hundred more, and severely damaged government buildings, customs warehouses, and banks, including the Imperial Ottoman Bank, the Salonica Bank, and the German Palestine Bank.¹⁰

Several Italians were attacked in the streets by way of reprisal, along with a Russian Jew "mistakenly supposed to be an Italian."¹¹ The Ottoman government responded to the bombardment by ordering all Italians living in the administrative districts of Beirut, Damascus, Aleppo, and the *mutesarriflik* of Jerusalem to leave within two weeks, warning that others might be expelled from the empire if there were further attacks.

The shelling of Beirut and bombardments along the coast of Yemen (nominally still an Ottoman possession but then gripped by an uprising) were driven by the stalled position of the Italian army in Libya. Expecting attacks in the Aegean, the Ottomans mined the "narrows"—the straits leading into the Sea of Marmara (Çanakkale Boğazı)—and positioned four merchant ships laden with stones in the channel leading into the harbor at Izmir, ready to be scuttled if necessary. Italian warships were seen in the Gulf of Edremit, and by November Italy was letting the powers know that it was prepared to attack the straits.

The question of whether Italy would actually go ahead filled the dispatches of European governments in the coming months. Their immediate concern was the protection of their commercial interests if the Ottomans responded by closing the straits. Britain's foreign secretary suggested to Russia that Italy could be asked not to attack the straits or launch hostile operations in neighboring waters. From Foreign Minister Sazonov came the reply that such a request could hardly be justified "as it might be regarded by her [Italy] as an attempt to restrict the field of her operations." Furthermore, he wished to keep on the friendliest terms with Italy, as it was seen as "a valuable counterpoise to Austria in the Balkans"[12] despite its membership in the Triple Alliance.

DANGEROUS DIRECTIONS

On April 18, 1912, an Italian flotilla of 24 ships appeared off Çanakkale after cutting the cable links with Imroz (present-day Gökceada), Tenedos (Bözcaada), Lemnos, and Selanik (Salonica). The further severance of communications in the southern Aegean included the link between Rhodos (Rhodes) and the mainland town of Marmaris. The telegraph offices on the island of Kos, at Izmir and nearby Çesme, and the military barracks at Samos were all subjected to naval bombardment.

On April 19, the forts guarding the "narrows" came under heavy attack. The British vice-consul at Çanakkale reported that the Italians started the barrage by firing on an Ottoman destroyer.[13] When an Ottoman fort returned fire, Italian warships lying thousands of yards off the coast pounded the forts with hundreds of shells in a three-hour bombardment. There were military and civilian casualties, and the government in Istanbul responded by closing the straits.

The war had now entered a new dimension. Libya had been invaded and annexed. That was acceptable to the powers, but by threatening British and Russian trading and strategic interests centering on the straits, Italy was forcing the powers to intervene. Dozens of ships—Greek, Rumanian, German, Russian, French, and British—were now bottled up between Çanakkale and the Black Sea. Shipments of grain, corn, petroleum (from Rumania), iron ore, timber, coal, and naphtha, passengers of all national descriptions, and thousands of British naval officers and men were stuck.

Russia was particularly affected, not because of trade with the Ottoman Empire, which was slight, but because almost half its exports (including almost all of its grain) were shipped to the outside world through the straits. As the closure had not been anticipated, many of these shipments were uninsured. By April 30, 150 merchant ships, mostly British and many carrying grain, were held up. Financial losses were accruing by the day, and perishable cargo (such as maize) soon likely to rot.[14]

The straits were mined, and mines also placed in the Gulf of Izmir, leading to tragedy on the night of April 29 when the steamer *Texas*, American flagged but owned by a local company (the Archipelago-American Steamship Company), hit a mine and sank with the loss of about 70 lives. Under pressure from the powers, the Ottoman government agreed on May 1 to reopen the straits, but this was delayed for three weeks, ostensibly by bad weather and mine removal.

Refusing to give guarantees to the powers that it would not threaten the straits again, Italy kept up its pressure.[15] On May 4, thousands of troops were landed on Rhodes. The Ottoman garrison withdrew to the mountains and resisted the invasion before finally being overwhelmed in a nine-hour battle on May 15. These actions, followed by the bombardment of Marmaris on May 18, were met with an Ottoman decree ordering all Italians to leave Ottoman lands within two weeks. The expulsion order (not the bombardments) caused a "storm of indignation" in Italy. Expressing outrage and seizing the opportunity to put further pressure on the government in Istanbul, the Italian foreign minister found himself unable to judge "what measures the force of public exasperation might not oblige the Italian government to adopt."[16]

The occupation of Rhodes was followed in November by the seizure of all other islands in the Dodecanese except Kastellorizo. When none of these measures forced the Ottoman government into submission, Italian policy began moving in even more threatening directions. In June, Chief of the General Staff, Albert Pollio, declared that Italy must engage in total war with the Ottoman state, must land troops at Izmir, and must encourage Balkan Christians to rise up and end the Ottoman presence in southeastern Europe once and for all.[17]

The continual widening of the war far from the North African coastline into the Aegean and the eastern Mediterranean could only be disturbing to the powers. A quick seizure of territory in Africa was one thing, but a drawn-out war that Italy seemed unable to win fell into another category. Both France and Britain had to consider the effect on Muslim opinion in their African colonies and (for Britain) on the Indian subcontinent. A more pressing issue for Britain was the Italian naval presence around the Ottoman coast. Admiralty policy, as it had developed over the previous century, was based on the principle that no power should be allowed to take permanent possession of any territory or harbor east of Malta, if such a harbor could be turned into a naval base.

No one could say what Italy might do with its new possessions, but the British position was that "the occupation of the most useless island should be resisted equally with the occupation of the best." Italian naval bases in the Aegean—were they to be developed—would "imperil our position in Egypt, would cause us to lose our control over our Black Sea and Levant trade at its source and would in war expose our route to the east via the Suez Canal to the operations of Italy and her allies."

The threat to European interests was general, given the volume of traffic passing to and from the Black Sea through the straits. Accordingly, the permanent occupation of any of the Aegean islands by Italy should be strenuously opposed.[18]

With war breaking out in the Balkans, the Ottomans had to end the conflict in Libya without delay. The British Foreign Secretary had already signaled, once Ottoman troops were withdrawn, "We should have no political objection to recognize the full and entire sovereignty of Italy over Libya," while reserving the right to consider the effects on British commercial interests.[19] Other European governments were certain to take the same view. Thus isolated, the Ottoman sultan had no option but to surrender his last African territory.

In the Treaty of Lausanne, signed at Ouchy on October 18, Italy agreed to respect Muslim religious rights and institutions in Libya. The sultan's name as *amir al-mu'minin* (commander of the faithful) could be uttered in prayers as before. His Imperial Majesty could maintain a local representative in Tripoli, and the Ottoman Shaykh al-Islam would have the right to nominate qadis to administer Muslim law. There were various other sweeteners, but the bitter pill had to be swallowed. The long period of Ottoman rule over Libya was at an end. Behind the token gestures of respect for the sultan's dignity, Italy had got away with an act of unprovoked, premeditated aggression.

The reaction of the young officers sent to defend Libya fluctuated between consternation, resignation, and anger, but following the attack on the empire by four Balkan states they had to return to Istanbul to defend the heartland. Support for the Sanusi resistance continued, however, and the sultan subsequently affirmed Libya's independence despite the Italian occupation.[20]

In the meantime, thousands of Muslims fleeing Italian and French occupation in North Africa were finding sanctuary in the Ottoman heartland. A Special Commission for the Refugees from Tripoli and Benghazi (*trablusgarp ve Bengazi mültecilerine mahsus komisyon*) was set up to resettle them.[21]

CONSPIRACY THEORIES

In the years between the restoration of constitutional government and the outbreak of World War I, the Ottoman Empire was deprived of peace when it most needed it. Strengths and weaknesses dictated who benefited and who lost within the European web of alliances. While the powers preferred client states to independent kingdoms, Russia, enfeebled by its recent humiliating defeat at the hands of Japan, could do nothing to stop Bulgaria's declaration of independence and the installation of Ferdinand I as its tsar.

Austria-Hungary was able to annex Bosnia-Herzegovina because, without Russian support, Serbia could not prevent it. Italy was allowed to take Libya because Britain hoped to wean it from alliance with Germany and Austria-Hungary, even while remaining suspicious of Italian ambitions in the Adriatic. The annexation of sovereign Ottoman territory by Austria-Hungary had to be swallowed by Germany—kept in the dark until twenty-four hours beforehand—because the two countries were allies and unity was essential in the face of the Anglo-Russian entente. If France said nothing about Italy's descent on Libya, that was because Italy had previously accepted its prior "right" to Morocco. What some called "diplomacy," others might regard as a basket of writhing snakes.

The restored Ottoman constitution had little value to the powers in and of itself. Despite initial expressions of pleasure (at least partly generated by the damage seen to have been done to Germany by the overthrow of the "palace camarilla"), the triumph of the Young Turks caused alarm. Some (including Winston Churchill) did recognize the vitality and authenticity of the CUP leadership and eventually came to the conclusion that the embassy in Istanbul had gone too far with its negative if not actively hostile attitude.

The ambassador, Gerald Lowther, was impressed with Talat Paşa and Dr. Bahaeddin Şakir when he first met them. They seemed "moderate" and "realistic,"[22] but it was not long before he was filing consistently critical and condescending reports on the CUP leadership. The rise of the Freedom and Accord Party (Hürriyet ve Itilaf Firkası), also known as the Liberal Union and dominated by a "westernized" social class more amenable to the British point of view, pointed the way forward for the Foreign Office.

Nabeel Audeh has brought out the snobbery underlying the way many figures in the British government spoke about "the Turks." In the sanctity of their diplomatic dispatches, ambassadors and other high officials were free to express their true feelings. The CUP was seen by some as a clique of suspect radicals whose commitment to reform was more apparent than real. "I entirely share your view," Sir Charles Hardinge, Permanent Under-Secretary of State in the Foreign Office, wrote to Sir Francis Bertie, the ambassador to France, "that it is desirable that this Young Turk Committee should disappear in the near future, otherwise they will in the course of time deteriorate and assume precisely the same position as that held previously by the Palace camarilla."[23]

Lowther gave vent to the most fantastic theories about the Young Turks. Many of these dispatches expose a deeply ingrained antisemitism within the British government.[24] Lowther portrayed the Young Turks as an occult cabal of Jacobin revolutionaries controlled by *dönmes* (Jewish converts to Islam who surreptitiously were still supposed to adhere to their original faith) operating from behind the cloak of Freemasonry. In Lowther's construction of what was taking shape in Istanbul, the Turks were looking to "international Jewry" for economic support.[25] This would lead to the liberation of the Ottoman Empire from foreign control and independence in the true sense. What "international Jewry" was seeking in return, through the "economic capture of Turkey," was the creation of an autonomous Jewish state in Palestine.[26] "Pan-Islamic" agitation among the Muslims of Egypt and Afghanistan—a theme certain to tweak a raw nerve in the Foreign Office—was supposedly another part of the Young Turk program.[27]

Lowther's opinion on these matters was strongly shaped by the embassy's chief dragoman, Gerald Fitzmaurice, the acknowledged expert on the complexities of the "oriental mind." A strong Catholic, Fitzmaurice had spent most of his working life in the Ottoman Empire, yet even toward the end of his career still "saw things through the spectacles of the Christian Missionary Societies" and treated "the Turks" with a contemptuous paternalism. They were "children," and sometimes naughty children.[28]

Fitzmaurice was also ferociously anti-German and deeply antisemitic, believing with Lowther (or leading him to believe) that the revolution had been "harnessed to the chariot of Pan-Judaism," as well as having been the product of international Freemasonry. While Salonica was the center of this alleged conspiracy, the tendrils reached across and beyond the region.[29]

The declaration of the Zionist program in the late 1890s and Theodor Herzl's subsequent visit to Istanbul was kindling for this conspiratorial fire. The sultan had said 'no' to the plan for a Jewish chartered company in Palestine. Therefore, so the Lowther line ran, the revolution had been launched in 1908 at the inspiration of Salonica Jews to get him out of the way. These bizarre views seemed to leave Sir Charles Hardinge at a loss for a response. "Most interesting reading," he remarked, before forwarding copies of Lowther's dispatch to Tehran, Cairo, and the India Office.[30]

Even after the war, conspiracy theories shaped the thinking of leading imperial administrators and generals, centering this time on the specter of an elaborate Kemalist-Bolshevist-Pan-Islamist-German plot to destroy British influence from the Bosporus to the Caucasus. The central plotline in John Buchan's late imperial novel *Greenmantle*—a Pan-Islamic movement supported by Germany but finally confounded by Richard Hannay after following the trail across Europe to its source in Constantinople— might have been fantastic, but the fantasy was firmly rooted in the British imperial mindset.

Between 1908 and 1912, the Young Turks made various approaches in Istanbul and London, seeking the support and understanding of the British government. They even raised the subject of an alliance on several occasions but were fobbed off. The refusal to offer a helping hand, and, even worse, the British role in the further partition of Ottoman territory, had a sobering effect. The Young Turks realized they were alone in a world of hard imperial considerations, with the single exception of the steadily strengthening relationship with Germany, taking advantage of the loss of British influence.

Ottoman-Sanusi resistance had checked the invasion of Libya. Unless Italy was prepared to spend more money and send another 100,000 men to join the 150,000 already there, adding more casualties to the list of 14,000 killed and 6,000 wounded so far, the expeditionary army would remain stuck on the coast. It was at this point, however, that the attack on the Ottoman Empire by four Balkan states forced a negotiated end to the war in Libya while ushering in another war infinitely more threatening. What was at stake now was not the fate of a North African province far from Istanbul but the Ottoman capital itself and perhaps what remained of the empire.

CHAPTER 8

"May God Be with You"

IN 1912, MONTENEGRO, Bulgaria, Serbia, and Greece launched the second major onslaught in thirty-five years on Ottoman lands in the Balkans. Attacked by Italy in Libya, distracted by uprisings in Yemen and Albania, still engaged in large-scale military reforms, and entering a new period of political instability on the home front, the Ottoman government was in no condition to meet this most serious threat of all. Political turmoil had continued unabated since the counterrevolution in 1909, or the "events" of that year as they are sometimes called. Adding to these troubles, rising prices contributed to the slipping grasp of the CUP and growing support for the Liberal Union or Liberal Entente Party, formed in November 1911.

The collapse of the government early in 1912 was followed by campaigns for new elections, with Kamil Paşa returning from Egypt to work for the Liberal Union. Voting in April resulted in an overwhelming victory for the CUP, too overwhelming, in fact, to be regarded as genuine. It took 95 percent of the seats in parliament after a campaign it was widely regarded as having corrupted through "manipulation and fraudulent practices."[1] The Liberal Unionists won only six seats out of 275 in the chamber.

In May, a pro-Liberal Unionist faction within the army, the "Savior Officers" (*halaskar zabitan*) incited turmoil in the army and threatened to overthrow the government. The resignation of both the war minister (Mahmud Şevket Paşa[2]) and the grand vizier (Sait Paşa) finally precipitated its collapse in July. A new above-party government was formed by Gazi Ahmet Muhtar Paşa.

In early August, parliament was dissolved after a vote of no confidence. New elections were called, and campaigning was underway when the elections were cancelled by royal decree on October 25 because of the war with the Balkan states. On October 29, Gazi Ahmet Paşa was replaced as grand vizier by Kamil in the hope that the latter's close relationship with Britain would be an advantage during the war. In November and December, Kamil used his position to have senior figures in the CUP arrested, but by this time a great crisis was at hand.[3] "Turkey in Europe" had been overrun almost to the shores of the Bosporus by armies incited by their kings, princes, and patriarchs to drive "the Turks" from the Balkans once and for all.

"Our love of peace is exhausted," Tsar Ferdinand of Bulgaria had declared in the cathedral at Starazagora on October 18. "In order to succour the Christian people of Turkey, there remain no other means to us than to turn to arms. . . . I order the brave Bulgarian army to march on the Turkish territory. . . . In this war of the Cross against the Crescent, of liberty against tyranny, we shall have the sympathy of all who love justice and progress. Forward! May God be with you!"[4] In Athens, King George declared "the holy struggle of justice and freedom for the oppressed peoples of the Orient." The religious references led the writer and Near East observer Francis Yeats-Brown to conclude that the war amounted to the "ninth crusade."[5] Similar ringing declarations were being made by the Ottomans: in this war, God was being asked to be on everyone's side.

Montenegro had already declared war on October 8 and the Ottomans on October 17. Serbia and Greece issued their declarations at the same time as Bulgaria. Greece, in fact, had jumped the gun by several hours, sending torpedo boats into Prevesa harbor to attack two Ottoman warships, as the Italians had done during their war (but at least after it had started). In the name of justice, humanity, and peace, hundreds of thousands of Muslims in Thrace and Macedonia were soon to be driven from their homes, or face death at the hands of soldiers and bandit gangs if they stayed. The effects of war on Christians, especially after their governments started fighting each other, were smaller in scale but no less devastating for those who suffered.

THE BALKAN "MOSAIC"

In any empire, the conflicts generated by history in the Balkan domains of the Ottoman Empire would have been a government's nightmare. The modern history of western European involvement in the Balkans, humanitarian and romantic as well as strategic and commercial, dates to the Greek rising of the 1820s. Sympathy for the Balkan Christians was universal in the Christian world. All were said to be yearning to be free of the Ottoman "yoke," even if they still had to bear the yoke of their own princes and ecclesiastics. Religion and conflicting irredentist claims were central pillars of their identity, giving rise to mutual suspicion, dislike, and distrust.

Each Christian group looked ahead to the recovery of territory swept from its grip centuries before by the Ottomans or Balkan Christian rivals. There was a Bulgaria, a Serbia, and a Greece but not a Big Bulgaria, a Greater Serbia, or a Greece expanded to the limits of the Megali Idea. Where the claims of these Balkan Christians clashed, they were prepared to kill each other as remorselessly as they had killed "the Turks." In the second Balkan war of 1913, Christians massacred or scattered other Christians from territory they had conquered and also took the opportunity to get rid of another religious group none of them liked: the Jews.

Although frequently applied to the Balkans, the word "mosaic" is out of place. Pieces in a mosaic should fit neatly together, which the pieces in the Balkan "mosaic" never did. The *salade Macédoine*, inspired by Balkan diversity, might be an appropriate metaphor, even if showing that what works in food does not necessarily work in politics. The recipe calls for vegetables to be cut up small, whirled in a spinner, and turned into a salad lightly bound with oil. In the Balkan spinner, the Christian states were the chopped vegetables turning at dizzying speed and great power intervention the oil, but somehow the mix never turned into a wholesome *salade Balkanique.*

For Greeks, Bulgarians, Serbs, and Albanians, the past was a blueprint for the present and a road map to the future. Borders imposed by the powers were arrangements they would rearrange as soon as the opportunity arose. Complaints of oppression and Ottoman misgovernment were often justified, but in truth, even if the sultan put in place all the reforms demanded by Balkan Christian rulers, the central problem would remain unresolved. Ultimately it was not reform that these rulers really wanted but the disappearance from their midst of all symbols of the Ottoman presence, government, institutions, and people.

As the sultan had no intention of relinquishing what was left of sovereign Ottoman territory in the Balkans, war was the only way ahead, if the Balkan states could agree on how to fight and share the spoils. Yet, individually, not one of these states was capable of taking on and defeating the Ottoman Empire. Until 1912, all they could do was wait for an opportunity.

Always, there was the risk of a falling-out among themselves, so the timing had to be right. Bulgaria's annexation of eastern Rumelia in 1885 had provoked an armed response by Serbia. The Serbian-Bulgarian war lasted just two weeks: the Serbs had been routed when Austria-Hungary stepped in and threatened Bulgaria with a war of its own unless it agreed to a ceasefire. Intervention by Austria-Hungary could well have triggered a European war, but under Russian pressure the Bulgarians agreed. They retained their territory, and the war ended with no change except a slight reduction in the size of the Serbian and Bulgarian armies.

To end the Ottoman presence in Europe once and for all, it was clear that these states would have to band together. The search for the right formula began in the 1860s. Military preparations were made well ahead of time, and by 1912 the time finally seemed right. The auguries were all favorable, and "having reached a *rapprochement*, the Balkan states were in a position to wage war against Turkey."[6] But what would happen if they went to war and actually won? Their *rapprochement* was paper thin, and the fact that they could agree at all was simply the measure of their common detestation of the Ottoman presence. Victory was bound to be followed by a fight over the spoils, for they had not agreed in detail, and that was where the devil awaited his own opportunity.

Lines on a map had failed to end the squabbling between states over territory and national identity. The ethnonational religious mix was too entangled to allow clear demarcation anywhere, at least by peaceful means. Bosnia-Herzegovina, for example, was about half Muslim. Christians—Serbian orthodox (the majority) and Croatian Catholics—constituted nearly all the other half. Serbian nationalists regarded Bosnia-Herzegovina as theirs by right, denied to them by the diplomats meeting at Berlin. For Serbia and Serbian nationalists, Austria-Hungary was the enemy. For Croatian nationalists, it was a Catholic umbrella under which they could shelter against all prevailing winds. The Muslims would have preferred to stay under Ottoman rule but now had no say.

Many Catholics had moved out of Bosnia-Herzegovina after the Ottoman conquest in the fifteenth and sixteenth centuries, but with the territories placed under Austrian-Hungarian rule in 1878 many moved into the province from across the region, gradually changing the demographic balance in their favor. On the other hand, Muslims, chafing under the restrictions of an alien bureaucracy, not just Christian but cumbersome and inefficient, soon began moving out, with numbers rising after the conscription law was introduced in 1882 and rising again after the annexation of 1908.[7]

In the adjoining *sancak* of Novipazar (Ottoman Yenipazar), the demographic mix was Serbian, Montenegrin, Albanian, Turkish, and Muslim Slav, creating plenty of space for rival national claims. Lying across the middle of the Balkans like a beached whale, and about as capable as defending itself from the aggressive states pressing against its borders, lay Ottoman Macedonia, roughly half Muslim and half Christian but with its Christians divided against each other along Bulgarian, Greek, and Serbian national lines.

The Serb population of Macedonia was a small minority, but the territory still lay within the envisioned borders of a Greater Serbia, to be redeemed at some point in the future. For the Greeks, Macedonia was Greek; for the Bulgarians it was Bulgarian, also to be redeemed in the future. Every other national group regularly produced arguments for claims that were as impossible to reconcile as just about everything else in the Balkans. Macedonian nationalists argued that the territory should have an autonomous national future of its own, absorbed by neither Greece or Bulgaria and uniting all Macedonian people irrespective of ethnicity and faith.

Mixed among the major Muslim and Christian ethnoreligious groups in the region were Vlach, also known as Wallachians, originating from the Rumanian region of Wallachia (Rumanian Orthodox Christians), Pomaks (Bulgarian-speaking Muslims, originally converts from Christianity), Bosniaks (ethnically Slav Muslims), Gagauz (ethnic Turkic Christians), Circassians (Muslim refugees from the Caucasus), Gypsies, and substantial Jewish communities (up to 1911 close to half the population of Salonica was Jewish). The Albanians were divided into two main linguistic groups, Ghegs (north) and Tosks (south), further subdivided into a patchwork of Muslim or Christian (Catholic and Orthodox) tribes. Predominantly Slav, Montenegro also had a substantial Albanian population.

Everywhere in the Balkans, memories of great victories and tragic defeats were as long as history itself. Territories and cities were invested with iconic meaning. Serbia would forever remain incomplete without the "return" of Kosovo. Albania was just as determined to retain it. For Bulgaria, the icons just across the Ottoman border were Edirne (Adrianople) and Kirkkilise (Lözengrad), with the grand prize of Istanbul (Tsargrad) not far away. Both Bulgaria and Greece coveted Selanik as well as Istanbul.

All of these cities had been fought over many times before ending in the lap of the Ottomans. History had bred in their Muslim, Christian, and Jewish inhabitants a live-and-let-live cosmopolitanism that, of its nature, stood at odds with the single-minded nationalism taking root across the Balkans since early in the nineteenth century.

"A fundamental doctrine of the Great Serb Idea," wrote Edith Durham, "is a refusal to recognize that history existed before the creation of the Serb Empire or even to admit that the Balkan lands had owners before the arrival of the Serb."[8] However, Serb nationalists were hardly alone in their obsessive navel-gazing. Greek and Bulgarian nationalists—not just the politicians but the prelates and the kings—thought much the same way. History was a bag into which they dipped for what they wanted and *only* what they wanted. They would kill the common enemy, "the Turks." Then, when the time came, they would kill each other. Not "they" in person, of course, but their people, largely illiterate and vulnerable to the exhortations of the kings, the politicians, and the priests.

BALKAN DYNASTIES

Of the Balkan monarchies, Nikola of Montenegro had succeeded to the throne following the assassination of his uncle Danilo in 1860. He ruled as prince until 1910 and then as king, supplying so many daughters to other royal households that he became known as the father-in-law of Europe. Ljubica (Zorka) married Petar (Peter) who was to become King of the Serbs, Croats, and Slovenes; Milica married the Grand Duke Peter of Russia; Anastasia (Stana) accepted George, Duke of Leuchtenberg as her first husband and after their divorce Grand Duke Nicholas of Russia as her second; Jelena became Queen Elena of Italy after her marriage to Victor Emmanuel III, and Anna married Prince Franz Josef of Battenberg. One of Nikola's daughters died in infancy and another at age sixteen. Two daughters never married.

Then there were the sons. Danilo, "as good as crazy" according to some,[9] married the Duchess Jutta of Mecklenberg-Strelitz; Mirko married Natalia Konstantinović, a cousin of Alexander Obrenović, the king of Serbia for a brief period; finally, Petar (Peter) broke with family tradition by marrying a commoner, Violet Wegner, born in the London suburb of Hackney, the strikingly beautiful daughter of a Scotland Yard detective. Violet (later Violette) was a music hall dancer, actress, and "chic *comedienne,"* as described in the popular press, whom Petar met in Italy.[10] Dynastically, though, it was Nikola's strategically wedded daughters who really counted. The observation that Europe was being conquered by "peaceful penetration" was inevitable.[11]

Greece's first king, Otto, was a Bavarian. The second was a Dane, born in Copenhagen as Wilhelm Ferdinand Adolf George of Schleswig-Holstein-Sonderburg-Glücksburg (in addition to being a Hesse on his mother's side) but crowned as George and ruling from 1863 to 1913. The British government marked his coronation with the gift of the Ionian Islands, which they had held since seizing them from France in 1815.

Serbia's recent history was especially volatile. Milan Obrenović succeeded to the throne after the assassination in 1868 of Prince Mihailo Obrenović, Milan's cousin, who had adopted him after he was abandoned by his mother. As he was only fourteen, Serbia was ruled as a regency until Milan came of age in 1872.

Milan's decision to attack Bulgaria after its annexation of eastern Rumelia in 1885 led to a crushing defeat and a sharp decline in his popularity. In 1889, he abdicated in favor of his son Alexander. His abdication and retirement into private life (later he returned to help his son stem growing Russian influence) came as a complete surprise.

As Alexander was also underage, Serbia was again ruled as a regency, this time under Queen Natalija until Alexander declared himself king in 1893, even though he was still only sixteen. That was a bold and popular move, but his later liaison with his mother's lady-in-waiting, Draga Maśin, was not. Actually, the liaison was acceptable but his plans to marry her were not. Draga was somewhat of a Balkan Wallis Simpson.[12] Whatever the secret of her mesmerizing grip on Alexander, his love for her seemed profound. The daughter of a provincial official and widow of a civil engineer, she was twelve years older than Alexander, for which reason she was frequently portrayed as a scheming older woman ensnaring a younger man. Disregarding public disapproval and the bitter opposition of both parents, Alexander was determined to marry. Adding to his problems, it was "widely believed" that Draga had been his father's mistress, amounting to "a curse on the land that could only be removed by her death."[13] Furthermore, Alexander was rumored to be thinking of naming one of Draga's brothers as heir apparent if their marriage turned out to be childless.

Despite these formidable obstacles, Alexander wed Draga, on August 5, 1900. Their marriage, and their lives, lasted almost three years. On June 11,

1903, a group of army officers broke into the royal palace late at night, blew open the door to the royal couple's bedroom with dynamite, and dragged them out of the cupboard where they were hiding. The king and queen were shot and slashed with swords before being thrown from the window still alive and left to expire where they landed. While one of the attackers cut off a finger to get Alexander's signet ring, the attack on Draga was particularly vicious.[14]

Elsewhere in the city, the president of the ministry (prime minister), the defense minister, Draga's two brothers (Nicodemus and Nicholas), and numerous other people were also murdered. Alexander's removal may have been desirable, wrote Edith Durham, but "not even in Dahomey would it have been accomplished with more repulsive savagery."[15] Western Europe in 1903 was "quite ignorant of the state of savagery from which the south Slavs were beginning to rise."[16] The brutality across the Balkans then and later was so great that the comparison with the African tribes of Dahomey was surely unfair.

The killers, including Draga's brother-in-law, had been mobilized by Colonel Dragutin Dimitrijević (known as Apis), one of the leaders of the ultranationalist Black Hand secret society when it was formed in 1911 and the Serbian War Ministry's intelligence chief in 1914 when the Archduke Franz Ferdinand and his wife were assassinated in Sarajevo. At his trial for treason in 1917, following the attempted assassination in Salonica of the Serbian prince regent, Alexander (son of Peter, installed as king of Serbia after the assassination of King Alexander and Queen Draga), Apis claimed to have organized the assassination of the archduke in 1914. Although he and other alleged conspirators were executed for the purported plot against the prince-regent, his admission to involvement in the assassination of the archduke seems to have carried as much if not more weight with his judges.

In fact, dynastic rivalries and King Alexander's pro-Habsburg proclivities, antagonizing more extreme Serb nationalists and Russia, with opposition politicians standing ready to reap the rewards, were the prime motives for the decision to kill him, not his marriage to Draga or any other accusation leveled against him. The Obrenović and Karadjordjević families had been at each other's throats for generations, and the assassination of Alexander, an Obrenović, put a Karadjordjević back on the throne for the first time in more than four decades.

The new king, Peter, who had been implicated in the plot against Alexander and Draga, appointed Nicola Pasić, an old adversary of both

Milan and Alexander, as prime minister. Crowned in 1904, Peter ruled until 1921. His early years were marked by scandal when his son and heir-apparent George kicked a servant down the stairs in a fit of rage, killing him and instantly forfeiting his claim to the throne, which settled now on his younger brother Alexander. Upon King Peter's death in 1921, Alexander, having escaped assassination in Salonica four years previously, inherited the Kingdom of the Serbs, Croats, and Slovenes (Yugoslavia from 1929). Dealing with this endless cascade of dynastic rivalries and conspiracies must have created continual headaches in Istanbul for the ministers assigned the task of bringing order to the Balkans. Readers doggedly trying to follow the same twists and turns may feel some sympathy for them.

The other two notable monarchs in the region were Ferdinand of Rumania (married to Queen Victoria's granddaughter, Princess Marie of Edinburgh, but also linked by family ties to the Bulgarian, Austro-Hungarian, German, and Russian royal households) and Ferdinand of Bulgaria, whose lineal background connected him to the French, Belgian, British, German, Portuguese, and Mexican royal families. Ferdinand's grand dream was to establish a new Byzantium, once Istanbul had been wrenched from the hands of the Turks. "Constantinople" was also the prize beyond compare for Russia and Greece, but all across the Balkans lay other cities and territories that kings, politicians, and army commanders swore they would fight to the death to recover.

PREPARING FOR WAR

Looking usually to France or Germany for training and weaponry, the Ottoman Empire and the Balkan states had been building up their military strength for decades. While preparing for war, the Ottoman state actively was trying to avoid one. The Balkan states, on the other hand, were preparing to launch a war against the Ottomans as soon as favorable circumstances arose (or could be created).

Montenegro, the first state to declare war, had an army of about 45,000 men, equipped mostly with German, Italian, and Russian weapons. Muslims were exempt from military service, which for all other men, in one form or another, lasted from the age of 18 to 62.[17]

Bulgaria had the largest and most powerful army and regarded war as inevitable.[18] Military service was obligatory for men between the ages of 20 and 46: Muslims were exempted here, too, and had to pay a tax instead (just like Christians in the Ottoman Empire up to 1908). The army's weapons (rifles, carbines, field and mountain artillery, breech-loading guns, howitzers, and multibarreled *mitrailleuse* machine guns carried by pack animals), supplied by Krupp, Mannlicher, Berdan, Schneider-Canet, and Maxim were the most modern on the market. The fledgling Bulgarian air force had about two dozen Bleriot, Farman, and Albatros aircraft, used for reconnaissance and propaganda (dropping leaflets) as well as bombing enemy targets. The navy, one cruiser and six torpedo boats, was negligible.

The Bulgarian general staff's strategies, influenced by French thinking, were based on an overwhelming attack in force. But Bulgaria's true strength was the patriotism and endurance of its common soldiers. Mostly illiterate, they were vessels waiting to be filled by the exhortations of their king, their officers, and their church. Mobilization was based on the expansion of a standing army of close to 62,000 to 459,819 men, including a "huge pool" of 343,343 trained reservists and about 70,000 *bans* (territorials).[19] The demands on the national budget were great. Of a total expenditure of 170 million *kronen* laid down in the 1911 budget, 37.5 million were set aside for military purposes.[20]

Fighting alongside the special units were tens of thousands of Macedonian Bulgarians enlisted in the Macedonian-Adrianopolitan Volunteer Brigade, "which was to become notorious for its atrocities," according to Leon Trotsky, a correspondent at the front.[21] Volunteers also included a contingent of 273 Armenians led by Andranik Ozanian and Garegin Ter-Harutyunyan (*nom de guerre* Garegin Nzhdeh).[22] Ozanian, an Ottoman Armenian who had taken a leading role in the Sasun uprisings of 1894 and 1904, later commanded Armenian units fighting alongside the Russians as they advanced into the eastern Ottoman provinces in 1915.

Serbia's regular army of 169,000, when fully mobilized, could be expanded to about 300,000 men, including reserves.[23] Compulsory military service in one form or another extended from the age of 17 to 50. The troops were armed with Mauser or Berdan rifles and Maxim *mitrailleuses*. The estimated 660 pieces of artillery on hand when war was declared included Schneider-Creusot field and mountain artillery and howitzers. The air force consisted of a handful of Farman, Blériot, and Deperdussin aircraft and two observation balloons.

Greece had a standing army of just over 125,000, which could be augmented from a national guard of 80,000 men and a national guard reserve of another 60,000.[24] All males were obliged to serve 35 years as regular army or national guard soldiers or reserves, beginning with two years of

conscription. Arms came from the same familiar group of European man-
ufacturers, which, selling to all sides, did well out of the war. Unlike the
other Balkan states, Greece had a real navy, small but effective, including
gunboats, torpedo boats, destroyers, one submarine, and the pride of the
fleet, the 10,000-ton armored cruiser *Georgios Averof.*

Ricciotti Garibaldi, who had fought alongside the Greek army in the
war of 1897, returned to fight again as the commander of an international
brigade made up of more than 2,000 Redshirts composed of Greeks, Cre-
tans, and assorted foreign Philhellenes. Garibaldi and his son Pipino, who
was with him, were son and grandson of Guiseppe, who had founded the
Garibaldini in 1860 to help struggling nations achieve freedom.

The contribution each state would make to the war on the Ottoman
Empire was sealed in a series of bilateral agreements. Preliminary arrangements came to fruition in 1912. In early March, Serbia and Bulgaria signed
a secret pact (formalized in April and followed by agreements between
their general staffs) under which Bulgaria would commit 200,000 troops
and Serbia 150,000 in the event of war breaking out between either of
them and the Ottoman Empire, Austria-Hungary, or Rumania. This was
followed by a "defensive alliance" between Bulgaria and Greece in May
and, separately, by an agreement between Montenegro, Bulgaria, and
Serbia in September. Greece also reached "gentlemen's agreements" with
Serbia and Montenegro.[25]

Sensitive territorial issues were all sidestepped in these arrangements.
Bulgaria and Serbia agreed to differ, setting aside a "disputed zone" in
Macedonia whose arbitrator would be the tsar (of Russia) if they could
not agree later on how to divide the spoils, but finally all four states were
agreed on a plan of action. While their unity was flimsy from the start,
it created the final impetus for war: all the four governments needed now
was a pretext.[26]

Facing this combination of Balkan forces was the Ottoman military.
Between the 1870s and 1912 the army had been subjected to overhaul and
reorganization under the direction of a German military mission led from
1883 by Brigadier General Wilhelm Leopold Colmar Freiherr von der
Goltz. This program was accelerated after the 1908 revolution, with British
officers called in to oversee naval reforms. One significant change was the
formal breakup of the notoriously poorly trained 64 Kurdish Hamidiye
tribal cavalry in favor of 29 light tribal cavalry regiments (*aşiret hafif suvarı
alayları nizamnamesi*) under the command of the regular army.[27] Despite
the change of name, the units were still generally known as the Hamidiye.

The empire had a standing army of 280,000 men. In case of war, an extra 450,000 could be mobilized for a total pool of 730,000 men.[28] Arms came from Krupp, Mauser, Martini-Henry, Maxim, Hotchkiss, and Schneider-Creusot but without enough rifles for the number of soldiers who needed them. Since 1908, representing a complete break with the past, non-Muslims (Jews as well as Armenian, Balkan, and Syrian Christians) had been called into military service. According to a military observer traveling with the Bulgarian army, this was a "fatal mistake" as Greeks, Serbians, and Bulgarians "were naturally an element on which little reliance could be placed."[29]

The Ottoman fleet was substantial compared to those of its enemies: 3 ironclads, 5 armored cruisers (armored along the side), 2 protected cruisers (with an armored deck), 2 torpedo cruisers, 11 torpedo destroyers, and 15 torpedo boats. In the air, Ottoman pilots flew 13 trainer or fighter aircraft. Some of its pilots had trained at the same Blériot flying school in France as Serb and Bulgarian aviators.

The Ottomans also had one Parseval airship. Air power was new, and, with Italy in Libya and then the Balkan states claiming "firsts" of their own, the Ottomans claimed the distinction of sending the first woman passenger into the air when Belkis Şevket Hanım, a feminist member of the Society for the Defense of Women's Rights (*mudafaa-i hukuki nisvan cemiyeti*), went aloft in a plane piloted by Fethi Bey in December 1913.

Compared to the Balkan states, there was "little enthusiasm for the war on the Ottoman side."[30] The army was still being reorganized and retrained, and much needed to be done to bring it into a state of readiness. Still, the Ottoman Empire had a far greater population than all the Balkan states combined (close to 20 million compared to just over 10 million [31]) and thus a much bigger pool of men of fighting age. The longer the war dragged on, the stronger the Ottoman position was likely to be, hence the determination of the Bulgarian military command to deliver a knockout blow in a swift campaign based on the deployment of overwhelming force.

Arranging the circumstances favoring war involved negotiations among the Balkan monarchs to bring them into alignment. Reginald Rankin, correspondent for *The Times* with the Bulgarian army, wrote glowingly of James Bourchier, his old schoolmaster at Eton and "the unattached diplomatist who has broken up the Turkish Empire in Europe."[32] Bourchier, the confidant of kings, prime ministers, and foreign ministers, shuttled across the region, primarily between Sofia, Belgrade, and Athens, convinced that "only a resort to arms could free the subject Christians from an intolerable persecution."[33] By 1910, Ottoman suppression of uprisings and the state of preparedness of the Serbian and Bulgarian armies had convinced him that the hour of destiny had arrived.

On the slopes of Mt Pelion in May 1911, Greek Prime Minister Eleftherios Venizelos told Bourchier that he had approved the signing of a draft alliance with Bulgaria against the Ottoman Empire. In the coming year, "defensive" treaties were initialed between the three most powerful states in the developing alliance: Bulgaria, Serbia, and Greece. By July 1912, all the heavy lifting had been done. Bourchier had done his small part, "and none too soon for the futures of the peoples his statesmanship was to liberate," in Rankin's view.[34] He was certainly a useful messenger in persuading Balkan kings and princes to sink their differences, but they hardly needed any encouragement in deciding to go to war.

INSURRECTION IN MACEDONIA

By 1911, the timing was almost right and the pretexts were accumulating. Their central breeding ground was Macedonia. The European powers—Britain, France, Italy, Austria-Hungary, Germany, and Russia—all had strategic interests in the Balkans that would affect the general balance of power. The Balkans were only one of many houses in their mansions, whereas for local states and dynasties it was their only house. Each had a room, but Macedonia was one of the finest. Whoever was able to move in "would have the predominant strategic position in the peninsula."[35]

All three of the principal contenders—Bulgaria, Greece, and Serbia—exercised their influence through churches and societies devoting themselves to cultural and missionary work to strengthen the national cause. In the decade leading up to the Balkan wars, however, while armed Greek guerillas (*andartes*) were also involved, it was two Bulgarian groups whose *komitadjis* (insurgents) took the lead in the insurrectionary struggle for Madedonia.[36]

One group was the Secret Macedonian-Adrianople Revolutionary Organization (SMARO), later the Internal Macedonian Revolutionary Organization (IMRO) by which name it shall be called from hereon. The second group was the Macedonian External Organization (EMRO). Both were Bulgarian movements whose vision for the future was a Macedonia in which the Bulgarian ethnic element would be dominant. IMRO was based in Selanik and campaigned under the slogan of an autonomous "Macedonia for the Macedonians," implicitly all Macedonians, irrespective of ethnicity or religion. EMRO, on the other hand, was based in Sofia and tied to the policies of the Bulgarian government, which sought the annexation of Macedonia, whatever concessions it might make to regional autonomy.

International interest in Macedonia was sharpened with the abduction on September 3, 1901, of the American missionary Ellen Stone and her pregnant Bulgarian traveling companion. The kidnapping was overshadowed two days later when an anarchist shot American President McKinley at the Temple of Music on the fairgrounds of the Pan American Exposition in Buffalo, New York. McKinley died on September 14. Miss Stone's companion gave birth in January, so the kidnappers had to move about with two women and a newborn and frequently crying baby.[37] They were released on February 23, 1902, after the American Board of Commissioners for Foreign Missions (ABCFM) raised the 14,000 Turkish gold lira (about $66,000) by public subscription and it was handed to the kidnappers. Part of the money seems to have spent on settling internal revolutionary disputes, the rest on funding the major uprising of 1903.

The tumult in Macedonia began to boil over in September 1902, when insurgents murdered Muslims in several parts of the Selanik *vilayet* in western Macedonia, and Christians were then murdered by Ottoman troops or civilians. By October, dozens of villages had been caught up in a rapidly spreading insurrection. So unprepared were the Ottoman forces that a supposedly impregnable mountain pass fell into the hands of the rebels at the cost of 350 Ottoman casualties.

An experienced British consul based in Selanik, Alfred Biliotti, who had witnessed at first hand the sectarian killings on Crete in 1897, confirmed some of the accusations made by both sides but dismissed others as exaggerated or otherwise not having any basis in fact. Overall, Biliotti wrote, the violence was not due to a spontaneous outburst of "Moslem fanaticism," as might be inferred from the statements of Bulgarian refugees, but was "the direct result of the native Bulgarians having allowed themselves to be drawn or forced by the bandits into a rebellion against Turkish authority or as the case may be of their having of their own free will initiated such a rebellion."[38] Greek civilians were reported to have been killed by Bulgarians across the region.[39]

In the name of liberating Macedonia, a group of Bulgarians calling themselves the *gemidzhii* (boatmen) stole into Salonica's harbor on April 28, 1903, set fire to the Messageries Maritimes steamship *Guadalquivir* with a dynamite charge,[40] and then bombed the city's central water and electricity plants the next day, cutting off the supply of both. This was the prelude to a bombing campaign across the city in which the main target was the Imperial Ottoman Bank. All the young revolutionaries, some of school age, were later killed (or killed themselves) or were captured by Ottoman forces.

On August 2, 1903, bands of IMRO *komitadjis* overran the military barracks in Kruševo on the eve of the feast of Ilinden (St. Elijah's Day) and declared a republic. Ten days later, Ottoman forces retook the barracks and crushed the uprising, inflicting exemplary punishment across western Macedonia. Intense fighting continued between *komitadjis* and Ottoman forces, whom IMRO accused of massacre and the widespread destruction of villages.[41] In this ethnonational turmoil, Greece was represented by its own armed bands. In July 1904, Pavlos Melas led a group of *andartes* into Macedonia, only to be killed by the Ottomans in October. In March 1905, *andartes* massacred scores of Bulgarians in the largely Bulgarian southern Macedonian village of Zagoricani, killing Bulgarians in other villages as well.

In the following years interethnic and anti-Ottoman violence continued without letup. On December 11, 1911, a terrorist bombing in the town of Stip ignited a massacre of Bulgarians by Turks. In Bulgaria, an outraged public called for intervention. On August 1, 1912, bombs exploded in the town of Kochana's two markets. The first market targeted was crowded with townspeople and shoppers or vendors who had come in from outlying villages when the first bomb went off at 9 a.m. The second bomb exploded ten minutes later. Ten people had been killed, and the response by Ottoman soldiers and police was ferocious. They ran amok despite the efforts of civil authorities to restrain them. Scores of Bulgarians were pulled out of their houses and killed and shops were looted. If it is true that the bombing was a provocation by IMRO "elements," it worked.[42] Kochana was only one more round in a long cycle of violence, but at a time the Balkan states had completed their military and political preparations for war, it pushed the region to the brink. In Sofia, the response to news of the massacre at Kochana was a call for war.

THE ONSLAUGHT

In a collective note handed to Montenegro on October 8, 1912,[43] the powers warned that they would condemn any belligerent action and would

not allow any changes to the territorial status quo in the Balkans. They
would continue to seek "reforms" benefiting the Christians living under
Ottoman rule only insofar as they were consistent with the sultan's sovereign rights and did not damage the territorial integrity of his empire.
These warnings had no effect at all on the Balkan states. Moreover, given
the massive changes to the territorial status quo allowed by the powers
when the war was over, the note was taken by the Ottoman government
as further evidence of their double dealing.

Again, it was not reform that the Balkan states had ever really wanted
but the end of the Ottoman presence in southeastern Europe, as represented by the sultan's authority, the symbols of Islam on the landscape
(mosques, tombs, madrasas), and the presence of a large Muslim population. Within an hour of the note's receipt in Çetinje, King Nikola
of Montenegro moved from mobilization to war, firing a symbolic shot
across the border at an Ottoman outpost.[44]

Whether they were play-acting to the end or really thought they could
still avert war is not clear, but Russia and Austria proceeded to hand the
same note to the governments in Sofia, Belgrade, and Athens. Undeterred,
they responded with cynical demands the Ottoman government could
not have been expected to accept, and did not.[45] As Montenegro was little
more than the mouse that roared, its declaration of war was the signal that
the three other Balkan states would soon be declaring war.

"CHAOS AND MUDDLE"

From the beginning, the war was a disaster for the Ottoman forces, the
worst, after the war of 1877–1878, in the empire's history. The conflict in
Libya had forced redeployment of troops not just to North Africa but the
Aegean coast. The government had the additional problems of rebellion in
Yemen and, within six weeks (on November 28), an Albanian declaration
of independence. In facing up to the Balkan threat, the military command
seriously miscalculated the time needed for mobilization and battle readiness (an initial twenty-five days compared to a revised estimate put out
in June of forty-five to fifty days).[46] Logistical problems were to hamper
the Ottomans on every front during the war, causing chronic shortages of
food and medicine down to the lack of sufficient field hospitals and even
dressing stations at the front.

After witnessing battlefield outcomes, war correspondent Ellis Ashmead Bartlett wrote, "It is impossible for me to describe severely enough the utter state of chaos, of mess, muddle and make-believe which exists throughout all branches of the army. Had the Turkish soldier been supplied with even one biscuit a day he might have held his ground against the invader, and I am convinced that he has been defeated more by sheer starvation than any other factor."[47]

Uncomfortable in their new uniforms and boots, many of the soldiers were not even familiar with the guns put in their hands and had to learn how to use them on the job. In the aftermath, Turkish critics of the war pointed to improvisation in the order of battle, the appointment of inexperienced commanders, the relatively old age of some of the troops and their lack of training and experience, the chaotic nature of the mobilization, and the fact that many troops arrived at the front hungry and exhausted and "in no condition to fight, let alone fight enthusiastically."[48]

Two "centers of gravity" lay at the core of Ottoman military planning.[49] One ran along an axis in Thrace stretching from Istanbul to Edirne and the Bulgarian border. The other ran through the Macedonian *vilayets* of Selanik, Kosovo, Işkodra, Manastir, and Yanya (Greek Ioannina). As Erickson has remarked, "Unfortunately, the existence of two distinct and widely separated strategic centers of gravity placed the Ottoman General Staff in a difficult position. Against a single enemy the strategic problem was solvable, but, against a coalition of enemies attacking each strategic center of gravity simultaneously, the strategic problem was unmanageable."[50]

Combined with the practical shortcomings already noted, the outcome for the Ottomans was disastrous. Driven by patriotic and religious fervor and launching bayonet charges that repeatedly broke the Ottoman defenses in eastern Thrace, the Bulgarians took one position after another with lightning speed. Besieging Edirne but skirting it for the time being, the Bulgarians moved on to Kirkkilese (October 22–24) where, according to *The Times*'s military correspondent, the Ottomans began well before a regiment of *redifs* (reserves), "out of condition, underfed, undertrained and practically without officers," lost their nerve and generated panic through the ranks. Officers tried to hold the line even to the point of shooting their own men, but a general "pell mell" flight ensued.[51]

The Bulgarians then moved on to Lüleburgaz. The battle for the town (October 29–November 2), fought by more than 250,000 soldiers along an extended front, ended in another resounding victory for the Bulgarians and effectively "settled the fate of Turkey in Europe."[52] Overrunning Ottoman positions, the Bulgarians told correspondent Leon Trotsky of encountering no resistance: "We found only dead men, not fewer than two or three hundred of them, plus a few badly wounded Turkish officers and soldiers. We finished them off with our bayonets, on the spot. That was the order, so as not to encumber our transports with wounded.... Don't ask me about that business: I can't bear to remember how we killed those unarmed, maimed half-dead men."[53]

The defeated Ottomans retreated in disorder to Çorlu before being driven further back to Çatalca, the last line of Ottoman defense before Istanbul, 50 kilometers away. Artillery fire could be heard in the city. Still hoping Istanbul could be captured, Ferdinand dismissed an Ottoman proposal for an armistice, but his army could go no farther. A combination of exhaustion, strong Ottoman defensive positions on a ridge of hills, a shortage of supplies as the army moved deeper into Ottoman territory, and the ravages of cholera had finally brought the Bulgarian advance to a standstill. However, while Istanbul remained beyond reach, the Bulgarians had dug in on the northern coast of the Sea of Marmara and the upper part of the Gelibolu (Gallipoli) peninsula.

THE FALL OF SELANIK

In Macedonia, the Ottoman campaigns had suffered a similar series of disasters at the hands of the Serbs and the Greeks. At Kumanovo (October 23–24), the Ottoman Vardar Army suffered the "rout of an empire" at the hands of the Serbs.[54] From Swiss sources came accounts of the complete demoralization of the Ottoman forces, with many Christian soldiers deserting during the battle. Some were later seen with white crosses on their fezzes, coming out of Üsküb, about 30 kilometers from Kumanovo, to greet the victorious Serbian forces in what British Vice-Consul Peckham described as "symbolic of the triumph of Cross over Crescent."[55] After the battle, as described by a witness, "extraordinary scenes of panic and excitement took place. The railway carriages were stormed. Panic-stricken men in flight pushed each other down from the roofs of the carriages."[56]

The behavior of the Serbs toward Muslims was described as cruel in every way and, according to one observer, "seems to have for its object their complete extermination."[57] The numbers were no doubt exaggerated, but even if not to the extent of hundreds, bodies of murdered Albanians were seen floating down the Vardar river.[58] Village Muslims headed for Üsküb, where the Muslim notables were in an equivalent state of panic as the Serbian army approached. The departure of Ottoman troops and foreign consuls on the morning of October 26 was followed by several hours of looting until the Serbian army arrived in the late afternoon and the town was surrendered.

While conquering northwestern Macedonia, the Serbs marched through Albania to the sea, capturing Prizren (October 22), Pristina (October 27), and the Adriatic port of Durres (November 28). Between them, Montenegrin and Serbian forces had also captured the entire *sancak* of Novipazar and Albanian Kosovo. By early October, Montenegrin forces were besieging Işkodra (present day Albanian Shkoder), but the town was too strongly defended by a combined Ottoman-Albanian garrison for it to be captured unless the Montenegrins could call on Serb support.

In Thessaly, the Greek army defeated the Ottomans at Sarantaporos on October 22 and Yanitsa (Yenice) on November 1–2, thereby positioning itself for the advance on Selanik. In the first week of November, Bulgarian and Greek forces were rapidly closing on the city, but the Greeks got there first. The Ottoman garrison surrendered without resistance on November 9, a Greek force entering the city just ahead of a Bulgarian contingent. King George arrived in triumph on November 12, only to be assassinated the following March by a Greek, variously described as a socialist, an alcoholic, a vagrant, and plain feeble-minded. The assassin was taken to Athens where, in the six weeks before he fell to his death from the window of a police station, his true motive for the crime was never established. Ottoman Selanik now became Greek Salonica.

The capture of Salonica, where the Greek population was substantially outnumbered, first by Jews and then by Muslims,[59] was the beginning of the end of its place in history as a cosmopolitan gem of the Near East. The great fire of 1917 destroyed its physical heart along the waterfront. Greek chauvinism in the 1920s, fascism in the 1930s and occupation by the Nazis, who transported 54,000–60,000 Jews to the Auschwitz-Birkenau concentration camp in 1943, finally extinguished what the city had been.

Having captured Salonica, the Greeks also turned their eyes toward Istanbul. "The primary operation of the Hellenic Army ought to be aimed towards the capture of the Hellespont [the Dardanelles]," the army chief-of-staff wrote to Crown Prince Constantine on November 18. Sufficient forces would have to be made ready for a landing at Gallipoli. "If this operation resolves itself successfully then enemy resistance before Constantinople can be shattered through the actions of the fleet."[60] The fleet had already been active in the Aegean, capturing Lesbos and Chios and launching attacks around Çanakkale in December, with Ottoman warships coming out of the straits and engaging the Greeks in artillery duels that caused damage to both sides but were otherwise inconclusive.

Bulgaria, unable to break through the Ottoman lines at Çatalca, joined by Serbia and Montenegro, agreed to an armistice on December 3. Delegates of the warring states met in London on December 16 to see whether they could thrash out an agreement. Greece, hoping for further territorial gains, did not sign the armistice but was still represented over the initial objections of the Ottoman government.

The talks bogged down over the future of Edirne and the Aegean islands. The Ottomans agreed that Bulgaria could have eastern Thrace to the west of Edirne but not the city itself. It refused to budge on the future of the Aegean islands, which it said it would have to retain. With talks deadlocked, the ambassadors of the powers met on December 17 to frame an imposed peace. A London settlement of Balkan problems would now replace the Berlin settlement of 1878 in what Richard Hall has described as the "last gasp of the Congress system"[61] as it had functioned since the Congress of Vienna in 1815.

THE POWERS PROPOSE

The British foreign secretary, Sir Edward Grey, chaired negotiating sessions that dragged into the new year. Their immediate concern was Serbian gains at Albanian expense. Austria-Hungary was insisting on the creation of an Albanian state with borders that would keep the Serbs and thus Russian influence away from the Adriatic. If Austria-Hungary were blocked, a European war had to be regarded as a possibility. Behind the scenes, the Balkan states and the Ottomans continued lobbying for their respective interests, but it was clear that the powers were going to impose a settlement that would meet their collective interests first.

While Macedonia had been lost forever, the Ottomans were determined to fight for eastern Thrace and the Aegean islands. The powers were not receptive. Greece had already captured most of the Aegean islands not in

Italian hands, and European sympathy and diplomatic negotiations would eventually ensure that they got the rest. In eastern Thrace, the powers drew a line from Midia (on the Black Sea) down to Enos (on the Aegean) and called on the Ottomans to cede everything to the west to Bulgaria.

On January 1, 1913, the Ottomans came up with a proposal to divide eastern Thrace along the lines of the Maritsa (Ottoman Meriç) river, surrendering the west to Bulgaria but leaving Edirne in Ottoman hands. However, it still insisted that the Aegean islands would have to be returned. This was completely unacceptable to Greece. Dismissing the Ottoman proposals, the Balkan states declared on January 14 that if their demands were not met, they would resume the war. Three days later, the powers handed the Porte a collective note advising it to cede Edirne and "leave to the powers the task of deciding the fate of the islands in the Aegean Sea." They would come up with an arrangement "which will exclude all menace to the security of Turkey."[62]

With its armies driven back on all fronts, the negotiating position of the Ottoman government was obviously extremely weak. On January 22, the council of ministers (the Grand Divan), presided over by the anglophile Grand Vizier Kamil Paşa, met behind closed doors to study the recommendations being made by the powers. No decision was taken other than to meet again the following day to frame a response, but it was widely believed that the government was ready to capitulate and even surrender Edirne.[63] The public shock was profound.

The following morning, Talat visited Kamil in the morning, urging him to resign. Receiving no reply, Enver (recently returned from Libya) and Talat broke into the government offices in midafternoon at the head of a large group of young officers. They then forced their way into the inner chamber where senior government ministers were meeting. In the shooting that broke out, Minister for War Nazım Paşa was shot dead by Yakub Cemil, who had served with Enver in Libya.[64] Two ministerial *aides-de-camp* and a gunman in the attacking party were also killed.

Kamil was forced to sign a letter of resignation, which Enver took straight to the palace for the sultan's endorsement. In the evening, the sultan appointed Mahmud Şevket Paşa as grand vizier, Talat as interior minister, and Ahmet Izzet Paşa as acting war minister. Kamil was put under house arrest before being allowed to leave for Cairo where he was reported to have suggested to the British Agent, Field Marshall Kitchener, that the Ottoman Empire be turned into a British protectorate as "the only means of preserving Turkey from extinction."[65]

APRIL ARMISTICE

On February 3, Britain and Germany advised the Bulgarian government to accept the Ottoman terms for a settlement but it rejected them and war resumed the same day. Having surrounded Edirne and cut it off from any possibility of relief, the Bulgarians now prepared to take it. Bombardment of the Ottoman forts ringing the city continued through February and March, with the continuing collapse of Ottoman positions in Macedonia reinforcing the desperate situation the empire had now reached.

On March 25, Bulgarian and Serbian forces launched a combined attack on all Ottoman fortified positions around Edirne. The storming and capture of the fort at Aivas Baba—the key position in the Ottoman defense—sealed the city's fate. The Ottoman commander, Mehmet Şukru Paşa, surrendering to the Serbs and then handed over to the Bulgarians, ordered an immediate ceasefire and exchanged pleasantries with Bulgarian officers while waiting for their monarch to arrive. Accompanied by his sons Boris and Cyril, Ferdinand drove into Edirne on March 29. At the military club he accepted Şukru Paşa's sword before gallantly returning it to him. The Ottoman general was then sent on to Sofia.

At the end of March, the Bulgarians made another attempt to break through the Ottoman lines at Çatalca but were repulsed. Both sides still had small victories, and with Edirne finally in the bag, Bulgaria agreed to an armistice on April 16. By this time, all Ottoman territory in Macedonia had been rolled up by the Balkan armies. Attention now came to rest on Albania, especially the Albanian town of Shkoder (Scutari), which had been besieged by Montenegrins since October but was strongly defended by a combined Ottoman-Albanian force (mostly Ottoman) of about 30,000 men.

In late January, the commander of the Ottoman garrison, Hasan Rıza Paşa, had been assassinated at the instigation of the man who replaced him, Esad Paşa Toptanı, an Albanian army officer and deputy in the Ottoman parliament. In February, with the Montenegrin offensive stalled, Serbia sent in a force of 30,000 men backed by heavy artillery. On March 28, the powers demanded an end to the siege. In the next three days, the Serbian-Montenegrin forced shelled the city and launched an unsuccessful assault, at which point the powers sent a fleet under the command of Rear Admiral Cecil Burney to blockade the coast of Montenegro.

The Serbs withdrew but the Montenegrins stayed until Esad Paşa handed the town over on April 22.[66] The Montenegrins then occupied

Shkoder until compelled to leave by the powers on May 5, ahead of Austria-Hungary possibly taking military action to drive them out. An international force was landed in Shkoder to keep the peace ahead of it being handed over to Albania.

On May 30, the Balkan states and the Ottoman government signed the Treaty of London in which the sultan ceded all European territory west of the Midia-Enos line except for Albania. It seemed Edirne had been lost for good. The sultan yielded sovereignty over Crete, now absorbed into the Greek kingdom and agreed to the powers deciding who should have title to the Aegean islands, taken from the empire, it must be remembered, in wars of conquest launched by Italy and Greece. The powers would decide the borders of Albania plus other matters connected with it.

Thus ended the first Balkan war. All the Balkan participants had gained much of the territory they wanted but not all. Tension over Salonica remained high between the Greek and Bulgarian forces in and around the city. Serbia was forced out of Durres, allocated to Albania, but in the territorial washup was given "compensation" in the form of most of Kosovo, the rest going to Montenegro. In the Serbian nationalist view, without Kosovo Greater Serbia could never be fulfilled. In the Albanian view, without Kosovo Albania could never be complete. Such was the irreducible nature of Balkan claims, with consequences to reverberate across the region down to the 1990s and later.

ALLIES FALL OUT

Disputes between the former allies over the division of Macedonia quickly reached boiling point. In and around Salonica, skirmishes between Greeks and the disgruntled Bulgarians had continued since the city's capture. Anticipating war with their former Bulgarian ally, Greece and Serbia signed two protocols of mutual support in May before concluding their Treaty of Peace, Friendship and Mutual Protection on June 1. It confirmed the Greek-Serbian border; it referred to the need for international mediation to settle the claims of both governments to territory held by Bulgaria; and it bound both governments to mutual defense in the event of Bulgarian aggression.

This was not long coming. On June 16, without informing his government, let alone seeking its consent, Ferdinand ordered an all-out attack on Greek and Serbian positions along the 300-kilometer-long line of demarcation. The next day, the government countermanded the order, causing temporary confusion, but by the end of the month the Bulgarians were attacking in full force.

The Bulgarian chief of staff, General Savoff, architect of the brilliant victories of the first Balkan war was confident they could be repeated. On June 30–July 1, the Greeks crushed the Bulgarian force at Salonica. Battlefield setbacks were compounded when Rumania, its demand for territorial "compensation" having been rejected, declared war on July 10 and advanced to within a few miles of Sofia. Now facing three armies, Bulgaria was compelled to agree to the armistice of July 31. In the Treaty of Bucharest (August 10), it was compelled to accept border rectifications favorable to its three enemies.

The collapse of unity among the Balkan states in 1913 was an opportunity that the Ottoman government quickly seized. On July 12, the military command began mobilizing a force of 250,000 men to recapture Edirne. On July 22, as the army was approaching Edirne under the command of Ahmet Izzet Paşa, the self-promoting Enver managed to join a forward cavalry regiment as it entered the city so he could say he was there first.[67] From the time they arrived, the Ottoman forces maintained "perfect order ... there was not a single case of aggression." Kurdish cavalrymen committed some excesses in an outlying village, for which they were court-martialed and shot, while soldiers who tried to set fire to a house were killed on the spot by an officer.[68]

Rubbing salt into the Bulgarian wound, the Ottomans then crossed the Bulgarian border and formed a provisional government of western Thrace before retreating when Bulgaria confirmed the Ottoman possession of eastern Thrace in the Treaty of Constantinople (September 29, 1913).

All the Balkan states gained from the second war, but some gained much more than others. Under the terms of the Treaty of Bucharest (August 10, 1913), Bulgaria added more than 16 percent to its territory along with several hundred thousand people. Serbia and Montenegro came out well, but the biggest winner by far was Greece, which expanded its territory by almost two thirds and increased its population by close to 70 percent. The spoils included Salonica and the islands in the north Aegean it had captured during the war, the fate of the others to be decided at later dates. On December 1, Crete was formally incorporated into the Greek kingdom.

Albania was declared an independent principality by the powers in July 1913 but without much of the territory it claimed as its own. It went through numerous constitutional transformations: principality (1914–1925); republic (1925–1928), kingdom (1928–1939); and republic again after World War II, before Balkan borders were redrawn yet again in the 1990s.

DIVIDING "ASIA MINOR"

Italy remained in occupation of the Dodecanese Islands and now used them as leverage in an attempt to gain a foothold on the Ottoman mainland. Under Article Two of the 1912 Treaty of Lausanne, it was obliged to withdraw immediately from these islands, once Ottoman troops and civil servants had been recalled from Libya. By June, 1913, it was reported to be ready to hand them over to Greece, with the exception of Astypalaia.[69] At the same time, it was connecting the islands to its drive for commercial expansion in Asia Minor, "Thus for the first time in my experience," wrote the British ambassador to Italy, "bringing these two questions to some extent into correspondence."[70]

After speaking to the French and Italian ambassadors, Grey was left with the impression that Italy feared the loss of the islands would be "the first step for some plan of dividing Asia Minor amongst the European Powers. I gathered that Italy was afraid that if Asia Minor were divided in this way, after all the islands had been annexed to Greece, there would be nothing for Italy."[71]

The message being sent to the powers was that Italy was looking for a trade-off. Now that it had grown to maturity in the "family of nations" (i.e., the imperial club), it was seeking some region in Asia Minor that would serve as a "modest outlet for its energies," with Adalia (present-day Antalya on the southern Mediterranean coast) specifically mentioned. The Ottoman ambassador to Rome believed that the recovery of the islands would be worth the "small blackmail" of "giving Italy something to show on the credit side," as its foreign minister had indicated, such as a concession for harbor works at Adalia.[72] He was apparently unable or unwilling to understand that it was most unlikely the islands would ever be returned to the Ottoman Empire.

The Ottoman presence in Libya was also used as a bargaining chip. Accusing the Ottomans of delaying their withdrawal, Italy claimed the right not just to hold the Aegean islands but to annex them unless and until such time as the Ottoman government paid for the expenses Italy had incurred during the occupation.[73] This was surely monumental cheek, but the Italian Foreign Minister, the Marquis di San Guiliano, claimed that, as Italy had been forced to remain in occupation of the islands by the Ottoman failure to withdraw from Libya, it was entitled to "compensation."

Italy could not withdraw from the islands without some form of indemnity: not money, which it knew the Ottoman Empire did not have, but perhaps a small share alongside the other powers of the commercial opportunities opening up in Asia Minor. According to the Italian foreign minister, retention of the islands was the only "lever" open to his government to get what it wanted.[74]

The Ottoman government now faced permanent loss of all the Aegean islands, those in the south taken by Italy and those in the north seized by Greece in the early stages of the first Balkan war. In December 1913, commenting on reports of a British proposal that Greece should be allowed to retain all but two (Imroz and Tenedos), the grand vizier expressed disillusionment and spoke "most bitterly" of England's attitude. "The Porte no longer believed what they were always being told, that she [England] or any of the other Powers wanted her [the Ottoman Empire's] regeneration. They wanted the destruction of Turkey."[75]

Shortly thereafter, Cemal Bey, newly appointed as minister for public works, asked the British ambassador whether it would be possible for Britain to take "rather a less negative line with Turkey than they have done in the past two years."[76] He would never consent to the islands being given to Greece. Should this happen, the Ottoman government would never rest until it had got them back. Autonomy could be granted but they must stay under Ottoman sovereignty.[77] In reality, however, the Ottoman government had neither the military nor the diplomatic means of retrieving what it had lost.

Early in 1914, the grand vizier expressed further regret at Britain's attitude toward his government. While it had tried to settle all outstanding questions, all its approaches had been met with coldness and now Britain was giving an impression of actual unfriendliness. Britain was creating difficulties between Greece and Turkey, and though he hoped for a friendly settlement he was "pessimistic as to the future."[78]

Used as a staging ground for military attack by the entente powers during the First World War and by the Germans in the Second, the Dodecanese Islands were retained by Italy until its surrender in 1943, after which time they were occupied by Germany until 1945. In 1947, Italy formally ceded the islands to Greece.

Of all the islands in the Aegean, the Turkish state retained only two large ones near the entrance to the Sea of Marmara—Tenedos (Bozcaada) and Imroz (Gökçeada)—plus the small Rabbit (Tavşan) Islands off the coast of Çanakkale. The disputed ownership of numerous uninhabited islets in the Aegean remains the cause of intermittent tension between Greece and Turkey.

CHAPTER 9

Massacre and Flight

WITH THE EXCEPTION of eastern Thrace, masses of Turks had finally been packed out of Europe "bag and baggage," as Gladstone had wanted as far back as the 1870s. The process was catastrophic for the people whose fate was being decided by kings and politicians fired up with ideas far grander than the small lives or deaths of those living in the territories they coveted. Greeks, Bulgarians, and Serbs attacked each just as viciously once their governments had fallen out with each other, but while the whole war zone was awash with refugees, it was the Muslims who bore most of the human cost.

From Thrace to Macedonia and Albania, they were massacred or driven from their villages by Balkan soldiers and the *çeteler* (bandit gangs) following in their wake, often with civilians joining in for a share of the spoils. Hundreds of thousands of Muslims streamed out of the interior, often attacked again on the way by armed gangs. They headed for the coast in the hope of finding a boat to cross the Aegean.

In Thrace, overloaded trains carried the living and the dying to Istanbul. Oxcarts and the people stumbling alongside them wended their way in the same direction. Countless thousands of men, women, and children died of malnutrition, epidemic diseases or exposure. Many more were to die after they thought they had reached safety in the Ottoman capital.

In its effect on civilian life, the Balkan war was the first great human catastrophe in the twentieth century, eclipsing in number and scale the annihilation of the Herero and Nama people by the German authorities in southwest Africa between 1904 and 1908, often described as the "first genocide" of the new century. The destruction of hundreds of villages and the massacre or dispersal of hundreds of thousands of civilians, reducing the Muslim majority in the conquered territories to a minority, set new benchmarks for the brutal century ahead. The attack by the Balkan states sounded a tocsin for the outbreak of the far bigger war two years later.

The standard central text on the atrocities that were committed remains the report issued by the Carnegie international commission of inquiry.[1] Some caveats must be expressed about its structure and balance. The report deals mostly with the atrocities Balkan Christians committed against each once their governments fell out. The atrocities committed against Muslims on a much greater scale are only cursorily surveyed. Furthermore, the president of the commission, Baron d'Estournelles de Constant, took up his task with a Gladstonian view of the historical suffering of the Christian population of the Balkans under Ottoman rule. It obviously pained him to have to single out the Greek army as the architect of some of the worst intra-Christian violence. Introducing the report, he wrote,

> I love Greece. The breath of her war of independence inspired my youth, I am steeped in the heroic memories that live in the hearts of her children, in her folk songs, in her language, which I used to speak, in the divine air of her plains and mountains. Along her coasts every port, every olive wood or group of laurels, evokes the sacred origin of our civilization. Greece was the starting point of my life and labor. She is for the European and American more than a cradle, a temple or a hearth, which each of us dreams of visiting one day in pilgrimage.[2]

There was nothing unusual in this starry-eyed view of Greece and its place as the font of western civilization. Most educated Europeans thought the same, but there was a dark side of which they knew little. The war of independence in the 1820s, finally won for Greece by the intervention of the powers, was preceded by a brutal assault on the Muslim population. More recently, the Greek government had fomented anarchy on Crete in 1897, so there were precedents for the shocking atrocities of 1912–1913. Acting as a good friend who can hardly ignore bad behavior, Baron de Constant wrote that it was out of a sense of responsibility to Greece that he felt compelled to tell the truth.

To understand the mood that prevailed in Istanbul just ahead of the First World War, the impact of the loss of the Balkans territories and the remorseless brutality of the crimes committed against Muslims must be comprehended. Refugees flooded into Istanbul and the towns of the Aegean coast from all directions. Photos show great lines of refugees trekking eastward through Thrace along boggy tracks, sometimes riding oxcarts but more often walking. Retreating soldiers stumbled along with them. An unknown number of people died where they fell from exposure, hunger, and disease, sometimes after drinking ditch water contaminated by the bloated bodies of dead animals. The districts the refugees left behind in eastern Thrace, Macedonia, and Albania had been laid waste. Hundreds of villages were destroyed. Those inhabitants who had not fled in time were slaughtered, by the dozen, by the hundreds, and even the thousands according to the reports of contemporary observers. They were stabbed, shot, bayoneted, or perhaps shut up in a mosque or a barn and burnt to death.

Only blind hatred could account for such cruelty and only the combination of ethnicity, religion, and nationalism already described and evident from early in the nineteenth century can explain that hatred. The starting point, in the words of Richard Hall, was "the abandonment of the Ottoman *millet* system and the adoption by the Bulgarians, Greeks, and Serbs of an exclusivist national ideology as the moral core of their new states."[3] This national idea had fueled Balkan Christian sentiment since the Greek war of independence in the 1820s and eventually enveloped most other ethnoreligious groups across the Ottoman Empire.

"EXTORTION AND EXTERMINATION"

The Carnegie report on the plight of the Muslim civilian population begins with the observation that in European opinion the first Balkan war was one of liberation, not what it was: a brutal campaign of physical extirpation pointing toward the desire to exterminate, repeating in Macedonia and Albania the horrors suffered by Bulgarian Muslims in 1877–1878. In the first weeks of the war, the report found, Bulgarian forces had systematically destroyed Muslim villages in many districts of Macedonia, setting buildings on fire before they moved on.

British documents are another primary source. In the Manastir (Bitola) *vilayet*, occupied by Serbs and Greeks, the town of Manastir having fallen to the Serbs on November 19, the British vice-consul estimated that 80 percent of the villages "inhabited exclusively by Moslems and of the Moslem quarters of villages with a mixed population" had been sacked and wholly or partially destroyed. Irregular soldiers and gangs of armed civilians from neighboring Christian villages were "probably" responsible.[4]

In the northeastern town of Strumnitsa, under mixed Serbian and Bulgarian control from the fall of 1912, the Muslims had been disarmed and then forbidden to leave their houses. Hundreds of Muslims were arrested and given the parody of a trial before being taken to the slaughterhouse and killed "in some cases after torture and mutilation."[5]

The town of Kilkiş (Greek Kilkis and Bulgarian Kukush) and outlying districts had fallen to the Bulgarians on October 30. According to a village notable, Ali Riza Efendi, disarmed Ottoman soldiers were butchered in Kilkiş by Bulgarian irregulars after the departure of Serb and Bulgarian regular army detachments. Hundreds of houses were burnt down in the district by bandit gangs who "shut the men up in the mosques and burned them alive or shot them as they attempted to escape."[6] Money and jewelry were also extorted from villagers in the region. The same Ali Riza Efendi was still in Kilkiş when the Greeks drove the Bulgarians out (June 19–21, 1913) and then, according to the evidence he gave to the Carnegie commissioners, "systematically and deliberately plundered and burnt the town." He took refuge in a Catholic orphanage.[7]

Accusations of Bulgarian brutality in Kilkiş were supported by the statements of Protestant missionaries and the head of the French Catholic mission. The Carnegie commissioners found that Bulgarian bands had been left to pursue "this work of extortion and extermination" for several weeks.[8]

In Serres, captured by the Bulgarian army on November 6, 1912, a British vice-consul visiting two months later wrote,

> How the massacre of more than 400 unarmed Mohammedans was subsequently permitted in front of the Government buildings and almost in the presence of the officer in command has yet to be satisfactorily explained. The victims were for the most part villagers who had taken refuge in the town. Part of the Moslem quarter was pillaged and burnt and a very large number of houses were looted. The principal mosque was converted into a Bulgarian church; others were razed to the ground."[9]

According to the head of the Muslim community, Bulgarian troops entered the town peacefully. Initially, this may have calmed the fears of the townspeople, but massacres soon followed. First, refugees from outlying districts were summoned to the prefecture and killed. "The massacre lasted three hours and resulted in the deaths of 600 Moslems [compared to the figure of 400 given by the British vice-consul]. The number of victims would have been incalculable had it not been for the energetic intervention of the Greek bishop and the director of the Orient bank."

Then it was the turn of the townspeople.

The Moslems of the town were then arrested in the cafes, houses and streets and imprisoned, some at the prefecture and others in the mosques; many of the former were slaughtered with bayonets. Bulgarian soldiers in the meantime entered Turkish houses, violated the women and girls and stole everything they could lay their hands on. The Moslems imprisoned in the overcrowded mosques were left without food for two days and nights and then released.[10]

Before withdrawing from the town during the second Balkan war, Bulgarian officers and gendarmes set fire to shops, cafes, and mills and pillaged not just Muslim property but Jewish and Greek homes.[11] According to a British report, Bulgarian forces in the districts of Serres, Drama, Gumulcina (Turkish Gümülcine and now Greek Komotini), and Dedeağaç met with "practically no opposition; yet they have laid waste the countryside and pillaged almost all the towns. The numbers of murders committed in the towns can be estimated but the horrors perpetrated in the villages will never be known with accuracy and were perhaps better left alone. It may be said that this is 'war' and inevitable; but the fact is, so far as the districts in question are concerned, it never was war but an unopposed raid."[12]

In the seaport town of Kavalla, captured by the Bulgarians in October 1912 (and seized from them by the Greeks in June 2013), a British vice-consul wrote on March 6, 2013, "At least seventy Moslems were killed. I saw myself the corpses of that number. They were killed by irregulars and had all been killed slowly with the bayonet. Many were mutilated." Dozens of villagers around Kavalla had been killed "in the most brutal fashion, either by Bulgarian irregulars or by the native Christian population; the latter, both Bulgarian and Greek, helping the former by supplying them with lists of Moslems to be killed or by directly taking part in the killing."[13]

By the next day, the vice-consul had increased the number of Muslim dead in Kavalla to 200, "methodically tortured to death on successive days." At Dedeağaç about 300 people were massacred and the Muslim quarter looted. "Women were stripped and their ornaments torn from them. Everywhere one hears of outrages on women and children. In the country, villages and farms were devastated, cereals pillaged, cattle driven off and peasants murdered."[14] At the same time, just before Bulgarian troops reached Drama, "Turkish troops" had destroyed the village of Plevna "on the pretext" that *komitadjis* were concealed there: about 150 Christian families had "perished."[15]

In territories contested by Albanians and Serbs, regular and irregular Serbian forces massacred Albanians out of hand. The defeat of the Ottoman Vardar army at Kumanovo in October shattered Ottoman authority across northwestern Macedonia, opening up Kosovo to Serb and Montenegrin conquest. Zigzagging across the middle of Macedonia, the Vardar river runs through Skopje, Üsküb under Ottoman rule, where the killing of Albanians started immediately after other Serbs captured the city. The British consul was told by the Catholic *curé* of Albanian prisoners being removed from the military hospital and thrown into the Vardar (dead or alive not clarified); of Albanians being shot or bayonetted on the streets; and of numerous other atrocities committed in the region.

At Ferisovich, Pristina, Prisrend, and numerous villages, thousands of Albanians were killed. They included Catholic *muhtarlar* (village notables) and women shot as they escaped from burning houses, their children then bayoneted "to save powder."[16] At Pristina, "on the admission of a Servian military doctor," 5,000 men were cut down by machine-gun fire. At Lyuma, 400 Albanians surrendered and were taken to Prisrend, where 2,000 Albanians were said to have been killed. Dozens of villages in the district were razed and their inhabitants also killed.[17] No doubt many of these figures were exaggerated. The British consul at Skopje said, for example, that the account of 1,200 people being killed at Ferisovich was a "half-truth," adding that many of the villages had provoked Serb reprisals.[18]

The two priests who spoke to the British consul in Skopje were not just Catholic but Albanian and thus, in his view, had "a double motive for exaggerating" to the detriment of the Orthodox Serbs. Nevertheless, arguments over numbers and responsibility should not be allowed to minimize the horror of what happened.

INFURIATED HORNETS

Having almost finished with the Muslims, the Balkan armies turned on each other like infuriated hornets in the second Balkan war. Earlier

Bulgarian atrocities against Muslims in Serres were followed by Greek atrocities against Bulgarians, after the Bulgarian retreat in the first week of July 1913. Irregulars and Greek civilian gangs hunted down Bulgarians, pillaged their homes, and in a girls' high school used as a prison, according to evidence submitted to the Carnegie commissioners, murdered 200–250 of their captives with knives and bayonets.[19]

On July 11, a fire broke out that destroyed an estimated two thirds of the town's 6,000 houses. It was a hot day, a strong wind was blowing, the Balkan-style houses were mostly built of wood and were quickly consumed. Blame was freely apportioned and just as freely denied. While the fire may have been deliberately set, clearly it could also have been started by an exploding artillery shell fired by Greek or Bulgarian forces.

Elsewhere, when the Bulgarians were driven out of Kilkis, the Greeks "deliberately burnt the town, destroying practically every building in it."[20] Across the reconquered region, Greek troops assisted by *andartes* had carried a systematic and wholesale "plan of extermination of the Bulgarian population."[21]

In Salonica, after the defeat of Bulgarian forces in early July, Greek soldiers killed and threw overboard several Bulgarian prisoners being taken by ship to Piraeus, including the Archimandrite Eulogius of the Bulgarian church in Salonica, the head of the Bulgarian community, and the secretary of the Bulgarian bank.[22] The last that was seen of the Archimandrite Eulogius from the ship was his black hair floating in the water.

The mutual hatred, expressed in speech and lurid propaganda posters, was so uniform that it would be invidious to single out one ethnoreligious national group. Each was determined to bend all others to its own will. In Serbia and even Macedonia, a British consul wrote, no Serbian official would admit that Bulgarians even existed: "All are Servians and will be made to behave as such." Bulgarians would never accept being defined as Serb or Greek, but between the two, their hatred of the Greeks was so intense that one man spoke of being prepared to accept Serb citizenship and speak Serbian "to avoid the worse fate of having to speak Greek and see his children brought up as Greeks."[23]

Such detestation was abundantly returned by Greeks. In letters home, soldiers wrote of the atrocities they were committing as they drove the Bulgarians from the territory they had conquered: "We have to burn the villages—such is the order—slaughter the young people and spare only the old people and the children." "Here we are burning the villages and killing the Bulgarians, both women and children." "We massacre all the

Bulgarians who fall into our hands." "We picked out their eyes [five Bulgarian prisoners] while they were still alive." "The Greek army sets fire to all the villages where there are Bulgarians and massacres all it meets.... God knows where this will end."[24] Hundreds of Bulgarian villages, as well as numerous Turkish villages, were left in ruins by the Greek army, with shops, mills, and nearly 15,000 houses—according to the Carnegie Report estimate—destroyed in the process.[25]

FORCED CONVERSION

Serbs, Greeks, and Bulgarians attempted to persuade the outside world that a conquered territory belonged to them by historical, cultural, and religious right. Edith Durham visited towns where the population was forced to declare it was Greek. An unarmed population was helpless before a big army, she wrote: "Many an English village would declare itself Choctaw if five thousand armed men bade it do so or be extirpated."[26] At Koritza, a "bogus meeting" was held to show that the people of the town had voted unanimously that they were Greek when they were Albanian. In the western Macedonian town of Moskopol (modern Albanian Voskopoje), "[The Greeks] sent out overnight a number of people who danced out to meet us like stage peasants crying 'Welcome to a Greek town.' Moskopol is in fact inhabited by Vlachs and Albanians. The imported gang went everywhere with us to prevent us discovering this fact."[27]

Reports of forced conversion and baptism at the hands of Bulgarians and of women made to remove their veils were common. In Thrace and Macedonia, Pomaks—ethnic Bulgarians who had converted to Islam after the Ottoman conquest—were being forced to convert back into the Christianity of the Bulgarian national church by priests accompanied by soldiers and *komitadjis*. Male Pomak villagers were being deported to Bulgaria, with the old men, women, and children left to bear the brunt of further persecution.[28]

While an ignorant and bigoted clergy might be blamed, according to one report, "The persecution is on too large a scale and too uniform in method to admit the hypothesis that the Bulgarian government has not connived [at it]."[29] In these districts, there had been little resistance by Ottoman troops and none by the civilian population, yet Bulgarian forces behaved "as though engaged in the suppression of a bloody and obstinate rebellion." The destruction of villages was "wholescale."[30]

EDIRNE OCCUPIED

While no corner of Macedonia or Thrace was exempt from all or some of the horrors described above, no history of this period is complete without an account of the siege and fall of Edirne, Adrianople to the Bulgarians. When the Bulgarian army swept forward into Thrace under the command of General Savoff, it surrounded Edirne on three sides and moved on. Success at the battle of Kirkkilise and the failure of the Ottomans to destroy the stone bridge across the Maritsa (Meriç) River at Mustafapaşa, a main crossing for the Bulgarian army, sealed Edirne's fate. Besieged, running out of food, its water supply cut off, its surrounding villages destroyed to deprive Ottoman troops of any cover, the city would be captured at the Bulgarian army's leisure.

By late October 1912, the ring around the Ottoman forts defending Edirne was complete, and by November a Serbian contingent had joined the blockading force. As winter advanced, conditions worsened both for the besieging troops and the population inside the city, swelled to 150,000 by 80,000 refugees pouring in from the surrounding countryside.[31] Heavy shelling destroyed whole quarters. The Bulgarians cut the water supply on November 4, and food supplies rapidly began to dwindle. The armistice in December, as European ambassadors tried to talk the Ottoman government into accepting their peace terms, brought some relief before the war was resumed and the Ottoman garrison surrendered on March 26.

The Bulgarian troops were exhausted by a long siege in wintry conditions, suffering from food shortages, and beset by typhus and cholera. The civilian population of the city was in its own desperate state, with its fall marked by Greeks, women as well as men, pillaging Muslim property and to "some extent also" that of Jews and Armenians. Even the Bulgarian consul returned to his house to find it had been robbed.[32] Theft and damage extended to the library at the sixteenth-century Selimiye mosque.

Captured Ottoman soldiers were herded onto Eski Sarai island in the Tunca river (a tributary of the Maritsa) to prevent the spread of cholera already afflicting them, according to the Bulgarians. There they ate grass and stripped bark from the trees, "as high as a man could reach."[33] The prisoners even gnawed at their leather footwear to survive. Disease, cold, malnutrition, exposure, and exhaustion accounted for thousands of deaths. Despite claims by the Bulgarian command that it was doing its best, the Carnegie committee noted "cruel indifference in general to the lot of the prisoners."[34] The former Ottoman governor of Edirne estimated the death toll on the island alone at 3,000.[35]

EXODUS FROM THRACE

Throughout the last few months of 1912 and into the first half of 1913, refugees and defeated soldiers flooded into Istanbul, filling mosques and government buildings turned into temporary accommodation and hospitals or sleeping rough in parks and on the streets. The muddy roads across Thrace were strewn with the bodies of the dead. At Hademköy, near the last Ottoman line of defense at Çatalca, the sick were penned within a barbed-wire fence surrounded by armed guards with fixed bayonets. So many soldiers had died from cholera that they were buried in common graves. An eyewitness watched 263 bodies being dragged into one by hooks.[36]

Ashmead Bartlett wrote of what he saw after traveling through the valley of Çekmece and reaching Hademköy.

> As we mounted the last slope which hides the valley in which Hademkeuy lies we were brought to a standstill by the awful babel of sounds that came from beneath us. We were gazing into the valley of the shadow of death. In the center of Hademkeuy lay a great square formed on one side by some barracks, on two others by lines of white hospital tents and on the fourth by the high road. This square resembled a successful fly-paper in midsummer. It was covered with the corpses of the dead and the writhing bodies of the living in all attitudes, some prone, some sitting, some kneeling, some constantly shifting, some with hands clasped as if in supplication.
>
> In some parts of the arena the dead were piled in heaps; in others those still living were almost as closely packed. This shocking lake of misery was being constantly fed by rivulets of stretcher bearers, bringing in fresh victims from the camps and forts and by others who crawled in of their own accord ... all the tracks leading to this impromptu morgue were clothed with the bodies of those who had died on the road.[37]

Another correspondent saw "dozens of dead horses lying in puddles and marshy streams" from which thirsty soldiers were drinking. The dead and the dying were lying in every ditch and "the nearer one gets to Hademkeui, the more frequent become the heaps of corpses by the road."[38]

The way to Istanbul was marked by burial mounds of villagers who had contracted cholera and had been left to die in the nearest open space. Trains carried the dead and dying into the city, along with those who stumbled along on foot. Struggling to cope with the flood, the authorities sought to disperse them on the other side of the Bosporus. Cholera stations were opened there as well as on the outskirts of the city. Indian doctors arrived to help the Ottoman Red Crescent deliver medical aid. Disease spread far and wide. According to a modern scholar of epidemics, "Soldiers discharged from the army in the aftermath of the Balkan Wars acted as carriers of infectious and parasitic diseases, causing epidemics throughout Anatolia" during the First World War.[39] The same diseases would also have been carried by infected and untreated civilians.

The Ottoman parliament set aside special funds to meet the emergency. As these ran out, it passed extra budgetary allocations and called on the banks to pitch in with loans. State land was allocated to the refugees and efforts made to find them work. While many Istanbulis did their best to help the refugees, "most resented their presence, if for no other reason than the pressure they exerted on existing facilities, the competition which they provided for low paying jobs and cheap rental housing and the diseases they spread. Unrest, conflict and turmoil continued as the refugees kept coming."[40]

Because of the military, social, and administrative chaos caused by the war, and the fact that the First World War followed so soon after, there was no time to count the dead, the wounded, and the refugees. Numbers can only be estimated, but with the ethnic cleansing of the 1990s still to come, the 1912–1913 Balkan wars were not yet the end of the continuing historical process to extirpate the Ottoman/Turkish/Muslim presence in southeastern Europe.

Extrapolating from population figures, Justin McCarthy has estimated that of the 2,300,000 Muslims living in the Ottoman regions conquered by the Balkan states, 870,000 remained by 1926. After the Balkan wars, 414,000 had settled in the remaining Ottoman lands, a further 399,000 had arrived by 1926, and 632,000 had died, amounting to 27 percent of the pre-1912 Balkan Muslim population outside Albania.[41]

In Aksakal's slightly different calculus, the Balkan Wars cost the Ottoman Empire 80 percent of its European territories, "home to a population of over 4 million or 16 percent of the empire's total population."[42] Stanford Shaw puts the number of refugees alone at 640,000.[43] Taking the longer and territorially broader historical view, Kemal Karpat estimates that from the early nineteenth century down to recent history, but mainly between the Crimean War and 1916, about 7 million Muslim "migrants" settled in Ottoman Anatolia from the Balkans, the Crimea, the Caucasus, and the Mediterranean islands.[44] As the vast bulk of these civilians either were driven out of their homelands or fled under duress, the word "migrant" seems somewhat inappropriate.

Insofar as the Balkan Wars were concerned, elimination of the Ottoman Muslim presence clearly falls into the category of ethnic cleansing. No military motive could be argued for the wholesale destruction of villages and the massacre of overwhelmingly defenseless civilians. Paul Mozjes writes that the wars were not only genocidal "but in the unusual category of multiple mutual genocides."[45] It remains a curious anomaly that in most books dealing with ethnic cleansing and genocide the human consequences of the Balkan wars are rarely mentioned.

Pride among Ottoman Muslims at last-minute victories, especially the recapture of Edirne, was surpassed by the overriding sense of shock, anger, humiliation, and bitterness at the loss of nearly all Ottoman territory in southeastern Europe. Emotional appeals were made by writers and parliamentarians not to forget what was lost, even if there was no possibility of it ever being regained. Just before the war, the poet Feyzullah Sacit jeered at these Balkan "microbes," these hands that "hadn't swung a sword" and had a "fat chance" of overwhelming the "scions of Suleyman."[46] Yet in the end, the microbes—and the donkeys, dogs, servants, and bandits, as others called them—had triumphed.[47]

The Ottoman commander in Salonica surrendered 26,000 troops in Salonica without a fight. It was shameful and meant, in the words of the writer Şevket Süreyya Aydemir, "Up to the last day we had been living in a world of dreams."[48] Calls for revenge filled the air, but impotently, as there was no chance of revenge against those who had taken the Balkans. The recapture of Edirne was salve to wounded pride but still small consolation compared to the vast loss of territory and people. The bitterness was extended to the European powers who were seen to have allowed all this to happen. There was a growing sense that the next war would be a final battle for survival against predatory powers for which the people would have to be prepared at every level.

AEGEAN BACKLASH

The flight to Istanbul and the eastern Aegean seaboard of hundreds of thousands of Muslims ejected from their homes in a war Christianized by the kings and politicians poisoned relations between Ottoman Christians (Armenians and Greeks) and Muslims. Ottoman Muslims must have heard countless stories from refugees of massacre and destruction by Balkan soldiers and civilian gangs. Nor were the Aegean islands occupied by Greeks during the war exempt from punishment. News spread quickly of what happened on Chios, a few miles off the coast just south of Izmir, after the Greek army landed. In a memorandum handed to the British consul-general in Izmir, Ottoman officials stated that

> the Turkish warehouses were looted, that the wife and daughter of a prominent local notable whom they named had been carried off by troops and that the houses of six other Turkish residents had been burnt. People who complained of the pillage to the Greek commander had, it was stated, been arrested and exiled. The Mejidie mosque was converted into a barracks. Sacred objects were trodden under foot or broken and a mausoleum connected with the mosque pulled down by the troops. The Muezzin, Hikmi (Sic) Effendi, was called out from the mosque and exposed to special indignities. His turban was twisted around his neck, he was severely beaten, then sent on board and exiled to Athens.

On top of this public humiliation, his watch and chain and money were reported to have been stolen by the Greek commander and the harbormaster.[49]

The element of deflected revenge (against the innocent) must be considered central in Muslim attacks on Christians in eastern Thrace, down the shores of the Sea of Marmara and along the Aegean coast. The desperate state of Balkan refugees would have continually fed the flames. Reports of arson, beatings, murder, and rape came in from many districts, as armed Muslim gangs descended on Christian communities.

The preponderantly Greek coastal town of Aivali (present-day Ayvalik) was a particular target, at one stage surrounded by Ottoman irregular forces threatening to burn it down and massacre its inhabitants.[50] Cattle and property were stolen, shops boycotted, and Christians prevented from harvesting their crops. British, French, Italian, and Austrian subjects were also harassed and boycotted for the role of their governments in the string of disasters that had overwhelmed the Ottoman state since 1908.[51]

Ryan Gingeras refers to British consular officials who "identified local offices of the CUP as the primary centers orchestrating the campaign."[52] However, it is clear that much mob and armed gang violence against Christians was spontaneous and that the government took measures to avert or suppress disorders. It settled Muslim refugees as far as possible from Christian villages and sought to prevent them from attacking Christian homes and churches.[53]

Talat Paşa was said even by the British, who had no time for the CUP, to be "acting with energy" in dealing with violence in the Izmir, Bergama, Aivali, and Edremit districts, sending cavalry against a band of "raiders," apparently Muslim refugees, at Phocaea (Foca) and arresting them when they decamped to Menemen.[54] He had visited the region and ordered a proclamation be put up in towns and villages warning that anyone found with arms would be shot.[55]

Visiting Edremit, the interior minister found that Greeks living in the town and 16 outlying villages had already "emigrated," but 41 people who had looted their empty houses had been arrested, and a battalion sent from Aivali was maintaining peace and security. The government was doing its utmost to prevent Greeks from leaving the region. As a result, 57 families from Burhaniye and 53 from another town had been persuaded to stay, as had 800 families at Kuçukköy and Greeks from Aivali.[56] Nevertheless, while claiming to have restored order, Talat admitted that "things had gone very far."[57]

Along the coast of the Sea of Marmara, displaced Turks returning to Tekirdağ (Rodosto), occupied by Bulgarian forces from November 1912 to July 1913, allegedly murdered 19 Armenians and pillaged houses on the pretext of searching for enemy soldiers and *komitadjis*. At Malkara (Malgara), 30 miles west of Tekirdağ, Armenians were again accused of treachery and ordered to hand in weapons and goods "stolen from the Muslims." Attacks and pillage followed before the elapse of the two days given for Armenians to hand in their weapons, ending only after the arrival of the *kaymakam* with a police escort, by which time 12 Armenians were reported killed and 87 houses and 218 shops destroyed by fire.

Numerous Bulgarian or Greek villages suspected of giving aid and comfort to enemy forces were set on fire, and many of their inhabitants massacred as the Ottoman army regained control of eastern Thrace and then occupied territory across the Bulgarian border for a short time.[58] The sources for these reports were usually Bulgarian or Greek and in many cases they were probably exaggerated, but the Carnegie commissioners clearly believed the substance was true.

Ottoman soldiers, irregulars, and civilians were all implicated in these reported atrocities. As they had done elsewhere, when referring to the crimes of Serbs and Bulgarians, the Carnegie commissioners accused Ottoman military authorities of seeking the "complete extermination" of the Bulgarian population of Thrace, in accordance with a "systematic plan."[59] The commissioners did not produce any evidence of such a plan, however, beyond the statements of refugees.

The Greek and Ottoman governments accused each other of the same thing: the mistreatment and deliberate expulsion of an unwanted minority. The British ambassador believed that although there was some exaggeration in what the Greeks were saying, "In one way or another, the Turkish authorities are replacing the non-Moslem element of Thrace by a purely Moslem population and ... great hardship accompanies the process." On the other hand, the "migrant" outflows could not be disconnected, "and it is a fact that the Musulman emigration preceded the Greek."[60] By June, the ambassador was inclined to believe that Talat and the grand vizier "may find it difficult to stop the movement which is being worked up by the Chauvinists of the Committee [of Union and Progress]."[61]

While leaving open the possibility that the government simply could not contain the violence,[62] he spoke of a "highly organized" movement to drive out the Greek population from the south coast of the Sea of Marmara to the Çeşme peninsula (south of Izmir). He did not directly blame the government: the "campaign of terror" had been facilitated by local authorities who "must have felt, until the Grand Vizier and Talaat Bey realized that things were going too far, that their attitude would not be displeasing to the central government." Reverting to a familiar theme in British dispatches, he spoke of evidence that this whole movement "has been encouraged if not organized by the Salonica Jewish element in the Committee and was economic in its object, which aims at replacing the Greek traders by Ottoman Jews."[63]

POPULATION EXCHANGE

The Balkan wars of 1912–1913 had the impact of a demographic earthquake. Hundreds of thousands of Balkan Muslims were driven into exile.

In the immediate aftermath, tens of thousands of Christians (Greeks and Bulgarians) fled their Ottoman homeland as Muslims took their revenge or—as some argue—the Ottoman government set in motion a deliberate plan of "Turkification."[64] If anyone must take first responsibility for these disasters, it is the Balkan states. They launched a war of aggression, and their people as well as the enemy suffered the consequences. Greece, in particular, captured an enormous amount of Ottoman territory but at the expense not only of the lives of its soldiers and civilians but of the safety of the Ottoman Greek population. The atrocities committed against Muslims poisoned Muslim-Christian relations on the other side of the Aegean, generating hatred, suspicion, and the desire for revenge against the nearest vulnerable target. The war of conquest launched by Greece in 1919 delivered a second demographic earthquake: the 1923 population exchange between Greece and Turkey. There was to be to no recovery, only the abandonment forever of a way of life and of homes in which families had lived for generations.

Population "exchanges" were on the table well before the mass "exchange" that marked the end of the Greek-Turkish war of 1919–1922. The Treaty of Istanbul, signed between Bulgaria and the Ottoman Empire (September 29, 1913), provided for the formal exchange of Turks and Bulgars living close to their shared border. Accordingly, 48,570 Muslims were sent from Bulgaria to eastern Thrace, and 46,764 Christians from Ottoman territory resettled in Bulgaria. Ryan Gingeras refers to studies indicating that the "forced migration" of Greeks was related to "a more general Ottoman attempt at an 'exchange of population,'"[65] but here it needs to be said that the Greek government was no less interested in such an exchange. In late April 1914, Talat was reported to have made arrangements with Prime Minister Venizelos some time previously for a population exchange.[66]

By May 1914, the grand vizier proposed that a mixed commission be set up "for arranging and regulating the exchange of populations between Thrace and Macedonia."[67] Venizelos had been thinking of an exchange "on a considerable scale" but was talked out of it, as it would be unpopular and might cause his downfall.[68] In June, "after repeated unofficial hints," the Greek ambassador to St. James's Court reported that the Ottoman government had made a definite proposal: the Turkish population of Greek Macedonia would be exchanged on a voluntary basis for the Greek population of the *vilayet* of Aydın (which included Izmir). Greece accepted this arrangement in principle, but within a few months none of it mattered.[69] World War I began, and in December 1914, the Greek-Ottoman population-exchange negotiations were called off.[70]

The rearrangement of the map of southeastern Europe at the Congress of Berlin precipitated the slide toward the First World War. Even by its own people, the government in Istanbul was seen as incapable of protecting its own domains, a truth reinforced time after time between 1878 and 1914. The penultimate point in this slide was reached when four Balkan states ganged up on a gravely weakened Ottoman state in 1912. The first shots fired in the Balkan wars, not the shots that killed Archduke Franz Ferdinand and his wife Sophie in Sarajevo on June 28, 1914, heralded the onset of the First World War.

Enmeshed in their own complicated web of alliances, refusing, failing, or unable to act on moral or legal principle during the string of assaults on the territory and integrity of the Ottoman Empire, the powers brought closer the thing they feared most: the collapse of the European balance of power.

PART III

The Last Ottoman War

CHAPTER 10

Into the Abyss

THE BALKAN WARS brought in their wake changes that determined where the Ottoman Empire would stand when the greater European war broke out. First, with some exceptions, the army command was discredited by such a humiliating defeat. Second, the losses of 1912, followed by the apparent readiness of the government to cede Edirne and agree to the partition of eastern Thrace, precipitated the raid on the Bab-i 'Ali on January 12, 1913. The government fell into the hands of the CUP, with Mahmud Şevket, the hero of the march on Istanbul and the suppression of the counterrevolution in 1909, appointed grand vizier, only to be assassinated on June 11.

The recapture of Edirne on July 21 propelled Enver, then a relatively junior officer (but married to a niece of the sultan), to the status of national hero. It was about this time that a group of young officers and guerilla fighters (*fedai*) around Enver coalesced into the propaganda, intelligence, and black operations group known as Teşkilat i-Mahsusa (Special Organization).

By early 1914, Enver had been appointed war minister and Cemal minister for the navy. Along with Interior Minister Talat, the triumvirate that would take the empire into the next war was now in place. The day after being appointed war minister, Enver purged the army of more than 1,000 officers up to generals and marshals who "had failed in the Balkan War, were inefficient or too old."[1]

After the defeat in the Balkans, another war was generally seen as inevitable within Ottoman political and military circles. A war for the recovery of lost Balkan territory, possibly in the company of a former enemy, Bulgaria, was one possibility—until the assassination of Archduke Franz Ferdinand initiated a European war. The empire would have to be prepared not just militarily or diplomatically but morally: women and youth were the chief targets of a broad campaign initiated by the CUP government to mobilize from the ground up. One way or another, the empire would be sucked into the vortex. To prevent the final partition of its lands, it would need a great-power ally.[2] Although ready to consider all possibilities, the most likely candidate, given the rebuffs suffered at British hands, was Germany.

On August 2, between the German declarations of war on Russia and France, the Ottomans signed a secret alliance with the kaiser's government to which neither side was fully committed even when putting pen to paper.[3] Some senior German diplomatic and diplomatic figures were markedly unenthusiastic about any binding treaty with an empire long regarded by many as heading for the knacker's yard.[4] The Ottomans remained ready to consider better offers or make offers of their own.

In May, Talat had made a "furtive offer" of an alliance with Russia when visiting the Crimea.[5] In July, Cemal suggested Ottoman readiness to "orientate its policies towards the Triple Alliance" when visiting Paris.[6] In August Enver followed through with a concrete proposal for an alliance with Russia *after* signing the secret alliance with Germany and *after* Britain had declared war on Germany. The terms were attractive but ultimately too complicated to be acceptable.[7]

Still, these approaches were a good example of the horse trading that continued even after war was declared. This might be called amoral, but diplomacy is an amoral world in which power prevails, not moral principles. These were the real rules of the game, and everyone had to play by them, however weak their hand. No one could guarantee the Ottoman Empire's survival, but which of the powers offered the best chance of its survival? It might have been Britain, but Britain had long since shown that it was not interested. Admiral Arthur Limpus of the Royal Navy was still advising the Ottoman navy, but the government had so lost hope that it did not even bother sounding Britain out on the possibility of an alliance.[8]

The "July crisis" brought on by the assassination of Archduke Franz Ferdinand in Sarajevo began with Austria-Hungary's declaration of war on Serbia (July 28). This was followed by Germany's declarations of war on Russia (August 1), France (August 3), and Belgium (August 4) and by Britain's declaration of war on Germany (August 4). The Ottoman government declared mobilization (*seferbirlik*) on August 3. Months later, however, largely because of a transport shortage, the mobilization of all units was still incomplete.

On Enver's orders, the straits were closed to foreign warships. The military was still in the process of sweeping reforms and short of all the logistical support necessary to armies in the field—from ammunition and artillery to food and clothing. It was in no condition to fight the war now taking shape on the near horizon.

Naval control of the Aegean was a dominant issue in the lead-up to the war. The rivalry between Greece and Turkey was intense, particularly after the addition of the armored cruiser *Averof* to the Greek navy in 1911. Both Greece and Turkey were purchasing warships where they could, many from Germany or Italy, and were also modernizing naval administration and strategies as fast as possible.

In 1910, the Ottoman government bought two aging German warships (built in 1891), renaming them the *Hayrettin Barbarossa* and the *Turgut Reis*. The following year, the government began negotiations for the purchase of two dreadnoughts being constructed in a British shipyard (Armstrong Whitworth) for Brazil, the *Rio de Janeiro* and the *Minas Geraes*. Brazil had been engaged in its own naval race with Chile and Argentina, but now that the three countries had resolved their differences it was cancelling the order. The possible Ottoman purchase of the *Minas Geraes* was superseded by a contract signed with the Vickers shipyard to build the warship that was to be known as the *Reşadiye*.

The Ottomans were still interested in purchasing the *Rio de Janeiro*, and negotiations continued against the background of the Balkan wars. Winston Churchill, First Lord of the Admiralty, wanted the ship sold to Greece. A loan was arranged for this purpose, but in early 1913 the Ottoman bid, underwritten by a French loan, was accepted, and the *Rio de Janeiro*, one of the biggest battleships in the world, was renamed the *Sultan Osman I*.[9] The cost of nearly 4 million pounds for the two warships was partly covered by increasing taxes on a range of goods and partly by donations from the general public. In July 1914, an Ottoman commander arrived with a final payment for the shipbuilders and a crew to take delivery of the *Sultan Osman I*. The *Reşadiye* was to be handed over at a later date.

In early August, guns were being fitted to the *Sultan Osman I*, just ahead of transfer to the Ottoman navy, when Churchill intervened on the grounds that it would be "contrary to the public interest that she [the *Sultan Osman I*] should be permitted to leave England at the present moment,"[10] a position fully supported by Russia. Both the *Reşadiye* and the *Sultan Osman I* were sequestered for the Royal Navy and renamed the HMS *Erin* and HMS *Agincourt*. The reason for the seizure was the fear that the ships would end up in German hands. Britain told the Ottoman ambassador that the ships, or alternatively the money, would be returned after the war but only if his government remained neutral.[11]

In fact, although the Ottoman government had signed a secret agreement with Germany, it had still not decided how or even whether to enter the war. There were factions for and against, leaving some room for diplomatic maneuver even with Britain.

The violation of this legal contract infuriated Istanbul and all those ordinary citizens who had pitched in with small amounts of money to help buy these ships. Muslims everywhere viewed the seizure of the ships as a brazen and illegal move by the British government. The Ottomans responded by canceling the naval agreement with Britain and sending the team of advisers headed by Admiral Limpus home.

An opportunity for payback came on August 10 when two German cruisers, pursued across the Mediterranean by British ships, arrived at the straits. The Ottoman government decided to let them through, and on August 16 the *Göeben* and the *Breslau* were incorporated into the Ottoman navy as the *Yavuz Sultan Selim* and *Midilli*. On September 23, their commander, Wilhelm Souchon, was given command of the Ottoman navy. Four days later, the Ottomans closed the straits to all international shipping, and on October 29, under Souchon's direction, the *Yavuz Sultan Selim* and the *Midilli* were part of the flotilla that shelled Russian positions in the Black Sea and took the empire into the war alongside Germany and Austria-Hungary.

Having signed a treaty of alliance, the Ottoman government had come under increasing pressure from Germany to end its position of armed neutrality. It was split among those cabinet members who did not want war at all, those who did not want to go to war until conditions were more favorable, and those who were ready for war immediately. Enver, in particular, was determined to push ahead with the German alliance, against the wavering of the grand vizier, Said Halim Paşa. According to one source, Enver had only authorized "maneuvers" in the Black Sea, not the sinking of Russian ships and the subsequent shelling of shore installations. Once there, however, "It was evident that Souchon ... would be inclined to provoke an incident."[12] Questioned after the war, the grand vizier clearly felt that he had been duped.

The Admiral and commander-in-chief of the fleet [Souchon] came to me and asked for permission to take the fleet to the Black Sea for important naval manoeuvres. According to him, the Sea of Marmara, being a calm sea, was not suitable for naval manoeuvres and firing exercises. Upon his insistence we granted permission, on the condition the warships would not enter the Black Sea as a single unit but go in one by one to perform manoeuvres at the entrance of the Bosporus and then return by the evening. The fleet accepted this arrangement and acted accordingly. Since cabinet was in control of the situation we felt that everything was safe. Upon being informed of the incident [the shelling of Russian positions] I exclaimed, "You are playing with the life of the country. . . ." My unfortunate experience has strongly convinced me that a grand vizier wields little power: he does not have any authority over the cabinet and is completely at the mercy of his ministers who do whatever they want without informing him.[13]

The particular minister he had in mind was obviously Enver. The notion that Germany dragged the Ottoman Empire into the war has been overtaken by the release of archival material showing that Souchon was obeying orders from the Ottoman war minister. According to the wartime diaries of Hakki Paşa, an Ottoman army general, Enver ordered Souchon to destroy the Russian fleet. According to a copy of the order found in the Turkish military archives by a PhD researcher, Souchon is told the Turkish fleet intended to establish "naval domination" of the Black Sea. Souchon is then instructed to "search and destroy the Russian fleet wherever it is and without declaring war." In a handwritten annotation, Hakki Paşa, who had known Enver since they were military cadets, affirms that the order was written on the instructions of Enver and translated into German by himself.[14] As for Russia, it anticipated an Ottoman attack and had instructed naval commanders in the Black Sea not to fire first so the Ottoman responsibility would be clear.[15]

All options were now abruptly closed off. Lamely, the government tried to apologize for the raid, claiming that the Germans had acted without authorization, but Russia declared war on November 2, followed by Britain and France on November 5. Sultan Mehmed V, whose position was close to the grand vizier's, was compelled to declare war on the three governments on November 11. Three days later, the *fetvas* enjoining all Muslims to support *jihad* was read in Istanbul's Fatih Mosque.

ABOLISHING PRIVILEGE

Even before the war, the Ottoman government had notified the embassies
of its intention to abolish the "capitulations"—the arrangements dating
back to the sixteenth century granting special privileges to European governments. Over time, as the empire's military capacity weakened along
with the sultan's ability to resist European demands, these privileges were
magically converted into extraterritorial "rights" allowing the powers to
have their own courts and postal services and to intervene on behalf of
their various Ottoman Christian protégés.

Such protection encouraged Christians to seek the further benefit of
foreign nationality, "which largely if not totally took them out of the legal
framework of the Ottoman state" and put them under the protection of a
foreign power.[16] These "rights" amounted to a humiliating derogation of
Ottoman sovereignty. They were not reciprocal of course: the notion of
an extraterritorial judicial system or postal service run within a European
state by the Ottoman government would have been regarded as laughable,
as would any "right" of the Ottoman government to intercede on behalf
of Muslims living in a European country.

The derangement of justice in the Ottoman Empire by a European
government was underscored in 1905 when a Belgian subject was found
guilty of attempting the assassination of Sultan Abdülhamit. Charles
Edouard Joris was part of a Dashnak team that planned to assassinate the
sultan as he was leaving the Hamidiye mosque attached to Yildiz Palace.
The plot (Operation Mare) had been set up in Bulgaria where one of the
conspirators managed to blow himself up while testing a bomb.[17] A carriage specially built in Vienna was imported into Istanbul and parked near
the mosque on July 21. The 80 kilograms of high explosive sitting in a concealed compartment was timed to explode 2 minutes 42 seconds after the
sultan left the mosque. The assassins had carefully reconnoitered the sultan's movements, and this was the exact time they had calculated it would
take him to reach his carriage. On this occasion, however, he dallied to
talk to the Shaykh al-Islam, and the bomb went off before he reached the
carriage, killing twenty-six people and wounding scores, including Greeks
and Armenians as well as Turks.

Joris—an anarchist as well as a Dashnak militant—was arrested,
brought to trial, and sentenced to death along with other members of the
group. The government in Brussels refused to accept the verdict, however,
and demanded that Joris be handed over for trial in Belgium, claiming that

an article in the 1838 Treaty of Commerce with the Ottoman government gave it the right of jurisdiction over its subjects.

There was no doubt of Joris's guilt and no question that he had been given a fair trial, but European opinion had long been accustomed to regard a fair trial in the Ottoman legal system as an impossibility. Neither was there much doubt of the outcome should he be tried in Brussels: most probably he would have to be acquitted, wrote *The Times*, "for the evidence that is available here [in Istanbul] would not be available there."[18] Even if found guilty, the sentence would most likely be light because of widespread sympathy for the Armenians.

The Ottoman government refused to hand Joris over and a stalemate set in that lasted until 1907 when the sultan released the Belgian as an act of clemency. Joris had tried to assassinate the sultan, killing over two dozen people in the process yet was able to return to Belgium a free man after just two years in prison. Not even this was sufficient for European opinion to view the sultan and his government more charitably. "Falsely Accused" and "Plans to Bury Him Alive Just Averted by the Actions of His Government" ran two of the newspaper headlines.

Foreign intervention in the Ottoman justice system on behalf of an assassin was extreme, but intervention on behalf of others who had fallen foul of the Ottoman legal system was not unusual. Ottoman citizens who had some claim to European or American nationality were in a strong position, but even those without it could look to the foreign powers, especially if they were Ottoman Christians accused of crimes against the state. How far a European government was prepared to go would usually depend on the level of public outrage at home, but the powers certainly had the capacity to compel the Ottoman government to release people who in their own country would have been prosecuted and jailed—even executed—for the crimes they had committed.

A Turkish Joris who tried to assassinate a European monarch, killing scores of people in the process, was hardly likely to have been released after two years in jail. There would have been no demands by the Ottoman government that he be tried in an Ottoman court. There would have been no cries of outrage at the sentencing and unfairness of the trial. Had there been, they would have been rejected out of hand, no doubt with an irritated snort—how dare they question the integrity of the European justice system!

Of course, the Ottoman legal system was wide open to criticism, but it was the law of the land, and, given that the government could not fully apply its own laws (however defective) in its own country, the capitulations were loathed, by the government and the Muslim public alike, generating resentment of the Christians who benefited from outside protection. European opposition to the threatened removal of this instrument of power from their hands was unbending, but the atmosphere of crisis created by Britain's seizure of the two ships in 1914 enabled action long contemplated.

On September 9, 1914, the grand vizier announced that the capitulatory regime would end on October 1: extraterritorial privileges were incompatible with national jurisdiction and sovereignty. The Europeans protested, none more angrily than the Ottoman government's new allies, Germany and Austria-Hungary, but in Istanbul and elsewhere across the empire the sultan's Muslim subjects poured into the streets to show their delight at the final removal of this European "yoke."

MOBILIZATION

Part of the leveling process after 1908 was the inclusion of non-Muslims for conscription. Many social or ethnoreligious groups were exempted from military service, including nomads, Yazidis, and religious figures—priests, rabbis, and the mosque functionaries (an imam, a muezzin, a *hafiz* or Qur'an reciter, and a caretaker allocated to each mosque)—needed to maintain religious life and public morale.[19] Previously able to pay an exemption tax, Christians were now faced with the same choices as Muslims: obediently accept conscription, evade it somehow, disappear after the call-up, or desert once recruited.

Erik-Jan Zürcher has observed that Christians felt themselves to be subjects of an Ottoman "nation" rather than its members, but there was no Ottoman nation as such.[20] The late nineteenth-century encouragement of an Ottoman sentiment embracing everyone irrespective of religious or ethnic background did not add up to conscious nation-building but was rather a tool intended to preserve the empire. Until very late in the day, this remained the objective of the Young Turks despite their emphasis on the Turkish element in the Ottoman imperial mix. It is unlikely that the vast bulk of Ottoman Muslims, with different ethnic roots and even adhering to different understandings of Islam, felt themselves to be members of a nation any more than Christians did.

In any case, once mobilization was declared, hundreds of thousands of young men were called up. Most came from Anatolia where they were the backbone of agricultural production. Mobilization was also applied to Iraq and Syria, but otherwise the Arab provinces remained untouched, as were remote regions where tribal authority was paramount and there was neither the "demographic control" or the state mechanism needed to be restored to impose recruitment on the local people.[21]

The military command calculated that about 2 million men (about 10 percent of the empire's population) could potentially be drafted for military service. On the basis of census statistics showing the number of men of fighting age, this might have been true, but nothing approaching such a number was ever mobilized. In reality, even the number of men serving at any one time was "drastically reduced by injury, illness, and desertion."[22]

By the end of September 1914, the military had 780,282 men under arms, a figure that declined as the war steadily took its toll of the soldiers serving on numerous fronts.[23] To the number of soldiers mobilized in the regular army must be added the paramilitary *jandarma*, various frontier forces, and volunteers among Caucasian and other Muslim *muhaciler* (refugees) who lacked the training given to regular soldiers and were often hard to control.[24]

The social implications of draining an empire of its young men, with the burden falling most heavily on the peasant population of Anatolia, will be discussed later, but even within its own limits, conscription was an ordeal for those called up. Conscripts would be instructed to carry enough food to last until they reached the recruitment center. Most would have to walk. Often, when they arrived, according to Beşikci, "local recruiting offices were not able to provide any supplies."[25] Newly enlisted men who could not be fed would be "sent home and told to return later."[26] There was likely to be insufficient barrack space for their accommodation, along with shortages of clothing as well as food. Even when the conscripts could be housed, they were likely to be crammed into rooms that were an incubator for diseases.[27]

A long tradition of Ottoman soldiers never being paid on time was maintained during the war. When pay did arrive, it would often be in the form of paper money that was disliked and distrusted by everyone into whose hands it fell. Soldiers might have no choice, but merchants and farmers often refused to accept it. When the Lebanese purchasing agent, Michel Sursock, sent his men into the Hawran to buy grain with paper money, the Druze and Arab growers told them to "go and tell your master that we would only sell our grain for gold and silver." They had to return to Beirut empty-handed.[28]

Certain groups were still able to pay a tax in lieu of exemption, but under a law passed in October 1916, conscription was permitted for those who had already paid the exemption tax; they were assured that the money would be returned later. Christians unsympathetic to the Ottoman government in the first place were likely to abscond or desert when called up. Some joined insurgent groups sabotaging the Ottoman war effort from behind the lines.

Hundreds of thousands of Muslims also deserted during the war, often taking their weapons with them. They could see what was coming and chose to live rough or turn to banditry rather than endure the rigors of military service. Some left to go home for the harvest or to look after families in need and, in particular, protect their womenfolk.

Government support for soldiers' families was never adequate, causing distress and resentment in the towns and villages from which they came. This can possibly be encapsulated in the demonstration by women in front of the War Ministry in July 1918. The women threw stones at the building, breaking windows, and crying, "Feed us or bring back our husbands or sons."[29] There were instances of Kurds in Dersim [Tunceli] and Harput [Elazığ] openly resisting the draft and disarming and scattering the conscription agents when they arrived.[30]

The core penalties for avoiding the draft or desertion were the same as in other armies: imprisonment or execution. In Jerusalem, the Syrian soldier Ihsan Turjman mentioned in his diary the hanging of two soldiers for desertion at the Jaffa Gate in March 1915, commenting, "What is a soldier supposed to do? The army pays each soldier 85 piastres a month and expects him to survive on it. Even then, most soldiers have not been paid one *matleek* [a fraction of one piaster] since the general call [November 1914]."[31] In Damascus, deserters were hanged in public, their bodies left exposed as a lesson and warning.

Distrust of Christians serving in the military had deep roots, given uprisings by Ottoman Christians and their support for or involvement in wars with Christian states going back to the Greek insurgency of the 1820s and even much earlier. On August 3, 1914, the War Ministry issued instructions that labor battalions, as far as possible, were to be formed from non-Muslims. Its concerns would seem to have been justified by armed Armenian resistance to conscription agents in Van and Zeytun between August and October.[32]

Provincial governors were already informing the central government that Armenians were receiving Russian weapons.[33] In late February 1915, following the Sarikamiş campaign, during which Armenian volunteer units supported the Russian army, Enver ruled that Armenians were to be excluded from all armed units. Some remained in the military throughout the war but usually as translators or medical personnel.[34]

BATTLEFIELD SKETCHES

The focus in "western" military histories is naturally on regions where allied armies were most deeply involved: Gallipoli, Mesopotamia, and Palestine. The "Arab revolt" instigated by the British, playing on the cupidity of the Sharif of Mecca, was no more than a sidebar, providing an exotic desert distraction from the horrors of mechanized warfare in France: sand, sun, palm trees, camels, and a straw-haired Englishmen dressed in dazzling white robes and a headpiece tailored to his specifications in Damascus instead of rain, mud, and rotting bodies in bomb craters on the western front. Fascination with the campaign at Gallipoli has never ended. Books on the campaign continue to appear in Britain and Australia, with military historians paying archival attention to the Ottoman view of the war only recently.

The surrender of General Townshend's expeditionary force at Kut al-Amara in 1916 and the entry of General Maude into Baghdad in 1917 after the retreat of Ottoman forces from Kut were the extremes of the Ottoman Mesopotamian campaign. There is much about these campaigns that has still only touched the surface of research. The resistance of Indian Muslims to fighting other Muslims, the Ottoman-British struggle for influence among the tribes, Shi'a resistance to conscription in Najaf and Karbala, and even just the weather, oppressively humid for much of the year and sucking the energy out of white troops from cold climates, all stand in further need of specialist studies.

Oil and domination of the gulf were prime considerations well ahead of the campaigning in Mesopotamia. The Palestine campaign—the Australian Light Horse racing across the desert at Beersheba and Allenby's entry into Jerusalem on December 11, 1917[35]—was colorful, but by this time the Ottoman ability to continue the war was already running out of steam.

The first six months of the war resulted in one failure for the Ottomans and one complete disaster. The failure was the drive across the Sinai toward the Suez Canal in February 1915; the disaster was the large-scale destruction of the Third Army at Sarıkamış, on the Caucasian front, the campaign ending about the same time.

The Suez operation was designed to tie up so much of the British force in Egypt that a landing at the straits would be out of the question.[36] Striking at the right point, it might be possible to cross the canal, establish a bridgehead, and capture Ismailia. Apart from any strategic achievements, an attack would demonstrate the empire's willingness to take on the British. The propaganda effect among Muslims was an important consideration: the presence of an Ottoman force on the canal might even encourage an Egyptian uprising. However, the operation was risky and a gamble even from the start.

Under the command of Lieutenant Colonel Friedrich Freiherr Kress von Kressenstein, chief of staff of the Eighth Corps of the Fourth Army, the Ottoman forces began moving forward on January 14, 1915, 25,000 men divided into two echelons. Logistical problems included finding 12,000 camels capable of carrying loads for the operation. These were brought in from as far as Najd along with regular soldiers and volunteers from the Hijaz.[37]

The troops set forth with a minimum of provisions: one kilogram per man, consisting of biscuits, dates, olives, and a gourd of water.[38] They marched during the day but only by moonlight as they drew closer to the canal. Logistics and numbers dictated that if the troops could not dig themselves in on the other side of the canal within four days they would have to withdraw.

In February, Ottoman troops crossed the canal but in daylight, later than planned, and were seen by the British.[39] They managed to establish a bridgehead of 600 men on the west bank, but already their positions were being shelled and their pontoon bridges destroyed. A second attempt to cross the canal was out of the question, and, with the Ottoman force now in an unsustainable position, the decision was taken to withdraw. After only two days, the troops began the march back to Beersheba (Bir Saba').

A gloss was put on the situation by describing the operation as a successful reconnaissance mission that had forced the British—expecting a second attack across the Sinai—to retain troops in Egypt, thus delaying the landing at Gallipoli.[40] The 600 men stuck on the other side of the canal were taken prisoner.

DISASTER IN THE MOUNTAINS

The disaster unfolding simultaneously on the other side of the empire was the decimation of the Ottoman Third Army in the battle of Sarıkamış.

The Ottoman advance on Sarıkamış was intended to clear the way to Kars, captured by Russia in the war of 1877–1878 and confirmed as a Russian possession in the Treaty of Berlin. The Kars *oblast* included the towns of Artvin, Ardahan, and Sarıkamış, just over 50 kilometers from Kars and close to the Ottoman border. The strategic route into Ottoman territory ran southwest through Horasan and Pasinler to the Ottoman garrison town of Erzurum, toward which the Russians had been advancing since the beginning of November 1914.

The Sarıkamış operation—an unexpected attack at the onset of winter, encircling the Russians, cutting off their retreat, and setting the scene for an advance on Kars—was Enver's idea. His apparent inspiration was the Battle of Tannenberg (August 26–30, 1914), when the German Eighth Army destroyed the Russian Second Army, with Russian casualties including 30,000 dead, but the differences were very great.

It was late summer when the battle of Tannenberg was fought in east Prussia and the onset of winter when Ottoman forces began advancing on Sarıkamış. The terrain was very different: lakes, swamps, and forests in east Prussia, which the Germans knew well from previous maneuvers, but towering mountains (3,000 meters or more) in northeastern Anatolia, unfamiliar to Ottoman troops. In winter, blizzards could quickly drive the temperature down to 40–50 degrees Celsius below freezing. Moreover, the German army could utilize a well-developed rail network to transport troops and supplies to the front whereas the Ottoman soldiers had to march. The German soldiers were well trained and equipped, compared to the Ottoman soldiers, who did not even have proper winter clothing.

The Ottoman offensive began on December 22. Snowfall slowed men and draft animals pulling artillery and supplies, but the campaign still opened well. The Ottoman forces reached Sarıkamış and within a week had come within "a hair's breadth" of trapping the Russian forces before a sudden change in the weather brought the offensive to a catastrophic end.[41]

Caught in mountain blizzards, the men began to freeze. Frostbite immobilized hands, and the severe cold quickly turned sandaled feet into blocks of ice. Groups of soldiers huddled together for warmth, but as hypothermia set in they fell asleep and died. An eight-minute film taken by British Pathé on the Caucasus front shows a seemingly endless line of crumpled bodies around a mountain trail. They are then seen being dumped over the side of wagons into trenches dug for burial.[42] Tens of thousands of soldiers simply froze to death.

With the weather halting the Ottoman advance, the Russians called in reinforcements and successfully counterattacked. Decimated through death or surrender the shattered Ottoman army pulled back. Thousands of soldiers and hundreds of officers had been captured. Enver praised the army for a campaign that "rivalled the glorious days of the Ottoman Empire."[43] In fact, it was more reminiscent of the worst days.

Failure during the planning stage to allow for the possibility of a dramatic change in the weather in such a hostile environment was a central reason for the Ottoman defeat. Enver's refusal to take the advice of experienced officers advocating pause and rest for their men rather than pushing ahead in such adverse conditions was probably another. Had the campaign succeeded, Enver would have entered history as one of the Ottoman empire's greatest military commanders. As it was, he will be remembered as the architect of perhaps its greatest battlefield disaster. By January 4, the Ottoman forces had begun to retreat. On January 8, Enver returned to Istanbul from Erzurum after reminding the troops "not to forget that Allah's help was with them all the time."[44]

Campaigning in the northeast and across the border into northwest Persia continued but from a severely weakened base. On December 22, 1914, the offensive capacity of the Third Army was given as 118,600 riflemen augmented by artillery and machine guns. By March 24, 1915, the number of fighting men had shrunk to 860 officers and 24,469 men.[45] Estimates of the dead from the Sarıkamış campaign fluctuate from 23,000 (the figure given in the official history of the Turkish army) to 90,000. A recently revised figure from the Turkish army puts overall losses at 60,000.[46] Thousands of men were captured and sent to prison camps in Siberia, and thousands more were wounded or listed as missing.

The Sarıkamış catastrophe, Michael Reynolds has written, deprived the Ottomans of "any strategic offensive capability in the Caucasus for three years. Not until 1918, after the disintegration of the Russian army, would the Ottomans be able to again mount substantial offensive operations."[47] Nevertheless, it can still be agreed that for the soldiers to get as far as they did in the most adverse conditions was a "remarkable achievement."[48]

TRIUMPH AT GALLIPOLI

The Gallipoli campaign in April was preceded by an Ottoman victory at sea. On March 18, a French and British flotilla set out to force the straits and sail into the Sea of Marmara all the way to Istanbul. They shelled Ottoman shore batteries as they entered the narrows. They thought they knew where the mines were, but their intelligence was outdated: a new line had been laid and the ships sailed straight into it. A French battleship was destroyed, while two British ships sank after being abandoned. Three others were badly damaged.

The failure of the sea offensive persuaded Britain to launch a land offensive on the Gallipoli (Gelibolu) peninsula. An attack on the straits was never intended to include the army: the naval operation was predicated on success and only because it failed did Secretary of State for War, Lord Kitchener, agree to the land operation, which initially he had vigorously opposed.[49]

For all that has been written about Gallipoli, there remain some historical curiosities. Theoretically a successful advance would have enabled the allies to link up with Russia in the Black Sea, but that was only the theory. Under the Constantinople Agreement, signed by Britain, Russia, and France on March 18, 1915 (the same day British and French ships were sinking in the straits), Russia's share of the territorial spoils when the war was won would include the Ottoman capital and the straits. This was such an extraordinary reversal of traditional British policy—as if the Great Game were ending in a surrender—that it can only be wondered what the British would have done had they actually succeeded at Gallipoli and moved on to the Ottoman capital. Would Britain have handed it over to Russia immediately (hardly likely) or held it in trust until the war was over, when changed circumstances might enable different policies?

The story of the Gallipoli landing a week after the naval defeat has been told a thousand times over and needs only noting rather than retelling. The significant exception in the narrative is perhaps the marginalized role of the 40,000 French troops, many of them Senegalese, sent to Gallipoli, suffering losses as heavy as the British and Australian and staying to the end. Gallipoli put Mustafa Kemal on the world stage for the first time. It was he who pulled Ottoman defenses together and held the line until reinforcements could arrive. Successive attempts by the allied forces to storm the heights failed before their final retreat (or "evacuation," to use the term favored in British and Australian histories) from December 1915–January 1916.

The withdrawal—or retreat—is portrayed as the one great Allied success of the campaign. A soldier quoted by military historian C. E. W. Bean remarks: "My goodness, if the Turks don't see this they must be blind."[50]

More than 100,000 men were pulled out of Anzac Cove and Suvla Bay in December and a further 35,000 from Cape Helles in January. In the official Allied narrative, an uplifting victory was snatched from the jaws of defeat, without any of the 100,000 Ottoman troops or their forward scouts on the heights above the Allied trenches realizing what was going on. Awareness apparently sruck them only at the last moment.[51] The Ottomans certainly knew when the evacuation was being completed from Cape Helles and made some attempt to hinder it, but perhaps by this time they were just glad to see the enemy go.

THE SIEGE OF KUT

In Mesopotamia, a British force had landed at Basra in November 1914. By April 1915, the Sixth (Poona) Division, under the command of General Charles Townshend, was inflicting such heavy defeats on the Ottoman forces that their commander, Süleyman Askeri Paşa, shot himself. Encouraged by their victories, the British advanced up the Tigris River toward Baghdad. Overwhelming the Ottoman garrison at Kut al-Amara in late September, the British continued north to Salman Pak, some 25 miles south of Baghdad. Here, the Ottoman force had dug in and after three days of fighting in November, with heavy losses on both sides, the British were forced to retreat to Kut al-Amara.

Anticipating a siege, Townshend laid in two months' supply of food for his 11,800 troops and fodder for the stock animals. By early December, the Ottomans had encircled the town. Townshend made no attempt to break out, and all attempts of a relief force from Basra to break in failed.[52] More than 1,000 pack animals were killed to feed the British soldiers, but there were no greens and by March, 1916, hundreds of soldiers had come down with scurvy. Almost no food was left. At first, Indian colonial troops—including Punjabis, Pathans, Sikhs, Rajputis, Muslims, Hindus, Jats, and Gurkhas—refused to eat meat, despite the exemption authorized by their princes. By mid-April, however, with their entire food allowance reduced to a handful of flour, they finally began eating horsemeat. Many had already died, and others were too weak to survive.[53]

By April 27, with fifteen troops dying a day and no grain at all now, either for the troops or the town's civilian population, Townshend attempted to negotiate terms of surrender with the Ottoman commander, Halil Paşa, "knowing I had not a biscuit up my sleeve to argue with."[54]

Given the lack of food, this was probably the literal truth. Townshend offered Halil a payment of 1 million pounds plus a guarantee that his troops would not fight the Ottomans again if he would let them go. Enver was informed and insisted on unconditional surrender.[55]

More than 13,000 British and colonial troops (mostly Indian) were marched into prisoner-of-war camps in Anatolia, 70 percent dying before the war ended. This was "the largest mass surrender of Imperial troops between Yorktown in 1783 and Singapore" and a "horrible embarrassment" for the British, writes Erickson.[56]

Townshend saw out the rest of the war from the Sea of Marmara islands of Heybeliada and Büyükada (Prinkipo), the second of which, a few years later, was the temporary resting place of Leon Trotsky. Townshend could hardly be regarded as a prisoner. He was received by the sultan and knighted by the king during his absence. The islands are beautiful, and Townshend's living conditions (including the use of a yacht) were so comfortable that he asked his wife to join him (she declined). He had asked Halil Paşa to look after his fox terrier, Spot, and when he returned to his home in Norfolk the dog was waiting for him.

Kut al-Amara and Gallipoli were the greatest Ottoman victories. In northeastern Anatolia, they steadily lost ground to the Russians who in February 1916, overran Erzurum. The Ottoman defenders burnt the government *konak* and some military buildings before retreating.[57] The Russians captured the Black Sea port of Trabzon in April. Bayburt and Erzincan followed in July. Van had fallen to the Russians in May 1915, after a successful Armenian uprising. Ottoman forces reentered the town in late July but soon retreated and were unable to return permanently until 1918.

In northwest Persia, the Russians overwhelmed the Ottomans in the battle of Dilman (April 1915). Campaigning continued across the region with heavy losses on both sides. By 1916, Ottoman forces were fighting in Macedonia, Rumania, and Galicia, with the "Arab revolt," led by Lawrence and Sharif Husain's son Faisal, opening a new front the same year.

In early 1917, Ottoman armies held their ground against two major British attacks in Gaza but in Mesopotamia were forced to withdraw from Kut al-Amara. British forces were then able to continue upriver to Baghdad where their commander, General Sir Frederick Stanley Maude, proclaimed the city's "liberation" on March 11: "Our armies do not come into your cities and lands as conquerors or enemies but as liberators."[58]

In October, the British broke Ottoman defenses at Beersheba and forced a fighting retreat of the Yildirim army group from Gaza. Jerusalem was surrendered on December 9. Two days later, General Allenby walked into the city through the Jaffa gate at the head of a representative contingent of British troops who had fought under his command. A cordon was placed around the central Muslim sanctuary, the Haram al-Sharif, and non-Muslims were forbidden from entering without the permission of the military and Muslim religious authorities.

BLACK OPERATIONS

Many more battlefield sketches could be written but one more at least warrants attention: the largely undercover role of the Teşkilat. The organization had numerous forerunners in Ottoman history, with a number of individuals who had been involved in intelligence or counterinsurgency missions in the Balkans or North Africa from 1908–1913 eventually turning up in its ranks. Brought under the aegis of the War Ministry by Enver in 1914, the Teşkilat was initially set up as a Department of Eastern Affairs with a mandate covering propaganda and intelligence work in eastern Anatolia and the Arab provinces of the empire, the Caucasus, Central Asia, Iran, Afghanistan, and India.[59]

These activities were not so different from the operations being carried out by Germany, Russia, and Britain across the same span of territories, but in conditions of war the locus of the Teşkilat's activities soon shifted to counterinsurgency and black operations near or behind enemy lines. The organization was well funded and took care of the families of its members with food and loans. It also had to pay agents, which meant competing with the British or the Russians in the same field. Senior members, or *ikhwan* (brothers), included Enver himself, along with a number of distinguished army officers (Süleyman Askeri and Halil Paşa, the victor at Kut al-Amara, among them), as well as individuals who had been prominent in political life or were to rise to prominence during the early years of the Turkish Republic. Others included Arab nationalists who were hardly going to support the allied war effort when Britain and France occupied their lands. Where Sharif Husayn of Mecca gambled on an allied victory, they hoped the German-Ottoman alliance would triumph.

Influential Arab figures connected with the Teşkilat included Nuri al-Said, an officer on the Ottoman general staff who crossed to the allied side after his capture and, as Prime Minister of Iraq, later became a central pillar of British influence in the Middle East. Stanford Shaw has estimated that at its height the *ikhwan* had about 30,000 "fighters or supporters" under its command.[60]

Given the demand for manpower at the front, the senior figures in the Teşkilat had to find recruits where they could. Refugees from the Caucasus were especially valuable because they were likely to have a sound knowledge of the terrain behind the lines if sent there. Some units were formed through the diversion of men eligible for conscription but not yet called up. Otherwise, volunteers came from many sources, including tribes and ethnic minority groups (such as Circassians, Kurds, and Laz), pious Muslims outraged by news of the atrocities committed against Muslims as the Russian army advanced, and educated professionals (doctors, engineers, journalists, and retired army officers) who served more in leadership positions.[61]

The darker sources of recruitment were bandit gangs who saw an official opportunity to carry on their trade and prisoners offered a commutation of their sentence if they volunteered their services. Many were in prison for minor offences, others were deserters, and some had been sentenced for murder. Despite the risks, life in the Teşkilat was a far better option than life in prison. The background of such people was ideally suited to the dirty work at hand, if also a main reason why regular military commanders wanted nothing to do with them. Lacking discipline, the Teşkilat bands "often acted [as] little more than bandits, ravaging villages and roads in Ottoman as well as enemy territory."[62]

The organization has frequently been given a leading role in the "relocation" of the Armenians and held largely responsible for the crimes committed against the convoys as they were being moved south. In fact, while some Teşkilat members were involved and held to account at wartime courts-martial, the movement of the Armenians was a much broader operation, involving provincial officials at the organizational level and an assortment of paramilitary forces following their instructions, "most likely" local police and gendarmerie units composed largely of Circassian and Kurdish tribesmen.[63]

CHAPTER 11

A Land in Despair

UNDERSTANDING WHY THE OTTOMAN EMPIRE was in such a weakened state by 1914, and why there was such collapse at various levels afterward, means returning to the cost of all the wars it had fought since the 1850s and all the uprisings it had to suppress. In 1914, about one third of government revenue was still being sequestered by the foreign-run Ottoman Public Debt Administration, established in 1881 to pay off European bondholders. Even with the best of intentions, the state did not have the revenue base needed to establish a modern state and society.

In terms of military needs, while a gunpowder and cartridge factory had been established in the late nineteenth century at Zeytinburnu, beside the Sea of Marmara, the empire was almost completely dependent on the importation of mostly German foreign weaponry. To fight well, however, a soldier also needs proper clothing, accommodation, a regular supply of decent food, and a health and sanitation system that protects him from illness and disease. In the premodern Ottoman Empire, many of these basics were missing when soldiers went to war.[1]

In an empire whose territories were regularly stricken with outbreaks of epidemic diseases, an awareness of the root causes led to health and sanitary improvements designed to head them off in the first place. As the Hijaz and its holy cities were part of the Ottoman Empire, the annual *hajj* was a testing time for the authorities. Many of the *hujjaj* (pilgrims) came from as far away as Java (Indonesia), Central Asia, and even China. They might arrive with an epidemic disease and transmit it in Mecca and

Medina or leave with it and infect others on the way home (if they did not die first, an additional honor for those making the pilgrimage).

Quarantine stations were set up to monitor ships moving between Ottoman ports, with vessels that had previously docked at a port where cholera or some other outbreak had been reported delayed for days until passengers were cleared by medical inspection. Because rats were regarded as carriers of disease, docks, granaries, and storehouses were inspected, but to properly eliminate the outbreak of plague diseases, Ottoman health authorities realized that the general standards of housing, sewage, sanitation, drainage, and water supply would have to be improved. While the Hijaz remained a priority, because of the *hajj*, their attention also turned to cities whose decaying infrastructures needed replacement or repair to meet the needs of a rapidly expanding urban population "to get rid of the filth that allows rats into a city" and spread epidemic diseases.[2]

These improvements only went so far. In Istanbul, muck of all descriptions—sullied household water and the offal and blood discharged from tanneries—poured into the *halic*, the estuary running inland from the Golden Horn, topping up what was already there from previous centuries. The stench of human waste was still there in the 1980s when a start was finally made in cleaning up the waters of the *halic* and the Bosporus.

Outside the cities, most markedly in the eastern provinces, there was little or no change. In towns and villages, rubbish accumulated in the streets and filth flowed through open drains, attracting flies and mosquitoes. Contaminated drinking water contributed to the spread of disease. The general level of health was poor. Smallpox, malaria, and tuberculosis were prevalent in many parts of the country as were many other diseases. In 1918, the American Committee for Armenian and Syrian Relief estimated that in some villages, 80–90 percent of the people were infected with syphilis.[3]

A problem specific to Istanbul was fire. Thousands of the wooden buildings dominating the hills were destroyed in the years leading up to 1914, and many more were to burn down during the war.

Whereas the Europeans were fighting a modern war in a modern environment, the Ottoman Empire fought a modern war largely in a premodern setting, with almost none of the infrastructure needed to support the war as well as the needs of the civilian population. Edward Erickson, writing that the army was "ill-equipped to fight a modern war," has drawn out some of the details: shortages of field guns, howitzers, machine guns (sometimes none at all at the battalion and company level), rifles, and ammunition; "chronic shortages of doctors, medicine and medical supplies,"[4] extending to food and clothing, and accounting for the photos of soldiers dressed in tattered uniforms, with makeshift footwear fashioned from rags or the hide of animals they had killed for food.[5] The boots and greatcoats of fallen Russian soldiers were highly prized and likely to be taken from dead bodies on the battlefield.

Even in harsh wintry conditions, some Ottoman soldiers only had sandals. In Palestine, one contingent could not advance across stony ground because it had no footwear at all. An honor guard for the German commander, Liman von Sanders, included soldiers wearing torn boots or shoes "while others were barefoot."[6] Stripping the bodies of dead British and Indian soldiers was their only opportunity "to find clothes, shoes and underwear." Prohibitions against seizing the clothing of the dead "bore no fruit."[7]

In the autumn of 1915, the Third Army Command sent a desperate message to the Supreme Military Command, informing it of the problems certain to arise from inadequate clothing and requesting "the immediate supply of as many greatcoats, shoes, clothes and tents as possible." But what the army did not have it could not provide, and, depending on where they had been sent, soldiers continued to freeze to death even in relatively warm weather in early spring.[8]

Even by the winter of 1916, many of the soldiers still had only summer clothing. "They don't have shoes and greatcoats. Most of the time they are wrapping rags around their feet, but of course that doesn't help much. Their feet remain naked anyway. The daily food supply is only one third of the suggested daily intake. The faces of the soldiers reflect their malnutrition."[9]

This report is not exceptional but rather representative of what the military command was being told by officers in the field. Food shortages extended even to the lack of bread. "With no food to eat," one NCO wrote, "the soldiers had been forced to walk for 15 hours with only a 30-minute break. Some were forced to do a five-hour armed guard duty while others were forced to stand on their feet for 20 hours. Everyone's feet were swollen and bloody. This wretched nation, these wretched soldiers . . . you would have to be an animal to look at them without crying."[10] In a village without water, so cold and snowing so heavily it was hard to stand, the soldiers "drink from the dirty water that had accumulated in the holes left by animals' shoes."[11]

Military shortages extended to supply wagons and draft animals, with motorization and aviation in the armed forces "almost non-existent."[12] Even if there had been more motorized capability, there were few roads able to support such vehicles. In particular, "roads" in the eastern provinces were mostly dirt tracks. Railways were an extremely limited transport option. Whereas France had laid its first railway line in the 1820s (British railway history goes back even further), the first line in the Ottoman empire, between Izmir and Aydın, was not constructed until 1860. While the government laid some lines, most were constructed by foreign companies, British, French, or German.

Railway construction in the Balkans, especially the Orient Express connection between western European capitals and Istanbul, was commercially attractive to foreign concessionaires and strategically important to the Ottoman government. The loss of the region in the 1912–1913 war left the empire with about 3,000 kilometers of railway line, compared to the tens of thousands of kilometers of integrated networks in France and Germany.

What this meant during the coming war was that whereas French or German soldiers could be transported close to the front lines, Ottoman soldiers frequently had to march hundreds of kilometers, often in difficult conditions across rugged terrain. Supplies would have to be carried on camels or bullock-drawn wagons along dirt tracks that quickly turned to glutinous mud in winter.

Logistics problems were particularly severe in the east. In the southeast, the break in the rail connection at Pozantı, the entrance to the Taurus mountains, meant that all goods had to be unloaded and carried through a mountain pass by pack animals until the line started again. Different gauges between different parts of the empire complicated transport even where there was a railway.

EPIDEMIC DISEASES

Reference has already been made to the enormous loss of life among soldiers and civilians from epidemic diseases in wartime, from the Crimea in the 1850s to the Balkans in the 1870s and to the Balkans again in 1912–1913, when the medical sector was as unprepared for another war as the military. To meet urgent needs, the Ottoman Red Crescent Society (Osmanlı Hilal-i Ahmer Cemiyeti) opened hospitals in Istanbul and

Gelibolu (Gallipoli) with all necessary staff and material provisions. More hospitals and clinics were opened across the empire after the First World War broke out, but supplies still fell well short of civilian and military demand. Shortages were particular acute in the eastern provinces, the hub of some of the biggest campaigns of the war. During winter, many villages in the mountainous regions were effectively sealed off from the rest of the country by meters of snow. The privations people had to endure as a daily fact of life are hard to imagine in a context where pharmacies, hospitals, a transport system, and other conveniences of modern life are taken for granted.

The death toll from diseases during Ottoman wars in the nineteenth century was extremely high. During the Crimean War (1853–1856), 24,500 soldiers died from disease compared to 10,100 in combat. The loss of life among both soldiers and civilians during the war with Russia (1877–1878) was even more calamitous, running into multiple tens of thousands: 300 to 500 people died every day just in Istanbul, apart from deaths in other towns or at the front. Extreme heat, lack of basic sanitation, and the number of refugees traversing Ottoman lands encouraged the spread of disease. Hospitals could not cope with the number of patients, and cemeteries did not have enough space to bury the dead. Old graves had to be opened to allow the interment of more bodies. If graves were not dug deeply enough, the stench could be appalling.[13]

In the Balkan War of 1912–1913, spotted fever, cholera, and dysentery killed tens of thousands of soldiers and civilians at the front, on the way to Istanbul, or in the city if they managed to arrive without being stopped at quarantine stations.

During the First World War, young men called into armed service often had to march to the front with inadequate supplies of food or water to sustain them on the way. For many, death from disease or malnutrition ended their war before it started. Of 10,000 troops who left Istanbul for Palestine, only 4,635 made it, the rest deserting or succumbing to illness.[14] Compared to British, French, German, and Russian statistics, the Ottoman military death toll was low, but civilian deaths were much higher.

With a population of 45.4 million, Britain suffered 885,138 military deaths; France, at 39.6 million, 1,397,800; Russia, with a population of more than 160 million, lost 1,811,000; Germany, with a population base of 64.9 million, 2,050,897. Civilian deaths in Britain amounted to 109,000; in France about 300,000; in Germany, 700,000; and in Russia,

1,500,000.[15] The main causes of death were disease, malnutrition, and the 1918–1919 Spanish flu pandemic, along with deaths resulting from military operations.

The Ottoman population in 1914, with the administrative districts of Baghdad, Basra, and Mosul uncounted, was 18,520,016.[16] Military losses of 771,844 between 1914 and 1918 included 305,085 dead (killed in action, dying of wounds, or missing) and 466,759 deaths from disease, substantially higher than the number of combat deaths. Some 68,000 Ottoman soldiers died from disease at Gallipoli alone, but the numbers were high everywhere. To these numbers[17] must be added those among the estimated 500,000 deserters who may have died from disease (or other causes such as malnutrition and exposure) or the badly wounded who may have died sometime later.

Because the empire was drawn into new wars immediately after the First World War ended, civilian deaths can only be estimated. The loss of territories where reliable statistics are unavailable further complicates the picture. In 1919, the Istanbul newspaper *Tasvir-i Efkar* (*Depiction of Ideas*) reported that of the 1,604,031 Muslims who fled from Russian and Armenian operations in the east, 701,166, or 42 percent, died on the way from various causes, including massacre, disease, and malnutrition.[18] These were just the registered refugees, so the real number would undoubtedly have been much higher. The *vali* of Erzurum said that in his province, of the 448,607 people who had fled, only 173,304 returned after the war.[19]

Analyzing the demographics, Justin McCarthy has arrived at an estimate of 1,190,000 Muslim civilian deaths in eastern Anatolia between 1914 and 1921, and 1,250,000 Muslim deaths in western Anatolia from 1914 to 1922, this period including the Greek invasion.[20] These figures do not include the number of Muslims who died in Transcaucasia during the fighting that followed the war.

Taking into account the death toll among other ethnoreligious groups during this period, beginning with Armenians (to be evaluated later in this study), Assyrians, and Greeks and counting also deaths from the Spanish influenza pandemic of 1918, civilian deaths during the war were clearly more than 3 million. Including military casualties, the death toll reaches about 4 million—by any measure a calamity of epic proportions that remains largely understudied.[21]

Looking at the outcome of all the wars fought between the Ottoman Empire and its enemies from the 1820s to 1922, and preferring low estimates, Justin McCarthy has calculated that about 5.5 million Muslims died and upward of 5 million were turned into refugees.[22] These estimates do not include the unknown numbers of people whose deaths or disappearances were never recorded.

IMPROVISED CLINICS

The most detailed work on the effects of disease on the Ottoman military has been done by Hikmet Özdemir. There were insufficient hospitals, insufficient numbers of medical staff, supplies, and beds. Hospitals were so overcrowded that soldiers often had to share beds or lie on the floor in wards or corridors. Soldiers with physical injuries were mixed with those suffering from infectious diseases.[23]

The need for sanitation, sterilization, and quarantine was hardly understood below the level of the medical staff. Soldiers might still be infested with lice or fleas, tiny insects that made life hell and survived all extremes of weather—unlike many of the soldiers. Washing and cleaning was minimal, and the stench arising from the combination of all these elements could be overpowering. Some "hospitals" were no more than hastily improvised clinics. In one shattered village, "only the stables were left to be used as a hospital."[24] Patients lay on beds resting on the earthen floor or slept directly on the earth. Healthy soldiers might be housed in barns with comrades suffering from typhus who died in the night, or they might be put up in damp, mud-brick dwellings at a time of extreme cold, falling ill as a result.

Arriving in one village, ravenous soldiers ate as much food as they could, mostly butchered livestock, and then used the streets as open-air latrines. The human waste was not only grossly obnoxious, making the streets impassable, but spread diseases from the serving men to the officers, with the number of those taken ill increasing by the day. The officer filing this account finally returned home after the war only to find his wife had died of typhus: "The whole world came crashing down on me. . . . I cursed my luck for not having died in battle."[25] Deaths of wives and other family members must have been the experience of many returning soldiers.

Another army officer, Halil Ataman, wrote of what he witnessed in the province of Sivas: "At the time there were carts driven by oxen coming from Suşehir. We could not believe what we saw. In every cart there were 5–6 clothed soldier corpses whose arms and legs were dangling [off the carts].... I was able to count the carts ... one, two, three, eight, yes, there were indeed eight carts full of soldier corpses."

Entering Suşehir, Ataman went to the town mosque, whose courtyard was filled with sick soldiers mingled with the bodies of some who were dead. Underscoring the two-way transmission of diseases between soldiers and civilians, his detachment is warned: "Leave this place at once, do not take anything, do not eat anything or even drink the water. This place is completely sick. I am the town's *kaymakam* [subgovernor], go on brothers, get out of this place at once."

The soldiers were met with the same message by the *kaymakam* at Refahiye: "Welcome to our township, but I am obliged to ask you to leave at once because there is an epidemic here. Seventy-eight people are falling ill each day and we are afraid that it will become worse. Do not buy any food from here and do not even drink the water."

Reaching the Narman district of Erzurum province, Ataman was met with even worse sights.

> I cannot stop myself from writing about Narman. It is very painful, but I am of the opinion that it is unfortunately necessary to speak about real national disasters. First of all, Narman is a miserable wreck of a village. I do not know how I am going to recount it, what I am about to recount is heart-wrenching, difficult to believe.... I was so shaken when I first saw it [the situation in Narman] that I was almost unable to remain standing and collapsed to the ground.
>
> At the entrance to the village one could see a huge pile of corpses, 80, maybe 100 meters in length. This lengthy pile is made up of the corpses of 2,500 or maybe more brave soldiers put on top of one another. Again, at the same place, there are more than 100 soldiers waiting with digging tools by a previously dug hole 50 meters in length and 15–20 meters deep. They were going to fill this hole with the piled-up corpses and cover it with earth. I asked them why they were waiting and they said, "The regiment's imam is coming to lead the [funeral] prayers, we are waiting for him."

The soldiers had not been killed in battle but had died of disease, and the grave Ataman was looking at was the fourth. "'See those high places that look like hills? Those are graves, too.'"[26]

The Erzurum region town of Nihan was still affected by the consequences of the Sarıkamış disaster when reserve officer Faik Tonguç arrived early in March 1915.[27] Mass graves had been dug and filled or were waiting to be filled. Houses were full of the sick and wounded. The soldiers had brought typhus and typhoid with them, and villages had been decimated by disease. Only the elderly seemed to be left.

The most shocking scenes awaited Tonguç in the village of Id, where the dead still lay in houses and the military barracks and where, walking through the muddy streets, "it was impossible not to step on the arm or leg of a corpse that had yet to be buried due to lack of time." Dogs "with terrifying stares" had grown fat from eating the dead. These were memories "that paralyzed one's emotions and thoughts and would never be erased from the mind for as long as one lived."[28]

Many doctors contracted the epidemic diseases they were trying to cure. Typhus alone killed a large number, along with other medical personnel. The death rate among officers and commanders was also high, while recurrent typhus epidemics alone killed tens of thousands of soldiers. Cholera, spotted fever, and dysentery added to these numbers on all fronts. Moreover, all these diseases jumped the front lines (if they had not already crossed from the other direction) and infected the enemy as well. In 1915, an American relief committee later estimated, typhus fever alone had killed 200,000–300,000 people.[29]

After Sarıkamış, the villages on the plains of northeastern Anatolia were "flooded by ill, disabled, and exhausted soldiers."[30] Hospitals were overwhelmed, with soldiers sent home on sick leave then spreading spotted fever and other diseases as they traveled. At Erzurum, when the sick could no longer be accommodated, many of them were sent to outlying villages, carrying their diseases with them, as Faik Tonguç and other officers discovered when moving across the region. In some places, the earth was frozen too hard for bodies to be buried.

To the numbers of civilians who died from disease, malnutrition, and general exposure, or were killed in intercommunal fighting, must be added those who froze to death after fleeing their towns and villages during a harsh winter. In eastern Anatolia, a large number of civilians fled the town of Bitlis ahead of the Russian advance in the summer of 1915. Returning after the Russian retreat, they fled a second time when the Russians advanced again in February 1916. Meters of snow lay on the ground, and snow was still falling when they set off. Some were so exhausted that they abandoned infant children by the roadside or under bridges, with an estimated 1,000 children dying of exposure within 50–60 kilometers of the city.[31]

SQUEEZING THE CIVILIANS

Over four years, the Ottoman Empire was bled almost dry of the means of survival: the balance between life support for the military and the civilian population always had to tilt toward the military if the war was to be won. Powers of requisition were given to a war-tax commission (*tekalif-i harbiye*), which operated branches across the empire. Its agents—*muhtarlar* or other *ayanlar* (notables)—were authorized to requisition whatever they thought necessary for the military, including land, buildings, means of transportation (mostly wagons and ox carts), businesses, goods held in depots and warehouses, food estimated to be in excess of civilian needs, and 50 percent of farm animals (mostly sheep, oxen, and goats[32] but also donkeys, mules, and camels) needed for food or transportation. Along the way, corrupt agents were not above making some profit for themselves.

Three zones of provisioning were established to meet military and civilian needs: central Anatolia, Istanbul, and the Arab provinces, with the army left to forage in regions not covered. The system worked so poorly in civilian hands that by 1916 the military was being instructed to supervise the collection of grain. By 1917, it had been given full responsibility for provisioning.

Requisitions extended to luxury goods, including silk stockings, caviar, and champagne. Clothing, from petticoats to children's clothing and shoes, was also seized. Rules and regulations did little to stop bullying and corruption by government agents and police. Accounts from across the empire suggest a high level of arrogance and disrespect at one end of the spectrum and cruelty and exploitation at the other. Scant consideration was shown for the real needs of the urban and rural population. The food allowed for household sustenance was often insufficient and the prices paid for expropriated goods always well below the real value—if paid at all.

Excessive grain seizures were the subject of frequent complaints. Most farmers operated on a very small scale: they had modest plots of land and even at the best of times never lived far above subsistence level. They could feed their families and perhaps make a small profit, but their lives were dependent on factors over which they had no control, market and weather fluctuations just two among many. In practice, requisitioning was so extreme that it was close to self-defeating. The seizure of farm animals and the conscription of young men needed for farm labor had devastating effects on the rural population from the Black Sea borders down to

Syria. The expropriation of grain and other crops reduced the peasant population to destitution. Farmers were left with little incentive (other than unquestioning loyalty to the government) to stay on the land.

Given that armies march on their stomachs, the severity of these expropriations undermined the war effort in the long term. The consequences, especially the shortage of farm labor, could be seen in the shrinking of the agricultural sector: the area under cultivation across the empire (but mainly in Anatolia and Syria) fell from 60 million *dunams* (about 15 million acres) in 1914 to 30 million in 1915 and 24 million by 1916.[33]

Farmers often did not hesitate to take their grievances to officials. Akın quotes the observations of the Sinop (Black Sea) parliamentary deputy Hasan Fehmi Efendi.

> Whomever I talked to said that for the sake of the country's salvation and as a sign of the sacrifice that was imposed on us by the nation "I had sent my father, brother, son," in brief ten or fifteen people from my family and relatives to the war. The news about the martyrdom of five, six, or seven of them reached us. Three or four of them are living with us, having been maimed in the war. Two of them have been taken prisoner. A couple are still at the fronts. Although I was deprived of all manpower, I managed to produce ten kilos of wheat, which was taken from me, disregarding my need for seed to plant three months from now, fodder for the draft animals that I employ in my fields and finally, my need for wheat for sustenance. I was not paid for any of this.[34]

Compounding the suffering involved in these exactions, peasants would be required to take the grain to government depots with the wagons and draft animals left to them after the requisition agents had removed the best of their stock. These journeys were likely to turn into a nightmare, with sick animals dying on the way, children and the elderly suffering from hunger and exposure, and the whole family exposed to attacks by bandit gangs out to take the grain for themselves. When farmers arrived at the depot, corrupt officials were likely to sequester some of the grain for their own profit.[35]

Similar accounts of the rural and urban population being bullied and exploited by officials and *jandarma* came from across the empire. These agents of the state would simply demand entry into homes, shops, and storehouses and take what they wanted, down to pots and pans in the kitchen, presumably to be melted down for the war effort but just as likely to be sold for a small profit. Like many others, poorly paid officials and police had to survive. Some would seize whatever opportunities came their way: villagers complained to army officers that they were being robbed and that no one cared for them. "It could be seen that they were swimming in poverty. Our hearts were aching."

At the same time, soldiers could be as bullying or thoughtless as any official, taking what they wanted from villagers unless or until their officers intervened. The *Hamidiye* cavalry remained notorious for their indiscipline. An NCO describes them as "good for nothing besides looting... [they] heed no officer... they are all ignorant... they shoot volleys whenever they see the enemy even if they are 5,000 meters away. They flee when the enemy approaches. Later they cut down, take and eat whatever they find in the villages that they enter. In short, every kind of sin is permissible for them."[36] They also absconded in large numbers. Even before the end of 1914, this soldier wrote after speaking to their commander, desertions had reduced the ranks from 38,000 to 7,000.[37]

PROFITEERING

Profiteering middlemen and the rich enjoying life as usual are part of the general story. Given the concession for wheat requisitioning across Syria, Michel Sursock, the scion of a wealthy Greek Orthodox family, was accused of hoarding grain and manipulating prices, connected and common practices among unscrupulous merchants. In the summer of 1918, when Syria was still gripped by famine, Sursock was said to be refusing to sell grain he had bought for 40 piasters a measure for less than 250 piasters, "even to save at least a portion of the children fed by the American relief organization."[38] Whether he died of typhus or perhaps was murdered remains unclear.[39]

In general, like all wars, the First World War created opportunities for a predatory class of wealthy entrepreneurs, corrupt officials, and greedy merchants. Writing from Istanbul, a German journalist observed, "Even at the end of 1916, with a population of well over a million, there were still unlimited stores of everything available for those who could pay fancy prices while by the beginning of 1915 those less well endowed with worldly goods had quite forgotten the meaning of comfort and the poor were starving with ample stores of everything still available."[40]

Food shortages began to appear the moment the war began. Partly this was because the military had priority over the use of transport; partly it was also because corrupt officials would refuse to shift supplies until they had been paid their cut; and partly it was because growers and contractors could not agree on prices. As a result, shipments of grain from the Syrian interior (the Hawran) to the coastal regions were frequently delayed. The urban population was worst affected as the mountain population had farm animals and could grow much of their own food for immediate consumption. The combined effects of shortages and hoarding by contractors and merchants were so severe that by February 19, 1916, Beirut had only five days of wheat and flour left.[41]

Wastage was also part of the story: consignments of sugar, grain, and cement were stored in the open while awaiting transport. In peacetime, primary produce was sold as soon as it was picked or harvested, so there was no need for depots; in wartime, perishable goods exposed to the elements while waiting to be moved were often ruined.

Attempts by Cemal Paşa, the governor of Syria, to ensure continuity of supplies were hampered by the nature of the system. Prices were supposed to be fixed, but farmers were compelled to deal with contractors who ignored regulations and forced them to give up grain they needed for their own survival. The contractors were likely to release a small portion for sale and withhold the bulk until prices rose. Third-grade wheat would be sold to the people for the price of first-grade or would not be sold at all. Millers and the bakers shared in these profit-seeking arrangements. By the middle of 1916, the situation was so disastrous that police seized mills and bakeries in Beirut and began distributing adulterated bread to the people, at first 250 grams a day per person, soon reduced to three days a week. Even this emergency measure was corrupted by the officer in charge: arrested, charged and sentenced to death, he shot himself in prison the day before he was to be hanged.[42]

"CAST US INTO THE SEA"

As might be expected, women were on the sharp end of war exactions.[43] They were idealized as the mothers of the nation and a central pillar of morale on the home front while having to assume responsibilities well beyond their traditional roles. Rural women had to run the farms in the absence of men. They had to plant, harvest, and take crops to market, exposing themselves to approaches by men, no doubt especially so if they were young. Frequently they were also required to transport food, ammunition, and other necessities to military depots, even while caring for children and perhaps elderly parents. Deprived of the usual protection of men, whether in the cities or rural areas, the war left many women destitute, desperate, and vulnerable to assault, including rape. In villages close to the front, they had to put up with soldiers billeted in their homes, eating their food, and exposing them to disease.

The mere entry of unknown men into the family home transgressed cultural values. At the end of this spectrum, lay the sexual violence that made no distinction between ethnic or religious boundaries. The knowledge that their womenfolk were exposed to the assaults of other men (including officials) and the need to protect them was clearly one reason for soldiers deserting, even at the risk of execution if caught.

As described by Yiğit Akın, the cumulative effects of war on their lives prompted ten women from a small village on the Black Sea coast to send a telegram of complaint to Talat Paşa on December 31, 1917. Describing themselves as the wives or mothers of soldiers, they "bitterly complained about the increasingly harsh policies of state and military officials, and the prevalence of poverty and hunger." Their flocks and farm animals had been expropriated for military needs. They had to run farms without the seed grain they needed for crops yet were under constant pressure to supply the military. People barely had clothes to put on their back and shoes on their feet. Accordingly, these women asked the minister of the interior to be moved to some other place or "cast us into the sea."[44]

Everywhere, social structures and moral standards were upended. In the cities, middle-class women might be reduced to selling their furniture or work as housemaids or charwomen. In desperation, some women turned to prostitution, which, large-scale and unregistered, Çiğdem Oğuz writes, "came to be considered as part of daily life," taking on "new forms," according to Ahmed Emin (Yalman), so that it became more common among Muslim women than non-Muslims.[45] Brothels were regulated and streetwalkers banned, to the extent of being banished from cities to distant locations with no rail link to the cities. Apart from the damage to moral standards, government control was driven by the need to curtail the spread of venereal disease.

Protecting women, augmenting the slender payments the state was able to make to families, and creating a workforce that could help meet military needs were the chief motives behind the establishment in 1916 of the Society for the Employment of Ottoman Muslim Women.[46] The organization acted as a conduit for channeling female labor into state or private workshops where they produced clothing, bedding, and such items for military use as sandbags, as well as fulfilling a moral responsibility by encouraging single women to marry. In 1917, under the aegis of the society, the War Ministry created a Women's Workers Brigade, which operated as an ancillary unit to the army, mostly engaged in clerical work once it was discovered that city women (the brigade was founded in Istanbul) were unsuitable for physical labor. Thousands of women eventually found work through the society, with their small salaries helping them to get through the war. The society opened avenues of employment that were previously closed to women, but as men were in charge at all levels, "It was definitely not a women's organization as some feminist writers of our day have argued."[47]

The consequences of war on the lives of the civilian population can partly be charted through inflation and price increases, which the state never managed to control, driven by shortages growing more extreme the longer the war continued. Food and fuel prices soon far exceeded the ability of many to pay. The cost of living rose from a base rate of 100 in 1914 to 1,424 in 1919. An *okka* (about 1.28 kgs) of sugar cost three piasters in July 1914, 62 by January 1917, and 140 by January 1918. An *okka* of potatoes cost one piaster in July 1914, 20 by September 1917, and 36 by January 1918. An *okka* of mutton cost seven piasters in July 1914, 28 by January 1917, and 120 by September 1918.[48] Ajay, writing of Beirut and Mt. Lebanon, noted that over two years (1914–1916) the price of flour increased by 1,200 percent, sugar by 1,900 percent, bulgur wheat by 700 percent, and kerosene by 2,000 percent. Similar rises affected the prices of olive oil, coffee, rice, macaroni, salt, potatoes, milk, and other foodstuffs along with such basic household items as soap.[49]

The same scale of price increases born of shortages across the board affected civilian life everywhere but most severely in the cities. The already poor were the first to suffer, followed by the middle class, and then the wealthy, until even they had to sell their possessions to buy the necessities of life. Expected to hand in their gold coins in exchange for paper money, civilians were caught in a bind: they needed money to buy food, but paper money, its market value continually depreciating, was often refused by food producers and merchants. They would only take gold, so the tendency among civilians was to hoard their coins. As in all wars, only the very rich were likely to come through the ordeal unscathed.

PLAGUE AND BLOCKADE

In Syria, a locust plague and the Allied blockade of the Mediterranean coast added enormously to the difficulties of the daily struggle for survival. Locust plagues are chronic in Middle Eastern history, but the plague of 1915 was then the worst in living memory. Indeed, the extent and density of the swarms had never been known "in any part of the world."[50] The locusts arrived in a massive swarm over southern Syria (Palestine) in March. Uncountable masses of these insects devastated all forms of vegetation, from shrubs and bushes in the municipal parks and gardens of Beirut, Jerusalem, Jaffa, Lydda, and Ramallah to ripening fruit and vegetable crops "of apricots, watermelons, musk melons, cucumbers, tomatoes, grapes, figs, and corn," as well as olive trees.[51]

Along the coast, swarms stripped citrus orchards of leaves and bark, leaving whitened skeletons behind when they moved off in search of more vegetation. Stocks of food stored from the previous year, as well as currently ripening crops, were ravaged. It was not just that they ate every "leaf and flower and fruit:" more awful still, wrote Margaret McGilvary, "They were carnivorous. There were numerous instances when mothers left their little children alone at home while they went to the fields and returning found little more than the skeletons, [their] clothing and flesh having been devoured by these horrible insects."[52] This was in Lebanon, but similar cases were reported in Palestine.

The locusts also descended on Egypt and Sudan and penetrated Jordan, as well as the Hawran grain-growing area of the Syrian interior.[53] After laying their eggs they moved on, leaving the destruction of their eggs as the priority. Bayard Dodge wrote from Beirut that once the eggs hatched, the young locusts "ate everything green with an unbelievable rapacity."[54] The Zionist settler Alexander Aaronsohn recorded that "not only was every green leaf devoured but the very bark was peeled from the trees, which stood out white and lifeless ... the fields were stripped to the ground. Nothing was spared."[55] Cemal Paşa "vigorously grappled with the situation," ordering all males between the ages of fifteen and sixty to collect twenty kilograms of eggs: those who did not collect were fined.[56] For a time, even as news of the war flowed in from all fronts, collection and destruction of locust eggs dominated public life. Not until October were all traces of the infestation finally cleared away. The following year, the grain harvest seemed promising until the *khamsin* sand storm blew across Syria and ruined it, reducing the expected yield of 2,750 kilograms per hectare to 625.[57]

The Allied naval blockades of the Mediterranean coast and the Black Sea were destructive in their own way. Imports of cotton thread, glassware, matches, nails, pharmaceuticals, chemicals needed for tanning and soap production, and fuel for irrigation pumps were all blocked. What could not get in was matched by what could not get out, these goods including tobacco (intensively grown around Bafra on the Black Sea), fresh fruit (the famous Jaffa oranges of Palestine), dried fruits and nuts, barley, olive oil, and the regular shipments of grain needed in the Hijaz.[58] In normal times, these goods were exported from Beirut, Mersin, Iskenderun, and Izmir. Now nothing could move. In ports on the Black Sea coast, the Russian blockade prevented shipment to Istanbul of cereal crops from central and northern Anatolia. With coal imports blocked, the government had to rely on the Black Sea mine at Zonguldak without being able to move its output by sea.

The Mediterranean blockade also prevented wheat shipments to Istanbul from southern Anatolia and Syria, where it was grown in the Hawran region and in southern Palestine. Increasingly, the Ottoman population was in desperate need of food, but with access to the sea closed and without rail transport to move produce in large quantities, or with the military having primacy on rail use where it was available, crops were likely to rot where they were harvested.

The same transport problems afflicted the supplies of food grown in the western provinces (eastern Thrace and the regions down the Aegean coast from the Sea of Marmara), with the same consequences there as elsewhere: shortages, rising prices, hoarding, and price-fixing.

On Mt. Lebanon, sericulture, a mainstay of the mountain economy with annual exports worth about 20 million francs, was killed off by the Allied blockade. Silk production had been developed in the nineteenth century through close cooperation with French spinners who came to Mt. Lebanon to take women out of their homes for training. This itself was a radical change for conservative mountain communities. In an annual pattern repeated decade after decade, silk moths laid eggs on the twigs of mulberry trees. These hatched into larvae that then fed on the leaves and eventually produced thread that was harvested by separating it from the cocoons in boiling water.

Before the outbreak of war, more than 180 spinning mills had been established on Mt. Lebanon. The final stages of production were celebrated as *mawsim al-qazz* (silkworm season).[59] Well forested, Mt. Lebanon was a rich source of timber for fuel, railway ties, and other military needs. The damage done to silk production by the naval blockade was terminal. Exports of spun silk and cocoons (mostly to France) came to an abrupt end and production and processing soon ceased. Without export and cash returns, sericulture was felled by the blockade as surely as the trees felled by an axe.[60]

In Palestine, the *Arab Bulletin* reported,

> Nothing comes in from the sea. Before the outbreak of the Arab revolt a certain amount of colonial goods, rice, sugar, coffee, etc. used to reach Damascus and Palestine from the Hejaz.... Now this scanty source of supply has been entirely closed.... Neither foreign nor home-made goods worth mentioning are coming from the North by railway; Palestine has to live exclusively on its own individual resources. Unless one has seen the country with one's own eyes one cannot realize what variety of essentials and all but essentials are absolutely non-existent in Palestine now. Manchester goods, leather, coal, iron, cement, iron nails, matches, tea, cocoa, chocolate, sugar, lubricating oils, drugs etc. etc. are entirely exhausted. People of wealth wear mere rags. Shoe-polish has been out of use for two years.

Previously, Palestine exported about 2 million boxes of oranges. Now the fruit rotted, and owners watched their orchards deteriorate for the lack of funds to maintain them.[61] The entire country was "dying slowly." In Haifa, Nazareth, Tiberias, Nablus, Jaffa, and Jerusalem, "The shops and stores are not only shut but empty." Even their doors had been removed.[62]

"GOD'S WILL"

As noted, the health of the general Ottoman civilian population was already poor when the war broke out.[63] Bodies already weakened by such afflictions as tuberculosis, trachoma, syphilis, and malaria were in no condition to resist the additional stresses that now came at them from many directions. Epidemic diseases traveled both ways between the military and the civilian population. However, whereas the military kept records, so it is possible to arrive at fairly accurate figures for the number of soldiers affected, civilians suffered and died in their villages or were treated in understaffed and overloaded hospitals where proper records might not be kept. Only estimates can be made of the number of civilians affected or dying from disease.

Whatever its defects, the military did have a health-care system. For civilians, there was health care, but it was too haphazard and subject to too many variables to be called a system as such. In eastern Anatolia, there were few doctors to attend to the ill and often no hospitals nearby to take them in. Villagers everywhere might not even be aware of the serious nature of an illness and certainly were unaware of the need for proper sanitation and hygiene. "Nobody came to us and told us that they were suffering from a disease in their village, neighborhood or house," the Balikesir (western Anatolia) Society of National Defense reported early in the war, following a typhus epidemic. "Although people travel from one village to another to seek advice when even one of their animals is ill, they have done nothing about this disease affecting human beings." Many died where they had lived all their lives. In some households, "no one remained alive."[64]

The war turned the empire into a vast incubator for the development and spread of diseases, with soldiers, deserters, and refugees carrying them wherever they went. While Christians had some additional help in the form of medical missionaries and foreign relief organizations, Muslims had to rely solely on a government that was incapable of giving them all the assistance they needed. The medical sector was poorly developed when the war began and the best efforts of officials, doctors, and the Red Crescent Society could only go so far in ameliorating the suffering of the civilian population. In any case, "The people believed that both health and illness were dependent on God's will and trying to be protected from disease would be tantamount to defying God's authority."[65]

In Jerusalem, wrote Sami Hadawi, "Epidemics of typhoid, typhus, malaria and dysentery spread like wildfire." Soldiers were lined up naked while their clothes were fumigated: "The odor and the dirt surrounding the operation was terrible. No precautions were taken by the army to take into account the presence of ladies living in the buildings overlooking the compound." Hadawi and his school friends were told to search their underwear for lice once in the morning and once in the evening: the precautions against infestation included keeping the hair cut short and carrying naphtha and mercury as a remedy if infected. The locust plague was followed by an outbreak of cholera.

Standing on his balcony in April 1915, Hadawi counted ninety-seven coffins on their way to the cemetery.[66] The still-stricken were shifted to hospitals and clinics, "but there aren't enough doctors and medicines," wrote the soldier Ihsan Turjman."[67] By May, he was writing, "Diseases are spreading like wildfire among the population, especially among Muslims—for they do not take the proper precautions, may God forgive us."[68]

In 1916–1917, a typhus outbreak in Beirut and on the mountain took the lives of 60,000–70,000 people.[69] In Beirut, during the winter "typhus raged," Margaret McGilvary wrote, "and in the summer, cholera, dysentery and pernicious malaria swept over the whole country. One passed four or five funerals each day on any route and the same coffin did service for every corpse in a district until it literally fell to pieces."

In villages and mountain towns like Aley, conditions were even more distressing: "The dead were gathered off from the streets in the morning and were thrown out on the hillside back of the town, where at night the jackals and hyenas found them."[70] Imported medicines were in short supply, while vitamin deficiencies due to the lack of fruit, greens, meat, and eggs were causing scurvy and increasing the incidence of such ailments as pellagra and trachoma.[71]

"BLACK MISERY"

The most harrowing tales have emerged from histories of the period. Weakened by illness, weakened psychologically, and exploited by the usual band of human parasites that thrive in times of war (corrupt officials, profiteering middlemen, and avaricious merchants), civilians in Syria were soon facing death from starvation. By the end of 1915, the supply of flour to Beirut had shrunk to a trickle, and neither there nor in Damascus was any grain available.

Food shortages soon turned into a catastrophe that spread across Syria. People scrounged for something to eat wherever it might be found. In Beirut, they rummaged through piles of rubbish and were seen "following behind moving animals picking food particles out of their dung."[72] They hovered around mills looking for grain in the droppings of horses and donkeys.[73] They ate dogs and cats when not fighting with them over scraps of food and were even seen clustering around ant mounds to take the grain the insects were carrying.[74] They ate fruit and vegetable peelings and bought blood from the butcher's shop so they could turn it into some kind of congealed food.[75] They ate animals found dead in the street. They ate grass, and they even ate each other: in Hardin, a village in the northern Lebanese district of Batroun, two sisters aged eighteen and sixteen were found to have lured children into their home so they could kill and eat them. Twenty-four skulls were discovered in a well. The sisters were taken to prison where it is said they died of starvation.[76] Cases of cannibalism were also reported in the mountain districts of Kisrawan and Shuf.[77] A priest heard the confession of a man who said he had eaten his own children,[78] while even if they did not kill them, some mothers were also said to have eaten the bodies of their children.[79]

The starving dropped dead in the streets of cities or in their mountain villages where, out of shame, men who could no longer provide for their families were walking away to die alone. Houses were stripped of anything that could be sold to buy food down to the roof tiles. Bodies might be unearthed in the search for gold dental fillings.[80] Whole villages were depopulated, with the skeletons of the dead lying unburied in their homes.[81] Many of those who survived were little more than living skeletons. So many were dying that the bodies were buried in mass graves. The scenes in everyday life were appalling: bloated children, emaciated women, and funeral processions everywhere. No sustenance was to be found in Beirut for villagers driven out of the mountains by complete impoverishment. "There were days," wrote Margaret McGilvary, "when on the walk of a mile from our house to the office Mr. Dana and I would pass as many as ten or twelve people either dead or dying by the roadside or with death only a few hours distant."[82]

Many others were witness to the same sights elsewhere. An agent of the Arab Bureau wrote from Beirut on June 25, 1916,

> I cannot describe to you the black misery that prevails at Outilias [Antilias], at Jedeide, Junie [Jounieh] and Burj and the neighborhood. The people are pale, thin and too feeble to stand upright. To look at them you would think they are living ghosts. The famine has hit hardest the middle class and the poor. On the 24th of June [1916] 14 persons died of hunger at Junie. During this morning (the 25th) five others have succumbed.... In the Kesrouan [Kisrawan] the famine has depopulated entire villages. Most of the sick whom I have visited have their bodies swollen up, especially the feet, through eating the weeds out of the field.[83]

The Damascus grain depots were reported to be empty. In Beirut, imported flour was arriving but in greatly diminished qualities. The town used to receive consignments of 60–70 tons a day but this had fallen to

15 or 20 tons and there were some days when "not a single sack" entered the depots and at present (June 1916) there was none. One schooner loaded with grain had run the coastal blockade, but with nothing close to the quantity needed to relieve the famine. Other vessels were sunk by Allied warships.

Flour was being ground from grain mixed with damp and black barley that had been stored for years. "The smell of it is disgusting and it has given rise to various forms of sickness." Grain could not be brought in by rail because "for the time being" all rail traffic was being used to transport troops to the Hijaz to put down the "Arab revolt." Paper money was disrupting commerce and supplies of food, as merchants "are hiding their stocks of grain in the cemeteries and at the bottom of wells so as not to be forced to sell them and to be paid in paper money which in their eyes has no real value."[84]

Where the living either could not or would not do anything to help, they simply shut out distressing scenes. By 1917, Edward Nickoley, employed at the Syrian Protestant College (long since the American University of Beirut), was writing in his diary of "starving people lying about" and of moaning children and weeping women "clawing over rubbish piles and ravenously eating anything they can find. When the agonized cry of a famishing people in the street becomes too bitter to bear, people get up and close the window tight in the hope of shutting out the sound."[85] Even in the great city of Istanbul, a dozen men were said to be dying of hunger every day by the beginning of 1916, while women were collapsing in the streets from exhaustion.[86]

Across Syria, out of a total population of about 4 million, the Arab historian George Antonius estimated that about 350,000 people died from starvation and disease and that the total death toll was probably close to half a million.[87] In Beirut or on Mt. Lebanon alone, estimates of the number of dead range from 100,000 to 200,000. Famine and the harsh nature of martial law and war left bitter feelings toward Turks that have not entirely abated even to the present day. "I pray to God that this war may bring about the dismemberment of the Turkish Empire, so that the poor, crushed nations may live again," wrote the poet Kahlil Gibran.[88] Many Ottoman soldiers stationed in Syria, on occasion reduced to eating grass like many others, and no doubt any wild plants thought to be nutritious, also died from hunger and exposure.

The victims of war in Syria included tens of thousands of relocated Armenians. Overcrowding and lack of sanitation and medical care had a deadly effect on this uprooted mass of people. German missionaries reported finding great numbers of bodies, with hundreds buried in mass graves in a single day, while the near-dead lay outside their tents stricken with dysentery and disease. At a *han* in Aleppo, wrote an eyewitness, "I found piles of putrefying bodies and among them people still alive, on the point of breathing their last. In other places I found piles of sick and starving people left to fend for themselves.... Most were suffering from typhus or dysentery."[89] At Meskene, north of Aleppo, a German consular official found "a wide belt" of excrement and garbage around an encampment for about 10,000 Armenians.[90] There were no latrines: every tent contained the sick and dying while others lay in the open. There and at other locations tens of thousands of Armenians died from disease and malnutrition.[91] At Deir al-Zor, overcrowding in the camp led officials in 1916 to order the transfer of more than 13,000 Armenians to Mosul. Few reached their destination, with thousands murdered on the way near the Khabur river, allegedly by Kurds, Chechens, Circassian, and Arab bands. Large-scale massacres were also reported at the Ras al-Ain camp, apart from the great number of people who died from disease there.

The ravages of war embraced Anatolia, Syria, Iraq, Iran, and the Caucasus. By the war's end, starving people were reduced to eating anything that might keep them alive, including grass, grain that could be dug out of animal droppings, leather sandals that could be boiled, and the straw that could be boiled from brooms. The entire land was devastated to an extent unimaginable in Europe, even in the regions of heaviest fighting. Towns and villages lay in ruins or had been virtually destroyed, with the eastern Anatolian provinces the worst affected.

In Iran, severe shortages of food in 1916 were followed by famine in 1917 and then outbreaks of cholera and typhus. The combination killed millions. In the struggle for survival, people ate dogs and other animals that had dropped dead from hunger or sickness. On occasions they too ate each other. This was rare but not unknown in the war-stricken regions (or in other wars in other places and at other times).[92] At Hamadan, wrote Arnold Wilson, 200 people were dying daily, and "children were being slain for food."[93] Major-General Lionel Dunsterville wrote that in Hamadan "two culprits, a mother and daughter, who had cooked and eaten one of the family (a boy six years of age) were stoned to death in front of the telegraph office by order of the religious authorities. In this case the offenders were women, who are of small account: and they had eaten a male child. There may have been cases equally bad where the culprits were male and the victims female, but I know of none such being brought to light."[94]

The same diseases spread among civilians everywhere, and the same shocking sights met the eyes of travelers. "When I was at Deli Abbas," wrote Kermit Roosevelt, "ghastly bands of skeletons would come through to us begging food and work." A *khan* on the outside of town had been turned into a poorhouse for starving women and children who had "drifted in" from across Kurdistan.[95]

Across the Kurdish regions of Iraq, Syria, and Iran, possibly a million Kurds had died by the time the war ended.[96] Cities, towns, and villages had been depopulated and ruined by fighting between colliding armies, their houses stripped even down to the timber on the walls. Most of Suleimaniye's mosques (19 out of 29) had been destroyed along with its Sufi lodges, bathhouses, markets, houses, and gardens, with some women selling their bodies to survive. The population had dropped from 20,000 to 2,500: "Dead bodies were collected in the bazaar every morning and in some cases people were eating their dead babies."[97]

In Rowanduz, the number of houses had been reduced from about 2,000 to no more than 60: "With its roofless crumbling walls," it looked more like a town in Flanders. "The whole country has in fact been laid waste by fire and sword, disease, pestilence and starvation."[98] Northwest of Sulaimaniye, the number of families in one tribe had been reduced from more than 150 to 7.[99] In another large tribe, the Baradost, the number of families had shrunk from 1,000 to 157. Out of its 81 villages, 52 had been destroyed by armies or abandoned because of sickness and famine.[100]

The levels of suffering were no different anywhere, not at Khanikin, Khoi, or Rowanduz.[101] Agricultural production had come to a stop. Stocks of farm and draft animals had shrunk to fractions of their prewar levels. "Stocks" of human beings had also been greatly diminished. Across the Ottoman Empire and in neighboring lands, the world created by the war was utterly dystopian, more like the setting for a science fiction horror story than the world that had existed up to 1914.

CHAPTER 12

Armenians in Arms

RELATIONS BETWEEN OTTOMAN MUSLIMS and Christians, already weakened by the upheavals of 1894–1896 in the eastern Anatolian provinces and 1909 in Adana, were further disturbed by the trauma of the Balkan wars. Balkan Muslims had been massacred and driven out of their homes by Greeks (as well as Serbs and Bulgarians). In retaliation, Muslims attacked Ottoman Greeks down the Aegean seaboard, driving them from their homes, boycotting their shops, and occasionally killing them.

Now that the Ottoman Empire was again at war—this time by choice—Christian communities came under suspicion again as potentially harboring fifth columnists. These fears were not groundless: the enemy was actively seeking to win the support of ethnoreligious national groups and the government would take no chances, especially where these groups were concentrated close to the front line. Within weeks of the Allied landing at Gallipoli, the government moved Greeks from the Çanakkale region farther south into Karesi (Balikesir) *sancak* with instructions that they were to be resettled at least an hour's distance from the coast. Others, from the villages and towns around Edirne, in eastern Thrace (Trakya), as well as the southern Marmara region, were sent well into the interior to see out the war. Possibly more than 100,000 "Rum" (Greeks) from northwestern Anatolia alone were resettled during this campaign.[1]

It was not just Christian Greeks or Armenians, however, but Christian and Muslim Albanians, Arabs, Kurds, and even the Zionist settlers of Palestine who had to be monitored with different levels of intensity according to the nature of the potential danger they were thought to represent.

The declaration of independence by Albania at the height of the first Balkan war (November 28, 1912) was regarded as a stab in the back by the Ottoman government. No doubt often unfairly, Albanians were not trusted for social reasons as well. Some were associated with banditry, and strict limitations were applied when Albanians entered Ottoman lands, with officials reportedly instructed to resettle them in central Anatolia or the southeast. By 1917, the government was banning the entry of all non-Muslim Albanians and prohibiting the settlement of any Albanians in Istanbul or the western provinces, except with specific official authorization.[2]

In northeastern Anatolia, the Muslim Laz people came under suspicion when the government heard that some of their notables had gone to Batum to discuss Russian support for a possible uprising. As a precaution, refugees from Georgia, part of the Laz homeland, were shifted from the border region.[3]

The Kurds represented a particularly complex problem. They had been a central element in the interplay across the border between Russia and the Ottoman Empire in the nineteenth century. But their own nationalism had begun to awaken after the Congress of Berlin and was rapidly developing by 1914. A very large number of Kurds fought in the Ottoman armies, though the loyalty of tribal leaders could not be taken for granted. Russia's strategic interest in the Kurds had a long history: it maintained a presence on the ground in eastern Anatolia through consulates and in the years before the war was subsidizing Kurdish tribes and uprisings with money and weapons.[4]

The Ottoman government fought back by agitating among the Kurdish tribes in northwestern Persia, but in its own domains it was hampered by the negative effects of conscription and alienation following the use of force to quell rebellions. While Russia wooed both Kurds and Armenians in the nineteenth century, by 1914 it still had not worked out "a coherent policy toward the Kurds, largely because Kurdish aspirations were bound to clash with Armenian ones."[5]

Resettlement of Kurds, while carried out with one eye on social, political, economic, and demographic considerations, was immediately driven by the need to deal with the huge flow of refugees from east to the west and south, increasing with the breakthrough victories of Russian forces in 1916. Between February and July, Trabzon, Muş, Bitlis, Erzurum,

Erzincan, and Baiburt were all captured, with Van falling to the Russians in May after a successful Armenian uprising. Russian-occupied territory, stretching inland from the border to Erzincan and narrowing to a point south of Lake Van, included much of the homeland claimed by Kurds and Armenians. Kurdish resistance and attacks by Cossacks and Armenians, along with starvation and the spread of epidemic diseases, led to the catastrophic situation for the Kurds that has been described.

Ottoman authorities did not distinguish between Muslims on the basis of ethnicity but of the hundreds of thousands of refugees moving out of the eastern provinces during the Russsian invasion and occupation, a very large number would have been Kurds along with Turks, Turkmen, Arabs, Chechens, Circassians, and others resettled from previous wars and now forced to move again. Others would have fled from northwestern Iran or the Russian Caucasus only recently.

While the immediate issue for the Ottoman government was where to resettle the Kurdish refugees, other motives were clear. Some were practical: the sharp decline in agricultural production meant that those used to working on the land could be put to good use in the more fertile regions of central or western Anatolia. However, the dislocation of such a large number of people of the same ethnic background also created opportunities for calculated demographic change.

The restriction of Kurdish resettlement to a small percentage (5–10) of the local population in the regions where they were sent furthered assimilation and sedentarization,[6] reducing the lawlessness traditionally associated in official Ottoman and foreign minds with tribal life. Furthermore, the process of resettlement separated masses of Kurds from their tribal chiefs. Such tactics, it should be mentioned, were of a piece with attempts by the European powers to shift populations and sedentarize tribes in lands they had occupied. In the nineteenth century, Russia had transferred Christians into regions from which Muslims had fled or had been driven out. In moving Kurdish refugees out of Kurdish (and Armenian) regions and non-Kurdish Muslims into them, the Ottoman government had this recent regional precedent.

While resettlement loosened a Kurdish thorn in the Ottoman side, the greater danger to Ottoman interests came not from tribal chiefs caught up in local rivalries but from advocates of Kurdish national identity. In this respect, some Kurds regarded Russia as a better option for the future and even served as auxiliaries to the Russian army. Kurdish nationalism was in an embryonic stage but still represented a threat to Ottoman state interests, further stimulating the resettlement of Kurdish refugees away from their traditional homelands.

The differences between Kurdish resettlement and the decision to "relocate" the Armenians were significant. The national idea had been developing among Kurds but perhaps not to the extent as among Armenians. Fellow feeling with other Muslims and respect for the sultanate-caliphate, no matter how attenuated by other loyalties, would partly have accounted for this. Armenians were barred from serving in military units, whereas Kurdish young men were conscripted for service along with everyone else. They fought and died on all fronts, and some rose to high rank in the army.

There were Kurdish brigands, Kurdish deserters, and Kurdish resistance to conscription and government authority in general, but, unlike the Armenians, there were no Kurdish bands deliberately sabotaging the Ottoman war effort from behind the lines. In a world of states whose identity at the time was being built on a fixed sense of national values and aspirations, Ottoman politicians were hardly unique in equating ethnic differences with danger. As understood by Michael Reynolds, Talat "recognized that Ottoman sovereignty over a poly-ethnic Anatolia would always be vulnerable in a world order that increasingly endorsed ethnic homogeneity as a criterion for statehood."[7]

The suffering of Kurdish refugees was immense, even if consistent with the terrible conditions endured elsewhere. They slept where they could find sanctuary, often in the courtyards of mosques. Government relief was never sufficient and sometimes nonexistent. Local people often could not help them because they had so little for themselves. Refugees ate whatever could be turned into food: animal blood,[8] "doves, street cats and dogs, hedgehogs, frogs, moles, snakes and the organs of slaughtered animals."[9]

TWIN-TRACK POLICIES

Of all ethnonational groups, the greatest perceived threat to the Ottoman government came from within Armenian communities, once but no longer collectively regarded as the "faithful community" (*millet-i sadika*). The Ottoman authorities and militant Armenian committees had been in conflict for more than three decades by the time the First World War broke out. The committees were well organized, had been stockpiling weapons since the late nineteenth century, and were able to

call on the armed and political services of Armenians won over to the
national cause who, though few in number among the general Armenian
population, were ideologically committed and numerous enough to concern the authorities.

From 1908 down to 1914, Armenian revolutionary politics ran along
two tracks. One was rapprochement with the CUP; the other was preparation for revolt when the right time came. At no time did the Dashnaks
or other militant organizations lose sight of the long-term objective: the
incorporation of "western Armenia"—eastern Anatolia from the Black
Sea down to the eastern Mediterranean—into an Armenian state. This
second track required continuous ideological and practical groundwork.
Small-scale uprisings had continued for decades, but by 1905 the Dashnaks had decided to eschew these local clashes in favor of preparations
for "large-scale movements in Van and Cilicia" in the context of moving
from "self-defense" to "revolutionary activity."[10] The tactics, reaffirmed at
their Fourth World Congress in 1907, were no different from what they
had been since the 1880s: uprisings, resistance to government forces, propaganda, and the assassination of Armenian "traitors."

Arms stockpiling continued across the east, especially in towns with a
substantial Armenian population such as Van and Bitlis. The arms seized
after 17 *jandarma* were killed by militants in Van included about 2,000
weapons, 5,000 bombs, and hundreds of thousands of cartridges. The
arms, including weapons not even available to government forces,[11] were
smuggled into the province in kerosene barrels loaded on camels.[12] Ruthless action was taken against government officials, informers, and Armenian notables who resisted the demands of the militants. Plots against
government ministers included the assassination of a former governor of
Van and a Hunchak plan to assassinate Talat.[13] The murder on December 10, 1912, of Bedros Kapamaciyan, the mayor of Van, popular with Muslims as well as Christians, was both punishment and warning. Those who
planned the assassination were said to have included Aram Manukian,
a Dashnak veteran of militant action in the eastern provinces who was
appointed "governor" of Van province during the short-lived period of
Russian occupation in 1915.[14] The violent interplay between Kurds and
Armenians continued in the background as did coordination between
the Dashnaks and the Armenian committees in Tbilisi.

In 1912, Arshak Vramian, a leading Van Dashnak, warned the *vali* of
Van, "in words that amounted to a threat," that if there were no improvements for the Armenians, Russia might be compelled to intervene.[15]

By 1913, he was in Tbilisi as Armenian committees (Dashnak, Hunchak, and Ramgavar) decided to form a single front. According to British Vice-Consul Molyneux-Seel in Van, they had agreed that the "Armenian nation" would be armed under Dashnak leadership and that political action would need the prior approval of all parties.[16]

Sean McMeekin has drawn attention to the need to focus attention on Russian manipulation of the Armenian question. In his view, British public campaigning for Armenian autonomy in the 1890s "ultimately served Russian interests far more than British or French." The Russians "believed they had the Armenians in their pocket and aimed unambiguously to exploit them" ahead of an invasion. After the 1908 coup and the massacre of Armenians in Adana, these intentions took shape in "operational" plans for sabotage in Istanbul by local Christians. The wooden bridges across the *halic* would be burnt and Russia would seize the city.[17]

Clearly, this was a plan—perhaps one of many plans—for taking the city when the time came, but the time had not come yet. While Russia had backed away from British attempts to impose "reforms" on the sultan in the 1890s, on June 8, 1913, the dragoman at the Russian embassy, M. A. Mandelstamm, unveiled a Russian Foreign Ministry solution to the problems of the eastern provinces that was similar in substance to the "reform" project of the 1890s. These revamped "reforms for Armenia" would create one province out of six.[18] It would have a governor-general *(vali umumi)*, a Christian Ottoman subject, "or better still" a European appointed by the sultan and approved by the powers. He would have full control of administrative appointments, with troops at his disposal if necessary, and he would have the support of European technical advisors. A provincial assembly would be elected on the basis of equal Muslim-Christian representation (in a region overwhelmingly Muslim). At the lowest administrative level, just as in 1895, the *nahiyes* or "communes" would be arranged in such a way as to allow "from the ethnographical point of view" the formation of homogeneous national groups.

Germany strenuously opposed the project, as did the Ottoman government, for which it represented what McMeekin has termed "a Trojan horse for Russian imperialism."[19] Cemal himself had no doubt that within a year the entire region would have been turned into a Russian protectorate "or at least occupied by Russia."[20]

In response, the Ottoman government came up with an unexpected plan of its own, dividing the entire empire into six "general inspectorates," two of which would be formed out of the six eastern Anatolian vilayets.

They would be placed under British authority. This was a clever move, compelling the British government to say out loud what the Ottomans must have known. Asked to assume this responsibility, Britain declined, explaining that "it could not undertake the appointment of officials for eastern Anatolia without Russian consent." This gave the Ottoman government an opening to say that it had been sacrificed to Russian interests.[21]

Negotiations over the reforms continued until February 8, 1914, when the Russian chargé d'affaires, Konstantin Gulkievitch, signed an agreement with Said Halim Paşa, Grand Vizier and Foreign Minister, establishing two inspectorates out of the six eastern Anatolian provinces. "Monsieur A will have the vilayets of Erzerum, Trebizond and Sivas and Monsieur B the vilayets of Van, Bitlis, Kharput and Diyarbekir."[22] They would have the same powers as drawn up for the governor-general. The search for suitable Monsieurs A and B ended in the selections of a Dutch colonial administrator, Louis Constant Westenenk, and Nicolai Hoff, a Norwegian army officer. Hoff was already in Van and Westenenk was preparing to leave for Erzurum when war broke out, bringing this hazard-laden plan to an abrupt and probably fortuitous end. On December 16, it was formally abandoned.

"THEATRE" AT ERZURUM

In July–August 1914, senior figures in the Teşkilat i-Mahsusa traveled to Erzurum, where the Dashnaks were holding their eighth world congress, with a proposal for Armenian autonomy in the *vilayets* of Erzurum, Van, and Bitlis and the two Russian governorates of Kars and Erivan in return for an anti-Russian insurgency, this depending, of course, on the Central Powers winning the war. The Dashnaks turned the offer down, "diplomatically explaining that Armenians on both sides of the border should stay loyal to their respective governments."[23]

Some authors have questioned whether such an offer was even made or whether it conformed to the terms described, but whatever was said, there must have been a lot of playacting by both sides.[24] As Reynolds has written, "The idea that a government in Istanbul would have been willing to delegate some of its control and authority [over/in] Erzurum, Van, and Bitlis to the Armenians following a victorious war is hard to imagine. The most obvious interpretation is that it was an act of theatre in which the Ottoman government made the Dashnaks an offer they knew the

Dashnaks could not accept and the Dashnaks politely and falsely promised their loyalty."[25]

In fact, the Ottomans believed that the Armenians were pretending submission while preparing for war. Once it was declared, they would join the Russian forces. If the Ottoman army advanced, they would remain silent but if it withdrew, armed gangs would launch operations already planned behind the lines.[26]

The attitudes of all great powers to ethnoreligious minorities were shaped, of course, by hard imperial and national considerations and not superficial displays of sentiment, as their proteges would have realized. Russia had not dropped its long-term objectives of capturing Istanbul and seizing the straits, but during the 1890s the relationship between the tsar and the sultan was harmonious. Like Britain, still its great imperial rival, Russia was not concerned with the Ottoman Empire for the time being. It had too many problems of its own. Internally, the empire was swarming with anarchists and revolutionaries of every ideological description, out to assassinate government ministers and the tsar if they could. The assassination of the tsar's predecessor, Alexander II, in 1881 had brought about a change of attitude more general than the determination to crush all revolutionary organizations and cells.

The Dashnaks believed Russia "will welcome our activities due to her historic enmity wth the Ottomans,"[27] but the change of official attitudes in the last two decades of the nineteenth century were to show that they were "somehow mistaken in their calculations."[28]

In the wake of Alexander's assassination, the Russian government set in motion a campaign of Russification intended to stamp out the dangers associated with ethnoreligious nationalism. The aim was assimilation and incorporation of multiple identities into one Russian national identity. Education, language, and religion were the main lines of attack. In Transcaucasia, the attempt to dismantle church authority began with the closure of parish schools in the 1880s. They were soon reopened but closed more forcefully in the 1890s.

In 1898, Prince Nikolai Golitsyn, a district governor and future prime minister, prepared a report that painted the Armenian church as the mother lode of revolutionary activities.[29] In 1903, its control of parish schools was transferred to the Ministry of Education, its properties to the Ministries of Interior, Agriculture, and State Properties.[30] The Dashnaks took the lead in openly defying these measures through demonstrations that were violently suppressed by police. In the coming two years, ahead

of the 1905 revolution, they were to collaborate with other radical movements in calling for the overthrow of the tsarist regime.

    Attempting to restore calm while the revolution was in progress, Tsar
Nicholas II (Alexander III having died in 1894), revoked the edict autho-
rizing the seizure of Armenian church property. To a degree, this restored
faith in the government among the clergy, the bourgeoisie, and even the
Armenian peasantry, who made public demonstrations of gratitude and
loyalty.[31] One has to suspect that local priests had a hand in this: no doubt
to the same degree, populist support for the goals of the Armenian revolutionary movements was weakened.

GREAT REWARDS

With war approaching, the Armenian committees and the Russian government realized they needed each other, or, probably more accurately,
could make use of each other for their own purposes. For the Armenians,
support for Russia and the other Entente powers seemed their best chance
of securing autonomy if not independence (at least not immediately)
when the fighting ended. For Russia, Armenian uprisings behind the
lines would be an invaluable addition to regular military operations. The
tsar himself hinted at the great rewards to come in return for Armenian
support. A flowery statement referring to Armenian heroes of the past culminated in the pledge, "O' Armenians! Together with your blood brothers
under the scepter of the Tsar you will finally fully feel the delights of
freedom and justice."[32]

    Russian approaches to the Armenians were matched by an Ottoman
counteroffer to Russian Armenians through their clerical and national
representatives in Tiflis (modern Tbilisi): in return for supporting the
Ottoman war effort, they would be given autonomy in Kars and Erivan
and all six eastern Ottoman provinces as well as Cilicia. This promise was
no more likely to be kept than the Russian guarantee: as the war was to
show, far from Russia delivering "freedom and justice." Where Armenians
abandoned or were driven from their homes, Cossacks were settled in
their place.

    Even by 1913, Russian consuls stationed in east Anatolian towns with
a substantial Armenian population were reporting general Armenian
enthusiasm for the Russian cause. By March, one consul wrote, the mood
across the Van *vilayet* had become "one of complete Russophilia ... the

Dashnaks are completely on our side." Within a month, he was reporting that Van city had become an "armed camp," and "all the Armenian
merchants are stockpiling guns in their stores."[33] In Tiflis, the Dashnaks
began recruiting volunteers, including hundreds arriving from Rustchuk
in Bulgaria. The Russian government was providing money and weapons
for the formation of armed cells along the border, and by late September
1914 seemed ready to incite uprisings when the time was right.

The contribution Armenians could make to the Russian war effort was
substantial: sections of the small Assyrian Christian tribal communities
in northwest Iran and southeastern Turkey also committed themselves to
the Allied cause, but Armenians had the numbers to make a significant
difference. Some 150,000 men were enlisted in the regular army, most
(including senior commanders) in the Army of the Caucasus. In addition,
there were the volunteer brigades (*druzhiny*) recruited by the Armenian
National Bureau in Tiflis from Caucasian Armenians, Ottoman Armenians, and Armenians arriving from other countries—the U.S. as well as in
Europe—to aid the Russian war effort and the Armenian national cause.
The Russian military also mobilized volunteer detachments from many of
the other Caucasian ethnoreligious groups, Muslim as well as Christian,
allotting them varying tasks.

The commanders of the Armenian brigades included Andranik Ozanian, Drastamat Kanayan (Dro), and Armen Garo (Karekin Pastermadjian). All had a long history of resistance to the Ottoman government.
Pastermadjian had taken part in the seizure of the Ottoman Bank in
Istanbul in 1896 but later entered parliament as a member for Erzurum
(1908–1912) before going to Tiflis to help organize the volunteer units.
Apart from Armenians in the regular army and the thousands of men
serving in the *druzhiny* squads, Armenian agents were sent across the border with arms and ammunition to organize sabotage of the Ottoman war
effort from behind the lines.

BLACK OPERATIONS

By the autumn of 1914, Russia and the Ottoman Empire were already
fighting a quasi war along their borders, with the Ottomans striving to
incite rebellion among Muslims living in territories Russia had captured
in the war of 1877–1878 and with Russia organizing insurgent bands in
Ottoman districts with a substantial Armenian population.[34] These black

operations—extending to northwest Iran—also involved Kurds as potential allies for either side.

In early November, Russian forces commanded by General Georgy Bergmann led the First Caucasian Army Corps over the border into the Eleşkirt valley and headed in the direction of Köprüköy. The Russians suffered heavy losses, encouraging Enver to press ahead with the Sarıkamış offensive. The Second Armenian *druzhina* had accompanied the Russian forces. Over eighteen days in early December 1914, the *druzhina*, wearing Russian uniforms and assisted by local Armenians, according to Ahmet Emin Yalman, massacred large numbers of Muslim civilians living on the plain between Eleşkirt and Beyazit. These events created "an unofficial state of war between the Armenians and the Turks."[35] Armen Garo played a key role in this campaign after Dro was wounded.

By December, 1914, the British warship HMS *Doris* was landing raiding parties around Alexandretta (Iskenderun), bombing shore installations, and spying out the terrain for a possible ground offensive.[36] At the same time, Ottoman intelligence reported that Armenian villagers in the mountains behind the coast were planning to attack Muslims with the aid of weapons and men landed from French and British ships. In February 1915, a delegation of Zeytunli Armenians traveled to the Caucasus to tell the Russian military command that they could raise a force of 15,000 men to cut Ottoman lines of communication but needed weapons and ammunition.[37]

From Cairo, Boghos Nubar, chairman of the Armenian National Assembly, encouraged the British to believe that such support was readily available, at the same time telling the French consul-general that Armenians, constituting 40 percent of the population of Iskenderun, in his estimate, were ready to support a French occupation of the Ottoman Empire.[38]

The Zeytunli Armenian promise of support for the Allied cause was backed up with major uprisings in 1915 (June) and 1916 (July–September) that tied up thousands of Ottoman troops. On the second occasion, the Ottoman siege of the town ended with the dramatic intervention of Allied warships and the transportation of thousands of people to refugee camps in Egypt (a fictionalized best-selling account of the siege by the Austrian novelist Franz Werfel appeared in the early 1930s under the title *Forty Days of Musa Dagh*).

Allied activities included liaison with Armenian spies, some of whom were caught as they attempted to board Allied warships. British warships continued to shell Ottoman towns and land raiding parties into 1915, but a new front in the eastern Mediterranean, positioning Allied forces at the intersection between Ottoman supply lines running into Iraq and Syria and posing a threat to Ottoman forces in eastern Anatolia, was never opened.[39]

By early 1915, reports of attacks on government officials, clashes with soldiers or *jandarma*, discovery of weapons caches, and the massing of armed men were coming from across the eastern and central provinces as well as the eastern Mediterranean, where the Armenians of Zeytun had been in a continuous state of renewed rebellion since late 1914. Other towns where Armenians were reported to be preparing uprisings included Trabzon, Amasya, Yozgat, Sivas, Tokat, Kayseri, Bitlis, Elazığ (Mamuret ül-Aziz), Van, Şebinkarahisar, and Diyarbakir. "Espionage centers" had been set up in Trabzon, Erzurum, Muş, Bitlis, Van, Sivas, and Kayseri to keep the Russians informed of the movements of the Ottoman army, with an "action committee" of Russians, Greeks, and Armenians established in Batum to gather information and foment uprisings on the Ottoman side of the border.[40]

Continuing clashes between Armenian bands and soldiers or *jandarma* prompted Enver to issue an order in February that no Armenian soldiers in the Ottoman army were to be given duties involving the use of arms. A few served as doctors and translators until the end of the war, but the great majority were transferred to labor battalions (*amele taburları*), which were used primarily to build or repair roads and railways or work on fortifications.

While "incidents" were not regarded as serious "at the time being," preparations were clearly being made for uprisings. Commanders were instructed to suppress any trouble, while sending out the message that loyal citizens would not be harmed.[41] There are only estimates for the number of Ottoman Armenians fighting as insurgents behind Ottoman lines. They range from 30,000 to more than 70,000. Measured against the size of regular armies, these numbers might seem small, but when an Ottoman army was hard pressed their contribution could be significant.

The Ottoman Armenian population was substantial, slightly more than 1.2 million by 1914, according to census figures, but probably considerably higher because of the undercounting of women and children and the avoidance of registration by Armenians so they would not have to pay the *bedel-i askeriye*, the military exemption tax. The numbers would have fluctuated dramatically during the war because of the ravages of death and disease and the flight of Armenians into the Caucasus or northwest Persia. By 1915, making allowances for all these factors, the total could have been no more than 1.5–1.6 million.

As the Ottoman population was counted for such mundane bureaucratic reasons as taxation, registering the number of young men available for conscription, and knowing the size of the population for planning purposes, the figures based on the official census are likely to be more accurate than the bloated and politically loaded estimates of the Armenian patriarchate or pro-Armenian outside observers.[42] Most Armenians lived in the central and eastern Anatolian provinces, creating a landscape into which Armenian insurgents could melt away unseen when not fighting.

COORDINATED UPRISINGS

A central issue in considering the fate of the Armenians is whether "military necessity" justified the *tehcir* (relocation) of hundreds of thousands of Armenian civilians in 1915. A non-Turkish scholar to have actually tracked Armenian operations through the lens of the Ottoman military command and tested the hypothesis is Edward Erickson. In January, Armenian activities were worrying but not regarded as a serious threat to the war effort; by April they definitely were.

The collapse of the Sarıkamış operation is the key to understanding the change in attitude. This disaster severely weakened the operational capacity of the Third Army in the region for which it was responsible, northeastern Anatolia down to Bitlis and Lake Van. Its fighting capacity was reduced from about 120,000 to about 20,000 men.[43] It was not able to prevent Russian occupation, and neither did it have the manpower to protect towns, villages, and lines of communication from attacks by Armenian insurgents. The defense of towns rested largely in the hands of *jandarma*, police, and volunteers, leaving villagers to fend for themselves as best as they could.

Between February and April, following the retreat from Sarıkamış, the record is scored with accounts of Armenian insurgent action in northeastern Anatolia that the military was not able to staunch. These "incidents" included attacks on soldiers and *jandarma* and the seizure of large quantities of weapons and ammunition. Armenians, equipped by the Russians with machine guns and artillery, had advanced along the Kotek-Pasin-Karakilise-Beyazit line, pillaging and destroying Muslim villages and, according to information sent to the army command in March, "massacring even the babies in their cradles." The women and children in neighboring regions were said to be fleeing into the interior.[44]

On March 6, a ciphered telegram reported that nearly 30,000 Muslim men had been killed around Kars and Ardahan, with houses destroyed and women and children driven into the snow. The Ottoman document does not specify whether Russians or Armenians or a combination of both were the perpetrators.[45]

Other sources confirm the ruthless treatment of civilians in this region. According to Michael Reynolds, when General Vladimir Liakhov recaptured territory from Ottoman regular and irregular (Laz and Ajar) forces in January 1915, "He ordered his Cossacks to kill Muslim natives on sight and burn every mosque and village and [he] reduced Artvin and the Chorokhi valley to a cinder." Armenian units took part in these actions, in which 45,000 Muslims were said to have been massacred in the Chorokhi valley alone.[46]

By the end of March, the government was convinced that large-scale coordinated uprisings across the eastern provinces were imminent. "Upheavals" would start in Van, Bitlis, Erzurum, and Şabinkarahisar, to be followed by Sivas, Kayseri, and Diyarbakir. On the evidence of arrested insurgents, an order had been issued for all males above the age of thirteen to register with Dashnak committees in preparation for mobilization. In a document sent by the government to army headquarters, it was remarked that "should the centers of upheaval be analyzed closely, it will be seen that they constitute the main points that are at a day's distance from the [Russian] border."[47]

The government was tracking the movements of Dashnak leaders, including Ruben Portakalian, Ruben Mgrditchian, Toros Karakashian, Aram Manukian, and Arshak Nersesian, who were organizing uprisings. Two former members of the Ottoman parliament from Van, Vahan Papazian (Goms) and Arshak Vramian, were also being watched.

Investigating claims of persecution by the Armenian patriarch, a government commission of inquiry found that "as of today [April 22] the Armenians are in a state of revolt and uprising, partially in the province of Sivas and totally in the province of Van. There is no doubt that Armenians living in other provinces are also waiting for the proper time to follow them." Far from being attacked, as the patriarch had claimed, it was Armenians who were on the offensive.[48]

In some towns (such as Van) armed Armenians had been challenging the authority of the state since the late nineteenth century but attacks in wartime fell into a different category. Ottoman Armenians who joined the enemy's war effort were regarded as traitors of the worst kind, stabbing the country in the back at a time of severe crisis. In similar circumstances, any government would take the same view, and it was not as if this treachery (as the Ottoman government regarded it) was ineffectual.

From the point of view of the Ottoman military, continuing attacks on convoys and lines of communication and supply, running from east to west and connecting up Anatolia with Iraq and Syria, were so serious as to threaten the entire war effort. At the time, and later during postwar political campaigning, Armenian delegates seeking statehood traded on the importance of armed Armenian support for the Allied cause.

THE BATTLE FOR VAN

There can be no objective judgment as to whether "military necessity" justified the removal of a large part of the Armenian population but the perception of an "imminent and existential threat to Ottoman national security" seems to have been real in the minds of military commanders and the heads of the government in Istanbul.[49] With insufficient troops available to send into the interior to deal with the threat behind the lines, the government picked up the option of relocating the bulk of the Armenian population in the eastern provinces, something Enver had considered earlier in retaliation for the number of Muslims being driven out of the Caucasus by the advancing Russian army.

Armenian attacks across the east from the Black Sea south toward the Mediterranean were now crystallizing into what the Ottoman military command regarded as a general insurrection. From various towns in the east, Armenians were reported to be sending information to the Russians on Ottoman army movements.[50] Small groups of soldiers were exposed to attack by insurgents, one in Muş involving the axe murder of four *jan-darma* near Geligüzan, a village prominent in the foreign outrage over the suppression of the Sasun uprising in 1894.[51] Large-scale confrontations with insurgents might last for many hours or even days, often ending with heavy losses for government forces.

Abutting the Russian border, the province of Van had been the setting for Armenian attacks on mostly Kurdish villages since late 1914. Massacre, plunder, and rape were all reported. By April 1915, the province was in a state of complete turmoil, with well-armed insurgents (bandit gangs as the Ottoman authorities would prefer to call them) attacking Ottoman troops amid reports of large-scale massacres of Muslim villagers.[52]

Although census figures did not differentiate among Muslims on the basis of ethnicity, most of the rural victims of Armenian attacks in Van were bound to have been Kurds, given their general predominance in the region. Needless to say, countervailing accusations of massacre came from Armenian sources.

In the sequence of cause and effect, the critical date is not April 24, which Armenians give as the beginning of the "genocide," but about a week to ten days earlier when military preparations inside the city of Van culminated in a full-scale uprising.[53] The immediate trigger for Armenians was the murder of a leading Dashnak figure, Ishkhan (Nikoghayos Mikaelian), allegedly at the instigation of the governor, Cevdet Bey. Several other Armenians were reported to have been killed with him when ambushed between Van and the village of Shatakh. Of the two other senior Dashnak figures in Van, Arshak Vramian was arrested at the beginning of the uprising, taken to Bitlis and later moved to Diyarbakir, where he was executed after a court-martial. Aram Manukian survived to be installed as governor of Van after the Ottoman withdrawal.

In the Garden Quarter, thousands of Armenians had prepared for open conflict by stockpiling weapons, breaking down walls between houses, digging trenches, manufacturing cartridges, and even sewing their own uniforms. A "defense council" had been active since late 1914, registering men and weapons, appointing leaders, and setting up a "provisioning council" and first-aid services.[54]

Within a month of open conflict breaking out, during April 15–20, the Armenians had overwhelmed government forces. Much of the city was destroyed early in the fighting, including the police headquarters, two military barracks, the post office, the Ottoman Bank, the tobacco *regie,* the former British consulate, and the offices of the Ottoman Public Debt Administration (Düyun-u Umumiye-i Osmaniye Varidat-ı Muhassasa İdaresi), imposed on the empire by the powers in 1881 to sequester revenue for payment of the Ottoman debt. Many of these buildings were burnt down or blown up by the Armenians, sometimes from tunnels dug beneath them.

On May 16, with Russian reinforcements approaching from the direction of northwest Persia where an Ottoman campaign at Dilman had just failed, the governor, his staff, and the mix of the *jandarma* and volunteers defending the city withdrew. The Armenians were jubilant, the secretary of their defense council writing of the dense smoke arising from burning government buildings.[55] In the few days before the arrival of a regular Russian army detachment, the victors turned on the Muslim civilian population with extreme savagery. Men were slaughtered and many women raped and killed but with more surviving than the men to provide eyewitness accounts.[56]

After the Russian military force entered the town, Aram Manukian was appointed the head of an Armenian republic before Van was placed under the authority of the Caucasian Committee of the All Russian Union of Towns (SOGOR), which appointed a Russian Armenian as its representative in Van. The main street was renamed Sogorskii Prospekt.[57]

Around the shores of Lake Van and across the province, Muslim villages were targeted for "clearing" operations by Armenian bands, with Cossacks sometimes involved in their attacks. The four Armenian volunteer battalions had converged on Van as the city fell. In the words of the authors of *Caucasian Battlefields,* the *druzhiny* under the command of Antranik, Hamazasp, and Dro "fought with great elan and drove the Turkish gendarmerie units from Vartan on the lake and from the two villages of Catak and Mukus on the road to Siirt." Other villages on the shore of the lake were captured on June 20 and 25.[58] Ottoman and Turkish sources describe a far more sinister side to these operations, as armed bands consisting of local Armenians and *druzhiny* militia moved around the lake. In Zeve, Mollakasim, Mollaselim, Karacik, and numerous other villages, thousands of people were slaughtered out of hand. The dead included refugees who had fled in the direction of Van after a Russian push across the border near Çaldiran to the northeast. About 2,000 had been taken in by the villagers of Zeve (previous population about 500), where one of the worst massacres was recorded. The menfolk attempted to defend Zeve from nearby hills, but the village was destroyed and almost all its 2,000–3,000 people killed, according to survivors.[59] About 80,000 Muslims fled Van in what has been known since as the *büyük kaçgın* (great flight). Many were also attacked and killed on their way out of the province.

To a degree, while differing strongly on the causes and course of the Van uprising, Armenian sources corroborate Ottoman documentary accounts. Yektan Turkyilmaz has written a valuable account from these sources on what happened at Van. He begins his chapter on the uprising with a visit to Muslim refugees in the missionary compound by Alexandra Tolstoy, a nurse in the Russian army and daughter of the great novelist, Leo. The refugees were sitting amid "filth and excrement all over the floor, no water either hot or cold." She speaks to a woman whose arms are hanging down in a strange fashion because they were torn out of joint by Armenians "in the fighting." Astounded, because she had only heard of "Turkish" atrocities, she is told by her American missionary companion of "slaughter on both sides ... here in Van we were able to observe the inhuman savagery of the Armenians. They had cut off women's breasts, it was said, they had pulled limbs from their sockets, they had broken arms and legs. I myself [the missionary is speaking] saw the victims of such beastliness."[60]

With the Ottoman authorities driven from Van, the Armenian population embarked on an orgy of looting, arson, and murder. According to the memoirs of Avetis Terzibashian, appointed mayor during the short-lived Russian-Armenian administration, Aram Manukian's first order was for the burning of houses so that "the Turks" would not want to return. The second order gave the "right" to Armenians to loot and burn "Turkish" houses. For three days, as allowed by the military committee, "we are plundering, slaughtering, and crucifying those who for thousands of years have plundered, pillaged, and crucified us," wrote a Dashnak militant.[61] Set upon by the "rabble," 2,000 defenseless (Muslim) women and children "were exterminated in one way or another," wrote a non-Dashnak Armenian observer.[62]

Having purged the city of its Muslim population, some of its residents rushed out to join the looting in the countryside. As Russian and *druzhiny* volunteer units—which had recently helped the Russian army overwhelm Ottoman forces in the battle of Dilman (April 15) in northwest Persia—advanced into Van, most Kurds fled. Where they did not, men were slaughtered, and some women and children abducted. In one Kurdish village held responsible for harboring bandits and engaging in plunder, an order was issued for it to be punished for twenty-four hours.

Wrote the deputy commander of the Armenian battalion that took part in this attack: "I should confess that unparalleled killings were carried out in this village both by the Cossacks and the Armenian volunteers. Weeping and screaming of the Kurdish women rose to the heavens ... [but] it was not possible to suppress the rage of the soldiers."[63] While this order was revoked by a Russian colonel, in areas that fell under Russian or Armenian control Kurdish villages were cleared of their inhabitants.

Writing from Erivan in August 1915, Manukian referred to what Turkyilmaz describes as his "exclusionist and exterminationist policies toward the Kurds."[64] Although Turkyilmaz describes Armenian violence as being part of a cycle of revenge rather than "a preplanned campaign of extermination,"[65] Manukian clearly sought to rid Van province of as many Muslims as possible, as a prelude to the establishment of an Armenian state.

While Armenians were overwhelming government forces in Van, Ottoman authorities were seizing stores of ammunition and dynamite and dozens of bombs in Diyarbakir. The Austro-Hungarian ambassador reported "widespread Armenian revolts" across Anatolia as well as massacres and the seizure of arms and arrests in Istanbul but "the Habsburg Empire must not interfere in any of the measures taken by the Turkish side. This is an internal affair of the Turkish government."[66]

CONFLICTING NARRATIVES

The Van uprising is a prime example of conflicting narratives that rarely touch each other. The American missionary Clarence D. Ussher and his assistant Grace Higley Knapp provided the outside world with details of crimes allegedly committed across Van province by Ottoman officials and soldiers. In his later memoir, Ussher claimed to have been in the presence of Cevdet Bey when the latter threatened to wipe out the Armenians: "I won't leave one, not one so high," the governor allegedly said, holding his hand below the height of his knee.[67] "Turkish" soldiers had been quartered in every Armenian village with instructions to begin massacres at a certain hour. According to Ussher, the general order read: "The Armenians must be exterminated. If any Muslim protects a Christian, first his house shall be burned, then the Christian killed before his eyes and then his [the Moslem's] family and himself."

The references to Muslim casualties are notional. Ussher talks of vengeance being wreaked on "the Turks" and of several being killed during the search for those in hiding. The "spirit of loot" took possession of Armenians, whose leaders "closed their eyes to what was going on. . . . Our protests were in vain for two or three days until the first madness passed."

On May 18, Russian-Armenian forces arrived: thousands poured through Van on their way to Bitlis, Ussher writes. The keys to Van were handed to General Nicolaieff, and Aram Manukian was declared governor of the province. In the meantime, "The Russians reported finding the villages full of dead bodies and the rivers full of them too. They sent out squads to burn these; 55,000 bodies were cremated." Ussher does not actually say that the 55,000 bodies were Armenians. Rather, he implies it and scoffs when Cevdet Bey claims that they were the Muslim victims of Armenians.

The Bryce-Toynbee atrocity propaganda publication of 1916 incorporates an Armenian newspaper account referring to 24,000 Armenians being killed in three days (April 15–18) and the decomposing bodies— by implication Armenian—that the writer claimed to have seen some time later around the shores of Lake Van.[68] In fact, the overthrow of the Van government by Armenians and the later "clearing" operations held around the lake in which a large number of Muslim villagers were killed indicate that many and very possibly most of the dead must have been Muslims.

For her part, Miss Knapp, the Van missionary, makes incidental references in her diary to some "acts of revenge" committed inside the city and to the "cleaning out" of villages around the lake by Russian-Armenian "volunteers."[69] Similarly, Taner Akçam refers to a "cleansing operation," as "the First and Second Armenian volunteer units saw success [sic] against the Turkish [sic] irregulars and attacked and looted Muslim villages."[70] When "the Turks" recaptured Van province a little over two months later, Akçam writes, "they killed the city's entire Armenian population."[71]

Seeing that virtually all Armenians had left the city and indeed the entire province, on the evidence of the missionaries, obviously this would not have been possible. After advancing on Bitlis but failing to capture the town, the Russians retreated to Van. On the night of July 30, according to Miss Knapp, "General Nicolaieff ordered all the Armenians of the Van province, also the Americans and other foreigners, to flee for their lives. By Saturday night the city was nearly emptied of Armenians and quite emptied of conveyances."[72]

On August 3, Van city was abandoned. According to missionary Ussher, 7,000 Armenians died on the flight into the Russian Caucasus, with many thousands more dying of dysentery after reaching what they thought was safety. Kurds attacked the Armenians during their flight, no doubt out of revenge for the killing of Muslims. The refugees, Ussher writes, included Armenians from Bitlis and Erzurum provinces: "During that week more than two hundred and seventy thousand refugees poured into the Caucasus and a friend told us later of seeing the Erivan plain filled with a shifting multitude overflowing the horizon."[73]

If Ussher's figure is correct, almost a fifth of all Ottoman Armenians crossed the border into the Russian Caucasus in August 1915 alone. Thousands more crossed into Russian Transcaucasia from the northeastern

Black Sea region. Few were allowed to return after the Russians consolidated their hold on the eastern provinces. In mid-August, a Russian force
reoccupied Van and held it until the collapse of the Russian war effort in
1917. When the Ottomans recaptured the city in 1918, it had been almost
completely destroyed. A new one had to be built in its place.

Ussher's accusation of extermination fits into the long history of Chris-
tian polemics against "the Turks" and Islam. In the late nineteenth century,
Sultan Abdülhamit was accused of setting in motion a "plan of extermination." Now the same charge was being leveled against "the Turks" again.
Ussher's memoirs were published in November 1917, but well before the
U.S. entered the war (April 6) he had been campaigning in America on
behalf of the Armenians. In early May, he addressed students at Harvard
University, telling them that several years before the war the Ottoman government had sent thirty-two regiments to Van to massacre the Christians,
withdrawing them only when Russia moved troops up to the border.

When the war broke out, he claimed the Armenians were hostile to the
Russians and had hurled them back into Russia, giving the Turks "a chance
to murder a great number of Russian women and children." The Armenians were then disarmed and made "the slaves of the Turkish soldiers."[74]
Such rank propaganda suggests that nothing Ussher wrote can be taken
at face value, including his account of his conversation with Cevdet Bey.
No Ottoman forces were moved to Van before the war with orders to
massacre Christians: where Ussher got this from only he would know.

In fact, while outbreaks of violence between Armenians and Kurds
continued in the years leading up to the war, Ottoman administrators in
Van were commended in British consular dispatches for their efforts to
maintain the peace.[75] A government commission inquired into the state
of the *jandarma*. A French officer had arrived as an advisor and a young
and energetic officer from the Ottoman general staff appointed as the
new commander. Foreign reports of ill treatment of the population were
"greatly exaggerated ... the gendarmerie authorities have made public in
every way possible that they will willingly listen to and investigate any
complaint against the gendarmes. They invite the villagers to bring any
such case to their notice."[76]

Ussher's further claim that Armenians hurled Russian forces back into
Russia after the war broke out is a complete inversion of the truth, given
the number of Armenians fighting with Russia, either in the regular army
or as volunteers in the *druzhiny* detachments, and killing Muslims in large
numbers.

ISTANBUL ARRESTS

There can be no doubt that the fall of Van, further exposing Ottoman supply lines and opening the way to possible Russian advances further south and west (Bitlis was finally occupied in February 1916), came as a serious blow to the Ottoman military command. Armenians regarded as a threat to the war effort had already been "relocated" from several districts (incuding Dörtyol, Osmaniye, Ceyhan, and Adana), but Van was the trigger for the general movement and resettlement of Armenians.

The first step was the closure on April 24 of the Armenian political committees—notably the Dashnaks, Hunchaks, and the Ramgavars—and arrest of their members or sympathizers in Istanbul and across fourteen *vilayetler* and ten *mutasarriflar* (subprovinces). It was emphasized that care should be taken "not to cause bloodshed between the Muslim people and the Armenian subjects."[77] In simultaneous searches, thousands of pistols and rifles (Mausers, Martinis, and Winchesters) and tens of thousands of bullets were seized in Istanbul—in churches as well as private houses—according to the German ambassador.[78] Other caches of weapons, ammunition, grenades, and dynamite were uncovered in Aydın, Izmir, Samsun, Trabzon, Kayseri, Sivas, Elazığ, Diyabakir, and Antep during the arrest of other Armenians.[79]

Those detained in Istanbul included the editor of *Sabah* (Morning) newspaper and political science professor Diran Kelekian, among other "upper-class" Armenians.[80] In other sources, there are extreme variations in estimates of the number of Armenians arrested in Istanbul or across the provinces on or after April 24, ranging from several hundred to several thousand.[81] Combined government figures put the number at several hundred.[82]

Yusuf Sarınay has shown from Ottoman documents that 235 Armenians were arrested in Istanbul on April 24. The next day, precise instructions were issued for 180 of the men to be sent to Ankara under armed guard by train that evening. The No. 164 train would leave Haydarpaşa station at 10:23 p.m., arriving in Ankara at the Sincan village railway station at 8:00 a.m.[83] From there, 60–70 were to be taken to the nearby town of Ayas and kept under arrest. The remaining prisoners were taken to Çankiri to be placed under house arrest. They would be obliged to pay for their own food and accommodation but were free to move around the town, on condition that they report to the police station every twenty-four hours. Some funds were provided by the government. A document sent from the Çankiri governorate to security headquarters on June 30, 1915, puts the number of detainees at 140.[84]

On August 31, 1915, the number detained in Çankiri was put at 155, of which number 35 had been found innocent and allowed to return to Istanbul, 25 had been found guilty and imprisoned at Ayaş or in Ankara, and 57 had been sent to Deir al-Zor. Of 7 foreign nationals, 3 had been deported and the others kept in custody. The remaining 31 had been pardoned and released to various towns in the western region, not including Istanbul or Izmir.[85]

Different documents give different numbers for Armenians held at Ayaş, either 60 or 71. All were accused of being members of the central committees of the Dashnaks and Hunchaks. One died and the rest were reported to have been released when the war was over and the armistice was signed.[86]

Raymond Kévorkian's version of the fate of the detainees is in accord with Sarinay at some points, while differing elsewhere. Kévorkian agrees that a number of Armenians were released soon after being detained, but whereas Sarınay merely refers to others being "exiled" to Deir al-Zor, Kévorkian is explicit in what he says happened to them when sent to Syria. In his account, after the release of some of the detainees, it was decided to proceed with "liquidation" of the rest.[87] "According to an Armenian survivor," he writes, 56 detainees from Çankiri were put on the road between July 8 and 11 "and slain to a man thereafter." A second convoy was dispatched on August 19, and a further 5 men sent off on the same date. Almost all were murdered, leaving only 37 detainees in Çankiri, a number close to the 31 Sarınay says were pardoned and released to live in towns.

Diran Kelekian, the *Sabah* editor who was initially detained, was close to a senior figure in the CUP, Bahaeddin Şakir. On the basis of this connection, he was released in early May on condition that he live outside Istanbul.[88] Kelekian chose Izmir but was later transferred to Çankiri anyway. On October 20, according to Kévorkian, he was sent under armed guard to Çorum to face a court-martial but was murdered between Yozgat and Kayseri.[89]

That Armenians in Istanbul were planning acts of sabotage and murder cannot be doubted. Armenians arrested in late 1914 confessed that they had been brought to Istanbul "to kill a man" and more specifically to kill Talat.[90] Furthermore, there is no doubt that the Armenian committees had a very active underground network in Istanbul linked to their bureaus abroad. The government claimed a plot was afoot to assassinate Enver as well as Talat, while the German ambassador wrote after the arrests on April 24, 1915, that Armenians had been planning to attack government offices on April 27, during celebrations for the accession of Sultan Mehmet V. On June 15, eighteen to twenty Armenians found guilty of planning assassination and sabotage were hanged in Istanbul.[91]

CHAPTER 13

The "Relocation"

LACKING THE MANPOWER to suppress continuing behind-the-lines sabotage of the war effort, the government picked up the equivalent of the current-day euphemism, "draining the swamp," by moving hundreds of thousands of Armenians in an operation called the *tehcir* (relocation). Such measures in wartime are ugly but hardly unique. Spain moved 400,000–600,000 people to camps in the process of suppressing the Cuban uprising of 1895–1896, which has gone into Cuban history as *la reconcentracia*. The U.S. moved civilians to "zones of protection" during its war with Filipino nationalists from 1898–1902. In South Africa, the British drove about 100,000 Boers and another 100,000 black African civilians into concentration camps during the Boer War (1899–1902). Russia moved up to 500,000 ethnic Germans from southern Russia and the Caucasus to Siberia in 1914.

About 117,000 Japanese Americans were interned during World War II. Not long after the war's end, British authorities in Malaya settled 500,000 ethnic Chinese in "new villages." At the tail end of the occupation of Algeria in the 1950s, French authorities moved up to 800,000 Algerians to *regroupement* centers. In Indochina, France also resettled about 3 million Vietnamese in "protected villages" (*agrovilles*) between 1952 and 1954, while millions of civilians were resettled in "protected" or "strategic hamlets" by the U.S. during its Vietnam involvement.

There are many differences between these situations as well as commonalities. Suffering, the loss of life, and the pain of being wrenched from an ancestral homeland are always involved. Unlike the Cubans or the Filipinos or the Algerians, however, the Armenians were not an occupied people, except in the minds of the militants. Rather, they were subjects of the sultan and citizens with the same rights and responsibilities as everyone else. Like civilians caught up in any war, the vast majority of Armenians would have been concentrating on survival, but insurgent activities were sufficiently threatening in the eyes of the military to justify the removal of all.

In December 1944, even though no Japanese-Americans were sabotaging the war effort, Supreme Court Justice Hugo Black also used the argument of military necessity when turning down the appeal by a Japanese-American citizen of his conviction for remaining in a designated military area in breach of an order excluding all citizens of Japanese descent.[1]

On May 26, the Ottoman military command recommended to the Ministry of the Interior that Armenians in densely populated areas of the eastern provinces should be moved to the south of Diyarbakir. This was followed on the same day by a message from the Interior Ministry (the Directorate for the Settlement of Tribes and Immigrants) to the Prime Ministry that it was necessary to transfer Armenians from the *valilikler* (governorates) of Van, Bitlis, and Erzurum; the *sancaklar* of Adana, Mersin, Cebel-i Bereket, Kozan, Maraş; and the *kazalar* (districts) of Iskenderun, Beylan, Cisr-i Şugur, and Antakya to the southern part of the *sancak* of Urfa, and the *sancaklar* of Deir al-Zor in eastern Syria and Mosul in Iraq. The process had already started under military command. The town centers of Urfa, Adana, Sis (now Kozan), Mersin, and Maraş were excepted from these instructions.[2]

On May 27, the government issued its "temporary law" covering the *tehcir* (relocation), and on May 31 the Council of Ministers issued a decree approving these measures and explaining why they had to be taken.[3] These can be reduced to "separatist aspirations"; armed attacks on soldiers and civilians; looting and plundering; passing information to the enemy; and stirring up hatred among "other subjects of the sultan." According to the instructions sent in code to provincial authorities, the Armenians were to be provided with food, shelter, and health care, with grain for planting or tools for artisans when they arrived at their destination. Restricting the number of Armenians to be resettled in any one location was a prime consideration. They should constitute no more than 10 percent "of Muslims and tribal members," and their places of resettlement should be at least 25 kilometers from the nearest railway line. Their property was to be held in trust, and, if sold, the proceeds were to be kept pending the owners' return.

Throughout this process it was emphasized that the decision taken was only to relocate the Armenians. "There is no intention like the complete destruction of the Armenian," Talat wrote, adding that it was "absolutely necessary to protect the convoys." Those who attacked them should be punished without mercy.[4]

RELOCATION EXEMPTIONS

There were many exemptions, including Armenian Catholics and Protestants, both of whose relocation was started and then stopped on Talat's orders[5]. Among others were parliamentary deputies and their families;[6] teachers; some merchants and tradesmen; employees of the Imperial Ottoman Bank, the tobacco *regie,* and the Public Debt Administration; civil servants; state railway administration staff and their families; army medical personnel and translators; and the families of Armenians who were ill or blind.[7] Children under the age of ten whose parents had been relocated were to be placed in orphanages "either existing or to be established" and given an education.[8] On the other hand, Armenians who had converted to Islam in the hope of avoiding the relocation were not exempted.

Even for Armenians who were not moved, concentrated populations were broken up. Thus, if there were more than five Armenian houses in a town or village, the family would have to shift to a Muslim village within their district. The Armenian population ratio could be no more than 5 percent of the host community. "Therefore," one directive stated, "in a Muslim village consisting of twenty houses there can only be a single Armenian house while in the villages or towns having more than a hundred houses, the number of Armenian houses can never exceed five."[9]

Suspicion pushed the relocation gradually westward, as far as İzmit on the shores of the Sea of Marmara. Instructions were issued to remove Armenians from Çanakkale, within the *sancak* or to Balikesir if necessary, after they were accused of having celebrated the Italian victory in the Libyan War.[10]

The Armenians of Istanbul remained under suspicion after the arrests of April 24 and subject to arrest when under suspicion, but they were not included in the relocation. Neither were the Armenians of Izmir. Not all those relocated were moved south to Syria or into Iraq. Some from the southeast were settled in Kastamonu, near the Black Sea coast; others were sent to Konya in central Anatolia and Balikesir (Karesi) in the west. Some were even moved to the outskirts of Urfa, replacing Armenians who had been shifted elsewhere,[11] but the clear intention always was to break up and disperse the Armenian population.

By October 27, 1915, Talat was already ordering an end to the relocation of Armenians from certain *valilikler* and *sancaklar*,[12] but tens of thousands were still on the move, with about half a million having arrived in Syria by February 1916. Government figures indicated a total Armenian population of 987,569 in nineteen provinces affected by the relocation, with 413,067 Armenians actually moved.[13] This is close to the 486,000 given in the Bryce papers on February 3, 1915.[14] This estimate is followed by a dispatch dated February 8: "I transmit herewith as copy of a report received from reliable sources in reference to the number of Armenian immigrants [*sic*] in this vicinity, between here and Damascus and in the surrounding country down to the Euphrates river as far as Der al-Zor, showing a total of about 500,000 persons."[15]

Dr. J. K. Marden, attached to the American Committee for Armenian and Syrian Relief (ACASR), wrote in 1917 that 486,000 individuals were receiving aid in February 1916.[16] An initial end to the relocation was ordered on February 21, 1915, but deferred to March 15 when the final instructions went out. Armenians still en route settled where they were at the time.[17] On December 7, 1916, the Ottoman Ministry of the Interior informed the grand vizier that a total of 702,900 Armenians had been relocated.[18] As might be expected, the figures fluctate greatly according to the source.[19]

SUSPECT "DOCUMENTS"

It was not just the negligence, cruelty, and criminal actions of officials or attacks by brigands and tribes that accounted for Armenian losses but the lack of almost everything that was needed to move them safely. There were no proper roads, only a few stretches of railway, little in the way of medical facilities, along with severe shortages of food for the soldiers as well as the civilian population. Neither was sufficient manpower available to protect the convoys.

Such a large-scale movement of a human population would have been difficult in times of peace. At a time of war, it proved to be completely impossible, feeding the accusations of genocide, a concept that did not exist in 1915 (but has been no bar to scholars applying the word retroactively) and which, in the case of the Ottoman Empire, has never been argued out legally in a court capable of handing down authoritative judgment.

Arguments against the wartime Ottoman government range from Bloxham's structural analysis of genocide taking place as the end result of a gradual "radicalization" of government policies[20] to Taner Akçam's accusation that the Ottoman government actually took a decision to wipe out the Armenians. In Akçam's view, it was "very likely" that "key decisions" concerning the massacre of Armenians were made "within the CUP" in March 1915. In his text, these "key decisions" for "the massacre" then slide seamlessly into a "decision for genocide" made by the CUP central committee "deliberately and after long consideration."[21] Akçam refers to postwar accusations, when Istanbul was occupied by the powers, but otherwise, building on supposition, speculation, and the utilization of suspect if not clearly falsified "documents," he produces no evidence to show that any such decision was ever taken.[22]

Talat's assassination in 1921 ended all further possibilities of exploring what he might, must, or should have known. He remains the central figure in an Armenian national narrative of planned destruction. On the Armenian National Institute website, he is described as the "principal architect" of the genocide.[23] Ara Sarafian writes that Talat was "clearly aware" that Armenians were being destroyed during the relocation and "obviously considered the ruin of Ottoman Armenians as a personal triumph."[24] For Göçek, Talat "governed an empire with a substantive non-Muslim, non-Turkish population that he intended to eliminate."[25] For Michael Reynolds, Talat's words when defending his actions left little doubt that "he understood the radically transgressive nature of his resolution of the Armenian question."[26] Taner Akçam quotes the view of the German scholar Ernest Jackh, that Talat "clearly saw the annihilation of the Armenian people as easing the political situation."[27] He also quotes the postwar allegations of Ottoman officials that Talat had sent them orders for the annihilation of the Armenians.[28] For Donald Bloxham, the nature of the deportations alone was sufficient evidence of "genocidal intent."[29] The Armenians were defenseless and without provisions, and attacks on the convoys fulfilled the desire of "radicals" for massacre. They were not being sent into regions where settlement was "possible if difficult" but into desert regions where, by implication, settlement was not possible, "natural attrition" taking a deadly toll.[30]

In fact, with war raging on the western front and in northeastern Anatolia, and the relocation having been decided, there was no other direction in which the Armenians could be sent but south. Furthermore, the eastern Syrian regions were not empty. Statistics for 1914 show that Deir al-Zor province—a main region for Armenian resettlement—alone had a town or village population of more than 60,000.[31] In line with the decisions taken in late May, however, the Armenians were to be kept separate from the settled population. The region was arid but divded by two river valleys, the Euphrates and the Khabur, a tributary of the Euphrates, both of which were settled and heavily cultivated along their banks.

The conditions of the Armenians, kept away from these more fertile settled regions, were shocking but mostly the consequence of completely inadequate food supplies, lack of proper sanitation, and the rapid spread of epidemic disease. If the Ottoman government is to be condemned, it is for failing to provide the safety and protection Talat had guaranteed, not for an unproven assertion that it sent the Armenians to eastern Syria knowing they would die.

The accusations against the government and Talat in particular must be weighed against a mass of documents, most bearing the interior minister's signature, instructing provincial officials to make sure that the Armenians were properly cared for and protected. In fact, the relocation turned into a disaster of epic proportions. Guarded only by thin lines of soldiers, *jandarma*, and other armed men, the Armenians were defenseless against onslaughts by tribal groups out for booty or perhaps taking revenge on wholly innocent and helpless people for attacks on Muslims by Armenian bands. Thousands died of disease, malnutrition, or exposure by the roadside or in makeshift camps even before reaching Syria.

The complicity of some of those entrusted with their protection suggests that while cowardice, negligence, and corruption were all involved, there was also a sense that the Armenians deserved what was coming to them. The bitter remarks of Ali Rıza Eti, the eastern-front corporal, were probably representative of the attitudes of many soldiers and civilians. "I wonder if something is going to be done to the Armenians at the end of the war?" he wrote in late 1914. The Russian enemy was receiving intelligence from Armenians who were deserting every day, and the soldiers must also have understood their treachery, "since every day they accidentally shoot three to five Armenians from each battalion. At this rate not a single Armenian will be left."[32] Blaming an Armenian for the death of a soldier he was supposed to be transporting to hospital but abandoned in a ditch, Ali Rıza took out his anger on Armenian hospital staff, mistreating some patients, giving the worst tasks to Armenian cleaners, and then having them replaced with Turks.[33]

In the short period after the war before his assassination in Germany in March 1921, Talat denied harboring any evil intentions toward the Armenians. The automatic response, of course, is that this is what he would say, but he is still entitled to his defense. According to Talat, the plan was only for Armenians to be moved out of harm's way so the military would have clear space to deal with the armed bands attacking the war effort behind the lines.

Talat admitted that the relocation had turned into a disaster, but,

> Whoever might have been in our place would have had to do the same thing for the safety of our country. Think a bit. At a time when our armies were in a life and death struggle with enemies who were vastly superior in both numbers and equipment the Armenians, who were our fellow countrymen, had armed themselves and revolted over the whole country and were cooperating with the enemy for the purpose of striking us in the rear. What other choice was there but to remove this race away from the war zones?[34]

While only a relatively small number of Armenians were involved in the insurgency, it was the bulk of the population—overwhelmingly innocent—that suffered. For this, Talat expressed "great pain and distress." However, he was the minister and must be held responsible for the consequences of his decisions, even if (questionable, if not completely rejected in the minds of some) he could not foresee the consequences.[35]

Cemal Paşa, demonized along with Talat and assassinated in Tbilisi on July 21, 1922, blamed Russia for the ill feeling created between Muslims and Christians. In his autobiography, he drew attention to the measures he took when appointed *vali* of Adana, including the execution of forty-seven Muslims found guilty of criminal acts and the allocation of funds for the rebuilding of Armenian houses. He wrote that he had "nothing to do with the deportations and Armenian massacres."[36] This is true: the relocation was not his decision, but he was stuck with the consequences. He had failed to secure support for his preference, which was moving the Armenians to central Anatolia on a line between Konya, Ankara, and the

Black Sea town of Kastamonu. If the bulk of Armenians were in Syria, that was only because he had persuaded the government that Mosul was an even worse option.

Furthermore, while Cemal ran Syria with an iron hand, there is abundant evidence of the measures he took to alleviate the suffering of the Armenians, providing medical care and support for orphans, increasing funding for food supplies, setting up workshops, and finding work for Armenians in government and municipal offices or private institutions. Many Armenians were able to leave the camps for the towns. Cemal also hanged army officers and Kurds found guilty of crimes committed against Armenians. While the mass of Armenians were penned in camps, some who had been working as state officials and had won the favor of Şukru Bey, the local director of the Department for the Settlement of Tribes and Immigrants, were permitted to settle in Damascus, Hama, Homs, and other towns located along the railway as long as they did not exceed 2 percent of the local population.[37]

Without casting doubt on the military reasons for the relocation, Cemal finally asked, "Could not the question have been solved in another way? Or would it not have been possible to protect the exiles from attacks en route?"[38] From the point of the Ottoman military, however, while the human cost of the relocation was shocking, the isolation of the insurgents and their exposure to military attack ended the threat to military supply lines.[39]

SPECIAL OPERATIONS

The relocation calls into question the role of the Teşkilat i-Mahsusa. This was a special-operations organization of the type many governments form at a time of war and maintain in times of peace to destabilize societies, overthrow governments, and assassinate political enemies.

Formally established in November 1913, the Teşkilat's operations were basically the same as any other intelligence organization from that time to the present. Its initial structure was based on an administrative committee and four regional desks (Rumelia, the Caucasus, Africa, and the eastern Anatolian provinces).[40] But in May–June 1915, the organization's name was changed to the Department of Eastern Affairs (Umur-i Şarkiye Dairesi).[41] The number of its desks was expanded to seven.[42] The regional desk core consisted of India, Egypt, Afghanistan, Africa, and an "eastern department," most probably responsible for the eastern Anatolian provinces and Transcaucasia.

The department functioned under the authority of the Ministry of War and was directly responsible to Enver. Its duties, covering the entire range of any intelligence organization, comprised reconaissance and information-gathering, counterintelligence, propaganda and disinformation, recruitment of agents in hostile countries, reconaissance, the dispatch of irregular units to fight alongside the regular army, and counterinsurgency. The upper ranks of the Teşkilat consisted of about 700 *ikhwan* (brothers), many of whom went on to play prominent roles in Turkish and Arab politics after the war.[43]

Beneath the *ikhwan* were the thousands of men who carried out orders in the field. Stanford Shaw has put their numbers, at the organization's height, at about 30,000, recruited from among men who had not been called up, including Muslim refugees from the Caucasus, tribal members, volunteer professionals (journalists, retired army officers, doctors, engineers), and even criminals whose sentences were commuted if they volunteered.[44]

The various magnets for joining the Teşkilat included patriotism, common Muslim identity, a regular salary, and, for the criminally inclined, an opportunity to profit from the misery of war. Corruption among officers and indiscipline among the ranks gave the organization a bad reputation even among the regular army. In the field, Teşkilat units "often acted as little more than bandits, ravaging villages and roads in Ottoman as well as enemy territory."[45]

In the opinion of some writers, Donald Bloxham, Taner Akçam, and Fatma Müge Göçek among them, the central government set out to annihilate the Armenians and used the Teşkilat as its main instrument of destruction.[46] In fact, the relocation was carried out by provincial officials under the instructions of the Ministry of Interior. Although some of its agents in the field were involved, and some were punished for their crimes, the relocation was not a Teşkilat operation. In an excellent graduate thesis, Polat Safi has made a detailed study of the Teşkilat from documents in the Ottoman archives. His description of the observations of one leading European scholar on the Teşkilat's role in the Armenian question as reductionist and often derogatory, as well as overgeneralizing and oversimplifying "the complex nature of the Teşkilat and its activities," would seem to apply to many others.[47]

CRIMES AND TRIALS

Attacks on Armenians are recorded in many Ottoman documents. According to one, "It has been communicated by the Governorate of Erzurum that a convoy of 500 Armenians removed from Erzurum has been massacred by the Kurds between Erzurum and Erzincan."[48] Elsewhere,

> According to the information received recently, massacres have been conducted in the province [of Diyarbakir] against the Armenians and Christians in general, without making any distinction between their sects. Particularly, from the individuals sent from Diyarbakir recently, it has been learnt that in Mardin, a total of 700 people consisting of Armenians and other Christians, also including the bishop, had been taken from their homes by night and killed by beheading like sheep.
>
> The number of individuals killed in that way until now has been estimated to have reached two thousand and it is feared that the Muslim people living in the neighbouring provinces could also rise up to massacre all the Christians unless the events are rapidly and definitely put an end to.[49]

Other reports speak of crimes committed by officials and the armed men supposedly guarding the convoys.

Agents of the state—police, *jandarma*, and senior provincial officials, as well as tribes out for booty or revenge (or both)—accused of criminal acts are named in the documents. Evidence indicated that Rifat Bey, the *kaymakam* of the Ulukişla district in Niğde *sancak* and Hasan Efendi, the *jandarma* commander, had murdered five Armenians and stolen the money hidden under their belts. The *kaymakam* was also accused of robbing a grocer and the *jandarma* commander of taking bribes from Armenians passing through the district. An Armenian girl had been taken away from her family and sent to Istanbul to be married to an army officer.[50]

In Konya, a member of the *jandarma* had been seen whipping Armenians at the train station in full view of other travelers.[51] In Sivas Cemil Bey, the *kaymakam* of the Sarkişla district, was dismissed for "improper conduct" toward Armenians, pending an investigation by a military prosecutor.[52] Hamit Bey, *kaymakam* of Pınarbası district in the same province, was similarly dismissed, pending his referral to a military tribunal.[53]

Again in Sivas, prosecution was recommended for the deputy *kaymakam* of Suşehri, Fahri Efendi, who had had allowed the pillage of Armenian property on the day of the relocation.[54] Officials elsewhere were singled out for negligence, failure to obey instructions, and intervening in the authority of neighboring districts.

Some Muslims (including Kurds) tried to protect the Armenians; some officials refused to be part of the relocation; and on the way or in Syria, many officials did their best to care for the Armenians within the constraints imposed by the war. The government funded the relocation with millions of *kuruş*, adding to this amount from other budgets according to need, but without ever meeting the needs of the Armenians or indeed those of the civilian population in general.[55]

As Talat set up the investigations and courts-martial of 1915–1916, and as there is the evidence of massacre in Ottoman documents, he obviously knew of the crimes being committed during the relocation. The trials are surely evidence that he did not sanction them.[56] In September 1915, the government established three commissions of inquiry to look into reports of attacks on the Armenian convoys and the complicity or negligence of officials. The high-level officials appointed to head these inquiries included Hasim Bey, a member of the Council of State; Hulusi Bey, president of the Court of Appeal; Muhtar Bey, civil services inspector in Ankara; Asim Bey, first president of the Court of Appeal; and Nihat Bey, an advocate from the Court of First Instance. The panels also included senior *jandarma* commanders.

The commissions were sent to three separate regions: the northwestern provinces as far inland as Eskişehir and Ankara; eastern Anatolia from the Black Sea down to Bitlis and Diyarbakir; and the southeast across what is now the Syrian border.[57] Their findings resulted in the court-martial of 1,673 people: 528 police, army, and intelligence officers; 170 civil servants up to the level of provincial subgovernors; and 975 gang members or civilians who simply joined in the attacks and pillaging. Charges included murder, assault, theft, bribery, extortion, and the forced marriage of Armenian women. By the middle of 1916, 916 individuals had been or were in the process of being prosecuted. Of this number, 67 had been sentenced to death and another 524 sentenced to prison terms of varying length.[58]

Research on this particular aspect of the war still has a long way to go, but for uncommitted and interested observers of the war situation, an obvious question arises: if the Ottoman government was determined to kill the Armenians, why was it prosecuting people accused of doing just that? Then there is the evidence in innumerable documents of government instructions that the Armenians were to be protected. Obviously, they were not. So, were the documents and the trials part of an immensely complex coverup, designed to conceal sinister intentions and actions? Or, do such accusations and insinuations come closer to an unfounded conspiracy theory rather than a far messier, disjointed, and disorganized reality?

From all the evidence of Ottoman maladministration and corruption, especially in the eastern provinces, leading up to the First World War, there is little reason to think that the government was capable of efficiently carrying out such an immensely difficult operation as the relocation of such a large number of people. However, if the army had decided the operation was necessary to save the empire, what was Talat to do, tell the generals that it couldn't be done, that the empire would have to collapse instead? Whatever the explanations, the outcome was ugly and brutal in the extreme.

BRYCE AND TOYNBEE

In Britain, the government made the most of the suffering of the Armenians. The most effective propaganda campaigns against both the Germans and the Ottomans were prepared under the direction of James Bryce. He was then nearing the end of a long life as a diplomat, distinguished historian, and activist for numerous communities he regarded as being oppressed, including all Christians living under Muslim rule and the Amazon Indians, whose exploitation on a British-owned rubber plantation he and Roger Casement had exposed.

In the 1890s, Bryce and Gladstone had agitated on behalf of the Armenians. Their suffering in 1915 gave Bryce a last opportunity to step forward. In 1916, he had already published his propaganda report on alleged German atrocities in Belgium, teaming up with Arnold Toynbee to prepare the collection of "documents" on the Armenians presented to the foreign secretary (Lord Grey) and published as a Parliamentary Paper (Blue Book).

Many of the claims made in the German report were shown to be fraudulent when the war was over, and Bryce's assertion that in the Armenian report he had bound himself to evidentiary standards observed in Britain and the courts of the Commonwealth is not borne out by the

contents of the Blue Book. Most of the evidence is hearsay, and most of
the "documents" are not documents at all but extracts from missionary
diaries, Armenian nationalist newspapers, and numerous letters from or
statements made by unnamed sources. They include an "especially well-
informed neutral source at Constantinople," an "authoritative source,"
"an Armenian formerly resident in Turkey," "letter from Mr. N, a foreign
resident at Constantinople," "a well-informed source at Bukarest," a "statement made by a foreign resident at Constantinople to a Swiss gentleman
at Geneva," and so on.

A vast amount of material has been written on the consequences of
the relocation. Much is based on what someone heard rather than what
they saw for themselves, but there is still abundant and credible eyewitness testimony in British, German, French, and American archival sources
as to the vast number of Armenians who were massacred or died from
other causes during the course of the war. Out of all this material, some
documents stand out because of what the author actually saw, as opposed
to what he or she had been told or surmised had happened. The author
of one such document, Leslie A. Davis, the U.S. consul at Harput from
1914–1917, compiling his report in 1918 on the consequences of the relocation, wrote that when he arrived in Harput (June 1914) "there seemed
to be nothing but good feeling between Mohammedan and Christian and
the Turks and Armenians appeared to be on friendly terms."[59]

This atmosphere quickly changed after war was declared and changed
even more when Armenians were moved from Harput and the town
became a transit point for other relocated Armenians being sent into
Syria. These "exiles" camping on the outskirts of the town were in shocking condition: "All of them were in rags and many of them were almost
naked. They were emaciated, sick, diseased, filthy, covered with dirt and
vermin, resembling animals far more than human beings." As soon as a
new group arrived, the earlier group would be moved along except for the
sick and elderly who could not move. Davis saw several hundred dead and
dying scattered around the camp, mumbling old men, emaciated women
and children with bloated bellies among them, some in convulsions.

With houses being searched for arms and ammunition and the missionaries themselves under suspicion (some of it justified, as he admits
to helping hide ammunition found on missionary premises), Davis was
soon referring to a "reign of terror." On June 23, 1915, he reported, several
hundred prominent Armenians, including the bishop of the Gregorian
church, most of the teachers at the missionary-run Euphrates College,

and many professionals and businessmen were sent away in oxcarts. Later, he heard that nearly all had been massacred somewhere between Harput and Diyarbakir.

Between July 1 and 3, thousands of Armenians were moved out of the town, at the same time that several hundred Armenians from Erzurum were arriving, Harput being a transit point during the relocation. All the men had been killed by Kurds en route and the women robbed, the *jandarma* "pretending" to be unable to protect them (but then providing them with clothing from village women).

Davis refers to reports of a massacre of 800–900 men outside the town on July 7, followed by the massacre later in the month of a party of forty Armenians despite a safe-conduct pass to Aleppo issued by the *vali*. All were killed by Kurds or *jandarma*, he wrote, with the exception of three women "saved for the harems of the murderers." He had heard of orphan children being taken to a lake 29 miles away and drowned.

In the autumn of 1915, Davis rode out to Lake Gölcük where "a Turk" had told him of seeing thousands of dead bodies. Even before reaching the lake, Davis saw several hundred bodies, mostly women and children. It seemed obvious to the consul that they had been killed "as so many could not have died from disease or exhaustion." Riding around a shore-line indented by deep valleys, more ghastly sights awaited him: "hundreds of bodies and bones in the water below," with heads sticking out of the sand at the edge of the lake. "It was rumoured," Davis wrote, "that many of the people who were brought here had been pushed over the cliffs by the gendarmes and killed in that way." A local Kurd said *jandarma* had brought 2,000 Armenians to one valley twenty days before "and had made the Kurds from neighboring villages come and kill them."

On a second visit to the lake with a missionary doctor several weeks later, Davis decided to see what lay on the far side. The terrible scenes were the same: more dead bodies, including women and children. In the course of their ride, the consul and the missionary were convinced that they had seen the bodies of "not less" 10,000 people, only the bones of some remaining but others apparently killed recently. "We noticed bay-onet wounds on many of them," Davis wrote. "It was a mystery how they could have been killed so closely together. There must have been a large number of gendarmes or Kurds to surround them in order to slaughter them in that way. All of the bodies were naked and many of them showed the signs of brutal mutilation which the gendarmes inflicted upon so many of the women and girls whom they killed." One group of bodies was still sitting upright in the hills around the remains of a fire, and personal effects including broken jugs and bowls, spoons, a sock, and "passports"—no doubt internal travel documents—indicated that this group had come from Erzurum and other places and had set up camp before dying, possibly of hunger.

Around the lake, Davis saw the evidence of terrible crimes but his conclusions about who was responsible were based on hearsay, rumors, or what he had assumed about people being pushed off cliffs and massacred, "as so many could not have died from disease or exhaustion." The campfire and personal belongings found in the hills indicate that some people at least were taken to the lake and abandoned to their fate. The state of their bodies indicated death from malnutrition or exposure. What is not arguable is that something truly shocking had happened on the shores of this lake.

There are many other accounts of massacres or of attacks on camps in Syria by Kurds and Circassians. Armenians also died in great numbers from malnutrition and disease. Their dead or dying bodies were observed by numerous witnesses along the route into Syria, or in and around its towns and encampments.

The scenes witnessed in what is now southeastern Turkey and across the border in north and northeastern Syria really were images from hell. An employee of the Vacuum Oil Company, Auguste Bernau, estimated that 60,000 Armenians had been buried around the Meskene transit camp, about 100 kilometers east of Aleppo, "carried off by hunger, by privations of all sorts, by intestinal disease and typhus which is the result. As far as the eye can reach mounds are seen containing 200 to 300 corpses buried in the ground pele mele [sic], women, children and old people belonging to different families."[60] Camp conditions were literally execrable, with no latrines and rubbish scattered everywhere.

It is not likely that a precise number for the Ottoman Armenians who died will ever be known. Hundreds of thousands survived the war, including an estimated half a million who took refuge in the Caucasus and nearly 600,000 estimated to be still living in Ottoman lands by the U.S. official responsible for "western Asia" at the Paris peace talks in 1919. [61] Thus, the often-given figure of 1.5 million dead—corresponding to the size of the entire Ottoman Armenian population—cannot be correct.

Some estimates in Armenian sources include the number of Armenians (not necessarily Ottoman) who died during the fighting (or because of it) that followed in the Caucasus after the war. The conflation of these figures from two separate periods between 1914 and 1923 is misleading.

The 1914–1918 war was one period, within which the relocation was a particular event. The subsequent fighting in the Caucasus among all ethnonational groups (Armenians, Azerbaijanis, Georgians, and Turks), involving as well outside participants (including Bolsheviks, White Russians, and British and German forces), was a different affair altogether.

The Armenian Genocide Museum in Yerevan (Erivan) puts the number of dead at 1.5 million "killed" (as opposed to dying for other reasons) from 1915–1923. Bloxham's 1914–1918 estimate is one million,[62] Kiernan's is up to 1.2 million,[63] while Göçek writes that the "western scholarly community is almost in full agreement that 800,000–1.5 million died."[64] Kévorkian puts the figure at 1.3 million, or 1.5 million if the number for those who died in Azerbaijan and the Caucasus is added.[65] Estimates by Turkish historians or foreign scholars specializing in Ottoman demographics fluctuate between 300,000 and about 600,000 Ottoman Armenian dead from all causes (not just massacre) for the duration of the war.[66]

The upper figure that has come out of their research tallies with Toynbee's estimate of 600,000 made just after the war.[67] All these figures have been challenged as either too high (for the Turks) or too low (for Armenians and historians who share their view of history). Still, given the size of the Ottoman Armenian population, even 600,000 is an enormous death toll.

THE COINAGE OF WAR

The coinage of war and war atrocities generally has two sides. The First World War is no different. War is all about extreme violence, inevitably extending to the civilian population and requiring both sides to disclaim atrocities and deliberate harm to noncombatants while allocating all wickedness to the enemy. There is rarely a situation in which the perpetrators of violence against civilians are all on one side and the victims are all on the other, but this is generally how the "Armenian question" has been framed in the western cultural mainstream and parliaments around the world. The Muslim victims of Armenian violence are mostly ignored. Perhaps it is not even known that they existed. Where references are made, the impression is that this violence was small scale, individual, and in any case justified by Muslim attacks on Armenians.

In fact, violence by Armenians was not small scale at all. It began well before the relocation, reached a peak during the Russian occupation of northeastern Anatolia and was then directed against Azerbaijani Muslims when Armenian forces were driven back into the Caucasus.

The Kurds of what is now northern Iraq were also the victims of extreme violence at the hands of Armenians. Traveling through the region in December 1918—January 1919, British army officer Major Kenneth Mason reported that after the Russians defeated an Ottoman force in northwest Persia in late August 1916, capturing two regiments and driving the rest back across the border to Rowanduz, "Armenian troops with the Russians massacred about five thousand Kurds, men, women and children by driving them off the cliffs of the Rowanduz gorge at the point of the bayonet." He remarked, "Even the Armenian can be a bit of a tiger when he has a defenceless prey." When the Russians withdrew from the region, "[T]hey took the precaution of wiping out almost every village on their line of retreat."[68]

As the major obviously did not witness this massacre, he was clearly repeating what he had been told, so his account has to be treated with the same skepticism that should be applied to Armenian accounts of Kurdish atrocities, but the basic fact of large-scale Armenian violence against Kurds during the war is no more to be doubted than extreme Kurdish violence against Armenians.

As Ottoman statistics did not differentiate between different Muslim ethnicities, only estimates can be made of how many Kurds died in the war as against Turks or Muslims of other ethnic backgrounds. In 1919, a Kurdish newspaper put the number of Kurds massacred in the Van/Bitlis region at nearly 400,000, further stating, "but they [the Kurds] thought the matter should stop there.... [W]e have got to live side by side with them ... let us do so peacefully." Kurdish tribal chiefs admitted Kurdish massacres of Armenians, blaming "the Turks" for instigating them but made a point that some tribes had protected Armenians.[69]

Documents in the Ottoman archives—real documents, not extracts from Armenian newspapers in the Caucasus or from distant anonymous correspondents that characterize the Bryce-Toynbee allegations—indicate that of the millions of Muslim civilians who died between 1914 and 1919, hundreds of thousands were killed by Armenians, Russian Armenians, or Russians, as variously described.[70] While all archival material must be read critically and skeptically, allowing for exaggerations and even untruths, the mass of evidence in these documents indicates that a far vaster number of Muslims died at Armenian hands than Fatma Müge Göçek's "at most 40,000 to 60,000."[71]

These documents are the records of what survivors told Ottoman military officials and civil administrators when the Ottomans were able to return to the eastern provinces in 1918. This primary source material was gathered at the time by senior military and *jandarma* commanders and commissioners of inquiry from local people and community leaders, including police, religious dignitaries, town and village notables, and heads of municipalities and province subdistricts down to *kaza* and the smallest communal *nahiye* level.

The same or similar accounts of terrible cruelty were told across the eastern provinces from the Black Sea to the Mediterranean. They came from cities, towns, and villages across the east, including Trabzon, Oltu, Kosor, Pasinler, Adilcevez, Karakilese, Eleşkirt, Kötek, Ardahan, Sarıkamış, Ardahan, Akçakale, Hinis, Kağizaman, Erzurum, Erzincan, Tercan, Hasankale, Bayburt, and Beyazit down to Kilis, Adana, and Maraş.

Atrocities elsewhere in the empire and across the former Russian border around Nahcivan and Erevan are included. The documents give details down to the town quarter *(mahalle)* or village. In many cases, full lists of the names of those murdered are included, often entire families down to small children. The names of their killers are also sometimes given, indicating that they were once either neighbors or at least well known to their victims.

These narratives are extremely unpleasant, raising the problem for the researcher of how far to go when describing them, but history without some of the detail is not history. The documents—genuine documents— tell of villagers burnt alive in barns and mosques; of beheadings and hangings; of murder by bayonet, axe, or flaying alive; of the trampling of men to death with horses; of babies thrown into bread ovens and other revolting and inhumane criminal acts; and of rape, of course, frequently followed by the victim's death.

Along with the slaughter, the documents give evidence of the destruction in villages and towns of houses, mosques, schools, government buildings, bridges, storage depots, bathhouses, Sufi lodges, and the tombs of saints, as well as the pillage and the theft of personal possessions and household goods (gold coins, jewelry, carpets, and bedding), large quantities of grain, and tens of thousands of cattle and livestock.

There is also the first-hand evidence of witnesses such as Ahmet Refik (Altınay), describing what he saw when entering devastated towns in the eastern provinces after Armenian forces had retreated. He traveled through the region in April–May 1918, as the head of a commission charged with investigating Russian and Armenian atrocities against Muslims. In Erzurum, Erzincan, and other places, he walked into scenes of sheer horror.

> I am in a place [Erzurum] destroyed by fire. This historical and devoted land of the Turks lay in ruins. Streets, buildings, mosques, madrasas and entirely destroyed houses are filled up with bodies.... Streets were all filled with bodies of women and children. Women's breasts and even private organs were nailed to walls. Children's lungs were hanging from telegraph wires. Entirely naked women's bodies with pierced abdomens were put in rows on both sides of the road. When we had seen this state of my unfortunate nation we became almost crazy. I wonder if civilized Europe will try to find out who are guilty of these crimes. History has never recorded such brutalities before."[72]

In Erzincan, where Armenians had slaughtered hundreds of Muslims and thrown their bodies into wells, "I am amidst ruins ... even the tiles of mosques were taken away.... [F]rom Trebizond to Erzurum there is nothing but ruins.... There is not a single living creature in any village."[73] In Tercan, his commission found, most of the buildings had been destroyed and the mosque turned into a church.[74]

The Ottoman general, Vehip Paşa, wrote of what he saw when returning to the east after the retreat of Armenian forces in 1918.

> All people old enough to use weapons were rounded up, taken to the Sarikamis direction for road-building and slaughtered. The remaining people were subject to cruelties and murder by Armenians after the withdrawal of Russian forces and were partly annihilated, the corpses thrown into wells, burnt in houses, mutilated by bayonets, their abdomens ripped open in slaughterhouses, their lungs and liver torn out, girls and women hung up by their hair, after all kinds of devilish acts.[75]

Between Çardaklı-Boğaz and Erzincan, the general had seen

> all the villages destroyed to the point that not one villager's hut has escaped destruction. The trees in all the orchards have been cut down and all the villagers are dead. History has not recorded

such atrocities as those committed by the Armenians in Erzincan. For three days we have done nothing but gather up the bodies of Muslims killed by Armenians then cast aside. Among these innocent victims are children not yet weaned, ninety-year-old men and women cut to pieces.[76]

Similar or worse scenes were witnessed by other military commanders, evidence of a hatred so transcendent that for many of the perpetrators, torturing and killing "the enemy" (civilian men, women, and children, the very young, and the very old) was not enough: the body had to be eviscerated and the parts put on display.

The scale of murder and destruction by Armenians was confirmed by U.S. Army Captains Emory H. Niles and Arthur E. Sutherland when they traveled across the eastern provinces in 1919 at the behest of the U.S. Congress. "Incredulous at first," they came to believe what they were told, on the basis that the testimony was unanimous and corroborated. Armenians had massacred Muslims on a large scale, "with many refinements of cruelty." The destruction of towns and villages they could see for themselves: many Muslim villages had been entirely destroyed, while Armenian villages remained standing. In Bitlis and Van, only the Armenian quarters were still standing. The whole country had been ruined and bitter hatred fomented among Muslims toward Armenians.[77]

Through such causes as massacre, disease, and malnutrition, the Muslim population of the eastern provinces had been reduced by up to 60 percent of prewar levels. Armenians died from the same range of causes, and the proportionate death toll was not greatly different, although in absolute terms, as the Muslim population was much greater, the number of Muslims who died was much higher. Justin McCarthy estimates that as a percentage of the prewar population the Armenian death toll in the six eastern provinces was "slightly higher" than Muslim losses. The general depopulation of some regions of the eastern provinces has been put at about 75 percent.[78] Apart from those who died, many Armenian civilians fled into the Caucasus or further abroad during the war or in its immediate aftermath. As a result, while a small Armenian community remained in Istanbul, the long historical Armenian presence in eastern Anatolia was extinguished.

More than a century later, Ahmet Refik's "civilized Europe" and its historians, while continuing to condemn "the Turks," are still ignoring the scale of the violence committed by Armenians against Muslims during the war. The contemporary phrase that fits the actions of armed Armenian bands in the eastern Anatolian provinces of the Ottoman Empire is "ethnic cleansing," only a step removed from the charge of genocide levelled at "the Turks." Armenian nationalists gave one Russian army officer the impression of wanting "to exterminate all Muslim residents of the areas we occupied," their savagery provoking "desperate Kurdish resistance" and complicating Russian military operations.[79]

Hard truths lie under the embellishments, the exaggerations and lies told for propaganda purposes to inflate or reduce the epic suffering of Ottoman Muslim and Christian civilians. This was not a "tragedy" born of elemental forces beyond human capacity to control but was entirely man-made, the consequence of actions flowing from decisions taken by governments at war. The Allied powers incited hatred of the enemy among their own people as well as among ethnoreligious groups they thought they could turn against the enemy: Arabs against Turks, Christians (Armenians and Assyrians) against Muslims (Turks and Kurds).

These governments advanced their own strategic objectives while damaging (if not destroying) the long-term national interests of their protégés by the time the war ended. The Assyrians ended up dispersed in Iraqi refugee camps, and while France sought to advance its own interests under the umbrella of an Armenian "protectorate" in the eastern Mediterranean, this project broke on the rock of Turkish national resistance. France was also forced to accept a smaller Syria. Losing their stake in Cilicia, the Armenians were then driven back by the Turkish nationalists in northeastern Anatolia and had to settle for an autonomous region established across the border by the Soviet Union. As for Britain, the only long-term beneficiary of its assurances was the Zionist movement, founded in Europe in the late nineteenth century and regarded as a useful tool in imperial planning.

In the second-level war generated among the civilian population of the Ottoman Empire, human beings divided into ethnoreligious categories did terrible damage to each other, committed terrible crimes, and inflicted the most wicked cruelties on people with whom they had once lived in relative harmony, including neighbors in the same or nearby villages. Such antagonism was not the product of anything as trite as "ancient hatreds" because Muslims, Jews, and Christians had a long history of living together amicably in Ottoman lands. There might have been problems and even sporadic outbursts of violence, but Jews and Christians were *ahl al-kitab*, "people of the book," who fitted into life beside (or with) Muslims and, in the great cities of the east (notably Baghdad and Istanbul), often prospered as merchants or advisers to Muslim rulers.

The match among generally pious people of religion in these lands was certainly more comfortable than in a secularizing Europe increasingly shaped and then divided by questions of national identity. These influences flowed into Ottoman lands through missionary schools and the manipulation by the powers of Christian minorities in the pursuit of their own strategic and commercial interests. Their manipulation continued during the First World War. Overall, the importation of "modernity" in all its aspects, but especially the national idea, quickly turned combustible in a multiethnic and multireligious empire. The First World War brought these destructive elements to a head.

PART IV

A Questionable Peace

CHAPTER 14

Onward to Baku

THE BIG WAR was over, but wars were not. On October 13, 1918, Talat, grand vizier since the previous year, resigned, fleeing the country on a German submarine early in November. On October 30, aboard the HMS *Agamemnon*, as it lay at anchor off the island of Lemnos, the Ottoman Minister of Marine, Rauf Bey, and Admiral Somerset Arthur Gough-Calthorpe, representing the Allied powers, signed the Armistice of Mudros (Turkish Mondros). French troops were landed in Istanbul on November 12, British troops followed the next day, and an Italian force arrived on February 7, 1919. It was an extremely humiliating moment for the Turks: for the first time since the conquest in 1453, although the Russians came close in 1878, Istanbul had been occupied.

With the war ended, the Allied powers moved quickly to make good on the territory they had been allocated through the wartime treaties. The notion that the Paris "peace" conference was actually a peace conference must be challenged. The negotiations did not bring peace to Anatolia and the Middle East, only more war. The mandates over Iraq, Syria, and Palestine, as well as the attempts to set up an Armenian protectorate in eastern Anatolia and an expanded Greek state in the west were all forcefully resisted. In every case, the interests and desires of the majority of people, and in the case of an Armenian protectorate and an enlarged Greek state, demographic common sense, were ignored for the simple reason that they did not suit what the powers wanted. Resistance and war were the results, because such policies could lead nowhere else.

Britain was now the dominant power in the region. Physically battered and materially drained, France was too severely weakened by the war to bolt down its Near East claims. For a brief period, its troops occupied the coal-rich region of Zonguldak-Karadeniz Ereğli along the Black Sea coast, but Syria was always the focal point of French strategic and commercial interests. Taking over what it had been allocated in the Sykes-Picot Agreement (May 16, 1916), France divided its mandated territory into Syria and "Grand Liban" (September 1920), later establishing the Republic of Lebanon (September 1926).

Under zone A on the Sykes-Picot map, stretching from Aleppo, Homs, and Damascus south to the boundary of Mandatory Palestine and eastwards to Mosul and Rowanduz, France was prepared to recognize "and protect" an independent Arab state or confederation of Arab states. The "blue" area of the map extended northward up the Syrian coastal littoral from the northern boundary of Palestine. From Iskenderun it extended west to Mersin, east to Mardin, and north to slightly above Sivas in the heart of Anatolia. In this vast swath of territory, which included the southeastern region known to Europeans as Cilicia, France could establish "such direct or indirect administration or control" as it desired or saw fit.

Similar provisions applied to Britain. It was allocated what is now Iraq, where it was prepared to recognize an Arab state, as well as a region stretching down into the Persian Gulf in which it was free to set up such forms of administration as it saw fit. In northeastern Anatolia, Russia, in return for acceding to Sykes-Picot, had been allocated control over "western Armenia," consisting of the Ottoman provinces of Trabzon, Erzurum, Van, and Bitlis.

In the bargaining that followed the war, France was compelled to drop any "protective" role over Palestine, as pledged in Sykes-Picot, as well as its claim to Mosul, which it yielded in return for a guarantee of a share in oil profits. Turkey also claimed Mosul, whose future, as part of the Iraq mandate under British control, was not to be decided until the League of Nations issued its ruling in 1925. Whether in the north or the southeast France's strategic concerns were strongly governed by commercial interests, as were Britain's in the territories it occupied.

Italian troops moved quickly to take territory along the Mediterranean coast, in line with wartime agreements. On January 21, 1919, an Italian force occupied Adalia (Antalya), assigned in the Treaty of St. Jean de Maurienne (April 26, 1917),[1] before extending its reach northwest to Konya and Isparta and towns on the southwest Mediterranean coast, including Fethiye,

Bodrum, and Marmaris. St. Jean de Maurienne also ratified the occupation of Aegean islands seized by Italy after its invasion of Libya. Italy was even assigned Izmir until Britain and France decided almost at the last moment that Greece should have it. Unlike Britain and France in their occupied territories, Italy had no apparent intention of establishing a permanent presence in the territory it occupied. Its sympathies quickly moved toward the nationalist government in Ankara. Whereas the British and French dug in their heels, the Italians correctly read the writing on the wall and retreated gracefully—a stark contrast compared to their brutality in Libya.

TERRITORY REGAINED

In northeastern Anatolia, the overthrow of the tsarist government in 1917 spelled disaster for the Armenians and triumph for the Ottoman military. Ottoman forces had surprised the Allies from the beginning of the war, with the sea victory at the Dardanelles (March 18, 1915), the victory on land at Gallipoli following the withdrawal of the last Allied troops from Cape Helles[2] (January 16), and the surrender of the besieged British army at Kut (April 1916). Ottoman armies fought well on other fronts, while suffering some serious setbacks and one full-scale disaster, the destruction of the Third Army at Sarikamış. The collapse of the tsarist government now opened the door to the recapture of lost territory in eastern Anatolia and an advance into the Caucasus.

Between February and March 1918, the Ottomans recaptured Trabzon, Malazgirt, Bayburt, Erzincan and the fortress city of Erzurum, defended by Armenian forces under the command of Andranik Ozanian. On March 3, 1918, the Bolsheviks, Austria-Hungary, Germany, and the Ottoman Empire signed the Treaty of Brest-Litovsk, formally ending Russia's participation in the war. Under the treaty, Russia ceded Ardahan, Kars, and Batum, the *elviye-i selase* (three administrative regions) that had been part of the Ottoman Empire until the war of 1877–1878. By April, Ottoman forces were moving deeper into what had been the Russian Caucasus. On April 5, they captured Sarikamış, which must have been a sweet moment against the disaster of early 1915. This was followed by the recapture of Kağızman, Van, Doğubeyazit, and then the victory on April 14 over the mixed Greek-Armenian force holding Batum.

The next major target in the eastern Black Sea region was the fortress city of Kars, which had fallen to a Russian army commanded by generals

Ivan Lazarev and Mikhail Loris-Melikov (Melikyan) in November 1877. Their force of 28,000 men was largely Armenian, and it was Armenians again who defended the city in 1918, finally surrendering to Ottoman forces on April 25. Lost to Russia for four decades, the recapture of Kars was another especially triumphant moment for the Ottomans. By the end of the month, the 1877 borders with Russia had been restored, clearing the way for further advances into the Caucasus that brought the Ottomans to within striking distance of the Georgian capital of Tbilisi by the end of May.

After six years of war (beginning in 1912 with the Balkan war), the advances in the Caucasus were extraordinary achievements, energizing, in Edward Erickson's view, "Enver Paşa's grand idea of a Pan-Turanic empire stretching beyond the Caspian Sea."[3] However, while this might have been Enver's dream, it was not shared by Mustafa Kemal, the outstanding officer under whose leadership the Turkish republic was established in 1923. His interests lay in securing national borders, not pursuing ideological goals beyond them. Michael Reynolds finds the Pan-Turanian thesis "untenable," arguing instead that the Ottoman drive into the Caucasus was based on "a sober vision grounded in concrete geopolitical reasoning and not any nationalist or proto-nationalist ideology of identity."[4] Fleeing the empire in November, Enver pursued his ideal and died for it while fighting with Muslim forces in Turkestan against the Red Army on August 4, 1922.

Although ideologically opposed, the Bolsheviks and the Turkish nationalists had developed a working relationship that suited them both, with the Bolsheviks dropping all Russian claims to Turkish territory (and indeed exposing the terms of Sykes-Picot) and the Kemalists willingly accepting Bolshevik arms and financial support. For the Bolsheviks, a Turkish national state would stand as a bulwark against the western powers, determined to destroy their movement at birth.

OLD FEARS AND NEW

The collapse of imperial Russia in 1917 was a major crisis for the entente powers. By 1918, fourteen countries, led by the U.S., Britain, and France, were funneling tens of thousands of troops into former Russian imperial territory to block the Bolsheviks and the Germans, now able, since the signing of the Treaty of Brest-Litovsk, to send troops from the eastern front to European battlefields. The war in Europe was far from won, and the collapse of the Russian government left great stocks of war materiel, shipped into Russian ports by the Allies, exposed to seizure by the Germans. Tens of thousands of Czech troops (the Czech Legions) who had been fighting alongside the Russian imperial army were now stranded along the Trans-Siberian railway after an agreement with the Bolsheviks to repatriate them collapsed. They were fighting the Bolsheviks but were also needed for the war effort in Europe. Intervention was aimed at extricating them.

The securing of Russia's main ports, Murmansk (on the Barents Sea), Arkhangelsk (the White Sea), Odessa (Black Sea), and Vladivostok, the home base of the Russian imperial fleet (the Pacific), was another prime objective. Manpower was a major problem in holding down the most critically strategic points in this great mass of territory. About 150,000 foreign soldiers were sent into the Russian homeland, but the Allies were still fully committed on the European front, and only a small number of troops were available to be sent into Russia. When the war ended, Britain and France also had to hold down the territories they had occupied in the Middle East.

Furthermore, war weariness had set in. Nowhere on the Allied side would public opinion support the dispatch of anything but small contingents of troops to a new theatre of war. The U.S. sent 13,000; France 15,000; Canada 4,800; Italy 2,500; Britain a few thousand; and Australia 150. Greece sent more than 23,000 but withdrew them after a few months because they were needed in Turkey. Japan's 70,000 were concentrated in the Far East, with the aim of taking territory for Japan, not for the European powers. The whole operation was disjointed and, as expected in an operation involving so many national forces, divided over priorities.

In northeastern Anatolia, following the signing of Brest-Litovsk, the military center of gravity had shifted to the Caucasus. Fighting in this arena of the "war of intervention" involved the Ottomans and all Caucasian ethnoreligious national groups (Georgians, Armenians, Azerbaijanis, and other Muslim ethnicities) along with White Russians and the Bolsheviks.

The Caucasus was a land bridge between the Black Sea and the Caspian. The then contested city of Baku lay on its western shore. Oil from the Caspian fields was the main commercial lure for the belligerents. Strategically, on the far side of the Caspian lay central Asia and the gates southward into Afghanistan and British India. In the minds of British imperial planners, the most strenuous efforts had to be made to keep this vast region out of the hands of the Bolsheviks or any other hostile force.

Old fears entangled with new ones now gripped the collective imagination of the British Foreign Office. Pan-Islam was one and Pan-Turkism (Pan-Turanism) another. In the British imperial mind, the Turks of Asia Minor had to be prevented from linking up with the "Tartars of the southern Caucasus and the Turks of northwestern Persia and beyond the Caspian, with the Turks of Turkestan."[5] If they were not stopped, the Turks could overrun not just Armenia, the southern Caucasus and northwestern Persia, possibly "even Afghanistan and Central Asia and gain for themselves a new reservoir of manpower in the shape of five or six million Moslem Tartars and Turks."[6]

If this were not already bad enough, the Bolsheviks were cooperating with the Turkish nationalists. Then there was Germany, still the Ottoman Empire's ally: even if the two were beginning to fall out over objectives in the Caucasus, nothing could be safely assumed.

A mandate over this unruly region seemed the best option for some British policymakers, but who could be asked to take it on? Perhaps the U.S. but certainly not France, which the government seemed to be contemplating, implying a French protectorate stretching from Iskenderun to Baku.[7]

Alarmed, the General Staff responded, "It would be most undesirable for the approaches to India from South Russia, the Black Sea and Turkey in Asia, which converge at Baku, to be placed at the disposal of an ambitious military power, which, although friendly to us at the moment, is our historical world rival."[8] In its view, only one candidate could possibly be considered: Britain itself.

There was to be no mandate over the Caucasus. Given the fragmented ethnoreligious national divisions in the region, it would have been a thankless undertaking. No one was keen. In which case, how could this region be held and made safe for the Allied powers? As none of the allies had troops to spare, perhaps local Christians, Georgians, and Armenians could be recruited in sufficient numbers to hold the Bolsheviks at bay. Britain was already arming the Armenians in northwest Persia, and now it began to look hard at the Armenian volunteer units and the huge pool of Armenians who had been fighting in the Russian army.

In December 1917, Andranik Ozanian, the veteran Armenian insurgent commander, told a British general he could supply 20,000 irregulars for 100,000 rubles and 40,000 for three months for 300,000 rubles but would require "40 British officers, pay, equipment, arms [?], supplies, machine guns, mountain guns, and pack transport from British or Russians."[9] General Nazarbekov, the commander of a new Armenian force, saw no difficulty in sending men to the Persian frontier where, over the next year in the northwest, Armenians, Assyrians, Kurds, and Ottoman forces were to be involved in bloody clashes.

In April 1918, the War Office authorized large payments to Georgians and Armenians so they could buy weapons. The British-owned Imperial Bank of Persia bought 60,808,000 rubles (about $230,000, a lot of money at the time[10]), of which 1 million rubles were paid to the "Turkish Armenian Committee" and 3 million were spent on buying arms for Georgian and Armenian forces. A further 2,808,000 rubles were sent from Tehran to Tbilisi, "final disposal not known."[11]

Arrangements were also made to send General Dunsterville, commanding 200 officers and about 200 NCOs (noncommissioned officers), into the Caucasus to organize "national forces."[12] The outcome was dismal. The British made no headway in attracting recruits from the estimated 150,000 Russian army Armenian soldiers still scattered over the region. Perhaps, like so many others, the soldiers were suffering from war weariness and just wanted to go home.

COMPETING FORCES

The chaos in the south Caucasus after the Bolshevik revolution could only help the Ottomans militarily and politically. Competing forces included Armenians, Georgians, Azerbaijanis, Bolsheviks, Social Revolutionaries, the "white" Russian Volunteer Army, its Cossack allies, as well as Germans and the British.

In April, 1918, Armenian, Azerbaijani, and Georgian delegates declared the Transcaucasian Democratic Federative Republic as a means of protecting their joint interests, which at the time were perhaps only a fraction stronger than their mutual differences. Within a short time, it was the differences that dominated. At a "peace" conference on May 11 with delegates from the republic, the Ottomans renewed their demands for control of the Aleksandropol-Etchmiadzin-Nahçivan-Julfa rail link—necessary for the transport of Ottoman troops to northwestern Persia—and unhindered use of all Transcaucasian railways "as long as the war against Britain continued."[13] These demands were unacceptable to Georgia and Armenia, and the fighting continued.

Between May 21 and 29, Ottoman and Armenian forces fought three major battles (Sardarapat, Karakilise, and Başabaran). The week-long battle for Sardarapat ended with a ceasefire, but as it prevented the Ottomans from advancing on Yerevan (Erivan), a short distance away, the Armenians claimed it as a victory. The Ottomans went on to occupy Karakilise (Armenian Vanadzor) after another fierce struggle but only after suffering severe casualties. Armenian forces also suffered heavy losses in these battles.

The Ottoman advance had caused disarray among the three ethno-religious groups in the Transcaucasian Republic, and each now went its own way. On May 26, Georgia withdrew from the *seim* (parliament), declared its independence, and put itself under nominal German protection in the Treaty of Poti. An armed clash near Tbilisi involving Ottoman troops and a German-Georgian force highlighted the growing antagonism between Germany and the Ottomans over now-conflicting strategic interests. Azerbaijan declared its independence on May 28, establishing its interim capital at Ganja (Elisavetpol) while maintaining the momentum of advance on the Caspian Sea port city of Baku.

On June 4, the three republics signed the Treaty of Batum under which the Ottoman Empire recognized the independence of each in return for territorial concessions restoring the pre-1877 Ottoman-Russian border. Disgusted by the concessions that had been made to the historical enemy, Andranik Ozanian broke with the Armenian republic, itself unhappy that it had no option but to accept the treaty because of the dominant Ottoman military position on the ground.

Through the Brest-Litovsk treaty the Ottoman Empire had gained almost 10,000 square miles of territory and 600,000 people in the Caucasus. The Batum treaty gave it another 8,000 square miles and 650,000 more people.[14] Ottoman forces were joined by Azerbaijanis as they advanced on Baku, claimed by Azerbaijan but held by the Bolshevik-dominated Baku Soviet (established November 13, 1917, and renamed the Baku Commune on April 13, 1918). In this ethnoreligious and political tangle, it should come as no surprise that by December, Georgia and Armenia were themselves at war over territory.

THE "MARCH DAYS"

The Azerbaijani alliance with the Ottomans was driven by Azerbaijan's military weakness and one particular event: the slaughter of thousands of

Muslims (mostly Azerbaijanis) in Baku by Bolshevik and Dashnak forces between March 30 and April 2, 1918. In the preceding months (December 1917–January 1918), clashes between Azerbaijanis and Russian soldiers in and around Elisavetpol had preceded the "March Days" in Baku. Azerbaijani suspicion of the Baku Soviet's inclinations were sharpened by the fact that Stephen Shaumian, chairman of the Baku Council of People's Commissars since April 25, was an Armenian.

The event that precipitated the March onslaught was the arrival in Baku of a small contingent of soldiers who had just disarmed a "pro-Bolshevik garrison"[15] in the Caspian coastal town of Lenkoran. These troops, ostensibly in Baku to attend a funeral, were members of what had been known as the Savage (or Wild) Division, established by the tsarist government in 1914 as a Muslim Caucasian cavalry drawn from Chechens, Ingush, Dagestanis, Ossetians, Azeris, and Karbadinians. During the war, the Savage Division had fought on the Russian western front. After the February revolution (March 1917), it had remained loyal to the Provisional Government in Petrograd. The division was formally disbanded in January 1918, but its soldiers remained active and armed.

On arrival in Baku their ship (the *Evelina*) was searched and the soldiers disarmed by the Soviet. When more Savage Division troops arrived, shooting broke out at the port, but these men were also eventually disarmed. Amid growing Azerbaijani agitation at the prospect of being overwhelmed by the 10,000 fighters available to the Soviet-Armenian alliance, even more Savage Division soldiers arrived in Baku. This time there was to be no disarming. Fighting broke out across the city with Bolsheviks and Dashnak Armenians on one side and largely Azerbaijani Muslims on the other. The Dashnaks shelled and plundered the Azerbaijani quarter. Over two days, thousands of Muslims were killed, the estimates beginning at 3,000 and going as high as 12,000. Many more fled the city so that "not a single Mussulman of any importance remained."[16] Shaumian later revealed that the Soviet had exploited the initial confrontation to overwhelm its enemies.[17]

On July 31, with Ottoman forces poised to attack, the Baku Soviet collapsed. Shaumian and twenty-five other "commissars" (among them journalists, a clerk, sailors, and a cavalry officer) fled to Krasnovodsk (present day Turkmenbaşı) in the Balkan province of what is now Turkmenistan, where they were captured and executed by anti-Bolshevik forces on September 20.[18]

MISSION IMPRACTICAL

Advancing on Baku at the same time as the Ottoman-Azerbaijani force was a small British contingent under the command of Major General Lionel Charles Dunsterville, transferred for the purpose from India's North-West Frontier. Dunsterville and Rudyard Kipling had gone to the same school at the same time, and the adventures of "Dunsterforce" on the way to Baku could have been plucked from a boy's own adventure penned at the high point of imperialism. The mission could be characterized (and was) as plain mad in the first place, but it also has defenders who argue for some strategic purposes having been served despite the ultimate failure to hold Baku.[19] Dunsterville's view of what went wrong and why has also been challenged from an Armenian perspective.[20]

Initially his brief was to go to Tbilisi and organize a Russian, Georgian, and Armenian force capable of resisting the Ottomans, but once Georgia was turned into a temporary German protectorate there was no point in going there. Eventually, the goal was set on keeping Baku and passage across the Caspian Sea out of the hands of "the enemy"—Germany, the Ottoman Empire, and the Bolsheviks—thus safeguarding the northern approaches to India.

This strategy did not preclude negotiations that suited Dunsterville and the Baku Commune, such as the exchange of motor vehicles for supplies of oil. Neither the British nor the Soviet government wanted "the Turks" in Baku, but neither could they agree to cooperate in trying to keep them out. For the Soviets, the British in Baku were the worst option and the British government felt the same way about them. The Turks were unlikely to be a danger to British interests in the east, Lloyd George told the War Cabinet on June 24, 1918, whereas Russia "if in the future she regenerated might be so."[21]

Dunsterville's small force, mostly Canadian, Australian, New Zealanders, and South Africans, was reinforced by a "splendid batch" of Russian officers sent from London, plus various other Russians, "refugees from the revolution who joined us later."[22] The main body was mobilized in Baghdad and set off on January 18. Heading to the Caspian Sea coast, reinforced incrementally on the way but still without any clear mission, the force gave aid to Armenian and Assyrian refugees and fought the Jangalis (adherents of Mirza Kuçuk Khan's antimonarchist and anti-imperialist "Jungle" movement in the province of Gilan). It was joined by anti-Bolshevik Cossack forces and began training Persian levies and irregulars, in the process accidentally enlisting "a complete gang of robbers."[23] Hoping to take a ship to Baku, the force was turned back by Bolsheviks holding the Iranian port of Enzeli (Bandar-e Anzali) and had to return to Hamadan.

The collapse of the Baku Soviet at the end of July and the establishment of the Central Caspian Dictatorship by a Menshevik, Social Revolutionary, and Dashnak alliance finally cleared the way for the arrival of Dunsterforce. The dictatorship appealed for British help and on August 10 an advance party was able to sail from Enzeli aboard the *President Kruger*. Dunsterville arrived on August 17 and soon afterwards met the five dictators running Baku.

The idea of five dictators rather than one amused Dunsterville, but "all five declared unanimously that they were not good enough to run things singlehanded."[24] Dunsterville had counted on the presence of a large and well-trained local force to defend Baku in coordination with his 1,000 or so men; the dictators, on the other hand, had expected 16,000 British troops to arrive and take the lead in defending the city. Either way, the combined force was not going to be nearly strong enough. The potential force of 150,000 Armenians whetting the British imperial appetite had turned out to be a wistful mirage. Disappointment arising from this apparent misunderstanding turned to anger when Dunsterville told the dictators on September 1, "No power on earth can save Baku from the Turks."[25]

Already by the middle of June the Ottoman Caucasian Army of Islam, commanded by Nuri Paşa (Nuri Killigil), a half-brother of Enver, was drawing closer to the city. By July 25, it had reached Alyat, less than 50 miles from Baku, and by early August it was positioned to capture it. Regarding the Caucasian Army of Islam as being "not up to much," Dunsterville also took a dim view of the Armenian soldiers tasked with defending Baku. He praised women fighters and pointed to individual acts of heroism but took the general view that the Armenian of Baku was not a soldier by instinct or training, "just an ill-fed undersized factory hand"[26] who lacked fighting spirit and was completely incapable of understanding anything about warfare.[27]

When he spoke to the dictators on September 1, Dunsterville said, "We came here to help you men fight the Turks, not to do all the fighting with your men as onlookers."[28] In the next fortnight, he threw himself into a last-ditch attempt to create a local force capable of defending the city. Some Russian reinforcements arrived, with British air support finally provided, but the task was hopeless. On the night of September 14, with

Baku surrounded, Dunsterville and his small band of soldiers left on two ships for Enzeli, thus ending "the adventures of Dunsterforce."[29]

Baku was now exposed to capture by the Ottoman-Azerbaijani force constituting the Army of Islam. Heavy attacks on outlying positions in late August were followed by a lull until the final advance on the day Dunsterforce departed. Baku's defenses collapsed under constant shelling and ground attack. Although guarantees had been given for the safety of the civilian population, the Army of Islam did not enter the city for a full day. In the interim, the city was swept by a wave of pillage and massacre as Azerbaijanis took revenge for the "March Days." Panic drove thousands of Armenians to the harbor or into the country, but thousands more were killed. An investigation by the Armenian National Committee put the death toll at more than 8,000. Other estimates go much higher.

Militarily, the dash to Baku was an Ottoman triumph, but by late September, after the decisive battle of Meggido (September 19–25), General Allenby had driven the Yildirim (Lightning) Army out of Palestine. "It was now apparent to all but the most diehard [Turkish] nationalist," writes Edward Erickson, "that the Turks were finished in the war."[30]

IMPERIAL RIVALRY

On March 13, 1921, Italy agreed to withdraw its troops from Anatolia in return for commercial concessions granted by the nationalist government in Ankara. However, along with Britain and France, it remained an occupying power in Istanbul and surrounding territories until peace was signed in 1923. Substantial differences began to emerge between France and Britain the moment the war was over, giving way to a familiar pattern of imperial rivalry. While France was too weak on the ground to demand that Britain uphold all the commitments made in the wartime treaties and had to relinquish its claim to Mosul and a stake in the future of Palestine, it still held a mass of valuable strategic and commercial territory.

In May 1919, the Syrian National Congress elected a government. In March 1920, it declared independence across all of historic Syria (including Palestine) and installed Faisal (the son of the Sharif of Mecca) as its king. On April 25, the San Remo conference confirmed the provisions of Sykes-Picot. And on the same day, the Supreme Inter-Allied Council declared France as the mandatory power for Syria (not ratified by the League of Nations until September 29, 1923).

On July 24, French forces that has been advancing over the mountains from Beirut overwhelmed a Syrian nationalist force in the battle of Maysalun, entering Damascus the following day. On September 1, France carved the Lebanese coastal and mountain flank out of Syria, creating Greater Lebanon (*Grand Liban*) and beginning the process of incremental partition of Syria that has continued to the present day.

In Anatolia, France had tied its strategic/commercial interests to the nationalist aspirations of the Armenians. The Treaty of Sèvres (August 10, 1920) obliged "Turkey" (still the Ottoman Empire) to recognize "Armenia" as an independent state in an area encompassing the provinces of Erzurum, Bitlis, and Van, as well as the Black Sea port city of Trabzon. South of this region, the Kurds were to receive autonomy and independence within a year—if they could convince the League of Nations that this was what they wanted. The boundaries of the proposed Armenian state had been drawn by President Woodrow Wilson whose government never signed Sèvres. In a region where Muslims constituted the overwhelming bulk of the population, an Armenian state could only have been established under the protection of outside powers.

As in the past, Kurdish leaders made their feelings known when visited by a British military intelligence officer in 1919. In their view, the phrase "Armenian vilayets" was a misnomer, as "between ninety and ninety-five percent of the population are Kurds."[31] They were not all nomads, as "vast numbers" were settled town-dwellers, and neither were they "savages." They had a national consciousness and were asking for a united Kurdistan and a government "based on proportional representation and placed under the mandate of a European power." The intelligence officer shared the Kurdish view that Kurds were in an "overwhelming majority in the six Armenian vilayets."[32] Clearly the imposition of an Armenian protectorate or state would have led to endless trouble, akin to the long-term problems created in Palestine by the establishment of a Jewish "homeland."

In any case, events on the ground soon overtook the deliberations of the diplomats. By May 1918, the Turkish nationalists had forced an Armenian retreat from northeastern Anatolia, and by the time Sèvres was signed France's attempt to take over Cilicia—Çukurova to the Turks—was rapidly running aground in the face of Turkish national resistance.

France's commercial-colonial lobby had long had its eyes on the fertile plains of this region, particularly the raw cotton needed to revive the French textile industry following the war's devastation. For imperial "defense" planners, France already had Algeria and Tunisia. A position

in the eastern corner of the Mediterranean would give it the deep-water
ports of Mersin and Iskenderun, as well as control over strategic railways,
especially the Taurus-Amanus tunnel system linking Istanbul to Aleppo
and Baghdad, placed under joint Allied control at Mudros. In its occupation of Cilicia, France was hampered by financial difficulties and an
insufficient number of administrators and troops on the ground, which
could only be supported and replenished by spending money the French
government could not afford.

Then there was the question of imperial rivalry. After all, as the British
prime minister, David Lloyd George, told his cabinet in October 1918,
"Britain had won the war in the Middle East and there was no reason why
France should benefit from it."[33] Having already succeeded in whittling
down France's territorial claims elsewhere, he proposed on May 21, 1919,
that if there was to be a mandate for Armenia, it should be given to the
United States.

A "DISGUSTING SCRAMBLE"

The U.S. president, Woodrow Wilson, had sent two commissions of
inquiry to the Near East. One, the King-Crane commission (formally the
Inter-Allied Commission on Mandates in Turkey, June–August 1919), was
tasked with sounding out the people of the region on what they wanted,
and if they had to accept mandatory administration, which of the Allied
powers they would prefer. The second, the American Military Mission to
Armenia, headed by Major General James G. Harbord and also dispatched
in 1919, was asked to make thorough inquiries across Anatolia and Transcaucasia in the light of American interests and responsibilities.

The mission's key finding was that as "Turks" were far more numerous
in the region than Armenians, even before the losses suffered during the
war, the "Armenian question" could not be settled in Armenia.[34] Harbord's alternative, "a single mandate for the Turkish Empire and the Trans-
caucasus," could hardly be said to be any more feasible. However, if the
U.S. were asked and accepted this single mandate, Harbord wrote, and
estimates of the number of troops that would be needed went as high as
250,000, he thought 59,000 "would be ample" to ensure security. Military
costs for the first year would be $88,500,000, with total cost more than
$275 million.[35]

Harbord's report was published on April 13, 1920. One has to assume that President Wilson saw an early draft, but he had always been sympathetic to Armenian aspirations (the State Department had drawn the boundaries of the Armenian state as envisaged in the Treaty of Sèvres). Several weeks earlier, he had made it clear that he would let Congress decide. Now, despite Harbord's negative findings, Wilson asked Congress on May 24 to approve a U.S. mandate over "Armenia." On May 27, the proposal was rejected by the Senate Foreign Relations Committee, and on June 1, by a vote of 52–23, the Senate said no.

Armenia was only one issue of many in the conquered Ottoman lands, and Wilson was becoming increasingly disillusioned with the European governments and what he called their "whole disgusting scramble." In his view, "When I learn of the secret treaty of Great Britain with Persia,[36] when I find Italy and Greece arranging between themselves as to the division of western Asia Minor, and when I think of the greed and utter selfishness of it all, I am almost inclined to refuse to permit this country to be a member of the League of Nations. I am disposed to throw up the whole business and get out."[37]

The League, written into the Treaty of Versailles (June 28, 1919), was Wilson's idea. On November 19, 1919, however, the U.S. Senate denied consent to the treaty on a 55–39 vote, thus blocking U.S. membership. A modified version was submitted again on March 19, 1920, and denied again on a 49–35 vote. The U.S. never signed the treaty and never joined the world body.

The King-Crane Commission report noted that Armenians would prefer to have an American mandate (if they had to have one at all), but its findings were not published until 1922, no doubt because they would have pushed public opinion toward support for a commitment the U.S. Congress was not prepared to make.

An extremely fluid movement developed across all occupied territories between 1918–1920. The arrival of Mustafa Kemal in the Black Sea port of Samsun on May 19, 1919, kicked off the Turkish national movement and the welding of disparate forces resisting occupation into a national army. Moving to the interior, Mustafa Kemal and his nationalist comrades mobilized the public by holding congresses in Erzurum (August 1919) and Sivas (September), having laid down the outlines of the national program at Amasya in June. The nationalists were confronting two immediate threats: the invading Greek army and the landing of French-Armenian troops in Cilicia. Both had to be fought simultaneously.

THE CILICIAN GAMBIT

There were substantial differences between the Armenia as envisaged by the victorious wartime powers and the Armenia of the Armenian nationalists. The "Armenia" endorsed by President Wilson conformed to the "western Armenia" of the Armenian Revolutionary Federation and would have incorporated the provinces of Van, Bitlis, and Erzurum into an Armenian state, as well as giving it the Black Sea port of Trabzon. The "Armenia" presented by the Armenian National Delegation at the Paris postwar settlement negotiations in 1919, however, extended this territory to the shores and the ports of the eastern Mediterranean, embracing Cilicia.

In this vast region, as virtually every observer on the spot had made clear over a long period of time, the central problem for the Armenians was demography. In 1914, Erzurum had a Muslim population of 673,297 compared to an Armenian population of 125,657; Bitlis had 309,999 Muslims and 114,704 Armenians; and Van had 179,380 Muslims and 67,792 Armenians. In the surrounding provinces, which could hardly be insulated from support for Muslims inside a minority Armenian state, the differential was even greater. Sivas, for example, had 939,735 Muslims and 143,406 Armenians.[38] These census figures were based on actual counts, whereas the numbers coming from the Armenian patriarchate—the deeply political national church—were estimates that had been grossly inflated ever since the Armenian delegation attended the Congress of Berlin in 1878 seeking support for Armenian statehood.

According to the patriarchate, Cilicia in 1912 had an Armenian population of 407,000 and 224,000 Muslims (Turks, Kurds, and "Turcomans"). However, the tabulations of the Ottoman government in 1914 based on each provincial subdistrict (*kaza*) show that the population consisted of 366,500 Muslims and 61,500 Armenians.[39] Of these two sets of figures, the Ottoman census figures were the more reliable, but France appeared (or chose) to believe the Armenian estimates.[40]

It was Boghos Nubar who, in 1916, had proposed the formation of an Armenian legion to "liberate" Cilicia. Supported by Britain and France, this Légion d'Orient was mobilized and trained in Port Said and Cyprus where it was augmented by volunteers from Europe, the U.S., and other countries. Units were sent to fight under General Allenby's command in Palestine before all four battalions of about 5,000 men, now called the Légion Arménienne, were shipped from Junieh, north of Beirut, to Cilicia after the armistice.

Two companies were sent to Iskenderun on November 21, 1918. The remaining troops, along with a company of Algerian *tirailleurs* (infantry), were dispatched to Iskenderun and Mersin toward the end of the year. The soldiers forming the French forces in Cilicia, the Troupes Françaises du Levant, included native-born French soldiers and officers and colonial African troops, as well as the Armenian battalions.

France was now making good on its commitment not just to protect the Armenian people but to create a "national home" for them in Cilicia. Such was the pledge made in December 1918, by Georges Picot, appointed after the war as France's High Commissioner for Syria and Armenia. Arthur James Balfour had made a similar commitment to the Zionists in November 1917, and the basic problem facing Armenian nationalists was the same as for the Zionists: how to establish a state in territories where they constituted a small minority. Accordingly, settling (or resettling) as many Armenians as possible in Cilicia was a central part of the French program. The French military governor, Colonel Edouard Brémond, estimated that 120,000 had arrived before the end of 1919, most moving north from Syria where they had been relocated. Many more were to come.[41]

In a majority Muslim area, a French army of occupation that included an Armenian legion, as well as a mass influx of Armenian civilians, was a formula for trouble. At the start, it would seem the encouragement of Armenian settlement was an attempt to change the demographics ahead of the establishment of an Armenian state-in-being under French protection.

At no stage did France have sufficient forces on the ground to impose order on the civilian population and simultaneously deal with a gathering Turkish nationalist insurgency. Given such a weak position at the beginning of 1919, General Allenby, the Allied commander of Occupied Enemy Territory (OETA), sent British troops into the region, including a brigade from India. The French force was placed under overall British command and the towns of Aintab (Antep), Maraş, and Urfa to the east of the Amanus mountains occupied by British forces until the French were able to take over at the end of the year. Only in November was full control of Cilicia formally transferred to France.

There was clearly an element of Anglo-French rivalry in the way Britain responded to the French predicament in Cilicia. In the short term, it had to help because the only option was the chaos that eventually enveloped the region anyway, but French ambitions also had to be watched and checked where necessary. The occupation of Syria in line with Sykes-Picot had to be accepted, but it was hardly in Britain's interests for the strategically important eastern corner of the Mediterranean to end up in French hands.

The focal point of British interests in 1919–1922 was the increasingly successful Turkish nationalist campaign against the Greeks in western Turkey. It did not want the nationalists to triumph anywhere but neither did it want France to benefit unnecessarily, perhaps to the point of helping out France's enemies in the southeast. Zeidner refers to "plausible evidence" that before withdrawing in October–November 1919, the British distributed "large stocks of arms to the Muslims."[42]

"TERRORISM" AND RESISTANCE

Attempts to calm the Muslim population were disrupted from the start by the indiscipline of the Armenian soldiers. Already by November 30, 1918, the French administrator in Iskenderun was reporting "acts of terrorism" against Muslims by Armenian legionnaires, with other reports of pillage by Armenian deserters in the nearby town of Dört Yol.[43]

In February 1919, fighting in Iskenderun between Armenian and Algerian troops was followed by reports of pillage and arson in the Turkish quarter. In response, the military authorities disbanded the Fourth Armenian battalion, shipping some of the soldiers to Port Said as a labor company and redistributing the rest among other Armenian units.

By the middle of the year, the French had broken up the Légion Arménienne, reducing its numbers to about 500 and assigning these soldiers to duties that limited their contact with the Muslim population to the essentials (i.e., guarding railway stations or escorting supply convoys). As that still left the *gendarmerie*, reconstituted in April 1919, with "suspicious" elements (presumably Muslim) being replaced by Armenians and other Christians, the complaints from Muslims of mistreatment and bullying were to continue.

Resistance to French occupation came from societies formed for the defense of Turkish rights and from Ottoman officials still holding their positions under the terms of the Mudros armistice but sympathetic to the national cause. Tribal leaders (Kurdish, Arab, and Turkmen) and the landowning and commercial notables (*eşrefler*) were important links for Kemalist officers dispatched to Cilicia to organize uprisings.

The French forces, whose officer corps included men who had served in North Africa, frequently resorted to the harsh tactics used to crush the Algerian resistance, including collective punishment. By the end of the first half of 1920, writes Yücel Güçlü, "about fifty villages in the plain between Adana, Kozan, and Osmaniye had been wiped off the earth. The houses of Turks were demolished and burned down, their personal belongings looted, their cattle carried off, and their crops destroyed."[44]

Antagonism overflowed in Adana. The chairman of the Society of Cilicians warned in February 1920, "The existence of a large number of Armenian revolutionaries who have come to Adana to be an element of trouble is not a good sign."[45] His prediction that Armenians were bent on ejecting "the Turks" (better described as Muslim, given that many inhabitants of Adana province were Kurdish or Muslims of other ethnic origin) was borne out in July when elements of the Christian population (Armenians, Assyrians, Greeks, and Chaldeans) ran amok and drove the Muslims from their homes.

About 40,000 fled into the countryside, leaving homes that were pillaged and burnt. According to an American Board of Commissioners for Foreign Missions (ABCFM) missionary teacher, Mary Webb, "Today this city [Adana] that was largely a Turkish city is entirely Christian. The Turkish shops were closed and one meets no Turks on the streets. They are said to be living in the fields, under trees, in great want and much sickness."[46] The violence of Armenians completely alienated the French authorities: not only had they disbanded the Armenian volunteer force little more than six months after its arrival in Cilicia but on occasion they hanged the Christian perpetrators of violence, while robustly rebutting the propaganda claims of massacre being made by Armenian committees abroad.[47]

The disorganized, decentralized, and somewhat haphazard nature of the Turkish national struggle began to change four days after the Greek landing on the docks at Izmir in May 1919 when Mustafa Kemal stepped ashore at Samsun, made his way to the interior, and began organizing a national government.

Resistance to the French gathered pace in 1920, with three events in particular affecting France's willingness to continue the occupation. The first was the battle of Maraş (January 20–February 10) spreading to outlying villages supporting the nationalist cause. This bloody operation cost the French hundreds of casualties and resulted in the destruction of much of the town through artillery shelling and the firestorm that followed[48] before the French withdrew with about 5,000 Armenians following, only for the whole military and civilian column to be engulfed in a blizzard. Thousands died in the fighting and the retreat.

This defeat—a great shock to French prestige and a corresponding boost for nationalist morale—was soon followed by a second loss at Urfa. There, the battle began with an attack on the French garrison on February 9 and ended with a negotiated retreat of French forces on April 11. Kurdish fighters then ambushed the retreating convoy near Urfa. Very few of the French soldiers survived.

By this time, the battle of Antep (April 1, 1920–February 9, 1921) had begun. This long campaign of attrition ended with a "hollow victory" for the French because of the widespread destruction and the flight of much of the town's population.[49] The nationalist government ordered the surrender so that it could concentrate on halting the Greek advance, but, in recognition of the endurance of its people, the recently established Turkish parliament, the Grand National Assembly, renamed the city Gaziantep, Holy Warrior Antep.

With nationalist forces overpowering French garrisons elsewhere, occupation authorities unable to control outbreaks of violence in towns and cities, and public opinion at home divided over the credibility of the Cilician operation and its heavy cost, the French government began looking for a way out. The dilemma was how to do it while upholding French prestige. Away from the battlefield, there had been continuous negotiations with emissaries of the Turkish nationalists along with a growing recognition that it was the government in Ankara and not Istanbul that represented the wishes of the people. The election of Alexandre Millerand as prime minister in November 1919, brought to power a man who was opposed to the more extensive occupation of Istanbul as proposed after the Treaty of Sèvres and only went along with it because of the British threat that if their allies would not join them, they would occupy the city alone.

France's gradual retreat from Cilicia drove the Armenian nationalists into a frenzy of anti-Turkish propaganda aimed at keeping the French troops in place, along with desperate but meaningless declarations of Cilician Armenian independence. The renewed cresting of anti-Turkish propaganda in 1920–1921 was tied to the continuing fight for Armenian statehood in London and Paris. However, the French ship of state had changed course too sharply to be turned around by propaganda and Armenian demands.

On March 9, 1921, in London, the next French prime minister, Aristide Briand (in his seventh of eleven governments), and the Foreign Minister of the Turkish government in Ankara, Bekir Sami, signed a Cilician peace treaty incorporating a cessation of hostilities, an amnesty, disarmament, and the withdrawal southward of all French forces into the *sancak* of Alexandretta (Hatay for the Turks). On October 20, the war was formally ended in the Treaty of Ankara (the Franklin-Bouillon agreement). The French flag over Cilicia was lowered for the last time the following January. Despite the reassurances of local notables and the Turkish nationalist government in Ankara, the French departure was followed by a massive outflow of Armenians.

ALLIES AT ODDS

A key element in this narrative is the falling-out between Britain and France. Whereas France was backing away, the British government remained determined to impose the Treaty of Sèvres to the letter. There were those, especially in the army, who had serious misgivings about British policy from the start, but for David Lloyd George "the Turks" were finished: they were a decadent race, while the Greeks "are our friends and a rising people."[50]

It was a long time before he could be persuaded that Mustafa Kemal was anything other than a bandit and outlaw. Speaking in late August, 1920, he remarked that Greek victories on the battlefield showed that Kemal "had no great value" and that the Turks were no longer a formidable people.[51] The defeat of the Greeks in the first and second battles of Inonu (January and March 1921) proved him badly wrong, and worse was yet to come for the Greek expeditionary force.

The slowest (or most unwilling) of the Allied powers to read the writing on the wall, the British government grew increasingly irritated with France as it negotiated with the nationalists "behind our backs."[52] After the signing of the Treaty of Ankara, British Foreign Secretary Lord Curzon accused France of a "breach of honor and good faith" that was also detrimental to British interests. Britain had been led to believe Henry Franklin-Bouillon had gone to Ankara as a private individual on a concession-hunting mission. Instead, what had transpired was an agreement that ignored key provisions of Sèvres.

Delineation of the border between Turkey and Syria favored the Turks: they would be permitted to use the Baghdad railway for military purposes while Mosul appeared to be "laid open" to them. It seemed that France would even welcome Mustafa Kemal's moves in that direction, even though (in the view being expressed) he was not as powerful as some seemed to think.[53] By December 1921, thanks to a combination of being "tricked" by France, Greece's refusal to accept Allied advice, and Turkish "intractability," Curzon had been compelled to conclude that Sèvres was "virtually dead."[54]

With French forces to be withdrawn in the coming year from the "neutral" zones at the straits and along the Anatolian side of the southern Marmara, relations further unraveled. The Cilician gambit ended in failure for France, mutual recriminations between the French and Armenians, and further death, devastation, and dispossession for the Christian and Muslim peoples of the region. Against the background of strengthening Turkish national resistance to the invading Greek army, it also set the stage for the withdrawal of France from occupied Turkish territory and reconciliation with Ankara. By September 1922, in the confrontation with the Turkish nationalists, Britain was the only man left standing.

CHAPTER 15

The Road to Izmir

EUROPEAN IDEALIZATION OF GREECE as the font of democracy, philosophy, and "western civilization," perhaps strongest among English "philhellenes," served the Greeks well throughout the nineteenth century. Here was a suffering Christian people that had endured centuries of life under the Ottoman yoke and deserved liberation.

Thanks to British, Russian, and French support, manifested at sea in the defeat of Ottoman and Egyptian ships in the Battle of Navarino (October 1827), Greece emerged in 1830 as an independent if incomplete state. Its irredentist claims included the Ionian Islands, Epirus, Thessaly, Crete, Macedonia, Thrace, Cyprus, and the western Aegean coast of the Ottoman Empire, plus all the offshore islands. By the end of the 1912–1913 Balkan wars, much of this territory had indeed been taken, leaving the future of Thrace, some of the Aegean islands, and the Ottoman Aegean seaboard yet to be determined.

Greece also supported the political aspirations of the Pontic Greeks along the eastern Black Sea coast, while realizing they were too far from the Hellenic homeland to be given much practical help. A substantial Greek minority also lived in communities scattered throughout the Ottoman interior, especially Cappadocia. The kingdom, enlarged to the limits of the Megali Idea of Greek nationalist imagination, would include all Ottoman lands with an ethnic Greek population, no matter how numerous the Muslims surrounding them. Its capital would be the city at the meeting point of the Bosporus and the Sea of Marmara, no longer Istanbul but Konstantinoupoli, the name preferred to this day by Greeks wherever they live.

THE WAR FOR CRETE

The successful expansion of Greece into territories claimed as part of the national homeland could only feed the appetite for more. At the same time, while there was widespread sympathy for Greek aspirations, particularly in Britain, Greece would not be allowed to take any action that might threaten the balance of power in Europe. This was demonstrated in 1886 after the Bulgarian annexation of eastern Rumelia when Greece appeared to be preparing for military intervention in the Epirus and southern Macedonia. Troops were mobilized and Ottoman forces blocked Greek irregulars crossing the border, but it was the opposition of the powers, who blockaded Greek ports, that ended this adventure before it started.

In 1897, irredentist aspirations found a new outlet in the crisis over Crete, the crisis itself having been stimulated by Greek agitation on the island, which had been a center of revolutionary action in the 1820s. The establishment of the Ethniki Etairia (National Society) in 1894 had created a powerful new locus for the fulfilment of the Megali Idea, its aim being "to inflame a large-scale conflagration within the Ottoman lands by provoking the Christians living in Epirus, Macedonia, and even Albania," thus turning European governments against the Ottomans "once more."[1]

In the disputes between the Ottoman state and Greece over Crete, there was fault on both sides. Under the Pact of Halepa (1878), the government in Istanbul had made substantial concessions to the Cretan Greeks, without the situation on the island calming down. An uprising had followed in 1889, and by the early 1890s further turmoil was brewing. Among the political class on the Greek mainland, it was believed that even autonomy for Crete could not be a permanent solution—only incorporation into the Greek kingdom would do. Greece's behavior as a new crisis over Crete developed disillusioned even many philhellenes. One of them, the correspondent Bennet Burleigh, wrote that he had never known a people "whose public affairs and business intercourse were so flagrantly conducted upon a basis of systematized delusion."[2]

Crete's population of about 300,000 was close to 80 percent Greek, but Muslims constituted the majority in many of the coastal towns. Throughout the nineteenth century, insurrections had marked Crete's history as frequently as Ottoman promises of reform. In the 1890s, agents of Ethniki Etaireia and the local Cretan organization Epitropi (the Commission) raised agitation to a dangerous new level. On the Greek mainland, where support for Ethniki Etaireia permeated all levels of society, public opinion was further inflamed by the claims of politicians that the Muslims of Crete were aiming to exterminate the Christians.

In May 1896, Muslims from outlying districts of Crete gathered in Canea (Greek Chania and Ottoman Haniya) to celebrate the *kurban bayram* religious festival. Fighting between Muslims and Christians ensued, ending only after Russian and Greek *kavasses* (consular guards) and several Muslims had been killed. "With them died Ottoman Crete," writes David Barchard.[3] By summer, Ethniki Etairia bands were crossing the Ottoman border into southern Macedonia and soon volunteers and weapons were also being poured into Crete to reinforce local insurgents. In early February 1897, seeking to control the situation, an international flotilla put the island under blockade. Britain, France, Germany, Austria-Hungary, Italy, and Russia all sent ships.[4] A "council of admirals," given authority over the island, landed an international force and in the coming months ordered the bombardment of Greek ports as well as positions on Crete.

On February 12, Prince George of Greece arrived in command of a naval flotilla consisting of a warship and several torpedo boats but was warned off by the admirals. Somehow slipping through the naval cordon three days later, two battalions of Greek troops (4,000 men) were landed under the command of Colonel Timoleon Vassos. This was an open breach of international law and surely more than just "ill-advised," as British prime minister, Lord Salisbury, put it.[5]

Vassos proclaimed *enosis* (union with Greece), and much of the island was quickly brought under the control of the Greek army and local volunteers. When the powers demanded that these forces be withdrawn, in return for a promise of autonomy, the Greek government refused.

The American-born British Conservative member of parliament, Ellis Ashmead Bartlett, who observed the war on the mainland, wrote that the landing of Greek troops on Crete inaugurated a deluge of blood and fire: "Everywhere the Christian insurgents rose and fell upon their defenceless Mussulman neighbours, plundering, outraging and in many cases massacring them."[6] In attacks on more than twenty villages in Sitia province, about 850 people were killed.[7] "Hundreds of wretched Mussulmans were butchered in the villages. Many were burned alive in their mosques. Women and children were mutilated. In fact, the worst of the Armenian horrors were paralleled by these Christian warriors."[8] The onslaught was only slightly mitigated by the Christians who took Muslims under their protection.[9]

George Curzon, undersecretary of state for foreign affairs, future vice-roy and governor general of India and foreign secretary, told the Commons the insurgents were "wandering up and down the mountains, exchanging shots with everybody whom they meet and, I am sorry to say, killing every Mohammedan of either sex who falls within their range."[10] To a large extent they were led by Greek officers. In Candia (Heraklion), 50,000 Muslims were protected by thin lines of European and Ottoman forces against 60,000 armed insurgents "ready at any moment ... to pounce on these people and inflict upon them the utmost cruelty."[11]

Despite these reports of massacre, philhellenic sentiment in Britain remained strong, especially against the background of recent reports of Armenian Christians being massacred in eastern Anatolia. In early March, besieged Muslim villagers living in the isolated southwest were saved by a Franco-British force that escorted them to the coast. The 2,047 Muslims taken back to Canea included 594 Ottoman soldiers "who had been saved from certain extermination," wrote the British consul, Alfred Biliotti, accompanying the joint force.[12]

On March 15, Greece mobilized, the reserves having been called up a month previously. Austria-Hungary, Germany, and Russia had been call-ing for a naval blockade of Crete and Piraeus, and Britain now agreed to a blockade at least of Crete. A small international force had already landed on the island and was now strengthened by 500–600 extra troops.

Greek nationalist irregulars further aggravated the developing crisis by crossing the border into southern Macedonia. The Ottoman government had tried to work around all violations of its sovereign powers, but finally it had to respond, and on April 17 it declared war. European and Amer-ican volunteers joining the Greek war effort included hundreds of men fighting under the leadership of Ricciotti Garibaldi (the son of Guiseppe and Anita) and the Italian socialist anarchist Amilcare Cipriani. Within a month, Greece had lost the war but went on to win the peace, as ratified in the Treaty of Constantinople (December 4, 1897). An autonomous regime for Crete was set up under the authority of a high commissioner, Prince George of Greece.[13]

The acknowledgment of Ottoman sovereignty in the terms negotiated was no more than a face-saving gesture for the sultan. Additionally, the war indemnity of 4,000 lira imposed on Greece was a fraction of what the war had cost the sultan's government.

In the year preceding the arrival of Prince George (December 1898), the admirals were in charge of an island from which Ottoman and Greek forces had still not been withdrawn and on which tens of thousands of Muslims driven out of their villages remained packed in the coastal towns. In early September, the admirals made matters worse by trying to take over customs revenue and replace Muslim customs officials with Christians. They succeeded in Canea and Rethymno, but when British officers arrived to take over the customs house at Candia, Muslim anger boiled over. In the onslaught that followed, Christians were chased down wherever they could be found.

Rioting and the destruction of property continued all day. Extra troops were landed and the town bombarded by a British gunboat. Between 300–500 local Christians are estimated to have been killed, along with up to 18 British soldiers, Britain's Greek vice-consul and his family (burnt to death in their home), and two other British subjects.[14] The 41 Muslims who died included 29 Ottoman irregular soldiers. In the aftermath, 17 people were hanged for the murder of soldiers and civilians. It remains difficult to understand how the admirals could not have foreseen the incendiary consequences of their actions.

With the arrival of Prince George in December 1898 and the withdrawal of the last remaining Ottoman troops, Crete passed out of the hands of the Ottoman Empire, even while nominally remaining under the sultan's authority. Greece had been richly rewarded for its aggression. As a Greek scholar has written, "After the exchange of thousands of despatches and notes between the powers, after the intervention of Europe and a crisis that threatened a conflagration in the Balkans and possibly a European war, the Greeks, totally defeated on the field of battle, secured what they had started out to get."[15]

The outcome of the war prefigured what was to happen when Greece, along with Bulgaria, Montenegro, and Serbia, attacked the Ottoman Empire in 1912 in the first Balkan war and emerged with its territorial conquests confirmed. In this period—the 1890s to 1914—there should be no failure to understand why the Ottomans no longer felt themselves able to trust in the good faith of the powers, collectively or individually.

BRITISH SYMPATHIES

A central theme in the Cretan crisis was the attitude of the British government. The attachment of the British to the Greeks was historical, cultural, and sentimental. England's greatest romantic poet of the early nineteenth century, Lord Byron, joined the struggle for Greek independence, giving money to the Greek navy and joining the insurgents at Missolonghi, where he died. "If I am a poet . . . the air of Greece has made me one," he wrote. Strategically, British involvement with Greece was strongly influenced by imperial rivalry in the Balkans, especially Russian support for Serbia. As much as the British government disapproved of Greek actions in 1897, it refused to commit itself to collective action at the point when it might have prevented war. When Germany, Austria-Hungary, and Russia wanted to blockade Greek ports, Britain was still holding out for administrative reforms that would give Crete a privileged autonomous position within the Ottoman Empire somewhat akin to Lebanon. Essentially, the policy was one of appeasement, of the philhellenes at home as well as the government in Athens, with the evident effect there of encouraging militancy rather than moderation.

Irrespective of the fact that Crete was Ottoman territory, Britain also proposed that both Ottoman and Greek forces withdraw from the island. Only at the end of March did Britain agree to a blockade of the Gulf of Athens, but by this time the powers were having second thoughts about the implications of deepening military involvement in the Near East.

Having finally agreed on collective naval action against the Greek mainland, the powers could not bring themselves to actually take it. They did, however, send a *note verbale* to both Greece and the Ottoman government on April 6, 1897, stating that if war broke out, the aggressor would be held responsible and "whatever the result of the war may be the Great Powers will in no case allow the aggressor to derive the least benefit from that."[16] In fact, the aggressor benefited greatly. The gains made, surfing along on British support, could only encourage the Greeks to keep going in their pursuit of the Megali Idea.

The outbreak of the First World War derailed any thoughts of further territorial acquisition in the near future. While Prime Minister Eleftherios Venizelos wanted Greece to join the Entente powers, King Constantine was determined that Greece should remain neutral. This tug of war, with the king ruling from Athens and Venizelos setting up a provisional government in Thessaloniki, backed by British and French forces, continued until the king's abdication on June 11, 1917, following the British blockade of the Greek coast and the landing of French troops at Piraeus. Constantine was succeeded by his son Alexander, who brought Venizelos back to Athens. On June 28, his government declared war on the central powers.

Internal turmoil, along with the accusation that King Constantine's "neutrality" had been governed more by dynastic, pro-German sentiment than Greece's best interests,[17] damaged the wholesome image of Greece in British eyes. With the war ending, however and Britain looking to the future, Greece soon resumed its place as a favored child and a "proxy"[18] for British interests in the Balkans and the Near East.

In January 1915, Britain offered Greece "most important territorial concessions" as an inducement to join the Allied war effort. Signing the Treaty of London on April 26, it also offered Italy an "equitable share" of the Mediterranean coast around Adalia (Antalya), adding Izmir to its share of the spoils in the Treaty of St. Jean de Maurienne in 1917. At the war's end, these commitments had to be rationalized within the remit of British strategic interests. As an expanding naval power looking for advantage in the Adriatic, the Mediterranean, and around the Horn of Africa, Italy represented a potential threat. Thus, while it could land some troops on the Mediterranean coast around Adalia, it could not now be allowed to have Izmir.

Out of strategic self-interest and sentiment, the obvious alternative for some leading British politicians was Greece. Despite wartime expulsions by the Ottoman government on the grounds of security, the entire coastline of the Sea of Marmara and the Aegean still had a substantial Greek population that could be considered largely sympathetic to the Greek national cause. However, there was a demographic problem: while the ratio of Christians to Muslims in Izmir was close, Greeks within the region were greatly outnumbered by Turks.[19] For this and other reasons, including Turkish nationalist resistance and support for their cause among Muslims in India in particular, senior military and political figures (including Lord Curzon and cabinet secretary Maurice Hankey) believed that the Greeks should never be allowed to set foot in Asia Minor.

Churchill, secretary of state for war and air, stated, "Venizelos and the Greece he represents (in whose future we have so great an interest) may well be ruined as a result of their immense military commitments in Smyrna."[20] General Henry Wilson, Britain's chief military advisor at Versailles, thought that landing the Greeks at Izmir would be both "mad and bad."[21] According to Count Sforza, Italy's high commissioner in occupied Istanbul, the Turks were far from dead, only "temporarily down and out."[22]

Such apprehensions were discounted by British prime minister David Lloyd George, a friend and great admirer of Venizelos. Lloyd George was a

Gladstonian liberal schooled in the ideals and prejudices of the late nine-teenth century. His love of Greek culture and history was matched by his detestation of the Turks. Neither he nor Venizelos could be deterred by warnings that Turkish nationalist forces would never give up Izmir and that a landing would end in disaster for Greece. Early successes after the landing on May 15, 1919, strengthened their confidence in victory.

In March 1920, General Wilson warned Venizelos that he risked ruin-ing his country. A war with Turkey and Bulgaria could last for years: the drain in men and money "would be far too much for Greece." Venizelos replied that "he did not agree with a word I had said."[23] For the Greek leader, Izmir was not just to be "occupied" (never a word he would have used) but incorporated into the Greek state forever.

Venizelos and Lloyd George continually underrated the battlefield capacity of Turkish forces, despite their often-impressive performance in the recent war and their known qualities of stubborn endurance. Here is Lloyd George on March 3, 1920: "The Turks were not formidable. Alone they had always been beaten even by Bulgaria a country half or even one-third the size of Turkey. Turkey possessed a false, sham reputation and the Allies were still living in dread thereof."[24] Again, on March 5: "He could not help thinking that the Allied Powers had so far been inclined greatly to exaggerate the power of the Turk. In his opinion it would be more correct to say that the Turk had been a great military power but now had ceased to hold that position."[25] As a people, the Turks were a nuisance and a curse. Wherever "the Turk" went he was a devastating agent who was now pleading for mercy when "he was not entitled to mercy. He was, in fact, the worst criminal of the whole of our enemies."[26] As for the Turk-ish military commander, Mustafa Kemal, Greek victories had shown he "had no great value."[27]

In December, Lloyd George returned to the theme of "the Turk" as "the curse of every land on which he had laid his hand," referring also to "Kemalists and other brigands." The treacheries of King Constantine were in no way comparable to the treacheries of the Turks.[28] Seeming to have haggling over the price of a carpet in Istanbul's covered market in mind, he said Mustafa Kemal was an Oriental who had to be treated as such: in his view, one of the great principles in dealing with Orientals was to let them make the first offer because if Mustafa Kemal knew Britain wanted to make peace with the nationalists he would raise his price.[29]

These remarks revealed yet again a mind so deeply steeped in preju-dice that it blinded Lloyd George to military realities and the singular leadership qualities of Mustafa Kemal, a man not just of great ability on the battlefield but educated, fluent in French and German, and widely read.[30] In August 1921, Lloyd George was still referring to the Turkish nationalists as having "a very exaggerated view of their own prowess" and "a contemptuous estimate of the Greeks' military capacity." However, the British prime minister was deluded. The Turkish nationalists had a very realistic grasp of their strengths and weaknesses and those of their enemy. Lloyd George had written that "the Turk accepts a fact in the end when it is really driven into his mind,"[31] when, if there was one mind into which facts had to be driven, it was his own.

Within a few weeks, the victory of the Turkish army in the Battle of Sakarya (August 23–September 13) was to show how disastrously wrong he had been all along. The battle marked the beginning of the end for the Greek army. Chasing the dream of the "great idea" in western Turkey had turned out to be a very bad idea indeed.

As the principal Allied supporter of the Greek attack, Lloyd George earned the mocking gratitude of Mustafa Kemal. On September 25, 1923, he said Lloyd George had been the real founder of the new Turkey "and that he intended to put up a public monument to him at Constantinople. It was the arrival of the Greeks at Smyrna that had enabled him to rally Turkish patriotism in defence of the Turkish homeland. Without that inducement he did not believe that he would have succeeded in resurrecting Turkey."[32]

INVASION AND OCCUPATION

Italy had suffered heavy loss of life on the battlefield: 650,000 dead and more than 1.5 million wounded, captured, or missing in action. Its delegation went to Paris expecting full territorial compensation for its sacrifices, as promised by its allies in the wartime treaties, but the mood had changed. Britain, in particular, was no longer prepared to pay what Italy thought was its due.

In January 1919, Lloyd George signaled that Britain was preparing to hand Izmir and the Aegean harbor town of Aivali (Ayvalik) to Greece. He had the support of France and influential philhellenes at home, while in Athens Venizelos constantly fanned the sparks into the blaze of occupation with accusations of massacre and the pending extermination of Christians by "the Turks." President Wilson still had to be convinced because a Greek occupation would violate his own principles of self-determination.

Italy had to be deceived for as long as possible. On April 24, its delegation walked out of the Paris "peace" talks in protest at the refusal of Italy's
wartime allies to hand over Dalmatia "within its present administrative
borders," as promised under the Treaty of London. While Italy was allocated islands in the Adriatic, on the mainland it was to be allowed only
the port of Zadar. The exclusion of Fiume (the present-day Croatian city
of Rijeka) was to have serious consequences in September when a force
of volunteers led by the Italian romantic nationalist poet Gabriele D'Annunzio drove out Allied forces and occupied the city.

Italy's absence from the negotiations allowed Lloyd George, Clemenceau, and Wilson to seal an agreement over Izmir behind its back. They
took the final decision just before the Italians returned to the conference
on May 5. Asked by Clemenceau whether "we should warn the Italians,"
Lloyd George replied, "not yet."[33]

On May 6, the Greek government was invited by the Supreme Allied
War Council to occupy Izmir in the name of maintaining order, at a time
order was not being disturbed. Italian and Greek warships were waiting
off the Aegean coast to see what would happen next. On May 12, Italy was
informed of an imminent Greek landing. When the Italian High Commissioner in Istanbul, Count Sforza, learned on May 14 that the Greeks
would actually land the next day, he was in a meeting with other high
commissioners. According to Wyndham Deedes, Britain's military attaché,
Sforza "got up and rushed from the room, banging the door behind him."[34]

Escorted by British and Greek warships, a Greek flotilla of fourteen
transports carrying about 20,000 men with their weaponry and pack
animals[35] left the port of Eleftheron (near Kavala in northern Greece)
on May 13 and headed for Izmir. The Allied deception of the Italians was
matched by their deception of the Turks.

At 9 a.m. on May 14, Admiral Calthorpe, in charge of the Allied side
of the operation, sent a message to the Turkish commander in Izmir, Ali
Nadir, that "the forts and fixed defences of Smyrna and its approaches"
were to be occupied by "allied forces" during the afternoon of that day.
Only at 11:30 p.m. did he inform the governor, Kanbur Izzet Paşa, that
a Greek force would be arriving early the next morning to occupy the
whole city.[36] Ottoman troops were to be kept in their barracks. Asked to
provide 100 Allied troops to help police and *jandarma* maintain order,
Calthorpe refused, agreeing only to the deployment of "small detachments
of soldiers" in the Muslim quarters of the city.[37]

Metropolitan Chrysostomos was informed of the "good news,"[38] and at midnight in the Aya Fotini Church the senior representative of the Greek government announced the military occupation of the city.[39] Overnight, while Greeks celebrated, the Redd-i Ilhak (Rejection of Annexation) society called on Muslims and Jews to meet in the Jewish cemetery. There, and at a mass meeting on the waterfront, speakers called for resistance to the occupation, while elsewhere reserve officers and civilians broke into the police armory to seize weapons.[40]

Having stopped at Lesbos (Midilli) on the night of the 14th, the Greek soldiers disembarked at various points along the Kordon (the central Izmir waterfront district) around 8 a.m. the next day. Metropolitan Chrysostomos was waiting to bless them. Perhaps 10,000 Izmirlis, plus Greeks who had come into the city from outlying areas, were there also, cheering and holding up Greek flags, garlands of flowers, and portraits of Venizelos. A contingent of *evzones* was marching past the military barracks and the *konak* (the governor's building) when shots were fired from the crowd, hitting several Greeks.

The gunman was Hasan Tahsin (the pseudonym of Osman Nevres), a journalist and former member of the Teşkilat who in 1914 had attempted the assassination of the Buxton brothers, Charles and Noel, during their mission to the Balkans to secure the neutrality of Bulgaria.[41] This "first shot," fired by a Turk, created pandemonium. Tahsin was chased and shot dead.[42] The Greek force then began firing at the government *konak* and the army barracks, breaking into it and taking soldiers prisoner.

Any hope that the occupation could be effected peacefully was now shattered. With murder, rape, and pillage spreading across the city, some 300–400 "Turks" (Izmir did have other Muslims in its population) had been killed by the end of the day and 2,500 arrested.[43] Because Izmirli men tended to wear the fez whatever their religious affiliation, some of the victims were actually Christians. Some soldiers taken prisoner were bayonetted on the waterfront, their bodies then thrown into the sea. Thousands of other captives—civilians as well as soldiers—were removed to a prison ship in the harbor.[44]

The newly appointed Greek governor-general of Izmir, Aristeidis Stergiadis, did his best to bring the situation under control, arresting many Greeks and spreading the message that discrimination against Turks would not be tolerated but already "the damage done to the cohabitation of Christian Greeks and Muslim Turks was irreparable."[45]

By the end of May, the Greek zone of occupation had been expanded
to include all towns about 100 kilometers distant from Izmir, including
Söke, Menemen, Torbalı, Selcuk, Manisa, Aydın, Turgutlu, and Ayvalik.
Ödemiş, Akhisar, Nazilli, Bergama, Alaşehir, Balikesir, and Edremit were
to follow in June. The capture of Edremit on July 1, 1920, moved the Greek
forces closer to the straits. On July 2, they occupied Bandirma and Biga on
the southern coast of the Sea of Marmara. Iznik and Bursa were captured
before the Greeks turned their attention to the western shore of the Sea
of Marmara, capturing Tekirdağ (Rodosto), Marmara Ereğli, and Çorlu
in eastern Thrace on July 20.

On August 4, it was the turn of Gelibolu (Gallipoli), with Uşak and
Afyonkarahisar falling on August 28, taking the Greek advance more than
300 kilometers into the interior. The zone of occupation had now been
extended down the Aegean coast from the Sea of Marmara almost as far
as Kuşadası, then occupied by Italian forces and to be occupied by the
Greeks for a short period in 1922 before the end of the war.

"COUNSELS OF DESPAIR"

By this time, the Greek occupation had been ratified in the Treaty of
Sèvres, which declared that Izmir was to be administered by the Greek
government while remaining under Turkish sovereignty. This was the idiosyncratic formula adopted after 1878 for the Austro-Hungarian occupation
of Bosnia-Herzegovina and for the Greek occupation of Crete after 1897.
The Greek zone of occupation was limited to the greater Izmir region,
with Britain's General George Milne drawing the line of demarcation.[46]

In March 1920, Venizelos complained that the Milne line was giving an
advantage to Turkish nationalist forces close to Izmir, consisting mostly of
irregulars buttressed by a small contingent of regular soldiers and officers.
Two months previously, General Milne had already adjusted the line in
favor of the Greeks. They were allowed to move a further 3 kilometers
forward, only for the Turks to pull back 4 kilometers where they "merely
sat down and laughed at the Greek troops." Venizelos begged the allies to
allow the Greeks to pursue the Turks for another 10–12 kilometers, apparently unaware, as Churchill pointed out, that General Milne, extending
the line again, had only the week before given Greek commanders permission to attack the Turks up to that distance.[47]

By July, the Greek army was advancing well beyond the Milne line. It met stiff resistance from Turkish irregulars, including bands led by the *efe* chiefs and their *zeybek* followers, forcing the Greeks to retreat on several occasions.[48] By January 1921, the army had moved northeast from Bursa into Hüdavendigar province (now Eskişehir) and was only about 230 kilometers from Ankara. However, it was also about 400 kilometers from its home base in Izmir. Logistics problems were accumulating, and the foot soldiers were showing signs of fatigue.

The Greek army's defeat in the first battle of İnönü (January 6–11, 1921) was followed by defeat in the second battle (March 26–31). These setbacks were a huge boost for morale among the Turkish nationalists. With King Constantine arriving in Eskişehir to talk to the generals and encourage the men, the Greek army moved south and began preparing for its biggest offensive yet. In the battle of Afyonkarahisar-Kutahya (June 27–July 20), it finally overwhelmed the Turkish forces. Instead of pursuing them, however, it stopped, allowing them to retreat to the Sakarya river and prepare for what would be a last-ditch stand in defense of Ankara.

By this time "counsels of despair had got the upper hand in Greece."[49] In June, a Greek flotilla headed by the flagship *Averof* sailed into the Black Sea from the Sea of Marmara and bombarded the port of Samsun. The following month, Greece built up its forces in eastern Thrace with the intention of marching on Istanbul. The Greek government actually asked the allies for permission to occupy Istanbul, raising the "scarcely imaginable folly" of its army marching on a city that was still under occupation by the powers. The allies said no and even raised the threat of force should Greece dare to proceed.[50]

The Battle of Sakarya (August 23–September 13, 1921) was fought near the town of Polatlı, about 80 kilometers from Ankara and close to the burial mound of King Midas at Gordion, the ancient Phrygian capital of Gordium where in the fourth century BC Alexander the Great is supposed to have cut the famous knot. Fighting on a 100-kilometer front, with all resources poured into the struggle by civilians, including food cooked by village women and items of clothing and other items donated in the name of national defense, the battle, following the biggest Greek offensive so far, ended in triumph for the Turkish army.

Sakarya marked the beginning of the end for the Greek army, even though that end was still some time coming. Greece had been unstable ever since the "national schism" caused by the conflict between Venizelos and King Constantine. On October 25, 1920, King Alexander died after being bitten by a monkey. In November, the government was voted out of power, Venizelos even losing his parliamentary seat. The man who had been instrumental in launching the war on Turkey now had to watch from the sidelines until he returned to government in 1928.

King Constantine returned from exile in December and resumed the throne, while the anti-Venizelist government continued the war, increasingly unpopular among the people. The major defeat at Sakarya almost a year later contributed to sagging morale among the troops, now very far from home. The army went on the defensive, as Greek politicians and generals argued over next steps and Britain contemplated the possible collapse of its anti-Kemalist policy on the battlefield.

Stalemate between the two armies lasted until August 13, 1922, when Mustafa Kemal launched the first of a series of offensives that drove the Greeks back to Izmir within a month. Victory in the battle of Dumlupınar (August 26–30, 1922) triggered the complete collapse of the Greek army. Kütahya was recaptured on August 30, and from that time onward, every single city, town, and village rolled up like a carpet in the Greek advance fell back into Turkish hands without any attempt by the Greek army to hold them. As one observer wrote, the Greeks headed for Izmir and the sea "like a half-demented mob of fear-stricken civilians."[51]

An advance contingent of Turkish troops entered Izmir on September 8, with the rest of the army following the next day. Most of the Greek army had embarked on September 8 from the nearby harbor of Çesme. As the army left, panic spread among the Greek population, with tens of thousands of desperate people packing the Izmir waterfront in the hope of escaping by sea.

Allied warships in the harbor were under instructions not to intervene, but the scenes along the quay were so shocking that eventually boats were sent to remove some of the people massing along the waterfront. Across the city, Turks began taking revenge on Greeks and Armenians they accused of betraying their country. In Mango's words, it was like "a murderous family quarrel."[52] On September 10, Metropolitan Chrysostomos, who had welcomed the Greek troops when they arrived in 1919, was brought to the governor's residence, accused of treason, and driven out into the hands of a mob, which stabbed, mutilated, and beat him to death.[53] On September 13, in an act crowning the suffering of Izmir, a great fire broke out that raged through the Armenian and Greek quarters and along the Kordon for four days.[54] Like Salonica, Izmir's cosmopolitan, multiethnic, multireligious history was just about at its end.

In the Treaty of Lausanne (July 24, 1923), it was decided to exchange about 1.2 million Greeks who had been living in Turkey for the approximately 400,000 Turks living in Greece. Whole cities, towns, and villages were emptied. Civilians, not politicians, paid the ultimate price for this war, in loss of life, property, possessions, and the land on which their forebears had lived for generations. The abandoned town of Kayaköy (Livissi) near Fethiye in southwestern Turkey was never resettled: its streets, houses, and churches overlooking a fertile valley stand today as testimony to the immense tragedy that engulfed its people because of decisions taken far from their homes.[55]

In Greece, the humiliating defeat of the army was followed by a military coup on September 11, 1922. Two weeks later, King Constantine was sent into exile, and in November the last commander-in-chief of the Greek army and five politicians, including former prime ministers, were sentenced to death and executed within hours. In London, David Lloyd George had recently been caught out in a cash-for-honors scandal when the coalition government collapsed on October 19, 1922, and he was forced to resign. The cause was the humiliating failure of foreign policy in the Near East, brought to a head by the confrontation with the Turkish army at Çanakkale.

TRAILS OF DESTRUCTION

In and out of Anatolia, the path of the Greek army was marked by massacre and willful destruction by troops and the civilians trailing in their wake. The reprisals taken by Turkish irregulars and civilians when they had the chance were equally vicious. Following Muslim complaints to the peace conference, the powers established an Inter-Allied Commission of Inquiry in July 1919.

By this time, the Commission had already received the result of one investigation carried out in the town of Menemen, north of Izmir, by a group consisting of Turkish, British, and Italian military, administrative, and medical staff. According to its report,

> All sorts of people, women, girls, children down to babies, more than a thousand persons, were basely assassinated. During the few

hours of its stay at Menemen the Commission was able to draw
up a list which, though incomplete, contains the names of more
than five hundred innocent victims.... The Hellenic agent, having opposed a thorough investigation and the exhumation of the
hundreds upon hundreds of corpses buried clandestinely by the
Hellenic military authorities, the identity of the victims could not
be established on the spot on the same day.... The massacres were
not confined to the town. They extended also to the surroundings,
to the fields, the mills, the farms where another thousand victims
may be counted. All the buildings outside the town, as well as several hundreds of houses in the town itself, were pillaged, sacked
or destroyed.[56]

The senior members of the Inter-Allied Commission of Inquiry were
Rear Admiral Mark Bristol (U.S.); General Bunoust (France); General
Hare (Britain); and General Dall'olio (Italy), with Turkish and Greek representatives allowed to witness the proceedings but not to vote on its findings. The Commission had an Italian secretary-general and a mixed support
staff. Between August 12 and October 15, 1919, it held forty-six meetings in
Istanbul, Izmir, Aydın, Girova, Nazilli, Izmir, Ödemiş, Menemen, Manisa,
and Ayvalik and took evidence from 175 witnesses. Its Aydın findings were
damning.[57] While the Greek population was "unquestionably persecuted
in 1914 and during the war," all citizens had been treated impartially under
the current *vali*, and Christians in the Aydın *vilayet* had been in no danger
since the armistice. Documents allegedly signed by Turkish police showing
Muslim plans to massacre Greeks were forgeries. Security in the *vilayet* of
Aydın and in Izmir in particular "in no way justified" the occupation of the
city's forts by the Allied powers or the landing of "Allied" (Greek) troops.
Their presence, in fact, had worsened the situation.
    On May 15–16, the Commission found, "countless acts of violence" had
targeted Turks and their homes, with people being murdered and women
raped, Greek civilians mostly being responsible for these acts although soldiers joined in. According to the Greek authorities, two people were killed
on the day of the landing; according to the Turks, 300–400 were killed or
wounded. The gradual extension of the zone of occupation beyond Izmir
was effected without the authority of the Allied powers.[58]
    The advance of the Greek army into the countryside, the search for
weapons, the behavior of armed Greek civilians, and the activities of brigands created a situation of chaos along the Aegean coast. Armed clashes

reached a peak in the town of Aydın, which Greek troops occupied before being forced to evacuate on June 29 after allegedly committing numerous atrocities in the district. According to the Turkish military commander for the region, referring to a "policy of extermination," entire villages and the Turkish quarters of towns were destroyed. In the town of Nazilli, Jews were killed as well as Muslims, with synagogues and mosques set on fire.[59]

In the short period before the Greeks were able to return to Aydın on July 4, vengeance was taken by Turkish civilians and *çeteler* (bandit gangs). In the Greek quarter, Michael Llewellyn Smith writes, quoting Arnold Toynbee's account, "women and children were hunted like rats from house to house and civilians caught alive were slaughtered in batches—shot or knifed or hurled over a cliff. The houses and public buildings were plundered, the machinery in factories wrecked, safes blown open or burst open and the whole quarter finally burnt to the ground."[60]

Thousands of civilians, Greeks and Turks, were killed. The reoccupation of the town was ordered by the Greek high command against the wishes of the Allied powers. The Inter-Allied Commission referred to a figure of 1,000 killed in or around Menemen on June 17, setting it against the findings of a French officer that 200 had died.

While allocating responsibility to both the Turkish and Greek authorities for what it was reporting, the Commission left no doubt as to where it thought the prime responsibility lay, concluding that the Greek presence was "incompatible with the restoration of law and order" and should be terminated in favor of occupation by Allied troops under the authority of the Allied Supreme Command in Asia Minor.[61]

The Commission's report was given to the Supreme Council (the Council of Ten) in Paris on October 7 but not discussed until November 8. In the course of an intense debate, Venizelos was given ample time to present his own view of the situation. Publication of the report would have been extremely embarrassing for the Allies, especially Britain. In addition, it would have strengthened Turkish national morale and probably stirred up Muslims even further in other British-occupied territories, especially India and Egypt, where the arrest of Egyptian nationalist leader Saad Zaghlul in March had already ignited a countrywide revolution. Under such pressures, the Commission's report was suppressed and never published.

In 1921, three representatives of the Inter-Allied Commission (British, French, and Italian) were sent on another fact-finding mission. This was a sketchy affair compared to the two months spent in 1919 investigating the situation down the Aegean coast to Izmir. The three commissioners spent nine days (May 13–22) traveling (on the sloop HMS *Bryony*) and taking evidence around Gemlik, Yalova, and Mudanya on the southern coast of the Sea of Marmara, several hours' sailing time from Istanbul.

A separate commission was sent to inquire into the situation around Ismid (İzmit). Neither commission had time to make a proper investigation (if that was ever considered), but both believed in the basic truth of what they were being told, notwithstanding probable exaggerations. In the *kazalar* of Yalova and Guemlek (Gemlik), occupied by the Greek army, the commissioners concluded, "There is a systematic plan of destruction of the Turkish villages and extinction of the Moslem population. This plan is being carried out by Greek and Armenian bands which appear to operate under Greek instructions and sometimes even with the assistance of detachments of regular troops."[62]

Maurice Gehri, representing the International Red Cross, accompanied the mission and used even stronger language when writing that for the last two months, "elements of the Greek army of occupation have been employed in the extermination of the Moslem population" of the Yalova-Gemlik peninsula.[63] The commissioners gave evidence of systematic burning and looting of Turkish villages by Armenian bands, joined by Greek soldiers. Whole villages had been destroyed and their Muslim population had disappeared. While it had not been possible to verify accusations of gross atrocities given by Turkish authorities, the commissioners stated, "it has, however, been definitely established that women and defenceless old men were shot or knocked on the head in the villages of Kapakli and Karaja Ali, sometimes even in their own houses."

Whereas in 1919, the commission had recommended that the Greeks be replaced by Allied troops, in 1921 the commission proposed the introduction of an Allied gendarmerie into these districts, "or at any rate that Allied officers should be attached to the various Greek commands for the purposes of surveillance."

The commission also condemned Turkish behavior, stating that "acts of violence and barbarism and massacres on a large scale were undoubtedly committed in 1920 by Kemalist bands or soldiers of the regular army against the Christian population of the region not occupied by the Greek army, east of Yalova, north of the lake of Nicea [present day Iznik] and in the region of Nicea." There are further references in the report to past events, to villages "destroyed by the Turks during the war and after the armistice," to villages "burned or destroyed by Kemalists during 1920," to acts of violence, barbarism, and massacre "committed in 1920 by Kemal-ist bands or by soldiers of the regular army," as well as more general refer-ences to "Kemalist excesses" and "Turkish bands of a more or less Kemalist persuasion."

In fact, it was not just "Kemalist bands" but civilians taking revenge when they could and bandit gangs out for what they could get. Religious affinity could be irrelevant. Muslim Circassians collaborated with the Greeks and along with other bandit gangs were allegedly used by them as "an instrument for the execution of Greek atrocities, with license to burn down villages, rape women, and rob and execute Muslims."[64]

The publication of British parliamentary papers—the "Blue Books"—is always governed by political considerations. Publication of the Inter-Allied Commission's much more detailed report in 1919 would have been deeply embarrassing to the British and Greek governments, so it was with-held for all time. Accordingly, what was the reasoning behind the govern-ment's decision to publish the shorter but still damning report of 1921?

Throughout the war the foreign press had run the most luridly exag-gerated articles about the criminal behavior of "the Turks," manifested in such headlines as "Millions of Greeks Massacred, Thrown into the Sea" (*Chicago Daily Tribune*, January 1, 1918); "1,000,000 Greeks are Put to Death by Turco-Teuton Forces in Asia" (*Washington Post*, January 1, 1918); "Turkey is Red with Blood of Slain Greeks" (*Chicago Daily Tribune*, May 12, 1918); and "Turks Parboiled 250,000" (*New York Times*, July 31, 1919).[65] Now, however, an Allied commission—not sensation-seeking newspapers publishing nonsensical reports—was accusing the Greeks of committing large-scale massacres. The findings of such an authoritative body would be hard to refute.

Lloyd George had backed the Greek invasion to the hilt and was still hoping for victory. The reports of Greek atrocities completely under-mined the propaganda campaign being waged against the Turkish nation-alists. The crimes committed by the Greek army and civilians were so gross that they could scarcely be denied, but the British government may have reasoned that the repeated references to "Kemalists," "Kemalist bands," and past "Kemalist excesses" in the Inter-Allied Commission report would attenuate moral outrage and, in the minds of readers, establish some kind of equivalence between the excesses of the two sides. In fact, while there was symmetry in the immorality of the crimes committed, there was no symmetry in their scale, as Arnold Toynbee and others were to make clear.

"ORGANIZED ATROCITIES"

During the war, Toynbee and Bryce had been pillars of the atrocity propaganda campaign against Germans and Turks. Now, visiting Ottoman lands in 1921 as a special correspondent for the *Manchester Guardian*, Toynbee turned his attention to atrocities committed during the Greek occupation. He compiled detailed reports of what he saw for himself or what he was told along the southern shores of the Sea of Marmara and along the Aegean coast. While he gave details of atrocities suffered by Greeks at Turkish hands, his reports were overwhelmingly an indictment of the Greek army, as well as the civilians who pillaged, looted, and killed in its wake. In his view, these atrocities were "organized from above."[66]

Under the heading "The War of Extermination," Toynbee listed hundreds of Turkish villages destroyed or pillaged.[67] His inquiries took him to Aydın where in June–July 1919, Muslims and Christians had slaughtered each other. Now all the mosques had been ruined or abandoned and hardly any Turks were to be seen. In Ismid (İzmit), Greek civilians had compromised themselves so deeply that "the entire native Christian population took its departure with the troops" after the Greek withdrawal in June 1921.[68]

Arriving in the town two days later, Toynbee saw some of the consequences of the Greek presence for himself: the corpses of Turkish wagoners and "one or two" bodies of Turkish women floating in the water; shops systematically looted except those protected with the sign of the cross chalked above the shutters over the owner's name; and arson in Turkish and Jewish quarters with cattle penned up and burnt alive. The principal mosque had been robbed of its carpets and furniture and "defiled," with slaughtered pigs left lying in the courtyard and the interior.[69] Three days before the evacuation, the male inhabitants of two Turkish quarters had been dragged to the cemetery and shot in batches. Toynbee was present when two mass graves were opened and saw for himself the bodies of Muslim men with their hands tied behind their backs. He estimated that about sixty had been buried in these two graves, but there were several more. Overall, about 300 people were missing.[70]

While referring to Turkish atrocities and the excesses of "Kemalist bands," it is condemnation of the behavior of the Greeks—army, irregulars, and civilians—that comprises the body of Toynbee's report. On the Yalova-Gemlik peninsula, "organized atrocities"[71] began in April 1921, not coincidentally, in Toynbee's view, following the Greek defeat in the second battle of Inonu, with Turkish "chettes" (*ceteler*) then retaliating. Many of the Greek irregulars were ordinary civilians brutalized by the war and now encouraged by the Greek army to put on a bandolier and fight.[72] In many cases, the victims of soldiers and irregulars alike were singled out because of their wealth, robbed, and killed. Sometimes the entire family would also be murdered and the house burned down to "cover the tracks" of their assailants.[73] Toynbee believed that after the Turkish victory in the battle of Inonu the purpose of atrocities on the Yalova-Gemlik peninsula was to "exterminate" Turks in districts "it was no longer convenient for the Greek army to hold."

Toynbee was writing in late 1921, but it was not until the retreat of the Greek army in September 1922 that the full scale of the destruction—committed during the occupation and then a scorched-earth pullback to the sea—could be exposed. Other reports came from numerous sources, including consuls, naval officers, and journalists both foreign and local. In town after town, mosques, hamams, hotels, shops, and private dwellings had been systematically destroyed by soldiers and their Greek and Armenian civilian accomplices, spraying kerosene and petrol on thousands of buildings. Civilians emerged from their houses to put the fires out at the risk of being killed.

Manisa, Turgutlu, Alaşehir, Menemen, and Salihli were among the worst affected. Many civilians were killed, and much of the previous civilian population was nowhere to be seen, probably having escaped into the countryside. Of Manisa, a U.S. naval lieutenant wrote, "It is hard to conceive of such complete destruction as we saw. Acres and acres were completely wiped out."[74] In Kasaba, only 200 of 2,000 buildings had not been destroyed. Alaşehir had a population of 38,000 people, but only 5,000 remained, and almost all of its 4,000 houses had been gutted by fire. All 12 mosques had been destroyed. In Salihli, most of the houses had been burnt down, along with hundreds of shops, hotels, flour mills, a cinema, two mosques, and a synagogue. Stories of rape, abduction, and murder were commonly told.[75]

The accounts of foreign observers can be supplemented by the large volume of official documents stored in the Ottoman archives, as well as material in other archival sources, including the British. In a report to Sir Horace Rumbold, senior Allied high commissioner in Istanbul, Sir Harry Lamb, British consul-general in Izmir, described the conduct of the Greeks during their retreat as "in every way indescribably disgusting." They had gone to pieces completely, and there seemed little doubt that in some places "they shut up Turks up in Mosques and then set the Mosques on fire."[76]

THE "CHANAK CRISIS"

The embarkation of the Greek army from Izmir left one critical issue to be resolved between Britain and Turkey before the diplomats met in Geneva to sort out the mess. By now—the autumn of 1922—the British government had been abandoned (as it believed) by all of its wartime allies. It was prepared to sign a peace with the Turkish government but only on its own terms, which included control over the straits and approaches to the Sea of Marmara. This last phase of the Turkish war of independence has passed into British history as the "Chanak crisis."

Having defeated all enemies but one, Turkish forces advanced up the coast toward the "neutral zone" declared by the occupying Allied powers. Britain believed the Turks had to be prevented from crossing the straits, so on September 12 the commander-in-chief of Allied forces, General Charles Harington Harington, crossed them himself with a small force and occupied Çanakkale. The signal to the Turks was that if they dared attack, it would be at the risk of war with the three Allied powers, Britain, France, and Italy.[77]

Churchill had opposed the landing of the Greeks before they even stepped onto the quay at Izmir, but the straits were a raw nerve in the imperial body and now that it was being twitched by the Turks, he threw his support behind Lloyd George. Not just the Commonwealth and Dominion governments but Rumania and the Kingdom of Serbs, Croats, and Slovenes (Yugoslavia from 1929) were approached to see whether they were willing to send troops to help: in return Curzon would support their admission to a European conference to draw up a new treaty covering the straits.

Facing the possibility of war, Italy and France now let the British know that they had gone as far as they were prepared to go in confronting the Turks. Count Sforza, Italy's representative on the Allied council in charge of the occupation of Istanbul, had made it clear that Italy would not fight Turkey or even put its troops at risk of being attacked by the Turks. On September 19, Harington informed the War Office that the French commander had told him the French detachment at Çanakkale was to be pulled back to Gallipoli at once.

In Paris the next day, Prime Minister Raymond Poincaré heard the British arguments for taking a strong stand at the straits before explaining to Curzon why France differed. First of all, it had no forces available to send to the Near East. Furthermore, when the French commander sent forces to the Anatolian side of the straits, it was an "on the spot" decision made in a spirit of *camaraderie*. It was not as if his government had taken a decision to put them there, and neither had it ever agreed to send troops to force the Kemalists to accept the neutrality of the zones held by Allied forces.[78] An entire army would be needed to defend the Allied position at Çanakkale. The allies were facing imminent peril, and he was not prepared "to expose French soldiers to that peril. In his opinion Mustapha Kemal could cross tomorrow if he wished to do so."[79]

Continuing their discussions two days later, Poincaré "lost all command of his temper," wrote Curzon,

> and for a quarter of an hour shouted and raved at the top of his voice, putting words into my mouth which I had never uttered, refusing to admit the slightest interruption or correction, saying that he would make public the insult to France, quoting a telegram from Athens to the effect that the British Minister had asked the Greek Government to furnish 60,000 men for the defence of Thrace[80] and the Straits and behaving like a demented school-master screaming at a guilty schoolboy. I have never seen so deplorable or undignified a scene. After enduring this for some time I could stand it no longer and, rising, broke up the sitting and left the room.[81]

They managed to resume their discussion, but the bitterness was to endure. With Poincaré refusing to give way, Curzon said that if the French weren't going to help, Britain would not hesitate to act alone. This was bluff. Britain had no intention of acting alone.

The problem was that it could not recruit any worthwhile allies. The Governor-General of Australia had just delivered a message from the Australian prime minister, Billy Hughes, like Lloyd George, of Welsh heritage if not birth, saying the news that Britain intended to take strong action against the Kemalists "came as a bolt from the blue." Speaking frankly, wrote Hughes, "the Australian people are sick of war. In their view, war except in defense of vital interests is not only a blunder but a crime." While Australians understood the importance of the straits, they had no sympathy with King Constantine's ambitious projects; they did not understand why the Dominions had not been consulted before Britain took action; and neither did they understand why the Greeks had not been restrained long before. The Dominions ought not to be asked whether they would join after Britain had in effect committed them. In short, "In a good cause we are prepared to venture our all," in a bad one "not a single man."[82]

On September 29, Curzon told ministers gathered for a meeting at his home that Turkish forces at Çanakkale "had advanced to a point where they were in close contact with British troops. They had actually reached the barbed wire of our position and were making grimaces across it."[83] One has to imagine that British troops pulled faces back. In any case, it was the "threat" to the straits that had to be dealt with forcefully, not face-pulling by Turkish soldiers.

Curzon said he had told the Kemalist representative in London, Nihat Reşit, that General Harington would demand the withdrawal of Turkish forces. If they were not withdrawn, they would be fired upon. Again, having failed to secure any worthwhile support for war against the Turkish nationalists, this was bluff. No ultimatum was ever delivered to Mustafa Kemal, though one was prepared. Instead, Harington, acting on his own, and in frequent communication with the Kemalists, withheld a demand that would have taken the crisis a very dangerous step further.

It was effectively the end. Australia had said no to the request to join the fight against the Turks, Canada had dithered, New Zealand had offered to send a small contingent of troops, and Jan Smuts had avoided giving an answer.[84] There was discussion of involving the Greeks, but they were a spent force. Rumania and the embryonic Yugoslav state could not be of much help even if they agreed. Britain would have to face the Turks on its own, which would mean sending a large army into another war in defense of what was clearly a lost cause.

It would have been a mad venture, so strongly opposed at home by the press, the public, the generals, and the politicians that it almost certainly would never have been launched in the first place. The card metaphor is doubly appropriate: the allies had played all the cards in their hand; now the whole house of cards they had constructed in 1919 when they invited Greece to occupy Izmir had collapsed.

On October 11, British, French, Italian, Turkish, and Greek delegates signed an armistice at Mudanya, which took east Thrace out of Greek hands, ceding it to Turkey, and froze the situation along the straits pending final decisions at a peace conference. On October 15, Ankara was declared the Turkish capital (dismaying the diplomats who contemplated having to serve there), and on October 19 a Turkish nationalist force arrived in Istanbul. That same day, David Lloyd George resigned after the Conservatives withdrew from the coalition government in protest at his mishandling of the "Chanak crisis."

The Treaty of Lausanne was signed in July 1923, establishing Turkey within its present borders. Twelve years of continuous war since the Italian invasion of Libya in 1911 had finally come to an end. The achievements of the Turkish nationalists in defeating all their enemies, straight after an enormously destructive war, were truly extraordinary. One more great tragedy followed—the Ottoman-Greek–Greek-Turkish population "exchange"—but like any house whose roof has fallen in and walls have collapsed, a lot of debris remained to be cleared.

CHAPTER 16

End of the Line

ON JANUARY 30, 1923, Greek and Turkish delegates meeting at Lausanne signed a convention on a population exchange of ethnic Greeks from Ottoman lands and ethnic Turks from Greece. Such an exchange had been on the cards ever since the Balkans war. Now, following the devastation of the Greek-Turkish war, and the conclusion that the two communities could no longer live together in the same country, the two governments picked up the option of a formal exchange.

Fridtjof Nansen, the League of Nations High Commissioner for refugees, was given the task of overseeing the exchange of the 200,000 Greeks who remained in Turkey and the 350,000 Turks living in Greece. Together with Greeks who had left Ottoman lands since the Balkan wars (having "migrated," fled, or been driven out according to how these events are described and who is describing them), the exchange affected about 1.2 million Greeks who had been living along the Aegean coast, in central Anatolia, and in the Pontus region of the Black Sea.[1] Close to 400,000 ethnic Turks had to leave Greece. Exceptions were made in the agreement for Greeks living in Istanbul and Turks living in western Thrace. The exchange was naturally devastating for people compelled to leave their ancestral homes at short notice.

Small Greek communities remained but successive wars with Greece since 1897 had cast a shadow over their lives in Turkey. In the decades after the First World War, the shadow was only to lengthen. In 1942, non-Muslim minorities were targeted in the imposition of a capital or "wealth tax" (*varlik vergisi*). Those to be taxed were divided into four categories:

M (Muslim), G (*gayrimüslim*, or non-Muslim), E (*ecnebi*, or foreigner), and D (*dönme*, or a Jewish convert to Islam). This was an arbitrary tax, with no right of appeal, justified through the need to control prices and combat speculation and black-marketeering. It fell disproportionately on Greeks, Jews, and Armenians, who constituted the bulk of the business, commercial, and manufacturing classes, and (to a lesser extent) on foreigners.

The *varlik vergisi* raised hundreds of millions of lira for the state. Although non-Muslims amounted to no more than a few hundred thousand in a population of nearly 19 million, they paid more than 50 percent of the money raised. Many non-Muslims were forced to sell homes, businesses, and factories: those who could not pay were detained until they could pay or made to pay off their debt through forced labor far from home. A number died as a result of their harsh treatment. Most of those punished came from Istanbul. The *varlik vergisi* remains a shameful chapter in Turkish history, a vindictive and spiteful measure enacted against vulnerable communities. It further weakened minority trust in the state, but for the Greeks, another bout of mistreatment amounting to persecution was soon to come.

In the early evening of September 6, 1955, rioters, incensed by reports that Atatürk's former home in Salonica (now the Turkish consulate) had been bombed, attacked Greek apartment buildings, businesses, churches, and schools in central Istanbul. Up and down the fashionable Istiklal Caddesi (Independence Avenue), the Rue Pera of Ottoman times, windows were smashed and shops looted in a nine-hour rampage. Thousands of buildings were destroyed or severely damaged and twelve or thirteen people killed (more according to some estimates). In the aftermath, this usually charming thoroughfare looked as though it had been strafed from the air. Obviously, only Greeks would have attacked Atatürk's former home, or so it was assumed by the rioters. Only later did inquiries reveal that the bombing and the assembling of a mob was a Turkish "false flag" operation. A small bomb had been planted in the grounds of the Salonica consulate, not in Atatürk's former home and not by a Greek but a young Turk.

At his trial on the Marmara Sea island of Yassiada in 1961, the former Turkish prime minister, Adnan Menderes, overthrown in 1960, was charged with organizing the riots along with other offenses. However, this accusation clearly served the interests of the junta that overthrew him: the truth seems murkier and more complex, involving individuals the military would not have wanted prosecuted. The central role seems to have been played by a military intelligence unit, with elements of the press coopted to heighten a sense of crisis.

The international background was the developing crisis over Cyprus, whose future was at the time being discussed at tripartite talks in London between Greece, Turkey, and Britain. Greece wanted Cyprus to be declared independent, while on the island the former Greek army officer, George Grivas, was leading a terrorist campaign at achieving *enosis* (union) with Greece. A dramatic act putting Greece in a bad light would clearly serve the purposes of the Turkish government. Years later, in September 1990, the Turkish government cleared Menderes and the two senior ministers executed with him, Fatih Rüştü Zorlu and Hasan Polatkan, of wrongdoing and pardoned them posthumously.[2]

Some 10,000 Greeks left Istanbul after the 1955 riots (or pogrom as they have also been described), and more fled in 1964, after Greek Cypriot ultranationalist armed gangs massacred Turkish Cypriots. About 50,000 Turks still live in western Thrace, while Istanbul and the islands in the Sea of Marmara remain homes to 2,000–3,000 Turkish nationals of Greek origin and upward of 50,000 Turkish Armenians.

ABOLITION OF THE CALIPHATE

On July 24, 1923, the belligerent states and other interested parties, including Japan and the short-lived Kingdom of Serbs, Croats and Slovenes (Yugoslavia from 1929), signed the Treaty of Lausanne, formally ending all conflicts between them. The 143 articles dealt with borders and administrative, financial, and legal matters and the status of minorities. Italy still occupied the Dodecanese islands, but otherwise, with the exception of Tenedos (Bozcaada), Imroz (Gökceada), the Rabbit (Tavşan) islands, a few kilometers off the north Aegean coast, and one or two pieces of contested rock that on occasion still cause tension between Greece and Turkey, the Aegean islands all went to Greece.

Turkey acknowledged the British annexation of Cyprus. The border between Turkey and Syria was settled according to the Franco-Turkish pact (the Ankara agreement) of October 20, 1920. However, this was to change when the autonomous *sancak* of Alexandretta (Iskenderun) within the French mandate for Syria was established as the State of Hatay in 1938 and incorporated into Turkey as the province of Hatay in 1939.

The contested status of Mosul remained an issue until the League of Nations decided in 1925 that it should go to Iraq and not Turkey, thereby bringing the oil wealth of Kirkuk and Mosul under the control of the Turkish (later Iraq) Petroleum Company, dominated by British, French (initially), Dutch, and U.S. interests.

Turkey still had two governments when the fighting stopped. This was resolved on November 1, 1922, with the abolition of the sultanate on the vote of the Grand National Assembly and the resignation of Tewfiq Paşa, grand vizier in the sultan's government and the last in Ottoman history.

The fate of Mehmet VI, who had succeeded as sultan-caliph after the death of Mehmet V on July 3, 1918, now had to be decided. Mehmet had good reason to fear for his life or to fear being put on trial. He had run a government under occupation and had cooperated fully with the allies in trying to destroy the nationalist cause. He had gone as far as sponsoring a "caliph's army," armed by the British, to prevent the nationalists reaching Istanbul. His government had sentenced Mustafa Kemal to death in absentia, and both he and the government in occupied Istanbul were regarded by the nationalists as traitors.

On November 15, a messenger arrived at British headquarters in Istanbul with a message from Yildiz Palace. The sultan wanted to leave Istanbul immediately: would Britain help him as it had said it would? General Harington visited the sultan at the palace and secured a signed letter requesting his removal from Istanbul under British protection. At 8:00 a.m. on November 17, Mehmet VI, accompanied by his son Ertuğrul and eight members of the royal household, slipped through a palace side door into the Yildiz barracks, then occupied by a battalion of Grenadier Guards. The royal party was then taken in two military ambulances to the naval base at Tophane where it was escorted aboard HMS *Malaya*. By 9:30 a.m. Mehmet VI was on his way to Malta, later taking up permanent residence in San Remo until his death in 1926. Although a line of Ottoman sultans established in 1299 had finally come to an end, this still left open the future of the caliphate.

Elected as successor to Mehmet VI by the Grand National Assembly, but only as caliph, Abdülmecid II had no role to play in the life of the republic and plenty of time, if he chose, for his hobbies of butterfly collecting and oil painting.[3] By early 1923, the Turkish press was filled with reports of impending "reforms" that would change the status of religion and affect the standing of the royal family. The caliphate might have sentimental value for Muslims around the world, but in the new Turkey it dangled like a useless appendage. The time had come to finally cut the thread.

On March 2, 1923, the People's Party (Halk Firkası), later the Republican People's Party, adopted four draft bills. The first declared the caliph deposed and the institution abolished. The second decreed that all members of the royal family—the caliph and all princes and princesses of the blood plus spouses—must be sent from Turkey within ten days and never allowed to return. They would be given a year to wind up their affairs, but all imperial property—mostly their palaces—would go to the state.

The third draft abolished the Ministry of Religious Affairs, replacing it with a directorate whose chief officer would be appointed by the president of the republic. There would no longer be a Shaykh al-Islam. All schools would be placed under government authority, with a theological faculty established at university level and schools opened for the training of mosque functionaries (the forerunners of the present *imam-hatip* schools).

The fourth draft changed the status of the chief of the general staff. He would no longer have a ministerial position and henceforth would be appointed by the president on the nomination of the prime minister but would be independent in the exercise of his powers.

On March 3, all four drafts were adopted by an overwhelming vote of the deputies in the Grand National Assembly. The Ottoman caliphate now belonged to history.[4]

The director of public security had already been sent to Istanbul and, on receiving instructions from Ankara, went to Yildiz Palace late at night to inform Abdülmecid II of his deposition. He was given only a few hours to arrange his departure. Early in the morning of March 4, the last Ottoman caliph, his son, and other members of the royal household were driven to the railway station at Çatalca, between Istanbul and the Bulgarian frontier, the last line of defense for the capital during the Balkan war.

The government had given Abdülmecid a passport in the name of M. Abdul Mecid, son of Abdul Aziz, and some money for travel expenses but nothing for his maintenance. He was put on the Orient Express and left his now defunct empire for good. Settling in Paris, "Abdulmecid Efendi" would have led an impoverished life until his death in 1944 but for the financial help of the Nizam of Hyderabad. Other members of the royal family soon followed him into exile. In Friday prayers, the caliph's name was dropped in favor of prayers for the republic. Abolition of the caliphate was followed by the establishment of a *khilafat* movement by Indian Muslims, but otherwise it was received with surprisingly little opposition in the Muslim world, perhaps because of the widespread admiration for Mustafa Kemal and the achievements of the Turkish nationalist movement against the common imperial enemies.

PROPERTY RIGHTS

The threads still needing to be tied up included the fate of Armenians and Greeks who had been "relocated" and the mass of property they had left behind. Between 1918 and 1920, the government in Istanbul took various measures to facilitate the return of Christians and other displaced persons and ensure the return of their property. Pressure from the occupying powers (especially Britain) was a clear element behind the edicts that were issued, but there is no reason to think that the government's intentions were not genuine. It sought to create as favorable a situation as possible ahead of peace talks, opinion was positive in both Turkish and Armenian newspapers, and there was a natural desire to clear away the mess of the war and to a degree offset the negative effect of wartime anti-Turkish propaganda.

On October 18, 1918, with the armistice of Mudros (Turkish Mondros) to be signed on October 30, followed by the arrival in Istanbul of the occupying powers on November 13, the government authorized the return of all those who had been relocated or otherwise displaced by the war. The decree was sent to the provinces two days later.

In view of the shortage of food, refugees who had been living in the provinces of Erzurum, Trabzon, Van, Bitlis, Diyarbakir, and the *sancak* of Erzincan would be given permission to return "only after obtaining information from the local authorities on the existing situation at the places in question ... they shall return in groups to be sent one after another as a means of security."[5] Further instructions were issued for the return to their original faith of people who had been subjected to forced conversion; for the release of Armenian prisoners; for orphaned Armenian children to be handed over to relatives or guardians; and for property to be returned to its original owners.

The return of this mass of displaced people was to be organized by the General Directorate for the Settlement of Tribes and Immigrants (Aşair ve Muhacirin Müdüriyyeti Ummumiyesi).[6] This would be an enormously

complicated operation—not just because of the financial cost or the logistics, that is, how to actually return people to their homes, but because of
the obvious difficulties they would face once they arrived. In the eastern
provinces, Muslims who had suffered during the war were likely to resent
the return of Christians associated with the Allied war effort, while refugees living in "abandoned" properties were likely to resist eviction.

The practical problems were daunting for a new government emerging
from a massively destructive war. Transport and food would have to be
found. Where homes no longer existed, other accommodation would have
to be provided. Stock and seed would have to be found for returning farmers. Tribunals would have to decide the legitimacy of claims to property
(a Mixed Commission had been established at the British embassy for this
purpose) and to punish those who had stolen it or used it for their own
ends. This alone was going to be enormously complicated.

Despite these obstacles, large numbers of displaced Greeks and Armenians were able to return with government help from late 1918 through
1919. Others made their way back independently. Steamers were used to
transport refugees to the eastern Black Sea or to return them to Anatolia
from other ports. By February 1919, more than 170,000 were estimated
to have returned. In March, the government released a figure of 232,679,
and in June the British authorities estimated that 276,015 had returned.
On February 3, 1920, the newspaper *Ileri* reported that 335,883 Greeks
and Armenians had returned since the armistice. To this number must
be added perhaps 250,000 Armenians who had followed the French army
into Cilicia, only to flee after the French withdrawal in 1922.

Returning to a devastated land to find a home in ruins or one in which
someone else was living and then having to apply to a tribunal for their
removal was hardly an incentive to stay. Many Armenians subsequently
emigrated to the U.S. and other lands. For the Greeks, most of those who
chose to remain were forced to leave in the population exchange of 1923.

While the nationalist government in Ankara wanted to get over the
consequences of the war as soon as possible, its immediate tasks were to
consolidate its authority and meet the desperate needs of the people, not
claims being made on the basis of past suffering. At Lausanne, Ismet had
argued that the return of a mass of Armenians would constitute a security threat. Subsequently, Armenians who had left the empire without
passports were not permitted to return. Decrees passed by the previous
government in Istanbul were superseded by new laws and ad hoc measures that over time extinguished the question of "abandoned" Armenian

property in the eyes of the state, if not even now in the eyes of the original owners or their heirs.

This issue is too complex for more than a few cursory remarks, but some examples can be given of how it was resolved. One is the rejection of "proxy" claims to property by Greeks from the Pontus who had left for Istanbul or Greece.[7] Elsewhere, in situations where the owners were dead and no heirs had come forward, the property was sold (most probably for a price considerably less than its real value). In a situation of such devastation, however, what was "real value," and who would have the money to buy at the "real value"? When ownership could not be established, proceeds were often given to charities for the care of Christian orphans and other dependents.

A large amount of immovable property was taken over by the government for state-building purposes. Factories had to be restored or built to meet the basic needs of the people. Previously, trade, commerce, and industrial production (such as it was) had largely rested in the hands of the minorities. Now that they had gone, a national economy had to be developed by and for Muslims.

Some property went to nationalist institutions and associations. Some ended up in the hands of officials and the families of "martyrs," the title given not just to soldiers but to leading figures in the wartime CUP government. A law passed in May, 1926, gave abandoned Armenian property to the families and aides of a number of senior figures in the wartime government, including Talat, Cemal, Bahaeddin Şakir, and Kemal Bey, the *kaymakam* of Boğazlian, who had been executed in Istanbul after a trial held under the aegis of the occupying powers.[8] After the Şey Sait rebellion in 1925, abandoned Armenian property was also used for the resettlement of Kurds.[9]

In the analysis of one scholar, the laws passed and the practices of the state indicate that it had no intention of returning properties to their rightful owners but aimed "to legitimize the liquidation and depredation of the abandoned Armenian properties."[10] In the circumstances of the time, the question of whether any other solution would have been possible must remain moot. The enormous destruction of Muslim property should surely be part of this discussion but is rarely if ever raised.

In the eleven years between 1912 and 1923, the entire population of the Ottoman Empire had passed through a long period of severe trauma. Defeat and humiliation in 1912–1913 were followed within five years by an even more shattering defeat. The vast majority of people had survived,

but not yet as a people with a common identity and purpose. The damage
done physically and psychologically through war and the dismemberment
of territory was so great that politicians, doctors, and neuropsychiatrists,
looking at demographics and medical conditions, "feared that the nation
may not survive for long."[11]

The need to rejuvenate and build up the "human stock" led to a debate
over "positive" eugenics through sterilization and the "negative" eugenics
actually applied by restricting marriage to couples who passed physical
and mental tests decreed under the Marriage Hygiene Law of 1930.[12]

Political revival was achieved by closing the ranks around a rigid defi-
nition of national identity, underpinned in the 1930s by pseudoscientific
and pseudohistorical notions ascribing to Turkic peoples a primal role in
the development of all languages and civilizations. Plurality, difference,
and ethnoreligious diversity had destroyed the empire and could not be
allowed to destroy the nation established amid its ruins. Identity would be
decided—or rather dictated—by the state. But what the Ottoman Empire
had failed to resolve in the nineteenth century the republic was still struggling to resolve almost a century after its foundation.

AN EPIC SAGA

The Ottoman Empire in its last century is a saga of epic proportions.
Thanks to war and the self-interested power calculations of kings and
politicians, millions of innocent people died or were driven from their
homes forever. The common cliché about the empire was the "sick man
of Europe," but this was a patient for whom few felt any compassion.
On the contrary, most awaited the right moment to take advantage of
his ailments. The sick man's death was followed by an unseemly scramble,
rather like distant relatives pouring into the house of a dead man and
grabbing what they can before the will is read.

The sultan's empire had been squeezed from without (calculating
powers) and within (revolutionary committees and scheming Balkan
monarchs). Indeed, the field was rich with glittering opportunities. The
empire was afflicted with all the problems one might expect of a premod-
ern/preindustrial state. Reform was held back not just by dilatory or lazy
officials but by the chronically parlous condition of the empire's finances
and the ramshackle condition of Ottoman bureaucracy.

The educated elites were fractional in number compared to the illiterate masses, conservative, clinging to religion, and suspicious of change.
Reform, as they understood the word, threatened to turn their world
upside down. Needless to say, reform also threatened the interests of local
power-holders in distant provinces. Their world was static, unchanging
from one generation to the next, and that was how they wanted it to stay.

Although the empire had been absorbed into the world economy,
it was only as a producer of agricultural goods, tobacco, citrus fruits, dried
fruits, and the cotton and silk feeding the textile mills of Europe. There
were small workshops but no industry. Capital for the development of
the infrastructure essential to "modernization" could only be found on
the European money market, but financial incapacity naturally increased
the risk to the European lender and the commission costs to the Ottoman borrower. Eventually the government's failure to service debts led to
substantial foreign control of the economy through the establishment of
the Public Debt Administration.

These political, economic, social, and diplomatic threads were to end
in the tangle that was the Ottoman Empire in the final stage of its decline.
Undoing this tangle proved beyond the efforts not just of the government
in Istanbul but the European powers. Their great fear was of the careless
action taken somewhere—most likely in the Balkans—that would plunge
them all into a general war. Whatever the circumstances, whatever the
legal rights and manifest wrongs in any situation, their priority was the
maintenance of the balance of power in Europe. This was the sacred cow
that trumped all other considerations until killed by the shots fired in
Sarajevo.

Throughout the last stage of its life, the sovereign rights of the Ottoman government were repeatedly trampled underfoot with the tacit or
active support of the European powers. What the law said had little place
in the calculations of European governments: the morality of civilization,
progress, and humanitarian concern was simply the cloak thrown over
self-interest. The real rules were those of the imperial game, which meant
that the old powers would take what they wanted when they could and
would be understanding of the claims made by new players. Everyone had
to receive a fair share of the pie, except the Ottoman Empire, which of
course *was* the pie, cut up slice by slice.

This remorseless pattern of behavior was to be continued in the agreements signed after the First World War. The decisions taken in Paris and

San Remo ended the war by starting the fires of new ones: the imposition of mandates and the allocation of territory to Greeks and Armenians that could not be justified demographically and was bound to meet with armed resistance by the Muslim (largely Turkish, Kurdish, and Arab) population.

An expanded Greek state in western Turkey and an Armenian state in eastern Anatolia could have been established only through ethnic cleansing or some other form of suppression of the rights of the Muslim majority. Palestine can be regarded as the template of what would have happened in 1918–1920 had the wishes of the Allied powers come to fruition.

Despite the rhetoric of liberation, the collective aspirations of the population in the newly conquered territories counted negatively or positively only to the extent that they served the interests of the occupying powers. Their policies were to end in great suffering for their Christian protégés as well as the Muslim and Christian Arabs whose claims to Woodrow Wilson's right of "self-determination" were being subverted while the ink of the "fourteen points" was barely dry. The Arabs were deceived, the Armenians walked away from the Paris peace conference empty-handed, and the cries of the dispersed Assyrians for a place in the sun justified by their gallantry during the war went unheeded. In street parlance, these wartime allies of the Allied powers were used up. Only the Zionists, a small European settler community in Palestine, benefitted.

For all these reasons, the notion of Paris as a "peace" conference has to be challenged and even upended. It was a conquerors' peace, framed according to their interests and no one else's. The decisions taken by the statesmen led to resistance and war: they must have known it but thought they had the power to impose their wishes on these partitioned lands. In the short term, their calculations proved correct but at the expense of even more lives. In the long term, the decisions taken during the war and rationalized afterwards in the "peace" negotiations have haunted the Middle East ever since.

The First World War, as experienced by the Ottoman state and society, is largely absent in "western" histories except for military campaigns. Even then, they are written from an Allied point of view. The studies by Leila Fawaz, Yiğit Akın, and a small number of other scholars open a window into the general suffering of the Ottoman civilian population, but they remain the exceptions.

Much has been written on the crimes committed by "the Turks" against Christians from the late nineteenth century until the end of the First World War but very little on the crimes committed against Muslims.

This study may serve to correct the imbalance by helping to bring these largely ignored Muslim victims of war into the picture—not "back" into the picture because they were never there in the first place. No history worthy of the name can be produced as long as they are kept in the shadows.

The binary ranging of Christian victims of violence on one side and Muslim perpetrators on the other is entirely false. It might suit propagandists and nationalist politicians for whom the acknowledgment of common suffering, common criminality, and common innocence threatens the foundations of a national identity based on a one-sided view of history, but it prevents those still caught up emotionally in this catastrophe from reaching common ground.

The true binary is between the innocent and the guilty, irrespective of ethnoreligious national background. Acceptance of the irrefutable evidence that the "other" also suffered terribly might enable individuals and national groups still divided by what happened more than a century ago to reframe their perspectives and even step on the path toward reconciliation.

Epilogue

THE PAST ALWAYS LEAVES SCARS on the present and the future. This study began with one maxim, so we might as well finish with another, equally well used. This time, it is from the Bible (John 8:32): "And you will know the truth, and the truth will set you free." A nice idea, but what is the truth? Where is the truth in everything described in this study, the precise truth and not just the truth as retailed in the correspondence of diplomats and journalists and the stories told by the survivors of extreme suffering and violence?

Precise, detailed truth about the past is not attainable. The historian can only draw as close as possible to what he or she thinks is the truth. No wise historian would ever claim to know *the* truth. Even then, one person's history will not be the same as anyone else's. Despite a matrix of facts, the "history" of historians must be based on selection and interpretation. There will always be other facts and other interpretations another person will think more important, but two core truths can be established, especially about the First World War as experienced by and in the Ottoman state. One is the large-scale suffering of Christians: Armenians, Greeks, Assyrians, and others. The second is the large-scale suffering of Ottoman Muslims: Turks, Kurds, Arabs, and others.

The first core truth has been so deeply embedded in "western" cultural consciousness as to hardly need repetition. The second, by comparison, still has almost no place at all outside the writings of a small number of historians. The Turkish voice is largely muffled in debate over the fate of the Ottoman Armenians. Members of distant parliaments who know little or nothing of late Ottoman history are among those who do not hesitate to pass judgment. The implicit signal they send to "the Turks" is, "We know your history better than you, and we won't listen until you admit *we* are right and *you* are wrong."

Those writers who do admit they are right are applauded; those who disagree are shut out of the discourse, such as it is, except to be vilified. This attitude is deserving of research in itself, given its resemblance to the orientalist attitude to the Ottoman Empire that prevailed across Europe and in the U.S. during the nineteenth century.

The mass of information needed to understand the First World War is enormous. Very few scholars have the language skills to access it. The Turkish military archives (ATASE) alone are the repository for 41,591 documents on the 1911 Libyan war with Italy, 902,800 on the 1912–1913 Balkan wars, and 3,671,470 on the First World War.[1] Then there is all the other material, the government documents covering all aspects of the war, from food supply to health and transport, as well as the memoirs and secondary sources. This is surely a formidable mountain to climb, even for fully qualified Ottoman historians, yet there is no shortage of distant observers who seem sure of the facts. This applies in particular to the fate of the Ottoman Christians. Parliamentarians are entitled to their opinion, but when they have no specialized knowledge of Ottoman history, when they are relying not on independent research but on the media handouts of a lobby, they obviously cannot pass credible judgment. Yet pass judgment they do, all the time.

After the war, Halil Ataman traveled through Europe. In Vienna, he met an Armenian. They shared a hotel room and after the Armenian resumed his journey, Ataman found that he missed his company.[2] Returning from captivity in Siberia, Ziya Yergök met an Armenian while waiting for the train in Baku. He was in the station restaurant paying for a meal when a man who had been looking at him intently approached and said, "Hey Ziya Bey, what are you doing in these parts . . . you don't recognize me, perhaps? I am Midiciyan Vaham, your fellow townsman from Erzurum."

Before Yergök could say very politely, "I know many Armenian fellow townsmen, but I don't remember you," the man said, "While Your Excellency was on the Ninth Army Corps staff I was its rice supplier."

After a complaint from the military Provisions Department, a committee had been established under Yergök's presidency to investigate the quality of Vaham's rice. Continuing, Vaham said, "You came to the storehouse where the rice was located and inspected it at length. Do you remember? I was that rice supplier."

Yergök replied, "Now I remember. How are you doing?"

"Don't ask," Vaham replied. "We are in a terrible state. I am here, my children are in Revan [Erevan], we are moaning in pain and torment."

Yergök sympathized fully: "We experienced such a war that even if you gather all the wars fought in history, the blood that was shed would not amount to the blood that was shed in this war. The whole world was turned upside down. You can see our condition. Don't worry, we are not behind you in suffering torment and pain."

They chatted while waiting for the train. Yergök expressed his pleasure at meeting a fellow townsman and friend in this foreign place. After remarking, "God willing, there will not be another war for a long time and people will live comfortably," Vaham told him to run for the train and insisted on paying for his meal.

"After thanking him and shaking his hand I ran to the train and rejoined my friends," Yergök said.[3]

Ali Rıza Eti, a corporal, harbored deeply bitter feelings toward the Armenians, blaming one for abandoning in a ditch a wounded young soldier he was supposed to be taking to hospital. The young man later died. "I can't stand it," Ali Rıza wrote. "I begin to cry. May God grant him mercy. Just think of the villainy of the Armenian private. I wonder, will we remain as brothers, as citizens after the war? By my account, no! It is rather easier for me to take my revenge." He was angry enough to think of killing three or four Armenians in the hospital by dosing them with a chemical poison.

Yet after the war, Ali Rıza took care of two Armenian women who had lost their husbands. According to his granddaughter, "We used to refer to these two Armenian sisters as aunts. My grandfather was their elder brother. They would call my father *uşak*, meaning son, and would call my mother the bride. They were like members of the family. We remained as friends until their passing from this world."[4]

These are only a few straws in the wind. People reacted to the war in different ways, and still do, but a high level of suspicion and bitterness based on the recollections of survivors is general. In the eastern provinces of Turkey, a poll carried out in 2014 among the people of Erzurum revealed strongly negative feelings about Armenians. Asked whether they would marry an Armenian woman, 72 percent of the respondents answered, "Absolutely not." Asked whether they would allow one of their young women to marry an Armenian 91 percent again responded, "Absolutely not." There were also broadly negative responses to the question of whether the respondents would go into business with an Armenian or work for one.

This was the harsh side of the poll. Other questions revealed that 69 percent would employ Armenian workers, 81 percent would allow their young women to be examined by an Armenian doctor, and 83 percent would allow their children to attend classes taught by an Armenian teacher. The sad part of this, of course, is that there are no Armenians left in Erzurum to treat patients or teach.

Of the 4,200 people polled, 39 percent had lost family members to Armenian violence during the war period; 27 percent had not; and 34 percent were unsure. Yet despite this, 79 percent of the respondents thought the borders with the Republic of Armenia should be opened.[5] Such support for an open border seemed to indicate a willingness to get on with the present and open the way to a more positive future.

The border, psychological as well as physical, divides two groups of people: Armenians in their homeland and diaspora, Turks in their country and diaspora, each national group harboring negative and distrustful feelings toward the other. The driver of this poisonous atmosphere is the inability of the two national groups to resolve their differences over what happened during the First World War and its immediate aftermath. Greeks, Assyrians, and others are similarly divided from "the Turks."

Reconciliation is not helped by the endless repetition of one core narrative at the expense of another. Unfortunately, for reasons of national pride or identity, the mutual empathy that lies at the heart of reconciliation cannot be allowed in such tellings of history. Like arm-wrestling, the debate over what happened in the war (insofar as there *is* any debate) apparently must continue until one hand is forced to the table and victory can be claimed.

The First World War was like other wars but worse than all others fought up to 1914 in its industrial scale of death and destruction. Moral precepts are always turned upside down in war: what is condemned in peacetime is justified in war and even glorified. On the home front, the families of the fighting men rejoice in the killing of the enemy, forgetting that a human being lives inside a uniform. Hatred of the enemy is deliberately induced so he can be killed without compunction—and universally it is "he": men fight the wars, women and children are often the first victims.

War brutalizes and can brutalize to the most shocking degree. People who would not raise a hand against their neighbors will slaughter them at a time of war. This was true of all ethnoreligious national groups across the Ottoman Empire during the First World War. There were no exceptions. Attempts to create categories of civilian suffering on the basis of who suffered the most are surely distasteful. What would the criteria be anyway? If a body count, far more Ottoman Muslim civilians died in the war than Christians. If the level of suffering, how would the living know what the dead experienced in the seconds or minutes before their death? Yet they have no shortage of advocates seeking to draw political advantage from their fate.

In war, all antagonists claim the same moral high ground, even when stooping to fight by the same immoral means as the enemy. In victory or defeat, what remains after the last bullet is fired are the innocent dead, and there were millions of them, men, women, and children in the Ottoman Empire between 1914 and 1922: Armenians, Greeks, Assyrians, Maronites, other Christians, Turks, Kurds, Circassians, Muslims of other ethnic backgrounds, all long since buried in the soil of the Ottoman Empire. Is this to be their only brotherhood, or can their descendants find a way to the acceptance of painful truths that will release the trap in which they are all caught?

Notes

INTRODUCTION

1. Including Justin McCarthy, *Muslims and Minorities: The Population of Ottoman Anatolia and the End of the Empire* (New York: New York University Press, 1983), and McCarthy, *Death and Exile: The Ethnic Cleansing of Ottoman Muslims, 1821–1922* (Princeton, NJ: Darwin Press, 1995).

2. Leila Tarazi Fawaz, *A Land of Aching Hearts: The Middle East in the Great War* (Cambridge, MA: Harvard University Press, 2014).

3. Yiğit Akın, *When the War Came Home: The Ottomans' Great War and the Devastation of an Empire* (Stanford, CA: Stanford University Press, 2018).

CHAPTER I

1. Roderic H. Davison, *Reform in the Ottoman Empire, 1856–1876* (Princeton, NJ: Princeton University Press, 1963), 54.

2. Ibid., 13.

3. Ibid., 15.

4. Afaf Lutfi al-Sayyid Marsot, *Egypt in the Reign of Muhammad Ali* (Cambridge: Cambridge University Press, 1984), 243.

5. Murat Birdal, *The Political Economy of the Ottoman Public Debt: Insolvency and European Financial Control in the Late Nineteenth Century* (London: I. B. Tauris, 2010), 20.

6. Marsot, *Egypt in the Reign of Muhammad Ali*, 247.

7. The attention given to reforms in the nineteenth century can take attention away from the earlier reforming drive in Ottoman history. Sultans and their advisers were usually aware of the empire's weaknesses, even if they were not capable of putting in place the changes needed to correct them.

8. Şevket Pamuk, *A Monetary History of the Ottoman Empire* (Cambridge: Cambridge University Press, 2000), 189.

9. See Virginia H. Aksan, *Ottoman Wars, 1700–1870: An Empire Besieged* (London: Pearson Longman, 2007), 306–342.

10. Ibid., 385–388.

11. M. Şükrü Hanioğlu, *A Brief History of the Late Ottoman Empire* (Princeton, NJ: Princeton University Press, 2008), 7.

12. Pamuk, *A Monetary History*, 189.

13. Not to be confused with the "great debasement" of currency in England (1544–1551) during the reign of Henry VIII.

14. Pamuk, 188.

15. Eldem, *A History of the Ottoman Bank*, 93.

16. Pamuk, *A Monetary History*, 193.

17. Şevket Pamuk, "Prices in the Ottoman Empire, 1469–1914," *International Journal of Middle East Studies* 36, no. 3 (2004):454.

18. A now-archaic Turkish word for document or bank note applied to paper currency as well. They were first issued during the crisis of 1839–1840.

19. Pamuk, *A Monetary History*, 202–203; see also footnote 203, quoting Stanford Shaw.

20. Eldem, *A History of the Ottoman Bank*, 27.

21. The European term for the *kuruş*.

22. Davison, *Reform in the Ottoman Empire, 1856–1876*, 112n90, quoting Damad Fethi Paşa.

23. On the rise and fall of the Banque de Turquie and the consequences of the Mirès affair, see Eldem, *A History of the Ottoman Bank*, 66–82.

24. Bilal N. Şimşir, ed., *British Documents on Ottoman Armenians*, vol. 1, *1856–1880* (Ankara: Turkish Historical Society, 1989), no. 16, Russell to Bulwer, Foreign Office, July 4, 1861, 42.

25. Eldem, *A History of the Ottoman Bank*, 79.

26. Ibid., 79–80; Davison, *Reform in the Ottoman Empire*, 111–113.

27. Davison, *Reform in the Ottoman Empire*, 111.

28. Hanioğlu, *A Brief History*, 92. The exchange rate at the time was 1.1 lira to the pound sterling. To give some idea of the relative purchasing power of these amounts of money, the same goods and services bought for 100 pounds in 1870 would have cost 6,260.9 pounds in 2017. The relative figure for 1880 would be 6,618.47 pounds. Goods and services purchased for 217 million pounds in 1870 would have cost 13,586.15 million pounds in 2017. The relative figure for 1880 would be 14,362.08 million, putting the modern equivalent of the total Ottoman debt in 1875 between 13.5 and 14.3 billion pounds. The bank of England's relative figures differ somewhat, but both sources make it clear that their calculations are approximate. According to its calculations, goods and purchases costing 100 pounds in 1875 would have cost 11,334.69 pounds in 2018. See UK National Archives currency converter: www.nationalarchives.gov.uk/currency/convertor/#currency-result.

29. Şimşir, ed., *British Documents on Ottoman Armenians,* vol. 1, no. 8, enclosing circular addressed by Sir H. Bulwer to Her Majesty's Consuls in the Ottoman Dominions, Constantinople, June 11, 1860, 10–13.

30. W. E. Gladstone, *Bulgarian Horrors and the Question of the East* (London: John Murray, 1876).
31. Eldem, *A History of the Ottoman Bank*, 136.
32. André Autheman, *The Imperial Ottoman Bank* (Istanbul: Ottoman Bank Archives and Research Centre, 2002), 91.
33. Ibid.
34. The Imperial Ottoman Bank was controlled by committee from London and Paris, run by British and French directors in Istanbul, and acknowledged as the exclusive financial agent of the Ottoman government in 1874.
35. Autheman, *The Imperial Ottoman Bank*, 92.
36. Ibid., 94.
37. The reaction of villagers to these demands is raised in Şimşir, ed., *British Documents on Ottoman Armenians*, vol. 1, no. 216, enc. Trotter to Layard, Erzurum, June 12, 1879, 457–459.
38. Ibid., no. 349, Wilson to Layard, Constantinople, April 12, 1880, 708.
39. A silver coin worth five *kuruş*. All countries whose monetary system was based on bimetallism (a fixed value for gold and silver in the coinage) were badly affected in the 1870s by the massive amounts of silver pouring into the international market from the Comstock Lode in Nevada. For the effects on the Ottoman Empire, see the complex monetary maneuvers undertaken by the government, as described by Eldem, *A History of the Ottoman Bank*, 145–153.
40. Şimşir, ed., *British Documents on Ottoman Armenians*, vol. 1, Wilson to Layard, no. 349, Constantinople, April 12, 1880, 708.
41. Ibid., 709–710.

CHAPTER 2
1. Şimşir, ed., *British Documents on Ottoman Armenians*, vol. 1, no. 11, Skene to Bulwer, Aleppo, August 4, 1860, 28.
2. Ibid., no. 145, enc. Trotter to Layard, Diarbekir, December 21, 1878, 310.
3. Ibid., 308.
4. Sena Bayraktaroğlu, "Development of Railways in the Ottoman Empire and Turkey" (master's thesis, Atatürk Institute, Boğaziçi University, 1995), 27.
5. Alan Bodger, "Russia and the End of the Ottoman Empire," in *The Great Powers and the End of the Ottoman* Empire, ed. Marian Kent (London: George Allen and Unwin,1984), 79.
6. For more on rail construction see Carter Vaughn Findley, *Turkey, Islam, Nationalism, and Modernity: A History, 1789–2007* (New Haven, CT: Yale University Press, 2010), 166–169.
7. See *The Famine in Asia Minor: Its History Compiled from the Pages of the "Levant Herald"* (Istanbul: Isis Press, 1989).
8. Ibid., 47.

9. Ibid., 3.
10. Ibid., 4.
11. The *tanzimat* (reorganization) period of reforms began in 1839. While, as a specific period of reform, it ended in the 1870s, many important reforms were still introduced by the Sultan Abdülhamit.
12. Moshe Ma'oz, *Ottoman Reform in Syria and Palestine, 1840–1861* (Oxford: Oxford University Press, 1968), 226.
13. See UK Parliamentary Papers, Turkey No. 8 (1881) Cd. 3008, *Reports on the Administration of Justice in the Civil, Criminal and Commercial Courts in the Various Provinces of the Ottoman Empire*, inc. in no. 13, report on the courts of the Konya *vilayet*, quoted in Jeremy Salt, *Imperialism, Evangelism and the Ottoman Armenians, 1878–1896* (London: Frank Cass, 1993), 23–24.
14. Vambéry Papers, FO 800/33, Vambéry to Sanderson, July 1, 1895.
15. Ibid., FO 800/32, Vambéry to Currie, October 22, 1889.
16. As demonstrated in the rise to all-encompassing power of Turkey's President, Recep Tayyip Erdoğan.
17. Jelle Verheij, "'Les frères de terre et d'eau': sur le rôle des Kurdes dans les massacres Arméniens de 1894–1896," in *Islam des Kurdes*, eds. Martin van Bruinessen and Joyce Blau, *Les Annales de l'Autre Islam* 5, special issue (Paris: INALCO-ERISM, 1998), 268, quoting Stephen Duguid.
18. Davison, *Reform in the Ottoman Empire*, 118.
19. Şimşir, ed., *British Documents on Ottoman Armenians*, 1:28.
20. Feudal "lords of the valley."
21. Şimşir, ed., *British Documents on Ottoman Armenians,* vol. 1, no. 11, Skene to Bulwer, Aleppo, August 4, 1860, 28.
22. Whether Ottoman society could accurately be described as feudal is the subject of a typological inquiry by Halil Inalcik. See "On the Social Structure of the Ottoman Empire: Paradigms and Research," in Inalcik, *From Empire to Republic: Essays on Ottoman and Turkish Social History* (Istanbul: Isis Press, 1995), 27–72.
23. The *ayan* served the central government as a valuable local intermediary. Assigned greater responsibilities (and greater opportunities) as the power of the central government weakened, the *ayan* became closely identified in the nineteenth century with corruption, oppression of the peasantry through the imposition of licit and illicit taxes, and the misuse of political power.
24. Şimşir, ed., *British Documents on Ottoman Armenians*, 1:28.
25. Ibid.
26. Ibid., no. 145, enc. Trotter to Layard, Diarbekir, December 21, 1878, 309.
27. Davison, *Reform in the Ottoman Empire*, 136–171.
28. Ibid., 146.
29. Ibid., 148.
30. Ibid., 150.

31. Ibid., 149. For a detailed examination of provincial government see Stanford S. Shaw, "The Origins of Representative Government in the Ottoman Empire: An Introduction to the Provincial Councils of 1839–1876," in Shaw, *Studies in Ottoman and Turkish History: Life with the Ottomans* (Istanbul: Isis Press, 2000), 183–231.

32. Şimşir, ed., *British Documents on Ottoman Armenians*, vol. 1, no. 147, enclosing Kiamil [Kamil] Paşa to Eldridge, Aleppo, December 16, 1878, 316.

33. Ibid., no. 164, Malet to Salisbury, Constantinople, February 25, 1879, 340–341.

CHAPTER 3

1. In 1897, Ottoman census figures for the six provinces showed a total Muslim population of 2,509,048 and 670,318 non-Muslims. On a percentage basis, Muslims constituted 78.91 percent of the population and Armenians (the largest non-Muslim group) 16.4 percent. See Kemal H. Karpat, *Ottoman Population, 1830–1914: Demographic and Social Characteristics* (Madison: University of Wisconsin Press, 1985), 197. According to the census report of 1914, Muslims constituted 79.32 percent of the population of the six provinces and Armenians 16.47 percent. See Servet Mutlu, "Late Ottoman Population and Its Ethnic Distribution," *Nüfusbilim Dergisi/Turkish Journal of Population Studies* 25 (2003):22–24.

2. S. Aslıhan Gürbüzel, "Hamidian Policy in Eastern Anatolia (1878–1890)" (master's thesis, Department of History, Bilkent University, 2008), 6–7.

3. For an analysis of these issues see Janet Klein, "Conflict and Collaboration: Rethinking Kurdish-Armenian Relations in the Hamidian Period, 1876–1909," *International Journal of Turkish Studies* 13, nos. 1–2 (July 2007): 153–166.

4. Reşat Kasaba, *A Moveable Empire: Ottoman Nomads, Migrants, and Refugees* (Seattle: University of Washington Press, 2009), 91.

5. Martin van Bruinessen, *Agha, Shaikh and State: The Social and Political Structure of Kurdistan* (London: Zed Books, 1992), 179.

6. L. Molyneux-Seel, "A Journey in Dersim," *Geographical Journal* 44, no. 1 (July 1914), 51.

7. Karen Barkey, *Empire of Difference: The Ottomans in Comparative Perspective* (Cambridge: Cambridge University Press, 2008), 278.

8. Donald Bloxham, *The Great Game of Genocide: Imperialism, Nationalism, and the Destruction of the Ottoman Armenians* (Oxford: Oxford University Press, 2005), 15.

9. The sultan had "complete confidence" in Agop Zarifi Paşa, who looked after his personal finances. Donald Quataert, *Manufacturing and Technology Transfer in the Ottoman Empire 1800–1914* (Istanbul: Isis Press, 1992), 131.

10. Between 1893 and 1907, the census department was run by an Ottoman Jew, an Ottoman Armenian, and an American specialist in statistics. See Mutlu, "Late Ottoman Population," 7.

11. Ahmed Emin (Yalman), *Turkey in the World War* (New Haven, CT: Yale University Press, 1930), 214.

12. Ibid.

13. Bloxham, *The Great Game of Genocide*, on the sultan's "advanced paranoia," 46.

14. Gürbüzel, "Hamidian Policy in Eastern Anatolia," 31.

15. See Bloxham's reference to "Ottoman theocracy," *The Great Game of Genocide*, 39.

16. Amir Hassanpour has argued that the revolts of Bedir Khan (Bedirhan) and Shaykh Ubaydullah were not nationalist "because they aimed at the retention (Bedir Khan) and formation (Ubaydullah) of feudal-mini-states, none of which had any resemblance to a modern state, with elected, representative government, citizenship, the rule of law, separation of powers, etc. Both projects treated the majority population, the peasants, as rai'yats, subjects rather than citizens, and Ubaydullah would have opted for a theocratic regime." See Amir Hassanpour, "Ferment and Fetters in the Study of Kurdish Nationalism," review of Hakan Özoğlu, *Kurdish Notables and the Ottoman State: Evolving Identities, Competing Loyalties, and Shifting Boundaries* (Albany: State University of New York Press, 2004), published on H-Turk, September 2007, http://www.h-net.org/reviews/showrev.php?id=13540.

17. Susan Meiselas, the Magnum photographer, has produced a magnificent textual and photographic history of the Kurds from the nineteenth century onwards. See Meiselas, *Kurdistan in the Shadow of History*, with historical introductions and a new postscript by Martin van Bruinessen (Chicago: University of Chicago, 2008).

18. He was sent to exile in Medina.

19. Gürbürzel, "Hamidian Policy," 37.

20. Ibid., 31.

21. Ibid., 34. On today's map, Ottoman Kurdistan conforms to Erzurum, Van, Bitlis, Muş, Dersim (Tunceli), and Diyarbakir.

22. Şimşir, ed., *British Documents on Ottoman Armenians*, vol. 2, no. 93, Dufferin to Granville, Therapia, August 23, 1881, 271.

23. Wadie Jwaideh, *The Kurdish National Movement: Its Origins and Development* (New York: Syracuse University Press, 2006), 83. For more on Shaykh Ubaydullah and his family, see Mehmet Firat Kiliç, "Sheikh Ubaydullah's Movement" (master's thesis, Department of History, Bilkent University, 2003).

24. Martin van Bruinessen, "The Sadate Nehri or Gilanizade of Central Kurdistan," in *Mullas, Sufis, and Heretics: The Role of Religion in Kurdish Society: Collected Articles*, by Martin van Bruinessen (Istanbul: Isis Press, 2000), 201.

25. H. F. B. Lynch, *Armenia: Travels and Studies* (Beirut: Khayats, 1965), 2:1.
26. Hassanpour, "Ferment and Fetters in the Study of Kurdish Nationalism."
27. Gürbüzel, 88.
28. Ibid., 89.
29. Ibid., 90. Most probably, as Gürbüzel points out in her excellent study, the petitioners were referring to the activities of Armenian revolutionary societies.
30. Ibid., 90.
31. Verheij, "'Les frères de terre et d'eau,'" 255.
32. Ibid., 264.
33. Ibid., 269.

CHAPTER 4

1. See Stanford J. Shaw, "A Promise of Reform: Two Complimentary [sic.] Documents," *International Journal of Middle Eastern Studies* 4, no. 3 (1973):359–365. See also Sinan Kuneralp, ed., *The Queen's Ambassador to the Sultan: Memoirs of Sir Henry A. Layard's* [sic] *Constantinople Embassy, 1877–1878* (Istanbul: Isis Press, 2009), 473–474 (Layard was Austen Henry Layard, not Henry Austen Layard).
2. Şimşir, ed., *British Documents on Ottoman Armenians*, vol. 1, no. 10, Consul C. Blunt to Sir H. Bulwer, Smyrna, July 28, 1860, inc. "answer to queries," 16–22.
3. Ibid., no. 23, Palgrave to Stanley, Trebizond, January 30, 1868, inc. "Report on the Relative Position of Christian and Mahometan Subjects in the Eastern Provinces of the Ottoman Empire," 50–53.
4. Ibid., no. 12, Skene to Bulwer, Aleppo, August 20, 1860, 31.
5. Ibid., no. 11, Skene to Bulwer, Aleppo, August 4, 1860, p.27.
6. Kamal Salibi and Yusuf K. Khoury, eds., *The Missionary Herald: Reports from Ottoman Syria, 1819–1870* (Amman: Royal Institute for Interfaith Studies, 1995), vol. 2, 344.
7. Keith M. Greenwood, *Robert College: The American Founders* (Istanbul: Boğaziçi University Press, 2000), 219.
8. The Bulgarian nationalist and college professor Stephen Paneretoff.
9. Greenwood, *Robert College*, 207–208.
10. Ibid., 219–220.
11. Musa Şaşmaz, *British Policy and the Application of Reforms for the Armenians in Eastern Anatolia, 1877–1897* (Ankara: Turkish Historical Society, 2000), 91–92.
12. For the positive effects of the heavily modified "reforms" that were accepted in 1895, see Şaşmaz, *British Policy,* 254–269.
13. Louise Nalbandian, *The Armenian Revolutionary Movement: The Development of Armenian Political Parties through the Nineteenth Century* (Berkeley: University of California Press, 1963), 28–29, from the "two spoons"

speech made by former patriarch Mgrdich Khrimian on his return to Istanbul after representing the Armenian cause in Berlin.

14. Kuneralp, ed., *The Queen's Ambassador*, 445.
15. Ibid., 50.
16. Gladstone's *Bulgarian Horrors and the Question of the East.*
17. Layard arrived in Istanbul in April 1877.
18. Kuneralp, ed., *The Queen's Ambassador*, 699–700.
19. Ibid., 438.
20. Sarkis Atamian, *The Armenian Community: The Historical Development of a Social and Ideological Conflict* (New York: Philosophical Library, 1955), 97.
21. Ibid., 104.
22. Ibid., 99.
23. Kuneralp, ed., *The Queen's Ambassador*, 444.
24. Ibid.
25. Ibid.
26. Ibid., 445.
27. Gerard J. Libaridian, "What Was Revolutionary about Armenian Revolutionary Parties in the Ottoman Empire?" in Ronald Grigor Suny, Fatma Müge Göçek, and Norman M. Naimark, eds., *A Question of Genocide: Armenians and Turks at the End of the Ottoman Empire* (New York: Oxford University Press, 2011), 101.
28. Atamian, *The Armenian Community*, 105.
29. According to the Hunchak program. See Guenter Lewy, *The Armenian Massacres in Ottoman Turkey: A Disputed Genocide* (Salt Lake City: University of Utah Press, 2005), 12.
30. Şimşir, ed., *British Documents on Ottoman Armenians*, vol. 3, no. 343, Home Office to Foreign Office, Whitehall, January 5, 1895, inc. police report, 476–477. It was, of course, such activities that inspired Joseph Conrad to write *The Secret Agent.*
31. Şimşir, ed., *British Documents on Ottoman Armenians*, vol. 2, no. 41, Clayton to Trotter, Van, November 9, 1880, 151.
32. Ibid., no. 62, Goschen to Granville, Constantinople, March 17, 1881, inc. Clayton to Trotter, Van, February 15, 1881, 196.
33. Ibid., no. 75, Bennet to Goschen, Marash, June 7, 1881, 237.
34. Ibid., vol. 3, no. 18, White to Salisbury, Constantinople, March 28, 1891, inc. no. 1, Hampson to White, Erzurum, March 21, 1891, 33–34.
35. Ibid., no. 318, pro-memoria communicated by Rustem Pasha, London, December 10, 1894, annex I, memorandum by Cyrus Hamlin on "Huntchagist Revolutionary Party," written December 23, 1893, 443–445.
36. Ibid., vol. 4, no. 53, Lascelles to Salisbury, St. Petersburg, August 9, 1895, 69.
37. Verheij, "'Les Frères de terre et d'eau,'" quoting a British report, 240.
38. Ibid., 240.

39. Şimşir, ed., *British Documents on Ottoman Armenians*, vol. 3, no. 281, Currie to Kimberley, Therapia, November 4, 1894, inc. 1, "memorandum," 394–396.

40. Ibid., 395.

41. Ibid., no. 281, inc. 2, "Reply of His Majesty the Sultan to Preceding Memorandum," 396–398.

42. Ibid., no. 277, Currie to Kimberley, Therapia, October 15, 1894, 388.

43. Ibid., no. 274, Currie to Kimberley, Constantinople, October 9, 1894, 385.

44. Ibid., Currie to Kimberley, Therapia, October 15, 1894, 387.

45. Ibid., 387.

46. Ibid., no. 281, Currie to Kimberley, Therapia, November 4, 1894, 393.

47. *Ottoman Archives, Yildiz Collection, the Armenian Question*, vol. 1 (Istanbul: Historical Research Foundation, 1989), Zeki Paşa to Ministry of National Defence (War Ministry), "Ongoing military operations to suppress the rising at Talori and a report of the latest situation," September 16, 1894, 289–301.

48. Ibid., 291–292.

49. Ibid., 293.

50. Ibid., coded telegram, commander-in-chief of the Fourth Army to Department of General Staff, "Crimes committed by the Armenian insurgents in the region of Talori," September 26, 1894, 325.

51. Ibid., 325–326.

52. Ibid., "Ongoing military operations," 299.

53. See Justin McCarthy, Ömer Turan and Cemalettin Taşkıran, *Sasun: The History of an 1890s Armenian Revolt* (Salt Lake City: University of Utah Press, 2014), 188 and 169. Avedis K. Sanjian, in an older book, *The Armenian Communities in Syria under Ottoman Dominion* (Cambridge, MA: Harvard University Press, 1965), claims 20,000 people were massacred at Sasun, 278.

54. Edward Erickson, *Ottomans and Armenians: A Study in Counterinsurgency* (New York: Palgrave Macmillan, 2013), 52.

55. *The Ottoman Archives, Yildiz Collection, the Armenian Question*, vol. 2, General Staff Correspondence Department to the Prime Ministry, "Administrative, economic and military measures to be taken in order to relieve the tension around Bitlis, Moush and its vicinity," sent "after July 1895," 285–299.

56. Ibid., 297–299.

57. At a protest meeting in St. James's Hall, Lady Henry Somerset described the sultan as the "harem despot of Constantinople." See, for example, "The Atrocities in Armenia," *The Times*, May 8, 1895, 10. There was a lot more in the same vein.

58. Turkey No. 5 (1896) Cd. 8100, inc. 2 in no. 3, Fitzmaurice to Currie, Ourfa, March 16, 1896, quoted in Salt, *Imperialism, Evangelism and the Ottoman Armenians*, 97.

59. See, for example, Şimşir, ed., *British Documents on Ottoman Armenians*, vol. 3 (1891–1895), no. 10, inc. 3, Vice-Consul Devey to Sir W. White, Van,

January 12, 1891, "Memorandum on the misleading views respecting in certain newspapers, in particular the *Daily News*, and upon the condition of Kurds and Armenians generally," 16–19. Examining articles published in the previous year, Devey found that more often than not that they were "either wholly without foundation or most grossly distorted." He singled out the *Daily News* for publishing articles on the massacre of Armenians and the desecration of a church, events that had never taken place and "scarcely call for serious attention." These remarks call into question the veracity of the *Daily News* correspondent in Istanbul, Edwin (later Sir Edwin) Pears, who built a life in the Ottoman Empire around his work as a barrister in the consular courts. His reports on the "Bulgarian atrocities" in the 1870s were written on the basis of information provided by American missionaries, notably George Washburn, whose deep hostility to the Ottoman government and support for Bulgarian nationalists has already been noted. Pears recorded his experiences in his autobiography, *Forty Years in Constantinople: The Recollections of Sir Edwin Pears, 1873–1915* (London: H. Jenkins, 1916).

60. FO 800/33, Vambéry to Sanderson, Budapest, November 1, 1895. See *Imperialism, Evangelism*, 146.

61. Eldem, *A History of the Ottoman Bank*, 171n13.

62. Subsequently renamed Süleymanlı.

63. *Ottoman Archives, Yildiz Collection, the Armenian Question*, vol. 2, General Secretariat to the Cabinet, Yildiz Palace, "The Armenian uprising at Zeitoun and the measures to be taken against the intervention of foreign states during quelling [of] the rebellion," December 25, 1895, 377–85.

64. United States National Archives (USNA), Despatches from U.S. Ministers to Turkey, 1818–1906 (microcopy T46), no. 686, Terrell to Olney, enc. letter from consul Frederic Poche at Halep, November 2, 1895. Poche put the Armenian rebel force at 12,000 men, dropping to 10,000 through death and desertion, with the Ottoman force at about the same number.

65. Vahakn Dadrian, *Histoire du génocide Arménien* (Paris: Stock, 1999), 231.

66. Eldem, *A History of the Ottoman Bank*, 237.

67. Ibid., 237.

68. Ibid., 235.

69. Ibid., 241.

70. *Annual Register* (London: Longmans, Green, 1897), remarks made by Salisbury on January 31, 1897, 16.

71. Libaridian, "What Was Revolutionary," 100.

72. *Annual Register* (London: Longmans, Green, 1896), 16.

73. Büyük Elçi (ambassador).

74. Vambéry, *The Story of My Struggles* (London: Thomas Nelson, n.d.), 331.

75. Kuneralp, ed., *The Queen's Ambassador*, 255.

76. Ibid., 380.

77. Ibid., 385–387.
78. Ibid., 689.
79. Ibid.
80. Paul Knaplund, *Gladstone's Foreign Policy* (New York: Harper, 1935), 153.
81. Sir Alfred Lyall, *The Life of the Marquis of Dufferin and Ava* (London: Thomas Nelson, 1905), 302.
82. Kemal H. Karpat, *The Politicization of Islam: Reconstructing Identity, State, Faith, and Community in the Late Ottoman State* (Oxford: Oxford University Press, 2001), 158.
83. Gordon Waterfield, *Layard of Ninevah* (London: John Murray, 1963), 372.
84. See Ayşe Betül Kayahan, "My Father Abdülhamit II," *Daily Sabah*, February 26, 2014, for the recollections of the sultan's daughter, Ayşe Osmanoğlu. Kemal Karpat has written his own appraisal of the sultan. See *The Politicization of Islam*, 155–182.
85. Lyall, *The Life of the Marquis*, 299–300.
86. Gladstone was clearly frustrated by Dufferin's reluctance to follow his hard line with the sultan, that "arch-liar and arch-cheat," as he described him, whom the ambassador should be trying to make uneasy and insecure. Knaplund, *Gladstone's Foreign Policy*, 153–154.
87. Kuneralp, ed., *The Queen's Ambassador,* 539.
88. Nabeel Audeh, "The Ideological Uses of History and the Young Turks as a Problem for Historical Interpretation: Considerations of Class, Race, and Empire in British Foreign Office Attitudes Towards the Young Turks 1908–1918" (PhD diss., Washington, D.C.: Georgetown University, 1990).
89. Audeh, 176.
90. USNA, Despatches from U.S. Ministers to Turkey, no. 366, Terrell to Gresham, December 23, 1894, quoted in Salt, *Imperialism, Evangelism*, 146.
91. Kuneralp, ed., *The Queen's Ambassador*, 381.
92. FO 800/33, Vambéry to Sanderson, March 28, 1897, quoted in Salt, *Imperialism, Evangelism*, 143.
93. FO 800/32, Vambéry to Currie, June 12, 1889. The FO note on the Vambéry Papers, 1889–1911 (FO 800/32-33), refers to them as the "correspondence of Professor A. Vambéry of the University of Budapest, a notable Turkish scholar with the ear of the Sultan who reported secretly on Turkish affairs to successive Permanent Under-Secretaries of State."
94. Taner Akçam, speaking to the Australian broadcaster Philip Adams during his program *Late Night Live*, ABC (Australian Broadcasting Commission) Radio, November 22, 2006.

CHAPTER 5

1. As Stanford Shaw has observed, "The Balkans as a concept of society or administration and the word itself appeared very rarely in Ottoman texts and then only in its most limited geographical meaning." Stanford J. Shaw,

Studies in Ottoman and Turkish History: Life with the Ottomans (Istanbul: Isis Press, 2000), 53.

2. Justin McCarthy, "Muslims in Ottoman Europe: Population from 1800 to 1912," in McCarthy, *Population History of the Middle East and the Balkans* (Istanbul: Isis Press, 2002), 139.

3. Ebru Boyar, *Ottomans, Turks and the Balkans: Empire Lost, Relations Altered* (London: I. B. Tauris, 2007), 61. The population of Ulcinj-Dulcigno—when part of the Venetian republic (1405–1571)—remains predominantly Albanian.

4. Ben Kiernan, *Blood and Soil: A World History of Genocide and Extermination from Sparta to Darfur* (New Haven, CT: Yale University Press, 2007).

5. Karpat, *Ottoman Population 1830–1914: Demographic and Social Characteristics*, 55.

6. Ibid.

7. Feroz Ahmad, "The Late Ottoman Empire," in Marian Kent, ed., *The Great Powers and the End of the Ottoman Empire*, 25.

8. See Mara Kozelsky, "Casualties of Conflict: Crimean Tatars during the Crimean War," *Slavic Review* 67, no. 4 (Winter, 2008):866–891.

9. Karpat, *Ottoman Population*, 67.

10. L. S. Stavrianos, *The Balkans Since 1453* (New York: Holt, Rinehart, and Winston, 1966), 393–394.

11. See J. A. MacGahan, "The Turkish Atrocities in Bulgaria: Horrible Scenes at Batak," *Daily News*, August 22, 1876, and *The Turkish Atrocities in Bulgaria: Letters of the Special Commissioner of the "Daily News" J. A. MacGahan. Esq. With an Introduction and Mr. Schuyler's Preliminary Report* (London: Bradbury, Agnew, 1876). Contrary estimates put the number of Bulgarian dead at several thousand or even lower. Layard regarded MacGahan's and Schuyler's reports as "exaggerated and one-sided." Kuneralp, ed., *The Queen's Ambassador*, 161.

12. European outrage and calls for intervention are detailed in Davide Rodogno, *Against Massacre: Humanitarian Interventions in the Ottoman Empire, 1815–1914* (Princeton, NJ: Princeton University Press, 2012), 141–155.

13. W. E. Gladstone, *Bulgarian Horrors and the Question of the East* (London: John Murray, 1876), 9.

14. Karpat, *The Politicization of Islam*, 147.

15. Bilal N. Şimşir, ed., *Rumeli'den Türk Göçleri/Turkish Emigrations from the Balkans*, vol. 1, *1856–1880* (Ankara: Turkish Historical Society, 1989), Layard to the Earl of Derby, Constantinople, January 9, 1878, 260.

16. McCarthy, "Muslims in Ottoman Europe: Population from 1800 to 1912," 142.

17. Karpat, *The Politicization of Islam*, 148.

18. Ibid.

19. Şimşir, ed., *Rumeli'den*, vol. 1, no. 56, Layard to Derby, Therapia, July 24, 1877, 157.

20. Ibid., Layard to Derby, vol. 1, no. 144, January 16, 1878, 273.

21. Kuneralp, *The Queen's Ambassador*, 503.

22. Ibid., 503.

23. Ibid., 111.

24. Şimşir, ed., *Rumeli'den,* vol. 1, no. 84, Layard to Derby, Therapia, August 17, 1877, reporting on a conversation with the representative of the Red Cross in Turkey, 188.

25. Ellis Ashmead Bartlett, *The Battlefields of Thessaly: With Personal Experiences in Turkey and Greece* (London: John Murray, 1897), 50–51. Facsimile edition: British Library Historical Print Editions, n.d. Ashmead Bartlett had reported the war of 1877–1878.

26. Ibid., 52. A large-scale massacre of Muslim men was reported to have been committed at Kezanlik, where, in September 1877, a funeral was held for Julian Layard, the ambassador's nephew, a military attaché at the embassy in Istanbul. Julian Layard died of typhoid fever in the Şipka pass while attached to the Ottoman army. He was later buried in Istanbul.

27. Kuneralp, ed., *The Queen's Ambassador*, 318.

28. Ibid., 233

29. Şimşir, ed., *Rumeli'den*, vol. 1., no. 185, inc. Blunt to Layard, Constantinople, February 1, 1878, 322.

30. Ibid., 323.

31. Kuneralp, ed., *The Queen's Ambassador*, 313.

32. Şimşir, ed., *Rumeli'den*, vol. 1, no. 249, Layard to Salisbury, Constantinople, April 13, 1878, inc. report from Dr. Dickson, 406–408.

33. Ibid., 407.

34. Ibid., no. 251, Layard to Salisbury, Constantinople, April 16, 1878, 411.

35. Ibid., 411.

36. Kuneralp, ed., *The Queen's Ambassador*, 328–330.

37. McCarthy, "Muslims in Ottoman Europe," 143.

38. The Treaty of San Stefano would have created a Bulgaria stretching from the Black Sea almost to the Adriatic. It was severely shrunk at the Congress of Berlin.

39. Stavrianos, *The Balkans since 1453*, 410.

40. Henri de Blowitz, *My Memoirs* (London: Edward Arnold, 1903), 292.

41. Roderic Davison, "The Ottoman Empire and the Congress of Berlin," in Davison, *Nineteenth Century Ottoman Diplomacy and Reforms* (Istanbul: Isis Press, 1999), 183.

42. Ibid., 182.

43. Misha Glenny, *The Balkans 1804–1999: Nationalism, War and the Great Powers* (London: Granta, 2000), 142.

44. Karpat, *Ottoman Population*, 55.

45. Karpat, *Ottoman Population,* 69.
46. Donald Quataert, "Agricultural Trends and Government Policy in Otto-man Anatolia 1800–1914," in Quataert, *Workers, Peasants and Economic Change in the Ottoman Empire, 1730–1914* (Istanbul: Isis Press, 1993), 24.
47. Şimşir, ed., *Rumeli'den,* vol. 2, no. 115, Layard to Salisbury, June 20, 1879, 328–329.
48. Kuneralp, ed., *The Queen's Ambassador,* 137.
49. Şimşir ed., *British Documents on Ottoman Armenians,* vol. 1, no. 116, Trotter to Salisbury, Erzeroum, November 13, 1878, 259–260.
50. Ibid., no. 206, inc. 3, Chermside to Layard, Marash, June 3, 1879, 424.
51. Ibid., inc. 5, appendix to Lieutenant Chermside's despatch of June 3, 1879, 438.

CHAPTER 6

1. Aykut Kansu, *The Revolution of 1908 in Turkey* (Leiden: Brill, 1997), 32–36.
2. Ibid., 40.
3. Ibid., 46.
4. Ibid., 55.
5. B. Destani, ed., *Ethnic Minorities in the Balkan States, 1860–1871* (Cam-bridge: Archive Editions, 2003), vol. 2, *1888–1914,* Lansdowne to Plunkett, Foreign Office, August 3, 1904, enc. "Report of the Imperial Austrian Civil Agent, Hofrath von Müller, on the Results of the Reforms in Macedonia During the First Half-Year, 1904," Monastir, July 10, 1904, 169–174.
6. All were murdered with the rest of the Romanovs in 1918.
7. Andrew Mango, *Atatürk* (London: John Murray, 2004), 77.
8. Kansu, *The Revolution of 1908,* 98.
9. An older study, Ernest Edmondson Ramsaur Jr., *The Young Turks: Prelude to the Revolution of 1908* (Beirut: Khayats, 1965), 14–51, remains a useful short guide to the evolution of the Young Turks.
10. Audeh, "The Ideological Uses of History," 85–86.
11. Ibid., 93.
12. Kansu, *The Revolution of 1908,* 174.
13. Audeh, "The Ideological Uses of History," 93
14. See the summary in Kansu, *The Revolution of 1908 in Turkey,* 238–239.
15. Aykut Kansu, *Politics in Post-Revolutionary Turkey, 1908–1913* (Leiden: Brill, 2000), 78.
16. Kemal Karpat writes that there was "no evidence that [the sultan] had any-thing to do with it." Karpat, *The Politicization of Islam,* 163.
17. Yücel Güçlü, "Armenian Events of Adana in 1909 and Cemal Paşa" (paper, Adana Conference, Turkish Historical Society, Ankara, June 2009), 2–3.
18. Ibid., 5.
19. Bedross Der Matossian, "From Bloodless Revolution to Bloody Counter-revolution: The Adana Massacres of 1909," *Genocide Studies and Prevention* 6, no. 2 (2011):158.

20. Ibid., 158–159.
21. Ibid., 161–163.
22. Ibid., 163.
23. Ibid., 160.
24. Tetsuya Sahara, *What Happened in Adana in April 1909? Conflicting Armenian and Turkish Views* (Isis Press: Istanbul, 2013), 105. In her account of "what instigated the violence," Fatma Muğe Göcek does not mention the murder of April 9, singling out instead the murder on April 13 of "an Armenian carpenter named Latfik." Perhaps he was another carpenter, but in his detailed account Tetsuya Sahara says he was killed because he was a spy. For whom is unknown, as the killer was never caught. See Sahara, *What Happened in Adana*, 108, and Göcek, *Denial of Violence: Ottoman Past, Turkish Present, and Collective Violence against the Armenians, 1789–2009* (Oxford: Oxford University Press, 2015), 205.
25. Raymond H. Kévorkian, *La Cilicie (1909–1921): des massacres d'Adana au mandat Français* (Paris: Revue d'Histoire Arménienne Contemporaine, Bibliothèque Nubar de l'UGAB, 1999), 56. Other scholars who have researched these events include Kemal Çicek, ed., *The Adana Incidents of 1909 Revisited* (Ankara: Turkish Historical Society, 2011).
26. Der Matossian, "From Bloodless Revolution," 160.
27. Güçlü, "Armenian events of Adana," 8–9.
28. James Creelman, "The Red Terror on the Cilician Plain: How the Moslem Frenzy Started by the Foolish Talk of a Christian Priest Spread Far Beyond Adana," *New York Times*, August 29, 1909.
29. Djemal Pasha, *Memories of a Turkish Statesman, 1913–1919* (New York: George H. Doran, 1922), 261.
30. This estimate is based on the population counts of 1906–1907 and 1914. The census figures of 1906–1907 show a Muslim population of 435,795, compared to a total Armenian population (Apostolic, Catholic, and Protestant) of 55,073, within a general population of 504,396. The figures compiled in 1914 show a Muslim population of 341,903 and a combined Armenian population of 57,685 within a general population of 411,023. See Karpat, *Ottoman Population*, 162 and 188–189.
31. Yücel Güçlü, review of *Talaat Pasha, Father of Modern Turkey, Architect of Genocide*, by Hans-Lukas Kieser, *Journal of Muslim Minority Affairs* 38, no. 3 (2018):445.
32. Djemal Pasha, *Memories of a Turkish Statesman*, 262.
33. Yusuf Sarınay, "Arşiv Belgelerine Göre 1909 Adana Ermeni Olaylari," in Çicek, ed., *The Adana Incidents*, 79.
34. Sahara, *What Happened in Adana*, 169.
35. Ibid., 169–172.
36. Güçlü, "Armenian Events of Adana," 8.
37. Sahara, *What Happened in Adana*, 176. The most exhaustive study of the "Adana events" has been published only recently. See Yücel Güçlü,

The Armenian Events of Adana in 1909: Cemal Paşa and Beyond (Lanham, MD: Hamilton Books, 2018).

38. Viscount Grey of Fallodon, *Twenty-Five Years, 1892–1916* (London: Hodder and Stoughton, 1926), 1:175.

39. G. Lowes Dickinson, *The International Anarchy, 1904–1914* (London: Allen and Unwin, 1926), 172.

40. Grey, *Twenty-Five Years*, 179.

41. Ibid., 181.

42. Ibid., 183.

43. Ibid., 192.

44. A substantial body of Ottoman documents on the Bulgarian declaration of independence, Austria-Hungary's annexation of Bosnia-Herzegovina, and the Cretan proclamation of union with Greece has been published in three volumes under the general heading of *Ottoman Diplomatic Documents on the Origins of World War One*. See Sinan Kuneralp and Gül Tokay, eds., *Ottoman Diplomatic Documents on the Origins of World War One: The Road to Bulgarian Independence, September 1908–May 1909* (Istanbul: Isis Press, 2008); Sinan Kuneralp and Gül Tokay, eds., *Ottoman Diplomatic Documents on the Origins of World War One: The Bosnian Annexation Crisis, September 1908–May 1909* (Istanbul: Isis Press, 2009); and Sinan Kuneralp, ed., *The Final Stage of the Cretan Question, 1899–1913* (Istanbul: Isis Press, 2009).

45. Ebru Boyar, *Ottomans, Turks and the Balkans*, 61.

46. Bilal N. Şimşir, ed., *Ege Sorunu Belgeler, 1912–1913/Aegean Question Documents, 1912–1913*, vol. 2, no. 131, Dering to Grey, Rome, October 15, 125 (Ankara: Türk Tarih Kurumu, 1989).

47. Told by Grey, *Twenty-Five Years* 1:57.

48. Raymond Poincaré, *The Origins of the War* (London: Cassell, 1922), 67–68.

49. Grey, *Twenty-Five Years*, 1:160.

50. Ibid., 164.

51. See "The Landing of Wilhelm II in Tangier, March 31, 1905. Report of Councillor von Schoen, Envoy in the Imperial Suite, to the German Foreign Office." *The World War I Document Archive*, wwi.lib.byu.edu/index.php/The_First_Moroccan_Crisis.

52. Ibid.

53. *Twenty-Five Years*, 227.

54. Ibid., 229.

CHAPTER 7

1. R. J. B. Bosworth, "Italy and the End of the Ottoman Empire," in *The Great Powers and the End of the Ottoman Empire*, ed. Marian Kent (London: Allen and Unwin, 1984), 60.

2. Ibid., 54, quoting Hardinge.

3. Joseph Heller, *British Policy Towards the Ottoman Empire, 1908–1914* (London: Frank Cass, 1983), 52.

4. Ibid., 54.

5. Down to tanks of wine for the soldiers. See "In Tripoli after Zanzur, Tanks of Wine for Soldiers at the Front, Cafés Gay as Paris," *New York Times*, October 2, 1912.

6. From Marinetti's *Futurist Manifesto* of 1909.

7. A few years later, the British war correspondent Philip Gibbs, reporting the Balkan War from the Bulgarian side, encountered Marinetti on a train. Marinetti was flirting with a Bulgarian beauty. Asked to recite his poem *The Automobile*, Marinetti took off his coat and threw himself into his performance "until the veins stood out on his forehead and his face was scarlet." His voice "rang out like a trumpet." See Philip Gibbs and Bernard Grant, *Adventures of War with Cross and Crescent* (London: Methuen, 1912), 126–127. Marinetti celebrated the fall of Edirne in his poem "Zang Tumb Tumb." See also Mark Almond, "The Forgotten Fascist Roots of Humanitarian Intervention: 100 Years of Bombing Libya," *Counterpunch,* April 5, 2011.

8. Almond writes that the prime minister, Giovanni Giolitti, lied to parliament when he said the war had cost 512 million lire: "But in reality off-balance sheet accounting hid another billion lire in costs of the war against the Ottoman Empire over Libya."

9. David G. Herrmann, "The Paralysis of Strategy in the Italian-Turkish War 1911–1912," *English Historical Review* 104 (1989):332.

10. See Commodore W. H. Beehler, *The History of the Italian-Turkish War, September 29, 1911 to October 18, 1912* (Annapolis, MD: Reprinted from proceedings of the United States Naval Institute, 1913), 58.

11. Stephen B. Penrose, *That They May Have Life: The Story of the American University of Beirut, 1866–1941* (New York: American University of Beirut, 1941), 147–148. Penrose puts the number of fatalities at 40.

12. Bilal Şimşir, ed., *Ege Sorunu Belgeler*, vol. 1, no. 56, Buchanan to Grey, St. Petersburg, March 5, 1912, 39.

13. Ibid., no. 178, Lowther to Grey, Constantinople, May 8, 1912, 125.

14. Ibid., no. 146, Grey to Lowther, Foreign Office, April 30, 1912, 97.

15. On July 19, a squadron of five Italian torpedo boats penetrated the straits but withdrew without incident.

16. Şimşir, ed., *Ege Sorunu Belgeler*, vol. 1, no. 218, Dering to Grey, Rome, May 24, 1912, 151.

17. Bosworth, "Italy and the End of the Ottoman Empire," 62.

18. Şimşir, ed., *Ege Sorunu Belgeler*, vol. 1, no. 264, Admiralty to Foreign Office, June 29, 1912, enc. "Italian Occupation of Aegean Islands and its Effect on Naval Policy," secret, 201–205.

19. Ibid., no. 335, Grey to Dering, Foreign Office, October 14, 1912, reporting on a conversation with the Italian ambassador, 260–261.

20. Karpat, *The Politicization of Islam,* 265.
21. Stanford J. Shaw, *The Ottoman Empire in World War I* (Ankara: Türk Tarih Kurumu, 2006), 1:548.
22. Heller, *British Policy Towards the Ottoman Empire,* 13.
23. Hardinge to Bertie, Foreign Office, May 5, 1908. Quoted in Nabeel Audeh, "The Ideological Uses of History and the Young Turks as a Problem for Historical Interpretation: Considerations of Class, Race, and Empire in British Foreign Attitudes to the Young Turks, 1908–191" (PhD diss., Georgetown University, 1990), 188.
24. Undoubtedly strengthened by Jewish refugees pouring out of Russia after the latest pogrom at Kishinev in 1903, repeated in 1905. The British response was the Aliens Bill (1905), with debate on the government side led by then-Prime Minister, Sir Arthur James Balfour. The object was to stop these refugees from reaching British shores.
25. Audeh, "The Ideological Uses of History," 47.
26. The Zionist movement calling for the establishment of a Jewish "chartered company" for Palestine was hardly representative of "international Jewry." Zionism was regarded with suspicion and dislike within Jewish communities everywhere. It was the British government that embraced it, for reasons of its own, ensuring the first stage of its success in Palestine.
27. Audeh, "The Ideological Uses of History," see "The Lowther Embassy's Judeo-Masonic-Young Turk Conspiracy Thesis," 234–259.
28. G. R. Berridge, ed., *Tilkidom and the Ottoman Empire: The Letters of Gerald Fitzmaurice to George Lloyd, 1906–1915* (Istanbul: Isis Press, 2008), 107.
29. For Fitzmaurice's remarks to his friend George Lloyd (a Freemason) on how the Grand Orient lodge controlled the CUP and was extending its "subterranean workings into Egypt on political lines," see Berridge, 13.
30. Audeh, "The Ideological Uses of History," 242.

CHAPTER 8
1. Hasan Kayali, "Elections and the Electoral Process in the Ottoman Empire 1876–1919," *International Journal of Middle East Studies* 27, no. 3 (August 1995):273.
2. Assassinated in June.
3. Kansu, *Politics in Post-Revolutionary Turkey, 1908–1913,* 429–30.
4. See Rankin, *The Inner History of the Balkan War* (London: Constable, 1914), 150–151. F. Yeats-Brown, *Golden Horn: Plot and Counterplot in Turkey, 1908–1918, as Seen "from the Inside" by a Prisoner of War* (London: Victor Gollancz, 1932), 85, has a slightly different version.
5. F. Yeats-Brown, *Golden Horn,* 75–77. The leadup to the war and the results on the battlefield are surveyed in André Gerolymatos, "Intractable Boundaries: Balkan Battlefields," chap. 7 in *The Balkan Wars: Conquest, Revolution, and Retribution from the Ottoman Era to the Twentieth Century and Beyond* (New York: Basic Books, 2002), 195–232.

6. Hellenic Army General Staff, Army History Directorate, *A Concise History of the Balkan Wars, 1912–1913* (Athens, 1998), 8.

7. Leyla Amzi-Erdoğdular, "Afterlife of Empire: Muslim-Ottoman Relations in Habsburg Bosnia Herzegovina, 1878–1914" (PhD diss., Graduate School of Arts and Sciences, Columbia University, 2013), 59, quoting Kemal Karpat for a total figure of 80,000–100,000 emigrants, 1879–1914. Some eventually returned.

8. M. Edith Durham, *Twenty Years of Balkan Tangle* (London: Allen and Unwin, 1920), 84.

9. Richard C. Hall, *The Balkan Wars 1912–1913: Prelude to the First World War* (London: Routledge, 2000), 6.

10. Violet's father William was a detective, elevated from sergeant first class. Violet, later HRH Princess Violette Ljubica, the name she adopted after marriage, died in Monte Carlo in 1960, nearly thirty years after her husband. Her path through life had been a remarkable one.

11. Durham, *Twenty Years of Balkan Tangle*, 36.

12. The wife of the abdicated British king Edward VIII (January 20–December 11, 1936).

13. Durham, *Twenty Years of Balkan Tangle*, 51.

14. See Yeats-Brown, *Golden Horn: Plot and Counterplot*, 72n1.

15. Durham, *Twenty Years of Balkan Tangle*, 74.

16. Ibid., 79.

17. See Reginald Rankin, *The Inner History of the Balkan War*, 551–559, for a useful summary of the respective strength of the Balkan and Ottoman armies. Different figures are given in different sources.

18. Stephen Duggan, "European Diplomacy and the Balkan Problem," *Political Science Quarterly* 28, no. 1 (March 1913):116.

19. Edward J. Erickson, *Defeat in Detail: The Ottoman Army in the Balkans, 1912–1913* (Westport, CT: Praeger, 2003), 68. Hall, in *The Balkan Wars 1912–1913*, 24, estimates that on the eve of war in 1912 Bulgaria had mobilized 599,878 men out of a population of just under two million males.

20. Lieutenant Hermenegild Wagner, *With the Victorious Bulgarians* (London: Constable, 1913), 96.

21. Leon Trotsky, *The War Correspondence of Leon Trotsky: The Balkan Wars, 1912–13*, trans. Brian Pearce, ed. George Weissman and Duncan Williams (New York: Pathfinder, 1991), 256.

22. Garegin Ter-Harutyunyan was to serve with the Armenian Legion attached to the Wehrmacht during World War II.

23. Erickson, *Defeat in Detail*, 69.

24. Ibid., 70.

25. Hall, *The Balkan Wars*, 12.

26. Hellenic Army General Staff, *A Concise History of the Balkan Wars*, 8.

27. Erickson, *Defeat in Detail*, 54.

28. Ibid., 59.

29. Wagner, *With the Victorious Bulgarians*, 112.
30. Hall, *The Balkan Wars*, 14.
31. Ibid., 18, for comparative statistics.
32. Rankin, *The Inner History*, x.
33. Ibid., 6.
34. Ibid., 15.
35. Barbara Jelavich, *History of the Balkans: Twentieth Century* (Cambridge: Cambridge University Press, 1983), 2:90.
36. Bulgarian and Armenian revolutionaries engaged in close cooperation. See Garabet K. Moumdjian, "Rebels with a Cause: Armenian-Macedonian Relations and Their Bulgarian Connection, 1895–1913," in *War and Nationalism: The Balkan Wars*, eds. Hakan Yavuz and Isa Blumi (Salt Lake City: University of Utah Press, 2012): 132–175. For the Ottoman government, of course, the *komitadjis* (Ottoman *komitacis*) and *andartes* were nothing more than bandit gangs.
37. The kidnappers were concerned that the baby's crying would attract unwanted attention. After the ransom was paid, the women and the baby were left beneath a pear tree near Strumica. Miss Stone was fifty-five years old and apparently quite formidable. "Have you ever found yourself in strong opposition to a determined middle-aged woman with a will all her own?" one of the kidnappers remarked later. "She assuming the attitude that you are a brute and you feeling it?" See Randall B. Woods, "The Miss Stone Affair," *American Heritage* 32, issue 6 (October/November 1981): www.americanheritage.com/content/miss-stone-affair.
38. B. Destani, ed., *Ethnic Minorities*, no. 216, Whitehead to Lansdowne, Constantinople, February 14, 1903, inc. no. 7, Biliotti to Whitehead, Salonica, January 31, 1903, 102.
39. Ibid., no. 399, Lansdowne to Egerton, Foreign Office, June 17, 1903, enc. 2, 139–140.
40. The ship had to be towed to Marseilles, where it was scrapped.
41. See for example B. Destani, ed., *Ethnic Minorities*, "Communication from the Macedonian Committee. News from the district of Kastoria," received on September 18, 1903, 151–166.
42. Hall writes that IMRO "elements" carried out the attack as a deliberate provocation. Hall, *The Balkan Wars*, 13. These "elements" may have been the pro-Bulgarian state faction inside IMRO. The attack does not seem to have been endorsed by the leadership or IMRO's cells in Macedonia.
43. The initiative was taken by the French Foreign Minister, Raymond Poincaré.
44. Durham, *Twenty Years of Balkan Tangle*, 230.
45. For a summary of these demands, see Ellis Ashmead Bartlett, *With the Turks in Thrace*, (New York: Doran, 1913), 28.
46. Erickson, *Defeat in Detail*, 67.
47. Ashmead Bartlett, *With the Turks in Thrace*, 179.

48. Handan Nezir Akmeşe, *The Birth of Modern Turkey: The Ottoman Military and the March to World War I* (London: I. B. Tauris, 2005), 127.
49. Erickson, *Defeat in Detail*, 65.
50. Ibid., 65–66.
51. Rankin, *The Inner History*, 271.
52. Ashmead Bartlett, *With the Turks in Thrace*, 152.
53. Trotsky, *War Correspondence*, 20
54. B. Destani, ed., *Ethnic Minorities in the Balkans*, no. 721, Paget to Grey, Belgrade, November 21, 1912, enc. Peckham to Paget, enc. 1, Üsküb, November 2, 1912, 258.
55. Ibid.
56. Ibid., no. 720, Paget to Grey, Belgrade, November 21, 1912, enc. "Notes of Events in Old Servia since beginning of War," 257.
57. Ibid.
58. Ibid.
59. Mark Mazower, *Salonica, City of Ghosts: Christians, Muslims and Jews, 1430–1950* (London: HarperCollins, 2004), 303.
60. Hellenic Army General Staff, *A Concise History of the Balkan Wars*, 97.
61. Hall, *The Balkan Wars*, 72.
62. Duggan, "European Diplomacy and the Balkan Problem," 120.
63. See Rankin, *The Inner History*, 413–15, for a summary of the proceedings.
64. Implicated in planning for a coup in 1916, Yakub was sentenced to death and executed for wartime crimes during the Allied occupation of Istanbul.
65. Audeh, "The Ideological Uses of History," 379.
66. Toward the end of the war, with Serbian support, Esad Paşa set up an Albanian republic in Durres as a rival to the provisional government in Tirana. Upon the outbreak of the First World War, he aligned himself with the Entente. He signed an alliance with Serbia and agreed to the annexation of southern Albania/northern Epirus by Greece. Passing into Albanian history as treacherous and double-dealing, his colorful life came to an end when he was assassinated in Paris in 1920.
67. Erickson, *Defeat in Detail*, 326.
68. Carnegie Endowment for International Peace, *Report of the International Commission to Inquire into the Causes and Conduct of the Balkan Wars* (Washington, D.C: Carnegie Endowment, 1914). Republished as *The Other Balkan Wars: A 1913 Carnegie Endowment Inquiry in Retrospect with a New Introduction and Reflections on the Present Conflict by George F. Kennan* (Washington D.C: Carnegie Endowment, 1993), 329–330. Henceforth, *Carnegie Report*.
69. Şimşir, ed., *Ege Sorunu Belgeler*, vol. 2, no. 14, confidential, Elliott to Grey, Athens, June 17, 1913, 19.
70. Ibid., no. 183, confidential, Rodd to Grey, Rome, December 6, 1913, 171.
71. Ibid., vol. 1, no. 519, Grey to Bertie, Foreign Office, January 10, 1913, 443.
72. Ibid., vol. 2, no. 228, Rodd to Grey, Rome, December 27, 1913, 217–218.

73. Ibid., vol. 2, no. 288, Rodd to Grey, Rome, January 16, 1914, enclosing memorandum by Signor Fusinato, 281–287.
74. Ibid., vol. 2, no. 277, Rodd to Grey, Rome, January 11, 1914, 268–270.
75. Ibid., vol. 2, no. 218, Mallet to Grey, Constantinople, December 22, 1913, 204–205.
76. Ibid., vol. 2, no. 232, Mallet to Grey, Constantinople, December 29, 1913, 221–225.
77. Ibid., vol. 2, no. 221. The loss of these islands was raised in September 2016, by Turkey's President, Recep Tayyip Erdoğan, when he said that through the Treaty of Lausanne (1923) "we gave away islands that you should shout across to." Visiting Athens in December 2017, he returned to the issue, referring to the need to "update" the treaty where it referred to borders and minorities. In October 2017, Turkish opposition leader, Kemal Kiliçdaroğlu, further stirred the nationalist pot when remarking, "Look at the Aegean islands. They are Greek islands. The islands that should be ours are occupied by Greece. The Greek flag is fluttering on islands belonging to Turkey. I want an answer to this, Erdoğan."
78. Ibid., vol. 2, no. 348, Mallet to Grey, Constantinople, February 3, 1914, 341–342.

CHAPTER 9
1. *Carnegie Report.*
2. Ibid., 2.
3. Hall, *The Balkan Wars,* 137.
4. B. Destani, *Ethnic Minorities in the Balkan States,* Lowther to Grey, Constantinople, February 22, 1913, enc. 2, "Note on Distress in District of Monastir," Vice-Consul C. A. Grieg, Monastir, January 21, 1913, 350–351.
5. *Carnegie Report,* 73–74.
6. Ibid., 74, 279.
7. Ibid., 279
8. Ibid., 74–75.
9. B. Destani, ed., *Ethnic Minorities,* no. 1, Bax-Ironside to Grey, Sofia, March 17, 1913, confidential, enc.1., Vice-Consul Young to Bax-Ironside, Philippopoli, March 7, 1913, 352–359.
10. *Carnegie Report,* report signed and sealed by Youssef Effendi, head of the Muslim community in Serres, 279–280.
11. Ibid.
12. B. Destani, ed., *Ethnic Minorities,* Bax-Ironside to Mallet, Sofia, February 27, 1913, enc. 1, 321.
13. Ibid., Lowther to Grey, Constantinople, March 15, 1913, enc. no. I, Morgan to Lowther, Cavalla, March 6, 1913.
14. Ibid., Bax-Ironside to Grey, Sofia, March 17, 1913, enc. no 1, Vice-Consul Young to Bax-Ironside, Philippopoli, March 7, 1913, 357.

15. Ibid., no. 1, confidential, Lowther to Grey, Constantinople, March 15, 1913, enc. 1, Acting Vice-Consul Morgan, Cavalla, March 6, 1913, 343–344.

16. B. Destani, *Ethnic Minorities in the Balkan States*, no. 179, Paget to Grey, Belgrade, March 7, 1913, enc. Peckham to Paget, Üsküb, February 28, 1913, 328.

17. B. Destani, ed., *Ethnic Minorities,* Paget to Grey, Belgrade, March 7, 1913, enc. 1, Vice-Consul Peckham to Paget, Üsküb, February 28, 1913, enc. 1 and 2, "memorandum on massacres of Albanians. Statements of Catholic curé of Üsküb," 328–329.

18. Ibid., 327.

19. *Carnegie Report*, 89.

20. B. Destani, ed., *Ethnic Minorities*, Marling to Grey, Constantinople, August 1, 1913, enc. Morgan to Marling, Salonica, July 25, 1913, 429.

21. Ibid., Bax-Ironside to Grey, Sofia, August 12, 1913, enc. memorandum from Vice-Consul Heard, 433–434.

22. *Carnegie Report*, 189–192.

23. B. Destani, ed., *Ethnic Minorities*, James Morgan, "Treatment of Bulgarian prisoners," n.d., 495–496.

24. *Carnegie Report*, 105 and 307–314, 315.

25. Ibid., 314–316.

26. *Twenty Years of Balkan Tangle*, 245.

27. Ibid., 246.

28. B. Destani, ed., *Ethnic Minorities*, confidential, no. 1, Bax-Ironside to Grey, Sofia, April 8, 1913, enc. 2, "Extracts from reports received by His Majesty's Government," 383.

29. Ibid., 384.

30. Ibid., 386.

31. Syed Tanvir Wasti, "The 1912–13 Balkan Wars and the Siege of Edirne," *Middle Eastern Studies* 40, no. 4 (July 2004):63.

32. *Carnegie Report*, 115.

33. Ibid., 111.

34. Ibid., 113.

35. Ibid., 341, "Oral depositions," no. 1. For the fate of the city, see also Syed Tanvir Wasti, "The 1912–13 Balkan Wars," 59–78.

36. Rankin, *The Inner History of the Balkan War,* 309

37. Ashmead Bartlett, *With the Turks in Thrace*, 260–261.

38. Rankin, 308–309.

39. Hikmet Özdemir, *The Ottoman Army, 1914–1918: Disease and Death on the Battlefield* (Salt Lake City: University of Utah Press, 2008), 6.

40. Stanford J. Shaw, *The Ottoman Empire in World War I* (Ankara: Turk Tarih Kurumu, 2006), 1:554.

41. Justin McCarthy, *1912–1913 Balkan War: Death and Forced Exile of Ottoman Muslims. An Annotated Map* (Washington, D.C.: Turkish Coalition

of America, n.d.). Extrapolating from population statistics, McCarthy goes into more detail in *Death and Exile*, 135–177.

42. Mustafa Aksakal, *The Ottoman Road to War in 1914: The Ottoman Empire and the First World War* (Cambridge: Cambridge University Press, 2008), 22.

43. Shaw, *The Ottoman Empire in World War I*, 1:549.

44. Karpat, *The Politicization of Islam*, 343.

45. Paul Mojzes, *Ethnic Cleansing in the Balkans: Why Did It Happen and Could It Happen Again?* Cicero Foundation Great Debate Paper 13/04 (Rosemont, PA: Rosemont College, 2013), 3. The author explores these themes further in his book *Balkan Genocides: Holocaust and Ethnic Cleansing in the Twentieth Century* (Lanham, MD: Rowman and Littlefield, 2011).

46. Engin Kiliç, "The Balkan War (1912–1913) and Visions of the Future in Ottoman Turkish Literature" (PhD diss., University of Leiden, 2015), 52.

47. Ibid., 53.

48. Ibid., 57.

49. Şimşir, ed., *Ege Sorunu*, vol. 1, no. 440, Constantinople, Lowther to Grey, December 21, 1912, 363–364.

50. Şimşir, ed., *Ege Sorunu*, vol. 2, no. 543, Erskine to Grey, Athens, June 16, 1914, 535.

51. Shaw, *The Ottoman Empire in World War I*, 1:558.

52. Ryan Gingeras, *Sorrowful Shores: Violence, Ethnicity, and the End of the Ottoman Empire, 1912–1923* (Oxford: Oxford University Press, 2009), 40. The American Hellenic Society accused the Ottoman government of persecuting Greeks "with the objective of annihilating Hellenism." See Carroll N. Brown and Theodore Ion, *Persecutions of the Greeks in Turkey Since the Beginning of the European War* (New York, American Hellenic Society and Oxford University Press, 1918).

53. Shaw, *The Ottoman Empire in World War I*, 1:556.

54. *Ege Sorunu*, vol. 2, no. 551, Mallet to Grey, June 17, 1914, 541–544.

55. Ibid., no. 555, Mallet to Grey, June 18, 1914, 546.

56. Ibid., no. 577, Grey to Mallet, Foreign Office, June 26, 1914, enc. telegram from Talat, 562–563.

57. Ibid., no. 580, Mallet to Grey, June 29, 1914, 569.

58. *Carnegie Report*, 127–135.

59. Ibid., 130.

60. B. Destani, *Ethnic Minorities*, no. 481, Mallet to Grey, Constantinople, April 15, 1914, 464–466.

61. Ibid., no. 532, Mallet to Grey, Constantinople, June 15, 1914, 525. Back in power after the coup of 1913, the CUP was widely seen as the savior of the country against the threat of partition. The suppression of the Liberal Entente following the accusation that a number of its members were involved in the June assassination of the grand vizier (Mahmud Şevket Paşa) left only the CUP contesting the elections of early 1914.

62. Ibid., 525
63. Ibid., no. 584, Mallet to Grey, Constantinople, July 5, 1913, 573–575.
64. See Matthias Bjornlund, "The 1914 Cleansing of Aegean Greeks as a Case of Violent Turkification," *Journal of Genocide Research* 10, no. 1 (March 2008):41–58.
65. Gingeras, *Sorrowful Shores*, 40.
66. Şimşir, ed., *Ege Sorunu,* vol. 2, no. 507, Elliot to Grey, Athens, May 22, 1914, 499–501.
67. Ibid., no. 508, Mallet to Grey, Constantinople, May 27, 1914, 503–504.
68. Ibid., no. 507, Elliot to Grey, May 22, 1914, 500.
69. Ibid., no. 517, Grey to Erskine, Foreign Office, June 10, 1914, 514–515.
70. A two-volume history of the Balkan wars examines the situation from the perspective of all participants. See Mustafa Turkeş, ed., *The Centenary of the Balkan Wars (1912–1913): Contested Stances,* 2 vols. (Ankara: Türk Tarih Kurumu, 2014).

CHAPTER 10
1. Akmeşe, *The Birth of Modern Turkey,* 161.
2. Ibid., 168.
3. In fact, the sultan was the commander-in-chief of the Ottoman military, and as he had not put his name to this agreement, preferring neutrality, its legality was questionable.
4. Ulrich Trumpener, "Germany and the End of the Ottoman Empire," in *The Great Powers and the End of the Ottoman Empire,* ed. Marian Kent, 132.
5. Alan Bodger, "Russia and the End of the Ottoman Empire," in *The Great Powers and the End of the Ottoman Empire,* ed. Marian Kent, 96
6. L. Bruce Fulton, "France and the End of the Ottoman Empire," in *The Great Powers and the End of the Ottoman Empire,* ed. Marian Kent, 161.
7. Bodger, "Russia and the End of the Ottoman Empire," 96.
8. Aksakal, *The Ottoman Road to War,* 91. See also Said Halim Pasha, *L'empire Ottoman et la guerre mondiale* (Istanbul: Isis Press, 2000), 97.
9. Shaw, *The Ottoman Empire in World War I,* 1:592–604.
10. Ibid., 620–621.
11. Ibid., 622. For a summary of these events, see also Roger Ford, *Eden to Armageddon: World War I in the Middle East* (New York: Pegasus, 2010), 12–13.
12. Aksakal, *The Ottoman Road to War,* 177.
13. Ahmet Seyhun, *Said Halim Pasha: Ottoman Statesman. Islamist Thinker. 1865–1921* (Istanbul: Isis Press, 2003). See also Said Halim Pasha, *L'empire Ottoman,* 117–118
14. Emre Kizilkaya, "How Did the Ottomans Really Enter World War I?" *Hurriyet Daily News,* August 10, 2015. Hakki Paşa's diaries were published by the journalist Murat Bardakci. The PhD student who uncovered Enver's order to Souchon was Ali Kasıyuğun. See www

.hurriyetdailynews.com/how-did-the-ottomans-really-enter- wwi
.aspx?pageID=517&nID=86679&NewsCatID=550.

15. Sean McMeekin, *The Russian Origins of the First World War* (Cambridge, MA: Belknap Press of Harvard University Press, 2011), 111.

16. Ayşe Özil, *Orthodox Christians in the Late Ottoman Empire: A Study of Communal Relations in Anatolia* (London: Routledge, 2013), 98.

17. For details of the planning see Garabet K. Moumdjian, "Rebels with a Cause: Armenian-Macedonian Relations and Their Bulgarian Connection, 1895–1913," in M. Hakan Yavuz, ed., *War and Nationalism: The Balkan Wars*, 132–175.

18. See the collection of articles from *The Times* in "The Joris Affair," Macquarie University Law School. www.law.mq.edu.au/research/colonial_case _law/colonial_cases/less_developed/constantinople/joris_affair_1906/.

19. Mehmet Beşikci, "Between Voluntarism and Resistance: The Ottoman Mobilization of Manpower in the First World War," PhD diss. (Department of History, Boğazici University, 2009), 33.

20. See Erik-Jan Zürcher, "The Ottoman Conscription System in Theory and Practice 1844–1918," *International Review of Social History* 43, no. 3 (1998), 437–449.

21. Beşikci, "Between Voluntarism and Resistance," 143.

22. Shaw, *The Ottoman Empire in World War I*, 1:148.

23. Beşikci, "Between Voluntarism and Resistance," 138.

24. Ibid., 244. The *muhaciler* were also subject to regular military service.

25. Ibid., 139.

26. Yücel Yanıkdağ, *Healing the Nation: Prisoners of War, Nationalism and Medicine in Turkey, 1914–1939* (Edinburgh: Edinburgh University Press, 2013), 16.

27. Yiğit Akın, "The Ottoman Home Front during World War I: Everyday Politics, Society, and Culture" (PhD diss., Department of History, Ohio State University, 2011), 34–35.

28. *The Arab Bulletin: Bulletin of the Arab Bureau in Cairo 1916–1919* (Oxford: Archive Editions, 1986) 1, no. 10 (July 14, 1916):3.

29. Beşikci, "Between Voluntarism and Resistance," 179.

30. Shaw, *The Ottoman Empire in World War I*, 1:168.

31. Salim Tamari, *Year of the Locust: A Soldier's Diary and the Erasure of Palestine's Ottoman Past* (Berkeley: University of California Press, 2011), 94.

32. Shaw, *The Ottoman Empire in World War I*, 1:166–167.

33. Pınar Kundil, "The Armenian Question According to *Takvim i-Vekayi*, 1914–1918" (Master's thesis, Middle East Technical University, September 2003), covers these events on the basis of the official gazette.

34. Ibid. In late 1914, Armenians still remained in public service as bureaucrats and doctors and ran businesses, sometimes together with Muslims. Courts remained open to the hearing of their grievances.

35. There was no grand entry on a white horse. Allenby walked into the city accompanied by a handful of senior officers, an act that impressed the Jerusalem notables who had surrendered the city.
36. As Enver told Cemal Bey. See Djemal Pasha, *Memories of a Turkish Statesman,* 137.
37. Ibid., 152.
38. Ibid., 149.
39. Ibid., 155.
40. Eventually, a second Sinai attack was made in July 1916. It too resulted in failure. On the delayed Gallipoli landing, see Djemal Pasha, *Memories of a Turkish Statesman*, 157–159.
41. Edward J. Erickson, *Ordered to Die: A History of the Ottoman Army in the First World War* (Westport: Greenwood Press, 2001), 60.
42. For the film, see www.turkeyswar.com/campaign/caucasus.html.
43. Erickson, *Ordered to Die*, 59.
44. Ibid., 59.
45. Ibid., 57, 64, for comparative figures.
46. The figure was issued in 2007 on the ninety-third anniversary of the battle of Sarıkamış by the office of the Turkish Army Chief of Staff (General Hilmi Özkök). See "Military Revises Death Toll of 1914 Caucasus Operation," *Hurriyet Daily News*, December 28, 2007.
47. Michael A. Reynolds, "The Ottoman-Russian Struggle for Eastern Anatolia and the Caucasus, 1908–1918: Identity, Ideology, and the Geopolitics of World Order" (PhD diss., Department of Near Eastern Studies, Princeton University, November 2003), 226.
48. Erickson, *Ordered to Die*, 61.
49. Grey, *Twenty-Five Years, 1892–1916*, 2:76–77. Kaiser Wilhelm II relates in his memoirs how in 1886, as a young man in the Foreign Office when Germany was developing a close relationship with the Ottoman Empire, he was entrusted with the task of "offering" Constantinople to the Russian tsar, which he did, at Brest-Litovsk. The reply was lofty: "If I wish to have Constantinople I will take it whenever I feel like it, without permission or need of approval from Prince Bismarck." The matter was dropped. See Wilhelm II, *The Kaiser's Memoirs* (New York: Harper, 1922), 14–15.
50. C. E. W. Bean, *The Story of Anzac* (Sydney, 1924), 2:866.
51. Jeffrey Grey, *The War with the Ottoman Empire* (Melbourne: Oxford University Press, 2015), 81.
52. The first relief force was led by Sir Fenton Aylmer who in 1895 had led the relief at Chitral, on the northwestern frontier, ending the forty-nine-day siege by Muslim tribesmen of a force commanded by Townshend.
53. See Leila Tarazi Fawaz, "The Forgotten Soldiers: India and Pakistan in the Great War," *Wilson Quarterly*, Winter, 2015. www.wilsonquarterly.com/quarterly/fall-2104-the-great-wars/forgotten-soldiers-india-in-great-war/.

54. Charles Vere Ferrers Townshend, *My Campaign in Mesopotamia* (New York: James A. McCann, 1920), 2:235.
55. This offer is not mentioned in his memoirs.
56. In February 1942, the Japanese army defeated Allied forces defending Singapore. Erickson, *Ordered to Die*, 151.
57. Sami Önal, *Tuğgeneral Ziya Yergök'un Anıları—Sarıkamış'tan Esarete (1915–1920)* [Brigadier General Ziya Yergök's Memoirs—from Sarıkamış to Captivity (1915–1920)], (Istanbul: Ramzi Kitapevi, 2007), 34. The general refers also to villages being burnt by Ottoman forces on the Pasin plain to prevent Russian forces from using them.
58. An equestrian statue of General Maude stood in the grounds of the British embassy until it was destroyed in the revolution of 1958.
59. See Shaw, *The Ottoman Empire in World War I*, 1:361–366, for a summary of members and financial resources.
60. Ibid., 373.
61. Ibid., 375–378.
62. Ibid., 379.
63. Shaw, *The Ottoman Empire in World War I*, 2:103.

CHAPTER 11

1. Birsen Bulmuş, *Plague, Quarantines and Geopolitics in the Ottoman Empire* (Edinburgh: Edinburgh University Press, 2012), see chapter 7, "Plague, Sanitary Administration and the End of Empire," 152–176.
2. Ibid., 153.
3. *Reconstruction in Turkey: A Series of Reports Compiled for the American Committee for Armenian and Syrian Relief* (New York, 1918), 72–73. Without doubting the presence of syphilis in rural communities, such a high figure needs to be regarded with caution, given the committee's missionary bias, its mandate to bring relief to Christian victims of the war, and its total disinterest in Muslim victims of the same war. The committee was the brainchild of former U.S. ambassador to the Ottoman Empire, Henry Morgenthau, New York philanthropist Cleveland Dodge, and James L. Barton, Foreign Secretary of the American Board of Commissioners for Foreign Missions (ABCFM), a man of pronounced hostility toward Islam. The committee's fund-raising activities were heavily based on propaganda, with posters showing women and children in distress and relying on a sword-wielding America for relief. The committee later became the American Committee for Relief in the Near East and subsequently the Near East Foundation, by which name it still operates. For James Barton's reflections on Islam see, among his articles and books, *The Christian Approach to Islam* (Boston: Pilgrim Press, 1918), in which he refers to the "defective character" of Muhammad (169) and describes Islam as a religion "destitute of spiritual power" (176), "a dominant force for evil" (177).

4. Erickson, *Ordered to Die,* 7.

5. Yanıkdağ, *Healing the Nation,* 21.

6. Nicholas Z. Ajay, "Mount Lebanon and the Wilayah of Beirut, 1914–1918: The War Years" (PhD diss., Department of History, Georgetown University, 1973), 173.

7. Özdemir, *The Ottoman Army, 1914–1918,* 39.

8. Ibid., 38–39.

9. Ibid., 43–44.

10. Ali Riza Eti, *Bir Onbaşının Doğu Cephesi Günlüğü, 1914–1915* [The Eastern Front Diary of a Corporal, 1914–1915], prepared for publication by Gönül Eti (Istanbul: Türkiye İş Bankası Kültür Yayınları, 2016), 15–16.

11. Ibid., 42–44.

12. Erickson, *Ordered to Die,* 8. The military had close to 100 aircraft at its disposal, used for reconnaissance and combat.

13. Özdemir, *The Ottoman Army,* 15.

14. Ibid., 33.

15. These figures are given by the Robert Schuman European Centre. See "Repares," www.centre-robert-schuman.org. Figures vary according to the source, but these are close to a consensus.

16. Karpat, *Ottoman Population, 1830–1914,* 190.

17. For scholarly estimates of Ottoman military casualties, see Erickson, *Ordered to Die,* 240; Özdemir, *The Ottoman Army,* 119–129; and Yanıkdağ, *Healing the Nation,* 18–20.

18. Shaw, *The Ottoman Empire in World War I,* 2:993.

19. Ibid.

20. Justin McCarthy, *Death and Exile,* 339. A general appraisal of the death toll can be found in Mehmet Fatih Baş, "War Losses (Ottoman Empire/ Middle East)," International Encyclopedia of the First World War, https://encylopedia.1914-1918-online.net/article/war_losses_ottoman _empiremiddle_east.

21. The Schuman Centre figure of 2,150,000 Ottoman civilian deaths would seem to be somewhat understated.

22. McCarthy, *Death and Exile,* 338. The figures for western and eastern Anatolia are based on internal refugees.

23. See Melanie Schulze-Tanielian, "Disease and Public Health (Ottoman Empire/Middle East)," International Encyclopedia of the First World War, https://encyclopedia.1914-1918-online.net/article/disease_and_public _health_ottoman_empiremiddle_east.

24. Özdemir, *The Ottoman Army,* 46.

25. This is one officer's story of his war experience and what met him when it was over. See Sami Önal, *Tuğgeneral Ziya Yergök'un Anıları—Sarıkamış'tan Esarete (1915–1920)* [Brigadier General Ziya Yergök's Memoirs—from Sarikamiş to Captivity (1915–1920)] (Istanbul: Remzi Kitabevi, 2007).

26. Halil Ataman, *Harp ve Esaret—Dogu Cephesi'nden Sibiriya'ya* [War and Captivity—From the Eastern Front to Sibiriya] (Istanbul: Türkiye İş Bankası Kültür Yayınları, 2014), 27–45.
27. Tonguç, Faik, *Birinci Dünya Savası'nda Bir Yedeksubayın Anıları* [A Reserve Officer's Memoirs of the First World War] (Istanbul: Türkiye İş Bankası Kültür Yayınları, 2015).
28. Ibid., 23.
29. *Reconstruction in Turkey: A Series of Reports compiled for the American Committee for Armenian and Syrian Relief,* 71.
30. Özdemir, *The Ottoman Army,* 53.
31. Mehmet Törehan Serdar, *Istiklale Açılan Ilk Kapı: Bitlis (İşgal ve Kurtuluşu)* [The First Door Opening to Independence: Bitlis (Its Occupation and Liberation)], (Bitlis: Bitlis Valiliği Kültür Yayınları, 2017), 78–79.
32. Shaw, *The Ottoman Empire in World War I,* 1:290.
33. Akın, "The Ottoman Home Front," 106n78. See also Akın, *When the War Came Home: The Ottomans' Great War and the Devastation of an Empire* (Stanford: Stanford University Press, 2018), 141–142.
34. Akın, "The Ottoman Home Front," 117.
35. Ibid., 119.
36. Ali Rıza Eti, *Bir Onbaşının Doğu Cephesi Günlüğü,* 88.
37. Ibid. The *Hamidiye* had been redesignated as the Tribal Light Cavalry (*Aşiret Hafif Süvari*) in 1910 but were still generally known as the *Hamidiye.* For more on the *Hamidiye* see Erickson, *Ottomans and Armenians,* 75–77.
38. As quoted in Leila Tarazi Fawaz, *A Land of Aching Hearts: The Middle East in the Great War* (Cambridge: Harvard University Press, 2014), 122–123.
39. Ibid., 123.
40. Harry Stuermer, *Two War Years in Constantinople: Sketches of German and Young Turkish Ethics and Politics* (New York: George H. Doran, 1917), 118. The author is hostile to the Ottoman government, but his accusations of profiteering through cornering the market were consistent with other complaints of wartime malpractices.
41. Ajay, "Mount Lebanon and the Wilayah of Beirut," 354.
42. Ibid., 368.
43. Elif Mahir Metinsoy charts the wartime experiences of women in *Ottoman Women during World War I: Everyday Experiences, Politics, and Conflict* (Cambridge: Cambridge University Press, 2017).
44. Akın, "The Ottoman Home Front," 133.
45. Çiğdem Oğuz, "Prostitution (Ottoman Empire)," International Encyclopedia of the First World War, https://encyclopedia.1914-1918-online.net /article/prostitution_ottoman_empire.
46. See Yavuz Selim Karakişla, *Women, War, and Work in the Ottoman Empire: Society for the Employment of Ottoman Muslim Women, 1916–1923* (Istanbul: Ottoman Bank Archives and Research Center, 2005).

47. Ibid., 173

48. Beşikci, "Between Voluntarism and Resistance," 179.

49. Ajay, "Mount Lebanon and the Wilayah of Beirut," 389. See also Ajay's appendix 8, "Data on Economic Conditions," 147–148, quoting from Ahmed Emin, *Turkey in the World War*.

50. See Sami Hadawi, "Sodomy, Locusts and Cholera: A Jerusalem Witness," *Jerusalem Quarterly* 53 (Spring 2013):7–27.

51. Stefanie Wichhart, "The 1915 Locust Plague in Palestine," *Jerusalem Quarterly* 56–57 (Winter 2013/Spring 2014):35.

52. Margaret McGilvary, *The Dawn of a New Era in Syria* (New York: Fleming H. Revell, 1920; reprint, Reading, UK: Garnet Publishing 2001), 180.

53. Fawaz, *A Land of Aching Hearts*, 94.

54. Quoted in Ajay, "Mount Lebanon and the Wilayah of Beirut," 335.

55. Alexander Aaronsohn, *With the Turks in Palestine* (Boston: Houghton Mifflin, 1916), 51.

56. Wichhart, "The 1915 Locust Plague in Palestine," 30.

57. *The Arab Bulletin: Bulletin of the Arab Bureau in Cairo, 1916–1919* (Cambridge: Archive Editions, 1986), 1:1916, bulletins 1–36, no. 33, secret, December 4, 1916, "Syria. Economic and Political Conditions," 505.

58. Fawaz, *A Land of Aching Hearts*, 89.

59. Ajay, "Mount Lebanon and the Wilayah of Beirut," 295.

60. In later decades, sericulture was reestablished but has never returned to the prosperity of the pre-1914 years.

61. *Arab Bulletin*, 2:1917, no. 48, April 31, "Syria/Palestine Present Economic Conditions," 172–187.

62. Ibid., 185.

63. Özdemir, *The Ottoman Army*, 94.

64. Ibid., 64–65.

65. Ibid., 186.

66. Hadawi, "Sodomy, Locusts, and Cholera," 19–22.

67. Tamari, *Year of the Locust*, 108.

68. Ibid., 129.

69. Ajay, "Mount Lebanon and the Wilayah of Beirut," 417.

70. McGilvary, *The Dawn of a New Era in Syria,* 204.

71. Ibid., 410.

72. Ajay, "Mount Lebanon and the Wilayah of Beirut," 401.

73. Fawaz, *A Land of Aching Hearts*, 105.

74. Ibid.

75. Ajay, Mount Lebanon," appendices, interview with Shekin Nassar.

76. Ibid., 429. These are possibly the same two women described as "living in the port area of the Lebanese town of Tripoli who had abducted, murdered, dismembered and eaten at least five children." See Fawaz, *Land of Aching Hearts*, 115, quoting Linda Schatkowski Schilcher, "The Famine of

1915–1918 in Greater Syria," in *Problems of the Middle East in Historical Perspective: Essays in Honor of Albert Hourani*, ed. J. Spagnolo (Reading, UK: Ithaca, 1992), 229–250.

77. Ajay, "Mount Lebanon," 427.
78. Rym Gazal "Lebanon's Dark Days of Hunger: The Great Famine of 1915–1918," *The National*, April 15, 2015. www.thenational.ae/world/middle-east /lebanons-dark-days-of-hunger-the-great-famine-of-1915-18.
79. Fawaz, *Land of Aching Hearts*, 105.
80. Ajay, "Mount Lebanon," 399.
81. McGilvary, *The Dawn of a New Era in Syria*, 205.
82. Ibid., 204.
83. *Arab Bulletin*, 1:1916, bulletin no. 10, Cairo, July 14, 1916, 3–5.
84. Ibid.
85. Rym Gazal, "Lebanon's Dark Days."
86. Harry Stuermer, *Two War Years in Constantinople,* 109.
87. George Antonius, *The Arab Awakening: The Story of the Arab National Movement* (London: Hamish Hamilton, 1938), 240–241.
88. Jean Gibran and Kahlil Gibran, *Kahlil Gibran: His Life and World* (Boston: New York Graphic Society, 1974), 288.
89. Schulze-Tanielian, "Disease and Public Health."
90. Guenter Lewy, *The Armenian Massacres in Ottoman Turkey: A Disputed Genocide* (Salt Lake City: University of Utah Press, 2005), 213.
91. Ibid., 214.
92. Amin Delshad "Exploring Great Britain's Role in Great Famine in Iran during World War I," Islamic Revolution Documentation Centre, Tehran, translated by Maryam Aliabadi, parts 1 and 2. www.irdc.ir/en/content/13734/print.aspx, and www.irdc.ir/en/content/13813/print.aspx. The famine is a major but largely unexplored issue in modern Iranian history. Millions of people died.
93. Sir Arnold T. Wilson, *Loyalties: Mesopotamia, a Personal and Historical Record*, vol. 2, *1917–1920* (London: Oxford University Press, 1931), 32–33.
94. Major-General L. C. Dunsterville, *The Adventures of Dunsterforce* (London: Edward Arnold, 1920), 110.
95. Kermit Roosevelt, *War in the Garden of Eden* (New York: Scribner's, 1919), 144.
96. Maria T. O'Shea, *Trapped Between the Map and Reality: Geography and Perceptions of Kurdistan* (New York: Routledge, 2004), 102.
97. David McDowall, *A Modern History of the Kurds* (London: I. B. Tauris, 2004), 108.
98. Kenneth Mason, "Central Kurdistan," *Geographical Journal* 54, no. 6 (Dec. 1919):330.
99. Ibid., 329.
100. Ibid., 339.
101. O'Shea, *Trapped Between*, 102.

CHAPTER 12

1. Gingeras, *Sorrowful Shores*, 43. Referring to the removal, resettlement, or "relocation" of Ottoman ethnoreligious groups during the war, Gingeras and others prefer "deportation," but surely inaccurately, as deportation is a government legal process ending in the ejection of nonnationals from within national borders. None of the Ottoman groups were deported but removed from where they were living to different parts of the empire.

2. Ibid., 47–48.

3. Shaw, *The Ottoman Empire in World War I*, 1:167–168.

4. Michael A. Reynolds, *Shattering Empires: The Clash and Collapse of the Ottoman and Russian Empires 1908–1918* (Cambridge: Cambridge University Press, 2011), 60, 63–64.

5. McDowall, *A Modern History of the Kurds*, 102.

6. Akin, *When the War Came Home*, 177.

7. Michael A. Reynolds, "The Ends of Empire: Imperial Collapse and the Trajectory of Kurdish Nationalism," 42, http://src-h.slav.hokudai.ac.jp/rp/publications/no14/14-04_Reynolds.pdf.

8. Shaw, *The Ottoman Empire in World War I*, 2:1002.

9. Uğur Umit Üngör, "Young Turk Social Engineering: Mass Violence and the Nation State in Eastern Turkey, 1913–1950" (PhD diss., University of Amsterdam, 2009, 223). As noted by both Üngör and McDowall, *A Modern History of the Kurds*, 108, cases of cannibalism were also reported from the Kurdish regions, among reports of cannibalism elsewhere.

10. Edward J. Erickson, *Ottomans and Armenians: A Study in Counterinsurgency* (New York: Palgrave Macmillan, 2013), 27.

11. Justin McCarthy, Esat Arslan, Cemalettin Taşkiran, and Ömer Turan, *The Armenian Rebellion at Van* (Salt Lake City: University of Utah Press, 2006), 112.

12. Hüseyin Çelik, "The 1915 Armenian Revolt in Van: Eyewitness Testimony," in *The Armenians in the Late Ottoman Period*, ed. Türkayya Ataöv (Ankara: Turkish Historical Society, Ankara, 2001), 97.

13. Erickson, *Ottomans and Armenians*, 108.

14. While the actual killing is generally ascribed directly to Manukian and other Dashnaks, the mayor's son has also been blamed. In this version, he was taken to a tavern by the Dashnaks and filled with alcohol before shooting the mayor on Manukian's orders as the mayor passed by in his carriage. Ibid., 91.

15. Tolga Başak, *British Documents on Armenian Question (1912–1923)*, ed. Yavuz Aslan, Vice-Consul Molyneux-Seel to Lowther, Van, December 6, 1912 (Ankara: Avrasya Incelemeleri Merkezi, 2018), 64.

16. Ibid., Molyneux-Seel to Lowther, Van, May 8, 1913, 77.

17. Sean McMeekin, *The Russian Origins of the First World War* (Cambridge, MA: The Belknap Press of Harvard University Press, 2011), 145–146.

18. Full text in Djemal Pasha, *Memories of a Turkish Statesman*, 266–271.

19. McMeekin, *The Russian Origins of the First World War*, 152.

20. Djemal Pasha, *Memories of a Turkish Statesman*, 271.

21. Ibid., 272.

22. Ibid.

23. Reynolds, *Shattering Empires*, 117.

24. McCarthy, et.al., *The Armenian Rebellion at Van*, 182.

25. Reynolds, "The Ottoman-Russian Struggle for Eastern Anatolia and the Caucasus, 1908–1918," 205.

26. Inanç Atılgan and Garabet Moumdjian, eds., *Archival Documents of the Viennese Armenian-Turkish Platform* (Klagenfurt/Celovec:Wieser Verlag, 2009), Istanbul to Ottoman Army General Headquarters, March 1–31, 1915, 86–118.

27. Onur Önol, "The Armenian National Movement in Tsarist Russia, 1870–1906" (Master's thesis, Department of International Relations, Bilkent University, 2009), ch. 4:1. Quotations are taken from the thesis as presented to the jury, of which I was a member.

28. Ibid., ch. 4:50.

29. Ibid., ch. 4:18.

30. Ibid., ch. 4:18–19.

31. Ibid., ch. 5:10.

32. Jamil Hasanli, "Armenian Volunteers on the Caucasian Front, 1914–1916," *The Caucasus and Globalization* 8, nos. 3–4 (2014):184.

33. McMeekin, *The Russian Origins of the First World War*, 150.

34. Erickson, *Ottomans and Armenians*, 147–148.

35. Ahmed Emin Yalman, *Turkey in the World War*, 218–219. The author gives a registered population figure for the region of 100,000, of which 10–12 percent was Armenian. In addition, there were six Kurdish nomadic tribes numbering 40,000. His claim that the "whole" Muslim population had been massacred, with only a small number escaping, seems exaggerated, even though civilian Muslim casualties in northeastern Anatolia were extremely heavy from the beginning of the war.

36. Erickson, *Ottomans and Armenians*, 156–158.

37. Lewy, *The Armenian Massacres in Ottoman Turkey*, 103.

38. Hasan Dilan ed., *Fransiz Diplomatic Belgelerinde Ermeni Olaylari, 1914–1918* (Ankara: Turk Tarih Kurumu, 2005), A. Defrance to Minister of Foreign Affairs Delcassé, November 21, 1914, 1:244.

39. A British force would have been in position to cut Ottoman lines of communication and supply to Iraq and Syria. As well, moving north from the southeast, lay the possibility of forming a joint front with Russia. However, as the eastern Mediterranean around Iskenderun was part of the territory France had earmarked for itself, it is reasonable to assume—despite Churchill's enthusiasm for a landing at Gallipoli—that French concerns about the establishment of a British military bridgehead in the eastern

Mediterranean affected Allied strategic thinking. Britain was the dominant power in the Middle East, and as subsequent events amply demonstrated, there was no guarantee that pledges made during the war would be upheld afterward. The possibility of a British military presence around Iskenderun and Dört Yol would surely have caused concern at the Quai d'Orsay

40. Atılgan/Moumdjian, *Archival Documents*, Istanbul to Ottoman Army General Headquarters, March 1–31, 1915, 86–118. The number and size of these Armenian brigades fluctuated during the war.

41. Hikmet Özdemir and Yusuf Sarınay, eds., *Türk-Ermeni Ihtilafı Belgeler/ Turkish-Armenian Conflict Documents* (Ankara: TBMM Kultur, Sanat ve Yayın Kurulu Yayınları 126, n.d.), Ottoman Army General Staff Headquarters to Department of Public Security, February 25, 1915, document 2.

42. Karpat, *Ottoman Population, 1830–1914*, "Summary of Ottoman Population, 1914," 188. The size of the Ottoman Armenian population has been a political football from the Congress of Berlin in 1878 to the present day. Justin McCarthy interprets both Ottoman census figures and Armenian estimates: "The Population of the Ottoman Armenians," in *The Armenians in the Late Ottoman Period*, ed. Türkkaya Ataöv (Ankara: Turkish Historical Society, 2001), 65–86. In *Crime of Numbers: The Role of Statistics in the Armenian Question, 1878–1918* (New Brunswick, NJ: Transaction Publishers, 2010), Fuat Dündar questions the reliability of the Ottoman census. There is an enormous difference between official census figures and the estimates of the Armenian patriarchate. Mutlu, "Late Ottoman Population and Its Ethnic Distribution," 23, concluded from a careful analysis of census figures that there was "no evidence supporting the patriarch's figures."

43. According to the Turkish General Staff archives, the strength of the Third Army on March 24, 1915, stood at 24,469 men and 860 officers. See Erickson, *Ordered to Die*, 64.

44. Atılgan/Moumdjian, *Archival Documents*, 98.

45. Ibid., 128

46. Reynolds, *Shattering Empires*, 144.

47. Atilgan/Moumdjian, *Archival Documents*, 98.

48. Özdemir and Sarınay, eds., *Turkish-Armenian Conflict Documents*, document 5, "Report of the Commission of Inquiry Invesgigating the Armenian Patriarch's Claims of Persecutions of Armenians," 16. See also the coded message sent to the general command from Hasankale, on April 22 dealing with the investigation of the claims of the patriarchate and the finding that "all the claims are nothing but lies and pretexts." See also *Arşiv Belgeleriyle Ermeni Faaliyetleri/Armenian Activities in the Archive Documents* (Ankara: Genel Kurmay Basin Evi, 2005), 1:124–125.

49. Erickson, *Ottomans and Armenians*, 221. See also Edward J. Erickson, "The Armenians and Ottoman Military Policy," *War in History* 15 no. 2 (2008):141–167.

50. *Arşiv Belgeleriyle*, 1:109–121.
51. Ibid., 119.
52. See, for example, the report of March 15 from Kemal, the *kaymakam* of Mahmudi in Van province, on the massacre of more than seventy villagers. They were shot, stabbed, bayonetted, beaten, and burnt in "kilns" (most probably bread ovens). Many of the women were raped before being killed, with other frightful atrocities described. *Arşiv Belgeleriyle*, 1:65–70.
53. The authors of the most detailed book on the Van uprising give April 20 as the starting date. See McCarthy et al., *The Armenian Rebellion at Van*, 200. Yektan Turkyilmaz writes that the fighting began on April 7, two days after the Armenian military committee ordered trenches to be dug in the Garden City and Citadel districts. See Yektan Turkyilmaz, "Rethinking Genocide: Violence and Victimhood in Eastern Anatolia, 1913–1915" (PhD diss., Department of Cultural Anthropology, Duke University, 2011). There can be no certainty as to when the first shots were fired in the city, perhaps a few days earlier, but by the 20th clearly the city was in the grip of a full-scale uprising.
54. McCarthy et. al., *The Armenian Rebellion at Van*, 198.
55. Quoted in Lewy, *The Armenian Massacres in Ottoman Turkey*, 97. Turkyilmaz, "Rethinking Genocide," who starts the uprising at an earlier date, writes that Cevdet Bey ordered a withdrawal from Van on May 3, with Armenian *druzhiny* volunteers and regular Russian forces entering the city between May 5 and 7. Numerous other sources give the date of withdrawal as May 16. The Van missionary, Grace Higley Knapp, in her diary, has the Russian forces entering the city on May 19. See *The Treatment of Armenians in the Otoman Empire 1915–1916, Documents Presented to Viscount Grey of Fallodon, Secretary of State for Foreign Affairs, by Viscount Bryce* (London: His Majesty's Stationery Office, 1916); and "The American Mission at Van: Narrative Printed Privately in the United States by Miss Grace Higley Knapp" (1915).
56. McCarthy et. al., *The Armenian Rebellion at Van*, 237.
57. See Halit Dündar Akarca, "The Russian Administration of the Occupied Ottoman Territories During the First World War, 1915–1917" (Master's thesis, Department of International Relations, Bilkent University, February 2002).
58. W. E. D. Allen and Paul Muratoff, *Caucasian Battlefields: A History of the Wars on the Turco-Caucasian Frontier, 1828–1921* (Cambridge: Cambridge University Press, 1953), 301.
59. Between 1978 and 1981, Hüseyin Çelik interviewed elderly survivors of the Van massacres. He published the interviews in a 1993 book, *Görenlerin Gözüyle Van'da Ermeni Mezalimi* [The Armenian Uprising in Van Through the Eyes of Witnesses]. For his summary of their accounts, see Çelik, "The 1915 Armenian Revolt in Van: Eyewitness Testimony," in Türkayya Ataöv, ed., *The Armenians in the Late Ottoman Period* (Ankara: Turkish

Historical Society, 2001), 87–108. The full statement by one of the survivors, Ibrahim Sargin, who described himself as the only child to survive the Zeve massacre, can be found in Justin McCarthy, et al., *The Armenian Rebellion at Van* (Salt Lake City: University of Utah Press, 2006), 247–251.

60. Turkyilmaz, "Rethinking Genocide," 267, from Katharine Strelsky and Catherine A. Wolkonsky, eds., *Out of the Past* (New York: Columbia University Press, 1981), quoting Alexandra Tolstoy's memoirs. The missionary referred to as "Sam" Sparrow was Ernest Alfred Yarrow. In 2005, while researching in Armenia, Yektan Turkyilmaz was arrested and charged with trying to take prohibited material out of the country. He was imprisoned for two months before being given a two-year suspended sentence and released.

61. Turkyilmaz, "Rethinking Genocide," 285.

62. Ibid., 314.

63. Ibid., 309–310.

64. Ibid., 317.

65. Ibid., 323.

66. Atilgan/Moumdjian, *Archival Documents*, Pallavicini to Foreign Minister, April 29, 1915, 166.

67. Clarence D. Ussher, *An American Missionary in Turkey: A Narrative of Adventures in Peace and in War* (Boston: Houghton Mifflin, 1917).

68. *The Treatment of Armenians in the Ottoman Empire 1915–1916*, vilayet of Van, no. 19, narrative of Mr A. Safrastian, December 2, 1915, as published in the Armenian journal *Ararat*, January 1916.

69. Ibid., vilayet of Van, no. 15, "The American Mission at Van. Narrative printed privately in the United States by Miss Grace Higley Knapp (1915)."

70. Taner Akçam, *A Shameful Act: The Armenian Genocide and the Question of Turkish Responsibility* (London: Constable, 2007), 146.

71. Ibid., 147.

72. Bryce and Toynbee, *The Treatment of Armenians in the Ottoman Empire*, Miss Knapp's diaries.

73. Ussher, *An American Missionary*, 314.

74. Clarence D. Ussher, "Dr. Ussher Told About Many Atrocities at Siege of Van: Turkish Outrages and Conspiracies by Germans Brought to Light," *Harvard Crimson*, May 3, 1917. Ussher's talk was given at a meeting of the Graduate School Society in Peabody Hall. www.thecrimson.com/article/1917/5/3/dr-ussher-told-about-many-atrocities.

75. Başak, *British Documents*, Molyneux-Seel to Lowther, Van, December 6, 1912, 63; and Mallett to Grey, Constantinople, January 6, 1914, 79

76. Ibid., Lieutenant Smith to Mallett, Van, June 10, 1914, 80–82.

77. Özdemir and Sarınay, eds., *Turkish-Armenian Conflict Documents*, no. 7, Minister of Interior to Governorates of Vilayets and Sancaks, April 24, 1915, 25–26.

78. Yusuf Sarınay, "What Happened on April 24, 1915? The Circular of April 24, 1915, and the Arrest of Armenian Committee Members in Istanbul," *International Journal of Turkish Studies* 14, nos. 1–2 (Fall 2008):78–79.
79. Ibid., 83n69. According to the Austrian consul in Trabzon, writing on May 5, a "huge quantity of arms and ammunition" was found in the Armenian Gregorian and Catholic churches, in the Armenian club, and in houses. Atılgan/Moumdjian, *Archival Documents*, 186.
80. Ibid., Austrian embassy to Foreign Ministry, Istanbul, April 29, 1915, 174.
81. Sarınay, "What Happened on April 24, 1915?" 77–78.
82. Ibid., 78, 83. Sarınay (83) quotes a government figure for the provinces of 252 arrested on April 24, in addition to the 235 arrested in Istanbul, but all numbers fluctuate according to the source or, in case of government documents, when the numbers were being counted.
83. *Turkish Armenian Conflict Documents*, no. 8, Ministry of the Interior to the Ankara Vilayet Governorate, April 25, 1915, 29.
84. Sarınay, "What Happened on April 24, 1915?" 79.
85. Ibid., 80.
86. Ibid., 81–82. Sarınay's article includes appendices translated from original Ottoman documents giving the names of all Armenians held at Cankiri and Ayaş. Human-rights lawyer Geoffrey Robertson writes of these events that on the night of April 24, several hundred Armenians "were seized and transported in ships to military prisons in Ankara"—an impossibility as Ankara is inland. No evidence is produced for his claim that "most" of these Armenians and thousands of others arrested in the provinces were subsequently executed without trial. See Geoffrey Robertson, *An Inconvenient Genocide: Who Now Remembers the Armenians?* (London: Biteback Publishing, 2014), 48. Carter Vaughn Findley, in *Turkey, Islam, Nationalism, and Modernity*, 210, also writes that on April 23–24, Enver ordered several hundred Armenians arrested "and executed." The question on the cover of the Robertson book is taken from a statement Adolf Hitler allegedly made on the eve of the Polish invasion. In fact, there is no proof that Hitler ever made any such remark. In diary extracts and notes of his speeches accepted as evidence at the Nuremberg trials, the Armenians are not mentioned. The account in which they do appear, written by an American journalist, was set aside by the prosecution on the grounds of insufficient reliability.
87. Raymond Kévorkian, *The Armenian Genocide: A Complete History* (London: I. B. Tauris, 2011), 528–529.
88. Özdemir and Sarınay, eds., *Turkish Armenian Conflict Documents*, no. 13, cipher message from Talat to the Kastamonu Vilayet Governorate, May 8, 1915, 42–43.
89. Kévorkian, *The Armenian Genocide*, 528–529.

90. *Arşiv Belgeleriyle Ermeni Faaliyetleri*/Armenian Activities in the Archive Documents, 3:209, 217, the evidence of Stephen's son "Abraham." Turkyilmaz, "Rethinking Genocide," 156, refers to a Hunchak plot to kill Talat. The plot was discovered on July 14, he writes, after which Hunchak offices were closed down and members of the organization arrested.

91. Kévorkian, *The Armenian Genocide*, 516, puts the number at 20 but Sarinay, "What happened on April 24, 1915?" 84n75, observes that two of the men were sentenced in name only as they were out of the country.

CHAPTER 13

1. Justice Hugo Black's arguments in Korematsu v. United States were identical to those of the Ottoman government in 1915. His starting point was Exclusion Order No. 54, which declared, "The successful prosecution of the war requires every possible protection against espionage and against sabotage to national defense material, national defense premises, and national defense utilities." The exclusion order was preceded by a curfew, which had been upheld in the Supreme Court after an appeal by an American citizen of Japanese origin "because we could not reject the finding of the military authorities that it was impossible to bring about a segregation of the disloyal from the loyal." The judgment that temporary exclusion of a whole group "was for the same reason a military imperative answers the contention that the exclusion was in the nature of group punishment based on antagonism to those of Japanese origin." Hardships were involved but "war is an aggregation of hardships," and when in conditions of modern warfare "our shores are threatened by hostile forces, the power to protect must be commensurate with the threatened danger." Calling the "relocation centers" concentration camps was unjustifiable, but regardless of their nature, "We are dealing specifically with an exclusion order. To cast this case into outlines of racial prejudice without reference to the real military dangers which were presented merely confuses the issue." Mr. Korematsu, from San Leandro, California, had not been excluded from the "military area" because of his "race" but because the U.S. was at war with Japan and because the urgency of the situation demanded the temporary segregation from the West Coast of all citizens of Japanese ancestry. About 120,000 Japanese-American citizens or residents were interned during the war. See Black, "Korematsu v. United States, 323 U.S. 214 (1944), Supreme Court, Opinion of the Court," (Ithaca, NY: Cornell Law School, Legal Information Institute), https://www.law.cornell.edu/supremecourt/text/323/214.

2. See Kamuran Gürün, *The Armenian File: The Myth of Innocence Exposed* (London: Rustum, Weidenfeld and Nicolson, 1985), 206 et. seq. for a summary of these decisions. See also Özdemir and Sarınay, eds., *Turkish Armenian Conflict Documents*, no. 26, confidential, Interior Minister to Prime Ministry, May 26, 195, 58–59.

3. *Arşiv Belgeleriyle*, 1:134–146.
4. Özdemir and Sarınay, eds., *Turkish-Armenian Conflict Documents*, 237.
5. Ibid., no. 63, Talat to various governorates and *sancaklar*, ordering a stop to the relocation of Catholic Armenians, August 3, 1915, 179. Also no. 72, Talat to "the governorates of various provinces and *sancaklar* on stopping the relocation of the Protestant Armenians," August 15, 1915, 200–201.
6. Ibid., no. 73, Talat to the governorates of various *valilikler* and *sancaklar*, August 15, 1915, 203.
7. Kemal Çiçek, in *The Great War and the Forced Migration of the Armenians* (Belfast: Athol Books, 2012), sums up the exemptions and the foreign reaction, 78–86.
8. Özdemir and Sarınay, eds., *Turkish Armenian Conflict Documents*, no. 38, Ministry of Education to the Governorates (*valilikler*) of Diyarbakir, Aleppo, Trabzon, Sivas, Bitlis, Elaziğ, Van, and the Maraş *sancak* on Settling Armenian Children in Orphanages, June 26, 1915, 118–119.
9. Ibid., no. 76, Intelligence Department, Supreme Military Command (General Staff) Headquarters to Interior Ministry, August 16, 1915, 209.
10. Ibid., no. 27, Interior Ministry to Çanakkale *mutasarriflik*, June 8, 1915, 90–91.
11. Çiçek, *The Great War and the Forced Migration*, 97.
12. Özdemir and Sarınay, eds., *Turkish Armenian Conflict Documents*, no. 133, Talat to Governorates, October 27, 1915, 353.
13. *Arşiv Belgeleriyle*, 1:159.
14. Bryce and Tonybee, *The Treatment of Armenians in the Ottoman Empire, 1915–1916*.
15. Ibid., ch. 18, "Vilayet of Aleppo," 139d.
16. Çiçek, *The Great War and the Forced Migration*, 206.
17. Münevver Güneş Eroğlu, "End of Relocation," ch. 4 in "Armenians in the Ottoman Empire According to Ikdam, 1914–1918" (Master's thesis, Department of History, Middle East Technical University, Ankara, 2003), 141 *et seq*.
18. Gürün, *The Armenian File*, 214.
19. Çiçek, in *The Great War and the Forced Migration*, 204, considering all the figures, arrives at his own estimate of about 600,000. In personal papers dealing with the numbers of Ottoman civilians uprooted by war, the Balkan War as well as the First World War, Talat arrived at the figure of 924,158 for Armenians "relocated" across the empire. See Murat Bardakçı *Talat Paşa'nın Evrak-ı Metrukesi* [Talat Paşa's Forgotten Papers] (Istanbul: Everest Yayınları, 2008), 77. Çiçek, *The Great War*, 206, observes, however, that this figure includes Armenians removed to the inner Anatolian provinces as well as those who fled to the Caucasus, amounting to "no less" than 300,000 people.
20. Bloxham, *The Great Game of Genocide*, 87.

21. Akçam, *A Shameful Act*, 162–164. The author's idiosyncratic approach to historical method has been subjected to two detailed critical reviews: Maxime Gauin, "'Proving' a 'Crime Against Humanity'?"a review of Taner Akçam, *The Young Turks' Crime against Humanity: The Armenian Genocide and Ethnic Cleansing in the Ottoman Empire* (Princeton, NJ: Princeton University Press, 2012), in *Journal of Muslim Minority Affairs* 35, no. 1 (2015):141–157; and Erman Şahin, "A Scrutiny of Akçam's Version of History and the Armenian Genocide," a review of Taner Akçam, *A Shameful Act: The Armenian Genocide and the Question of Turkish Responsibility* (New York: Metropolitan Books, 2006), in *Journal of Muslim Minority Affairs* 28, no. 2 (August 2008):303–319.

22. Akçam returns to his accusations in *Killing Orders: Talat Pasha's Telegrams and the Armenian Genocide* (London: Palgrave Macmillan, 2108). His source is the Armenian patriarchate in Jerusalem, where alleged copies of Ottoman documents are stored. None of the copies of Ottoman "documents" from this source have ever been shown to be authentic. Sean Patrick Smyth has written that far from being unearthed for the first time, as Akçam claims, one of the most incriminating telegrams was presented as evidence to the postwar tribunals in Istanbul and was even previously used in an article by Akçam and his mentor, Vahakn N. Dadrian. He finds problems with the dating, the language, and even the paper itself, concluding that the alleged telegram "cannot be taken at face value." See Smyth, "From Smoking Gun to Muddied Waters: The Alleged Telegraph of Bahaeddin Şakir," (Ankara: AVIM [Avrasya İncelemeleri Merkezi] Center for Eurasian Studies), June 5, 2017. www.avim.org.tr/en/Analiz/from-smoking-gun-to-muddied-waters-the-alleged-telegraph-of-bahaeddin-sakir. (Sean Patrick Smyth has contacted the author to point out that he should have referred to "telegram" in his article, rather than "telegraph." The Turkish word "telegraf" can refer to either, but telegram was correct.)

    In a meticulous examination of Akçam's clains, Ömer Engin Lütem and Yiğit Alpdogan demonstrate that the signatures on the "documents" Akçam uses are inconsistent with those on authentic Ottoman documents. See "Review Essay. *Killing Orders: Talat Pasa's Telegrams and the Armenian Genocide*," *Review of Armenian Studies* 37 (2018):45–82.

    Supporting Akçam's accusation that the CUP took a decision to wipe out the Armenians, Hans-Lukas Kieser writes in *Talaat Pasha: Father of Modern Turkey, Architect of Genocide* (Princeton: Princeton University Press, 2018), 261, that an "intent to kill" Armenians *en masse* was obvious by spring, 1915. Kieser's work has recently been subjected to a sharply critical assessment. See Yücel Güçlü's review essay of Kieser, *Killing Orders*, in *Journal of Muslim Minority Affairs* 38, no. 3 (2018):441–450.

    Kévorkian is even more specific than Kieser, if equally speculative, claiming a decision was taken sometime in March 20–25. See Raymond

Kévorkian, "The Extermination of Ottoman Armenians by the Young Turk Regime (1915–1916)," June 3, 2008. *SciencesPo. Violence de masse et résistance—réseau de recherche*, https://www.sciencespo.fr/mass-violence-war-massacre-resistance/fr/node/2646.

23. Armenian National Institute, www.armenian-genocide.org/talaat.html.
24. Ara Sarafian, *Talaat Pasha's Report on the Armenian Genocide, 1917* (London: Gomidas Institute, 2011), 8–10.
25. Göçek, *Denial of Violence*, 254.
26. Reynolds, *Shattering Empires*, 152–153.
27. Akçam, *A Shameful Act*, 126.
28. Ibid., 164, 181
29. Bloxham, *The Great Game of Genocide*, 86.
30. Ibid.
31. Karpat, *Ottoman Population*, 190.
32. Ali Rıza Eti, *Bir Onbaşının Doğu Cephesi Günlüğü*, 104
33. Ibid., 140.
34. Stanford J. Shaw, *From Empire to Republic: The Turkish War of National Liberation 1918–1922: A Documentary Study* (Ankara: Turk Tarih Kurumu, 2000), 1:61–62.
35. In February 1921, Aubrey Herbert, the former British intelligence officer, was asked by Sir Basil Thomson, assistant commissioner for crime at Scotland Yard and also director of intelligence at the Home Office, to go to Germany and interview Talat. This must have been in connection with the planned trials of close to 150 members of the wartime Ottoman government being held on Malta. Herbert had several meetings with Talat in the town of Hamm ("a miserable industrial village that seemed to be inhabited by potential suicides") and Düsseldorf. Talat defended his position on the Armenian question. He had already been sentenced to death by a court-martial in Istanbul, held under the auspices of the sultan's government, and a month after meeting Herbert was assassinated in Berlin by Soghomon Tehlirian, a Dashnak. The "Malta deportees" were never brought to trial. See Aubrey Herbert and Desmond MacCarthy eds., *Ben Kendim: A Record of Eastern Travel* (London: Hutchinson, 1924), 308–329.
36. Djemal Pasha, *Memories of a Turkish Statesman*, 279.
37. Özdemir and Sarınay, eds., *Turkish Armenian Conflict Documents*, no. 124, Şukru Bey to the Interior Ministry, October 22, 1915, 335.
38. Djemal Pasha, *Memories of a Turkish Statesman*, 280.
39. Erickson, *Ottomans and Armenians*, 212, writes that as an aspect of the counterinsurgency, the relocation was "arguably very effective."
40. Polat Safi, "The Ottoman Special Organization—*Teşkilat-i Mahsusa*: A Historical Assessment with Particular Reference to Its Operations Against British Occupied Egypt (1914–1916)" (Master's thesis, Department of History, Bilkent University, 2006).

41. Ibid., 125. Stanford Shaw gives the date for the name change as August 5, 1914. See *The Ottoman Empire in World War I*, 1:360.
42. Ibid., Safi, 128.
43. Shaw, *The Ottoman Empire in World War I*, 1:367.
44. Ibid., 373.
45. Ibid., 379.
46. Göçek, *Denial of Violence*, 20, writes that the *teşkilat* "carried out most of the mass killings outside of settled areas"; for Bloxham, in *The Great Game of Genocide*, 70, it became "an instrument of indiscriminate mass murder" in the development of a fully genocidal policy; for Taner Akçam, in *The Young Turks' Crimes Against Humanity: The Armenian Genocide and Ethnic Cleansing in the Ottoman Empire* (Princeton: Princeton University Press, 2011), 412, Teşkilat units were assigned "to carry out the annihilation of the Armenian convoys." For a comprehensive review of the origins, membership, and wartime activities of the organization, see Shaw, *The Ottoman Empire in World War I*, 1:353–456.
47. Safi, "The Ottoman Special Organization," 9.
48. Özdemir and Sarınay, eds., *Turkish-Armenian Conflict Documents*, no. 32, Talat, Cypher Message to Governorates of Diyarbakir, Elazığ and Bitlis, June 14, 1915, 107.
49. Ibid., document 55, Ministry of the Interior, Cipher Message to the Govenorate of Diyarbakir, July 12, 1915, 161.
50. Ibid., no. 97, Interior Ministry to Governorate of the Nigde *sancak*, September 6/7, 1915, 259.
51. Ibid., no. 101, Interior Ministry, Cypher Message to the Konya *valilik*, September 18, 1915, 267.
52. Ibid., no. 130, Talat, Interior Ministry, to Sivas *valilik*, October 24, 1915, 347.
53. Ibid., no. 131, Interior Ministry to the Sivas *valilik*, October 26, 1915, 349.
54. Ibid., no. 146, Talat to Sivas *valilik*, November 17, 1915, 389.
55. The costs of the relocation were augmented by the contributions of provincial governors. See Çiçek, *The Great War*, 98.
56. Kieser writes that one of Talat's friends knew that his talk of investigative commissions that preceded the trials were an "evasion." Hans-Lukas Kieser, *Talaat Pasha*, 280. The evidence of courts-martial, convictions, and death sentences indicates otherwise.
57. See *Arşiv Belgeleriyle*, Foreign Ministry to Ministry of Defence, classified, "about the delegations to be sent to the provinces," September 30, 1915, 1:234.
58. For details of the trials see Yusuf Sarınay, "The Relocations (Tehcir) of Armenians and the Trials of 1915–16," *Middle East Critique* 20, no. 3 (Fall 2011):299–315. Maxime Gauin refers to a *Washington Post* report of June 4, 1916: "Turks Avenge Armenians—Fifty-One Muslim Soldiers Are

Shot for Mistreating Christians." It seems reasonable to connect these executions with the 67 sentenced to death at the courts-martial. See Gauin, "Review Essay: 'Proving' a 'Crime Against Humanity'?" 157n85.

59. The consul's report to the U.S. government—"Report of Leslie A. Davis, American consul, formerly at Harput, Turkey, on the work of the American consulate at Harput since the beginning of the present war"—has been incorporated into Leslie A. Davis, *The Slaughterhouse Province: An American Diplomat's Report on the Armenian Genocide, 1915–1917* (New Rochelle, NY: Aristide D. Caratzas, 1990), edited with an introduction by Susan K. Blair. Needless to say, nowhere does Davis use the word "genocide." Harput is now a village overshadowed by its near neighbour, Elazığ, lying in the province of the same name. Lake Gölcük is now Hazar Gölü.

60. Quoted in Lewy, *The Armenian Massacres in Ottoman Turkey*, 213–214.

61. That official, George Montgomery, estimated that 594,000 Armenians were still living in the Ottoman Empire, in addition to 450,000 in the Caucasus, and 60,000 in Persia. See Lewy, *The Armenian Massacres*, 239.

62. Bloxham, *The Great Game of Genocide*, 1.

63. Ben Kiernan, *Blood and Soil: A World History of Genocide and Extermination from Sparta to Darfur* (Melbourne: Melbourne University Press, 2008), 415.

64. Göçek, *Denial of Violence*, 1.

65. Kévorkian, "The Extermination of Ottoman Armenians."

66. Gürün, *The Armenian File*, 277, puts the figure at no more than 300,000. Justin McCarthy arrived at 584,000 but modified his estimates upward by a further 250,000 if recent Armenian patriarchate estimates are accurate. Historically, as far back as the Congress of Berlin, they have not been. See Justin McCarthy, "The Population of the Ottoman Armenians," in Ataöv, *The Armenians in the Late Ottoman Period*, 65–85.

67. Arnold Toynbee, *The Western Question in Greece and Turkey: A Study in the Contact of Civilisations* (London: Constable 1922), 342.

68. Mason, "Central Kurdistan," 331.

69. *The Arab Bulletin* 4:1919, no. 113, July 17, 1919, 121.

70. See the two-volume collection *Ermeniler Tarafından Yapılan Katliam Belgeleri (1914–1919)* and *(1919–1921)* (Ankara: Prime Ministerial State Archives General Directorate, 2001) translated into English as "Documents on Massacre [*sic*] Perpetrated by Armenians." These hundreds of documents include the affidavits of villagers; depositions of members of village councils; reports of army commanders and inspectors; reports of provincial governors and deputies; accounts of judges and prosecutors; and some extracts from diaries kept by foreigners. Vol. 1 *(1914–1919)*, 375–377, gives a tabulated figure of 363,141 "Turks" (the dead would have included Kurds and Muslims of other ethnic backgrounds) massacred in these years. Vol. 2 *(1919–1921)*, 1053–1054, gives a tabulated total for these years of 154,964. Accordingly, the 1914–1921 total is 518,105.

71. Göçek, *Denial of Violence*, 216.
72. From Altınay's *Kafkas Yollarında: Hatiralar ve Tahassüsler* [On the Caucasian Roads: Memories and Feelings], first published in 1919 and quoted in Ismet Binark, ed., *Archive Documents about the Atrocities and Genocide Inflicted Upon Turks by Armenians* (Ankara: Grand National Assembly of Turkey, 2002), 37.
73. Ibid., 39.
74. Ibid.
75. Justin McCarthy, *Turks and Armenians: Nationalism and Conflict in the Ottoman Empire* (Madison, WI: Turko-Tatar Press, 2015), 176.
76. Ibid., 171–172.
77. Justin McCarthy located a draft copy of the report in the U.S. National Archives. See http://louisville.edu/a-s/history/turks/Niles_and_Sutherland.pdf. Also see "The Report of Niles and Sutherland: An American Investigation of Eastern Anatolia after World War I," 11th Türk Tarih Kongresi, Ankara, September 5–9, 1990 (Ankara: Türk Tarihi Kurumu, 1994):1809–53.
78. See McCarthy, *Turks and Armenians*, 184–185, for Armenian losses, and Allen and Muratoff, *Caucasian Battlefields*, 437, for the 75-percent estimate.
79. Reynolds, *Shattering Empires*, 158. See also Twerdo Khlebof, "War Journal of the Second Russian Fortress Artillery Regiment of Erzeroum from Its Formation until the Recapture of Erzeroum by the Ottoman Army, March 12th, 1918, Translated from the Original Russian Manuscript, 1919," posted by McCarthy, http://louisville.edu/a-s/history/turks/Khlebof%20War%20Journal.pdf. Mehmet Perinçek has done extensive research in the Russian archives and translated many documents into English and Turkish relating to Armenian involvement in the war. See his *150 Belgede Ermeni Meselesi: Rus Devlet Arşivlerinden* (Istanbul: Kırmızı Kedi Yayinevi, 2012).

CHAPTER 14

1. The Treaty of London (April 26, 1915), signed between the Triple Entente (Russia, Britain, France) and the Kingdom of Italy, had committed the three powers only to giving Italy "a just share of the Mediterranean region adjacent to the province of Adalia."
2. In Turkish: Seddülbahir Çikarması.
3. Erickson, *Ordered to Die*, 185.
4. Michael A. Reynolds, "Buffers Not Brethren: Young Turk Military Policy in the First World War and the Myth of Panturanism," *Past and Present* 203 (May 2009):138. See also Yalçin Murgul, "Baku Expedition of 1917–1918: A Study of the Ottoman Policy Towards the Caucasus" (Master's thesis, Department of History, Bilkent University, 2007).
5. Başak, *British Documents*, "Supreme War Council, British Section Note on the Military Situation in Armenia," December 3, 1917, 124–125.

6. Ibid.
7. Başak, *British Documents*, "Future Settlement of Transcaucasia," General Staff, War Office, December 5, 1918, 177.
8. Ibid.
9. Ibid., General Shore to DMI [Department of Military Intelligence?], London, December 20, 1917, 130.
10. According to the U.S. Bureau of Statistics consumer price index, 2018 prices were 1,562.96 percent higher than in 1918. Taking other small variables into account, the purchasing power of $230,000 in 1918 would have amounted to $382,480,800 in 2018. See www.in2013dollars.com/1918-dollars-in-2018.
11. Başak, *British Documents*, "Memorandum Regarding the Support Afforded to the Armenians," General Staff, War Office, April 29, 1918, 146–147.
12. Ibid.
13. Erickson, *Ordered to Die*, 186.
14. Bülent Gökay, "The Battle for Baku (May–September 1918): A Peculiar Episode in the History of the Caucasus," *The Turkish Yearbook* 25 (1995):31–32. www.politics.ankara.edu.tr/yearbookdizin/dosyalar/MMTY /25/2_bulent_gokay.pdf.
15. Audrey L. Altstadt, *The Azerbaijani Turks: Power and Identity under Russian Rule* (Stanford: Hoover Institution Press, 1992), 86.
16. Ibid. 86, quoting the British Vice-Consul in Baku.
17. Ibid.
18. The commissars and Bolshevik troops left Baku aboard thirteen ships on July 31 but were stopped at sea and returned to Baku on August 16. On September 14, in the turmoil following the Turkish takeover of Baku, Shaumian and the other commissars either escaped or were freed by sympathizers and sailed to Krasnovodsk where they were arrested and executed a week later.
19. See Edward J. Lemon, "Dunsterforce or Dunsterfarce? Re-evaluating the British Mission to Baku, 1918," *First World War Studies* 6, no. 2 (2015):133–149.
20. See Artin H. Arslanian, "Dunsterville's Adventures: A Reappraisal," *International Journal of Middle East Studies* 12, no. 2 (1980):199–216.
21. Gökay, "The Battle for Baku," 35.
22. Major-General L. C. Dunsterville, *The Adventures of Dunsterforce* (London: Edward Arnold, 1920) 10.
23. Dunsterville, *The Adventures of Dunsterforce*, 129.
24. Ibid., 233.
25. Ibid., 279.
26. Ibid., 237.
27. Ibid., 261.
28. Ibid., 279.
29. Ibid., 317.

30. Erickson, *Ordered to Die*, 200.

31. *The Arab Bulletin*, 4:1919, bulletins 108–114, no. 113, July 17, 1919, "Kurdistan," 119–122. The intelligence officer was Captain C. L. (Leonard) Woolley, who had excavated with T. E. Lawrence at Carchemish and later uncovered the royal tombs at Ur, in Iraq, after the war.

32. Ibid., 119.

33. Eleftheria Daleziou, "Britain and the Greek-Turkish War and Settlement of 1919–1923: The Pursuit of Security by 'Proxy' in Western Asia Minor" (PhD diss., University of Glasgow, 2002), 63.

34. Major General James G. Harbord, *Conditions in the Near East: Report of the American Military Mission to Armenia* (Washington, D.C.: U.S. Government Printing Office, 1920), 19.

35. Ibid., 23.

36. Not the Anglo-Persian treaty of 1907, which divided Iran into Russian and British "spheres of influence," but the agreement signed on August 9, 1919, giving Britain significant control over the Iranian government and greatly strengthening its strategic position at the top of the Persian Gulf.

37. Lloyd E. Ambrosius, "Wilsonian Diplomacy and Armenia: The Limits of Power and Ideology," in *America and the Armenian Genocide of 1915*, ed. Jay Winter (New York: Cambridge University Press, 2003), 134.

38. Karpat, *Ottoman Population*, "Ottoman Population 1914," 170–187. The demographic problem was the same as that faced by the Zionists in Palestine, with the important exception that the Armenians were native to the country.

39. Robert F. Zeidner, *The Tricolor over the Taurus: The French in Cilicia and Vicinity, 1918–1922* (Ankara: Turkish Historical Society, 2005), 50–51.

40. Ibid., 124.

41. Zeidner, *The Tricolor over the Taurus*, 95–96, including reference to an Armenian estimate in late 1920 that puts the number of Armenians in the region at 250,000.

42. Ibid., 176.

43. Ibid., 78–79.

44. Yücel Güçlü, *Armenians and the Allies in Cilicia, 1914–1923* (Salt Lake City: University of Utah Press, 2010), 118.

45. Ibid., 121.

46. Ibid., 124.

47. For documentary evidence of French displeasure with the Armenians see Maxime Gauin, "How to Create a Problem of Refugees: The Evacuation of Cilicia by France and the Flow of Armenian Civilians (1921–1922)," *Review of Armenian Studies* 67, no. 5 (2012):67–102.

48. Zeidner, *The Tricolor over the Taurus*, 181.

49. Shaw, *From Empire to Republic* 3, part 2, 1393–1401, for his summary of the battle for the town.

50. Daleziou, "Britain and the Greek-Turkish war," 29.
51. Bilal N. Şimsir ed., *Ingiliz Belgererinde Ataturk/British Documents on Atatürk, 1919–1938: April–December 1920* (Ankara: Turkish Historical Society, 2000), notes of conversation between the British and Italian Prime Ministers in Lucerne, August 22, 1920, 2:283.
52. Ibid., Earl Curzon to Lord Hardinge, Foreign Office, June 13, 1921, 3:380.
53. Ibid., conclusions of a meeting of the British Cabinet, November 1, 1921, 4:46–50.
54. Ibid., 4:127.

CHAPTER 15
1. Ekıncı, "The Origins of the 1897 Ottoman-Greek War: A Diplomatic History" (Master's thesis, Department of History, Bilkent University, 2006), 26.
2. Ashmead Bartlett, *The Battlefields of Thessaly*, 11–12.
3. David Barchard, "The Fearless and Self-Reliant Servant: The Life and Career of Sir Alfred Biliotti (1833–1915), an Italian Levantine in British Service," *SMEA (Studi miceni ed egeo-anatolici)* 48 (2006):5–53.
4. Germany and Austria-Hungary subsequently withdrew their ships.
5. Ekıncı, "The Origins of the 1897 Ottoman-Greek War: A Diplomatic History," 29.
6. Ashmead Bartlett, *The Battlefields of Thessaly*, 18. The hyphen is dropped from the author's name in the title of the book.
7. Barchard, "The Fearless and Self-Reliant Servant," 31.
8. Ashmead Bartlett, *The Battlefields of Thessaly*, 19.
9. Barchard, "The Fearless and Self-Reliant Servant," 31.
10. Ashmead Bartlett, *The Battlefields of Thessaly*, 19–20.
11. Ibid., 21.
12. Barchard, "The Fearless and Self-Reliant Servant," 29.
13. For further background on Crete from the late nineteenth century until 1913, see Sinan Kuneralp, ed., *Ottoman Diplomatic Documents on the Origins of World War One: The Final Stage of the Cretan Question 1899–1913* (Istanbul: Isis Press, 2009).
14. Barchard, "The Fearless and Self-Reliant Servant," 39.
15. Quoted in Stavrianos, *The Balkans Since 1453*, 471.
16. Ekıncı, "The Origins of the 1897 Ottoman-Greek War," 65
17. As the king had refused to join the Allied war effort, the accusation was inevitable but probably unfair and certainly carried too far. The king's dynastic connections were Danish, Russian, Prussian, and English, as well as German. Constantine's wife Sophie was the granddaughter of Queen Victoria and the sister of Victoria's grandson, Kaiser Wilhelm, neatly displaying the dynastic complications of the war.
18. The word used by Daleziou in "Britain and the Greek-Turkish War."

19. Claims have been made that Greeks were the majority within the plurality, but Ottoman population figures for the administrative district of Aydın (including Izmir) in 1914 were the following: Muslims 100,356, Greeks 73,676, and Armenians 10,061. See Karpat, *Ottoman Population, 1813–1914*, 174.

20. Daleziou, "Britain and the Greek-Turkish War," 146.

21. Shaw, *From Empire to Republic* 2:491.

22. Daleziou, "Britain and the Greek-Turkish War," 66.

23. Ibid., 119.

24. Şimşir, ed., *British Documents on Atatürk*, vol. 1, no. 141, Allied Conference, 10 Downing St., March 3, 1920, 421.

25. Ibid., no. 145, Allied conference, 10 Downing St., March 5, 1920, 434.

26. Şimşir, ed., *British Documents on Atatürk*, vol. 2, no. 66, Inter-Allied Conference Held at the Villa Fraineuse, Spa, July 7, 1920, 187.

27. Ibid., no. 102, Notes of a Conversation between the British and Italian Prime Ministers, Lucerne, August 22, 1920, 283.

28. Ibid., no. 189, Conference of Representatives of British, French and Italian Governments, 10 Downing St., December 3, 1920, 11:30 a.m., 439.

29. Ibid., no. 190, Notes of a Conference between Representatives of British, French and Italian Governments, 10 Downing St., December 3, 445. In this context of bargaining, Lloyd George's involvement in an attempt to bribe Enver out of the war is ironic. Sedat Çilingir has dug up fascinating material from the Lloyd George papers dealing first with an approach to Talat Paşa through the Ottoman legation in Switzerland and then through more focused dealings early in 1917 involving Enver's secretary, the arms manufacturer Basil Zaharoff and Sir Vincent Caillard, chairman of the Vickers arms company. See Çilingir, "Lloyd George and the Dissolution of the Ottoman Empire" (PhD diss., Department of History, Middle East Technical University, Ankara, 2007). The triangular relationship among Lloyd George, Zaharoff, and Venizelos sits at the center of this story.

30. His interests included history, philosophy, literature, and religion. Even at the height of the war (1916–1917), he was taking detailed notes from the books he was reading. See George W. Gawrych, *The Young Atatürk: From Ottoman Soldier to Statesman of Turkey* (London: I. B. Tauris, 2013), 55–56.

31. Şimşir, ed., *British Documents on Atatürk*, vol. 3, no. 259, "Extracts from British Prime Minister's Speech of August 16, 1921," Prime Minister's Speech, 602.

32. Ibid., vol 5, no. 149, Tyrrell to Curzon, Reporting on a Conversation with an American Journalist, September 5, 1923, 261.

33. Shaw, *From Empire to Republic* 2:490.

34. John Presland, *Deedes Bey: A Study of Sir Wyndham Deedes, 1883–1923* (London: Macmillan, 1942), 308.

35. By the end of 1919, the expeditionary force had been named the Army of Asia Minor and increased to about 60,000 men.

36. Çağrı Erhan, *Greek Occupation of Izmir and Adjoining Territories: Report of the Inter-Allied Commission of Inquiry (May–September 1919), SAM Papers* no. 2/99 (Ankara: Centre for Strategic Research, 1999), 7. See also Shaw, *From Empire to Republic*, 2:501–502.
37. Shaw, *From Empire to Republic*, 2:503.
38. Erhan, *Greek Occupation of Izmir and Adjoining Territories*, 7.
39. Shaw, *From Empire to Republic*, 2:503–504.
40. Ibid., 2:505–506.
41. Noel Edward Noel-Buxton, a seasoned campaigner for the aspirations of Balkan Christians, and Charles Roden Buxton had traveled to Bulgaria to persuade the government to remain neutral. Failing in this attempt, they traveled to Bucharest and met King Carol at the palace the night before he died. At the funeral, Hasan Tahsin, who had traveled from Istanbul, shot the brothers, wounding Noel in the jaw and Charles in the lung. Tahsin was sentenced to five years in jail but released after a year when the Germans occupied Bucharest. Noel visited him in prison and, speaking French, established some kind of rapport with his would-be assassin, later sending him a book and a rug. See Robert Vogel, "Noel Buxton: The 'Trouble-Maker' and His Papers," *Fontanus* 3 (1990):131–150. www.Fontanus.mcgill.ca/article/viewFile/37/38.
42. There are different versions of this event. Some sources say two *evzones,* named as Basil Delaris and George Papakostas, were killed. Consulted on these events, Mr. Uğur Belger, an Izmir historian, named a third victim, "Lieutenant Yannis," the standard-bearer, and the son of an Izmir *meyhaneci* (fish restaurant owner). Stanford Shaw refers only to "someone running in front of the *evzone* brigade carrying a Greek flag [who] fell dead," which suggests he may have been a civilian. Shaw also writes that Hasan Tahsin was not shot but beaten to death. Thirty-one when he died, Hasan Tahsin was born in Mustafa Kemal's home city of Salonica. His real name was Osman Nevres, but as a Teşkilat agent he traveled in Europe under the name of Hasan Tahsin. He had lived on the left bank in Paris where he studied social sciences at the Sorbonne and came under the influence of the socialism of Jean Jaures. At the time of his death, he was a journalist writing for *Hukuk i–Beşir* (Human Rights) newspaper. In 1974, President Fahri Korutürk unveiled the "first shot monument" (*ilk kurşun anıtı*) in Izmir's Konak square, dedicated to Hasan Tahsin and other "martyrs" killed on May 15, including *miralay* (colonel) Süleyman Fethi Bey, reportedly bayonetted twenty-two times for refusing to chant, "Vito Venizelos! (Long live Venizelos)." See Shaw, *From Empire to Republic* 2:508. Thanks to Uğur Belger of Izmir and Nuri Yildirim of Ankara for help with these details.
43. Çağrı Erhan, *Greek Occupation of Izmir*, 8.
44. Shaw gives a figure of 3,402. *From Empire to Republic*, 2:511.
45. Andrew Mango, *Atatürk* (London: John Murray, 1999), 217

46. General George Milne also drew the line of Greek occupation around Izmir.
47. Şimşir, ed., *British Documents on Atatürk*, vol. I, no. 149, Notes of an Allied Conference, with Venizelos Present, March 10, 1920, 444–452.
48. *Efe* has the meaning of a romantic bandit chief, colorfully dressed, well-armed, and brave, corresponding to the romanticized *haiduk* brigands of the Balkans. The *zeybekler* were his armed followers, usually young men from the villages. To this day, the dance they performed, the *zeybek*, is part of Turkey's folkloric tradition.
49. *British Documents on Atatürk*, vol. 5, no. 159, Henderson to Curzon, Constantinople, November 7, 1923, enc. Annual Report for Turkey, 1922, 285. The whole report continues between 274–355.
50. Ibid., 285–286.
51. Ibid., 350.
52. Mango, *Atatürk*, 345.
53. Ibid., 345. In 1992, the Greek Orthodox Church declared the archbishop a martyr and canonized him.
54. Arguments over who started the fire continue more than a century later. Differing claims have been made by consuls, missionaries, foreign or local businessmen, Allied military figures, and Turkish authorities. Armenians and Greeks are said to have threatened to burn Izmir to the ground rather than see it fall back into the hands of the Turks. Some sources blame just the Armenians. Others blame Turkish soldiers allegedly seen pouring petrol or kerosene into the streets to spread the blaze, the theory being that Turks wanted to expunge "infidel Smyrna" from the map, but to what degree could the Turkish nationalist government be held responsible? A neutral source here is the joint U.S.-Turkish commission established to settle the claims of American citizens for the loss of property in the fire and elsewhere in the Ottoman Empire during the war. Created on December 4, 1923, the commission had two American and two Turkish members. It issued its findings on October 13, 1934, when it recommended that the Turkish government pay the U.S. $1.3 million in the settlement of all claims. This was agreed by the two governments on October 25. The commission was presented with 800 claims, many of which it disallowed for one reason or another. In its appraisal of the situation in Izmir, it was stated that the American delegation to the commission "at no time took the position that Turkish authorities directed the destruction of the city." The commission did not believe that claims intended to prove direct responsibility for the actions of soldiers would stand up before an international tribunal. It referred to a case heard in a British court of appeal, involving claims made by the Guardian Assurance Company, in which the judge stated that "to my mind the kind of suggestion that the victorious Turkish Army sacked and burnt Smyrna has no foundation at all." Having regained Izmir

after three years of war, it would be "the very last desire" of the nationalists to burn it down. On the contrary, the Turkish high command had taken steps to maintain order, including dispatch of the fire brigade to put the fire out. Maynard B. Barnes, the U.S. vice-consul at Izmir, however, thought the nationalists "could have maintained order in the city had they so desired" and thus were to blame, writing later, however, "I do not believe it was the desire of the Turkish officials and of the better class Turks of the city to see any portion of Smyrna destroyed, even though it be Greek and Armenian quarters." With regard to the claim that the Turkish authorities "could have maintained order," it must be remembered that the army had only been in Izmir for four days when the fire started and remained far from exerting control over the entire city. See Fred K. Nielsen, *American-Turkish Claims Settlement: Under the Agreement of December 24, 1923, and Supplemental Agreements between the United States and Turkey, Opinions and Reports* (Washington, D.C.: U.S. Government Printing Office, 1937), 24–33. Mr. Nielsen was one of the commissioners. The report runs to 816 pages. Thanks to Fatma Sarıkaya of Ankara for providing a copy of this important source.

55. In the novel *Birds Without Wings* (2004), Louis de Bernières recreates the complex but peaceful relationships that prevailed between Greeks and Turks down the Aegean coast before the ambitions of politicians and the wars they launched destroyed their world.

56. Çağrı Erhan, *Greek Occupation of Izmir*, 9. The contemporary Turkish view of these events is given in *Greek Atrocities in the Vilayet of Smyrna (May to July 1919): Inedited [sic] Documents and Evidence of English and French Officers.* (Lausanne: Permanent Bureau of the Turkish Congress, 1919).

57. Erhan, *Greek Occupation*, 29–52.

58. On August 15, the Greek authorities responded to criticism by setting up courts-martial for those accused of criminal acts in Izmir. They convicted seventy-four people, including Greeks, Turks, Armenians, and "one Jew." Three of them were sentenced to death.

59. Erhan, *Greek Occupation*, 9–10.

60. Michael Llewellyn Smith, *Ionian Vision: Greece in Asia Minor, 1919–1922* (London: Hurst, 1973), 208.

61. Erhan, *Greek Occupation*, 51.

62. UK Parliamentary Papers, Turkey No. 1 (1921) *Reports on Atrocities in the Districts of Yalova and Guemlik and in the Ismid Peninsula* (London: His Majesty's Stationery Office), Cmd. 1478. See also Shaw, *From Empire to Republic* 2:521–537.

63. Maurice Gehri, "Mission d'enquete en Anatolie (12–22 Mai 1921)," in *Revue internationale de la croix rouge* 3, no. 31 (July, 15, 1921), quoted in Shaw, *From Empire to Republic* 2:526, and Arnold J. Toynbee, *The Western Question in Greece and Turkey: A Study in the Contact of Civilisations* (London: Constable, 1922), 278.

64. Gingeras, *Sorrowful Shores*, 120.
65. The *New York Times* article was an account from a representative of the American Committee for Relief in the Near East of how Greeks between Sinop and Ordu on the Black Sea coast had been "parboiled" in Turkish baths and then turned out half-clad into the snow to die of pneumonia and other ills.
66. Toynbee, *The Western Question in Greece and Turkey*, 266.
67. Ibid., 300 *et seq*.
68. Ibid., 297.
69. Ibid., 297–298.
70. Ibid., 297–298. In 1924, Toynbee's newspaper reports and his book cost him his Greek-endowed Koraes Chair in Modern Greek and Byzantine History at King's College, the University of London, when he was compelled under pressure to step down. Richard Clogg has written a book on the controversy, *Politics and the Academy: Arnold Toynbee and the Koraes Chair* (London: Frank Cass, 1986).
71. Toynbee, *The Western Question in Greece and Turkey*, 316.
72. Ibid., 282–283.
73. Ibid., 277.
74. Shaw, *From Empire to Republic* 4:1710.
75. Ibid., 1710–1716.
76. Ibid., 1700.
77. Ibid., see 1751–1752.
78. Şimşir, ed., *British Documents on Atatürk*, vol. 4, no. 215, Notes of Conference between Poincaré and Curzon at the Quai d'Orsay, September 20, 1922, 455.
79. Ibid., no. 217, Notes of Conference between French President, British Foreign Secretary and Italian Ambassador to France, Quai d'Orsay, September 23, 1922, Continuation of Previous Discussions, 463. Two British admirals were present for part of the meeting.
80. Curzon had envisaged the establishment of a buffer state in eastern Thrace under the control of the League of Nations.
81. *British Documents on Atatürk*, vol. 4, no. 243, Hadinge to Foreign Office, September 22, 1922, Telegraphic, "following from Lord Curzon," 512.
82. Ibid., no. 249, Churchill to the British Cabinet, September 23, 1922, "The Turco-Greek Situation. Co-operation of the Dominions," 530–542. The telegram from Governor-General with the message from Hughes to Lloyd George, 537–540, dated September 20.
83. Ibid, 597.
84. Shaw, *From Empire to Republic* 4:1754.

CHAPTER 16

1. The Pontic Greeks, with their distinctive culture, shaped as it was by the geography, demographics, and politics of the Black Sea region, had tended

to support Russia in its wars with the Ottoman Empire. The First World War and its aftermath were no exceptions. Russia had stimulated insurgency among the Pontic Greeks during the war. Following the landing of the Greek army at Izmir in 1919, the region was thrown into turmoil amid attempts to establish a Pontic Greek republic. Branches of Greek national societies were established. The Allied powers occupying Istanbul allowed Greek ships to pass through the Bosporus into the Black Sea to land arms and bombard the coast. National societies were established with the active support of senior Greek ecclesiastics. The activities of Greek insurgents led finally to the decision of the government in Ankara (June 9, 1921) to transfer all men between the ages of 15 and 50 to the interior. This was followed by an edict three days later to move the Greek population completely from the entire coastal region, which had been declared a war zone on June 3. General Nurettin Paşa, former governor of Izmir (and accused of handing over Greek Orthodox Church Metropolitan Chrysostomos to the mob that murdered him) was given responsibility for suppressing insurgent bands on the Black Sea coast and overseeing the "relocation" of the population, "in the process killing hundreds and burning many of their villages to the ground." According to a report tabled in the Turkish Grand National Assembly (GNA), 7,000 houses had been destroyed and 5,000 Greeks killed. Sent for trial on charges of cruelty and misconduct, Nurettin Paşa was eventually acquitted on the grounds that he had only done what was necessary to suppress a dangerous revolt that threatened the Turkish national cause. See Shaw's summary of these events, *From Empire to Republic* 2:582–596, from which the references to Nurettin Paşa are taken. See also Teoman Ertugrul Tulun, *The Pontus Narrative and Hate Speech* (Ankara: Centre for Eurasian Studies, 2017); for a Greek perspective, Konstantin Fotiadis, "The Pontian Genocide: From the Time of the Young Turks to the Advent of Mustafa Kemal," *AHIF Policy Journal* 3 (Winter 2011–12): http://ahiworld.serverbox.net/AHIFpolicyjournal/pdfs/Volume3Winter/06.pdf. As is always the case in these conflicted narratives, there is no agreement on numbers or precisely what happened.

2. For different interpretations of this event, see Dilek Güven, "Riots against the non-Muslims of Turkey: 6/7 September 1955 in the Context of Demographic Engineering," *European Journal of Turkish Studies* 12 (2011): https://ejts.revues.org/4538; also Alfred de Zayas, "The Istanbul Pogrom of 6–7 September 1955, in the Light of International Law," *Genocide Studies and Prevention* 2, no. 2 (2007):137–154.

3. Abdülmecid II was an accomplished artist, producing some outstanding examples of late Ottoman art, including the seascape *Sis* (Mist), influenced by the poem of the same name by the Ottoman man of letters, Tevfet Fikret, and portraits of his first wife Şehsuvar and his daughter Hanzade.

4. These events are summarized in *British Documents on Atatürk*, vol. 5, 274–355, enc. in no. 159, annual report on Turkey for 1922.

5. Adem Günaydin, "The Return and Resettlement of the Relocated Armenians (1918–1920)" (Master's thesis in Middle East Studies, Graduate School of Social Sciences, Middle East Technical University, Ankara, 2007), 19.
6. Ibid., 24–51.
7. Mehmet Polatel, "Turkish State Formation and the Distribution of the Armenian Abandoned Properties from the Ottoman Empire to the Republic of Turkey (1915–1930)" (Master's thesis, Comparative Studies in History and Society, Koç University, 2009), 120.
8. Polatel, "Turkish State Formation," 161. Irrespective of the crimes that were or may have been committed, the Istanbul trials were established in a city under occupation and run by a government cooperating with the occupation authorities against the nationalist movement. After conviction, Kemal Bey was executed in Beyazit square on April 10, 1919, and buried in Kadiköy with great ceremony. His guilt was rejected by the national government. On October 14, 1922, he was declared a martyr by the Grand National Assembly, and in the eyes of Turks he remains a martyr today.
9. Ibid., 152–156.
10. Ibid., 183. On the issues raised in this study, see also Uğur Ümit Üngör and Mehmet Polatel, *Confiscation and Destruction: The Young Turk Seizure of Armenian Property* (London: Continuum, 2011).
11. Yuücel Yanıkdağ, *Healing the Nation*, 225.
12. Ibid., 232.

EPILOGUE
1. These figures are given in Polat Safi, "The Ottoman Special Organization," 25.
2. Ataman, *Harp ve Esaret—Doğu Cephesi'nden Sibiriya'ya*, 380–384
3. Önal, *Tuğgeneral Ziya Yergök'un Anıları*, 249–250.
4. Ali Rıza Eti, prepared for publication by Gönül Eti, *Bir Onbaşının Doğu Cephesi*, vii–ix.
5. Gürsoy Solmaz, *İkinci Kuşak Anılarında Erzurum ve Civarında Ermeni Zulmü* [Armenian Oppression in Erzurum and its Surroundings According to Second Generation Memoirs], *Yeni Turkiye* 60 (2014):1–29. Many thanks to Mehmet Oğuzhan Tulun for digging up and translating this and the previous passages.

Bibliography

Aaronsohn, Alexander. *With the Turks in Palestine*. Boston: Houghton Mifflin, 1916.

Ahmed, Feroz. *From Empire to Republic: Essays on the Late Ottoman Empire and Modern Turkey*. 2 vols. Istanbul: Bilgi University Press, 2008.

———. *The Making of Modern Turkey*. London: Routledge, 1993.

———. "The Late Ottoman Empire." In *The Great Powers and the End of the Ottoman Empire*, edited by Marian Kent, 5–30. London: Allen and Unwin, 1984.

Ajay, Nicholas Z. "Mount Lebanon and the Wilayah of Beirut, 1914–1918: The War Years." PhD diss., Department of History, Georgetown University, 1973.

Akarca, Halit Dündar. "The Russian Administration of the Occupied Ottoman Territories during the First World War, 1915–1917." Master's thesis, Department of International Relations, Bilkent University, 2002.

Akçam, Taner. "Conversation with Philip Adams." *Late Night Live*. ABC (Australian Broadcasting Commission) Radio, November 22, 2006.

———. *From Empire to Republic: Turkish Nationalism and the Armenian Genocide*. London: Zed Books, 2004.

———. *Killing Orders: Talat Pasha's Telegrams and the Armenian Genocide*. London: Palgrave Macmillan, 2018.

———. *A Shameful Act: The Armenian Genocide and the Question of Turkish Responsibility*. London: Constable, 2007.

———. *The Young Turks' Crime against Humanity: The Armenian Genocide and Ethnic Cleansing in the Ottoman Empire*. Princeton, NJ: Princeton University Press, 2012.

Akın, Yiğit. "The Ottoman Home Front During World War I: Everyday Politics, Society, and Culture." PhD diss., Department of History, Ohio State University, 2011.

———. *When the War Came Home: The Ottomans' Great War and the Devastation of an Empire*. Palo Alto, CA: Stanford University Press, 2018.

Akmeşe, Handan Nezir. *The Birth of Modern Turkey: The Ottoman Military and the March to World War I*. London: I. B. Tauris, 2005.

Aksakal, Mustafa. *The Ottoman Road to War in 1914: The Ottoman Empire and the First World War*. Cambridge: Cambridge University Press, 2008.

Aksan, Virginia H. *Ottoman Wars, 1700–1870: An Empire Besieged*. London: Pearson Longman, 2007.

———. *Ottomans and Europeans: Contacts and Conflict*. Istanbul: Isis Press, 2004.

Aktar, Ayhan. "Debating the Armenian Massacres in the Last Ottoman Parliament November–December 1918." *History Workshop* 64, no. 1 (2007):241–270.

Allen, W. E. D., and Paul Muratoff. *Caucasian Battlefields: A History of the Wars on the Turco-Caucasian Border, 1828–1921*. Cambridge: Cambridge University Press, 1953.

Almond, Mark. "The Forgotten Fascist Roots of Humanitarian Intervention: 100 Years of Bombing Libya." *Counterpunch*, April 5, 2011.

Alparslan Teoman. *Sarikamiş*. Istanbul: Kamer Yayınları, 2014.

Altstadt, Audrey L. *The Azerbaijani Turks: Power and Identity under Russian Rule*. Stanford, CA: Hoover Institution Press, 1992.

Ambrosius, Lloyd E. "Wilsonian Diplomacy and Armenia: The Limits of Power and Ideology." In *America and the Armenian Genocide of 1915*, edited by Jay Winter, 113–145. Cambridge: Cambridge University Press, 2003.

Amzi-Erdoğdular, Leyla. "Afterlife of Empire: Muslim-Ottoman Relations in Habsburg Bosnia Herzegovina, 1878–1914." PhD diss., Department of Middle Eastern, South Asian, and African Studies, Columbia University, 2013.

Annual Register. London: Longmans, Green, 1896 and 1897.

Antonius, George. *The Arab Awakening: The Story of the Arab National Movement*. London: Hamish Hamilton, 1938.

Anzerlioğlu, Yonca. "The Revolts of Nestorian Christians Against the Ottoman Empire and the Republic of Turkey." *Muslim World* 100, no. 1 (2010):45–59.

The Arab Bulletin: Bulletin of the Arab Bureau in Cairo 1916–1919. 4 vols. Oxford: Archive Editions, 1986.

Arşiv Belgeleriyle Ermeni Faaliyetleri/Armenian Activities in the Archive Documents; vols. 1–2, *2005*; vols. 3–6, *2006*; vol. 7, *2007*; vol. 8, *2008*. Ankara: Genel Kurmay Basin Evi.

Arslanian, Artin H. "Dunsterville's Adventures: A Reappraisal." *International Journal of Middle East Studies* 12, no. 2 (1980):199–216.

Ashmead Bartlett, Ellis. *The Battlefields of Thessaly: With Personal Experiences in Turkey and Greece* (London: John Murray, 1897). Facsimile edition: British Library Historical Print Editions, n.d.

———. *With the Turks in Thrace*. New York: Doran, 1913.

Ataman, Halil. *Harp ve Esaret: Doğu Cephesi'nden Sibiriya'ya* [War and Captivity: From the Eastern Front to Siberia]. Istanbul: Türkiye Iş Bankası Kültür Yayınları, 2014.

Atamian, Sarkis. *The Armenian Community: The Historical Development of a Social and Ideological Conflict*. New York: Philosophical Library, 1955.

Ataöv, Türkayya, ed. *The Armenians in the Late Ottoman Period*. Ankara: Türk Tarih Kurumu, 2001.

Atılgan, İnanç, and Garabet Moumdjian, eds. *Archival Documents of the Viennese Armenian-Turkish Platform*. Klagenfurt/Celovec: Wieser, 2009.

"The Atrocities in Armenia." *The Times*, May 8, 1895.

Audeh, Nabeel. "The Ideological Uses of History and the Young Turks as a Problem for Historical Interpretation: Considerations of Class, Race, and Empire in British Foreign Office Attitudes Towards the Young Turks, 1908–1918." PhD diss., Georgetown University, 1990.

Autheman, André. *The Imperial Ottoman Bank*. Istanbul: Ottoman Bank Archives and Research Centre, 2002.

Barchard, David. "The Fearless and Self-Reliant Servant: The Life and Career of Sir Alfred Biliotti (1833–1915), an Italian Levantine in British Service." *SMEA* (Studi miceni ed egeo-anatolici) 48 (2006):5–53.

Bardakçı, Murat. *Talat Paşa'nın Evrak-ı Metrukesi* [Talat Paşa's Forgotten Papers]. Istanbul: Everest Yayınları, 2008.

Barkey, Karen. *Empire of Difference: The Ottomans in Comparative Perspective*. Cambridge: Cambridge University Press, 2008.

Barton, James L. *The Christian Approach to Islam*. Boston: Pilgrim Press, 1918.

Baş, Mehmet Fatih. "War Losses (Ottoman Empire/Middle East)." International Encyclopedia of the First World War. https://encyclopedia.1914-1918-online .net/article/war_losses_ottoman_empiremiddle_east.

Başak, Tolga. *British Documents on Armenian Question (1912–1913)*, edited by Yavuz Aslan. Ankara: Avrasya İncelemeleri Merkezi, 2018.

Bayraktoglu, Sena. "Development of Railways in the Ottoman Empire and Turkey." Master's thesis, Atatürk Institute, Boğaziçi University, 1995.

Bean, C. E. W. *The Story of Anzac*. vol. 2. Sydney: Angus and Robertson, 1924.

Beehler, Commodore W. H. *The History of the Italian-Turkish War, September 29, 1911 to October 18, 1912*. Annapolis, MD: Reprinted from proceedings of the United States Naval Institute with additions, 1913.

Bernières, Louis de. *Birds Without Wings*. New York: Knopf, 2004.

Berridge, G. R. ed. *Tilkidom and the Ottoman Empire: The Letters of Gerald Fitzmaurice to George Lloyd, 1906–1915*. Istanbul: Isis Press, 2008.

Beşikci, Mehmet. "Between Voluntarism and Resistance: The Ottoman Mobilization of Manpower in the First World War." PhD diss., Department of History, Boğaziçi University, 2009. Reprint, Leiden: Brill, 2012.

Binark, İsmet, ed. *Archive Documents about the Atrocities and Genocide Inflicted upon Turks by Armenians*. Ankara: Grand National Assembly of Turkey, 2002.

Birdal, Murat. *The Political Economy of the Ottoman Public Debt: Insolvency and European Control in the Late Nineteenth Century*. London: I. B. Tauris, 2010.

Bjornlund, Matthias. "The 1914 Cleansing of Aegean Greeks as a Case of Violent Turkification." *Journal of Genocide Research* 10, no. 1 (2008):41–58.

Black, H. "Korematsu v. United States, 323 U.S. 214 (1944), Supreme Court, Opinion of the Court." Ithaca, NY: Cornell Law School, Legal Information Institute. https://www.law.cornell.edu/supremecourt/text/323/214.

Blowitz, Henry de. *My Memoirs*. London: Edward Arnold, 1903.

Bloxham, Donald. "The Armenian Genocide of 1915–1916: Cumulative Radicalization and the Development of a Destruction Policy." *Past and Present* 181 (November 2003):141–192.

———. *The Great Game of Genocide: Imperialism, Nationalism, and the Destruction of the Ottoman Armenians*. Oxford: Oxford University Press, 2005.

Bodger, Alan. "Russia and the End of the Ottoman Empire." In *The Great Powers and the End of the Ottoman Empire*, edited by Marian Kent, 76–110. London: Allen and Unwin, 1984.

Bosworth, R. J. B. "Italy and the End of the Ottoman Empire." In *The Great Powers and the End of the Ottoman Empire*, edited by Marian Kent, 52–75. London: Allen and Unwin, 1984.

Boyar, Ebru. *Ottomans, Turks and the Balkans: Empire Lost, Relations Altered*. London: I. B. Tauris, 2007.

Brown, Carroll N., and Theodore P. Ion. *Persecutions of the Greeks in Turkey Since the Beginning of the European War*. New York: American Hellenic Society and Oxford University Press, 1918.

Bruinessen, Martin van. *Agha, Shaikh and State: The Social and Political Structure of Kurdistan*. London: Zed Books, 1992.

———. *Kurdish Ethno-Nationalism Versus Nation-Building States*. Istanbul: Isis Press, 2000.

———. *Mullas, Sufis, and Heretics: The Role of Religion in Kurdish Society: Collected Articles*. Istanbul: Isis Press, 2000.

———. "The Sadate Nehri or Gilanizade of Central Kurdistan." In *Mullas, Sufis, and Heretics: The Role of Religion in Kurdish Society: Collected Articles*, by Martin van Bruinessen. Istanbul: Isis Press, 2000.

Bryce, James, and Arnold Toynbee. *The Treatment of Armenians in the Ottoman Empire, 1915–1916: Documents Presented to Viscount Grey of Fallodon, Secretary of State for Foreign Affairs, by Viscount Bryce*. London: His Majesty's Stationery Office, 1916.

Bulmuş, Birsen. *Plague, Quarantines and Geopolitics in the Ottoman Empire*. Edinburgh: Edinburgh University Press, 2012.

Carnegie Endowment for International Peace. *Report of the International Commission to Inquire into the Causes and Conduct of the Balkan Wars*. Washington, D.C: Carnegie Endowment, 1914. Republished as *The Other Balkan Wars: A 1913 Carnegie Endowment Inquiry in Retrospect, with a New Introduction and Reflections on the Present Conflict by George F. Kennan*. Washington, D.C: Carnegie Endowment, 1993.

"Caucasus. Turkey in the First World War." www.turkeyswar.com/campasigns /caucasus.html.

Çelik, Hüseyin. "The 1915 Armenian Revolt in Van: Eyewitness Testimony." In *The Armenians in the Late Ottoman Period*, edited by Türkayya Ataöv, 87–108. Ankara: Türk Tarih Kurumu, Ankara, 2001.

Çiçek, Kemal. *The Adana Incidents of 1909 Revisited*. Ankara: Türk Tarih Kurumu, 2011.

———. *The Great War and the Forced Migration of Armenians*. Belfast: Athol Books, 2012.

Çilingir, Sedat. "Lloyd George and the Dissolution of the Ottoman Empire." PhD diss., Department of History, Middle East Technical University, Ankara, 2007.

Clogg, Richard. *Politics and the Academy: Arnold Toynbee and the Koraes Chair*. London: Frank Cass, 1986.

Creelman, James. "The Red Terror on the Cilician Plain: How the Moslem Frenzy Started by the Foolish Talk of a Christian Priest Spread Far Beyond Adana." *New York Times*, August 29, 1909.

Dadrian, Vahakn. *Histoire du génocide Arménien*. Paris: Stock, 1999.

———. "The Naim-Andonian Documents on the World War I Destruction of the Ottoman Armenians: The Anatomy of a Genocide." *International Journal of Middle East Studies* 18, no. 3 (1986):311–360.

———. "The Secret Young Turk-Ittihadist Conference and the Decision for the World War I Genocide of the Armenians." *Holocaust and Genocide Studies* 7, no. 2 (1993):173–201.

Daleziou, Eleftheria. "Britain and the Greek-Turkish War and Settlement of 1919–1923: The Pursuit of Security by 'Proxy' in Western Asia Minor." PhD diss., University of Glasgow, 2002.

Davis, Leslie A. *The Slaughterhouse Province: An American Diplomat's Report on the Armenian Genocide, 1915–1917*. New Rochelle, NY: Aristide Caratzas, 1990.

Davison, Roderic H. "The Armenian Crisis, 1912–1914." *American Historical Review* 53 (April 1948):481–505.

———. *Nineteenth Century Ottoman Diplomacy and Reforms*. Istanbul: Isis Press, 1999.

———. *Reform in the Ottoman Empire, 1856–1876*. Princeton: Princeton University Press, 1963.

Delshad, Amin. "Exploring Great Britain's Role in Great Famine in Iran during World War I." Translated by Maryam Aliabadi. 2 parts. Tehran: Islamic Revolution Documentation Centre. www.irdc.ir/en/content/13734/print.aspx, and www.irdc.ir/en/content/1383/print.aspx.

Destani, B., ed. *Ethnic Minorities in the Balkan States, 1860–1971*; vol. 2, *1888– 1914*. Cambridge: Cambridge Archive Editions, 2003.

Dickinson, G. Lowes. *The International Anarchy, 1904–1914*. London: Allen and Unwin, 1926.

Dilan, Hasan, ed. *Fransiz Diplomatik Belgelerinde Ermeni Olayları, 1914–1918.* 4 vols. Ankara: Türk Tarih Kurumu, 2005).

Djemal Pasha. *Memories of a Turkish Statesman, 1913–1919.* New York: George H. Doran, 1922.

"Dr. Ussher Told About Many Atrocities at Siege of Van: Turkish Outrages and Conspiracies by Germans Brought to Light." *Harvard Crimson,* May 3, 1917. www.thecrimson.com/article/1917/5/3/dr-ussher-told-about-many -atrocities.

Duggan, Stephen P. "European Diplomacy and the Balkan Problem." *Political Science Quarterly* 28, no. 1 (March 1913):95–122.

Dündar, Fuat. *Crime of Numbers: The Role of Statistics in the Armenian Question, 1878–1918.* New Brunswick, NJ: Transaction, 2010.

Dunsterville, Major-General L. C. *The Adventures of Dunsterforce.* London: Edward Arnold, 1920.

Durham, M. Edith. *Twenty Years of Balkan Tangle.* London: Allen and Unwin, 1920.

Edib, Halidé. *The Turkish Ordeal: Being the Further Memoirs of Halidé Edib.* New York: Century, 1928.

Einstein, Lewis. *Inside Constantinople: A Diplomatist's Diary During the Dardanelles Expedition April–September 1915.* New York: Dutton, 1918.

Ekıncı, Mehmet Uğur. "The Origins of the 1897 Ottoman-Greek War: A Diplomatic History." Master's thesis, Department of History, Bilkent University, 2006.

Eldem, Edhem. *A History of the Ottoman Bank.* Istanbul: Ottoman Bank Historical Research Centre, 1999.

Emin (Yalman), Ahmed. *Turkey in the World War.* New Haven, CT: Yale University Press, 1930.

Erhan, Çağrı. *Greek Occupation of Izmir and Adjoining Territories: Report of the Inter-Allied Commission of Inquiry (May–September 1919).* SAM Papers no. 2/99. Ankara: Centre for Strategic Research, 1999.

Erickson, Edward J. "The Armenians and Ottoman Military Policy." *War in History* 15 no. 2 (2008):141–167.

———. *Defeat in Detail: The Ottoman Army in the Balkans, 1912–1913.* Westport, CT: Praeger, 2003.

———. *Ordered to Die: A History of the Ottoman Army in the First World War.* Westport, CT: Greenwood Press, 2001.

———. *Ottomans and Armenians: A Study in Counterinsurgency.* New York: Palgrave Macmillan, 2013.

Ermeniler Tarafından Yapilan Katliam Belgeleri, vol. 1, *1914–1919;* vol. 2, *1919–1921.* Ankara: Prime Ministerial State Archives General Directorate, 2001.

Eroğlu, Münevver Güneş. "Armenians in the Ottoman Empire According to Ikdam, 1914–1918." Master's thesis, Department of History, Middle East Technical University, Ankara, 2003.

Eti, Ali Rıza. *Bir Onbaşının Doğu Cephesi Günlüğü, 1914–1915* [The Eastern-Front Diary of a Corporal, 1914–1915], prepared for publication by Gönül Eti. Istanbul: Türkiye İş Bankası Kültür Yayınları, 2016.

Evans, Laurence. *United States Policy and the Partition of Turkey.* Baltimore, MD: Johns Hopkins University Press, 1965.

Evans, Richard J. *The Third Reich in History and Memory.* London: Little, Brown, 2015.

The Famine in Asia Minor: Its History Compiled from the Pages of the "Levant Herald." Istanbul: Isis Press, 1989.

Fawaz, Leila Tarazi. "The Forgotten Soldiers: India and Pakistan in the Great War." *Wilson Quarterly* (Winter 2015): www.wilsonquarterly.com/quarterly /fall-2014-the-great-wars/forgotten-soldiers-india-in-great-war/.

———. *A Land of Aching Hearts: The Middle East in the Great War.* Cambridge, MA: Harvard University Press, 2014.

Findley, Carter Vaughn. *Turkey, Islam, Nationalism, and Modernity: A History, 1789–2007.* New Haven, CT: Yale University Press, 2010.

Ford, Roger. *Eden to Armageddon: World War I in the Middle East.* New York: Pegasus, 2010.

Fotiadis, Konstantin. "The Pontian Genocide: From the Time of the Young Turks to the Advent of Mustafa Kemal." *AHIF Policy Journal* 3 (Winter 2011–12): http:// ahiworld.serverbox.net/AHIFpolicyjournal/pdfs/Volume3Winter/06.pdf.

Fromkin, David. *A Peace to End All Peace: The Fall of the Ottoman Empire and the Creation of the Modern Middle East.* New York: Henry Holt, 1989.

Fulton, L. Bruce. "France and the End of the Ottoman Empire." In *The Great Powers and the End of the Ottoman Empire*, edited by Marian Kent, 141–171. London: Allen and Unwin, 1984.

Gauin, Maxime. "How to Create a Problem of Refugees: The Evacuation of Cilicia by France and the Flow of Armenian Civilians (1921–1922)." *Review of Armenian Studies* 67, no. 5 (2012):67–102.

———. Review Essay, "'Proving' a 'Crime Against Humanity'?" Review of Taner Akçam, *The Young Turks' Crime against Humanity: The Armenian Genocide and Ethnic Cleansing in the Ottoman Empire. Journal of Muslim Minority Affairs* 35, no. 1 (2015):141–157.

Gawrych, George W. *The Young Atatürk: From Ottoman Soldier to Statesman of Turkey.* London: I. B. Tauris, 2013.

Gazal, Rym. "Lebanon's Dark Days of Hunger: The Great Famine of 1915–1918." *The National*, April 15, 2015. www.thenational.ae/world/middle-east /lebanons-dark-days-of-hunger-the-great-famine-of-1915-18.

Gerolymatos, André. *The Balkan Wars: Conquest, Revolution, and Retribution from the Ottoman Era to the Twentieth Century and Beyond.* New York: Basic Books, 2002.

Gibbs, Philip, and Bernard Grant. *Adventures of War with Cross and Crescent.* London: Methuen, 1912.

Gibran, Jean, and Kahlil Gibran. *Kahlil Gibran: His Life and World*. Boston: New York Graphic Society, 1974.

Gingeras, Ryan. *Sorrowful Shores: Violence, Ethnicity, and the End of the Ottoman Empire, 1912–1923*. Oxford: Oxford University Press, 2009.

Gladstone, W. E. *Bulgarian Horrors and the Question of the East*. London: John Murray, 1876.

Glenny, Misha. *The Balkans, 1804–1999: Nationalism, War and the Great Powers*. London: Granta, 2000.

Göçek, Fatma Müge. *Denial of Violence: Ottoman Past, Turkish Present, and Collective Violence against the Armenians, 1789–2009*. Oxford: Oxford University Press, 2015.

Gökay, Bülent. "The Battle for Baku (May–September 1918): A Peculiar Episode in the History of the Caucasus." *Turkish Yearbook* 25 (1995):31–32. www.politics.ankara.edu.tr/yearbookdizin/dosyalar/MMTY/25/2_bulent_gokay.pdf.

Greenwood, Keith M. *Robert College: The American Founders*. Istanbul: Boğaziçi University Press, 2000.

Greek Atrocities in the Vilayet of Smyrna (May to July 1919): Inedited [sic] Documents and Evidence of English and French Officers. Lausanne: Permanent Bureau of the Turkish Congress, 1919.

Grey, Edward (Viscount Grey of Fallodon). *Twenty-Five Years, 1892–1916*. 2 vols. London: Hodder and Stoughton, 1926.

Grey, Jeffrey. *The War with the Ottoman Empire*. Melbourne: Oxford University Press, 2015.

Güçlü, Yücel. *Armenians and the Allies in Cilicia, 1914–1923*. Salt Lake City: University of Utah Press, 2010.

———. "Armenian Events of Adana in 1909 and Cemal Paşa." Paper delivered at the Adana Conference, Turkish Historical Society, Ankara, June 2009.

———. *The Armenian Events of Adana in 1909: Cemal Paşa and Beyond*. Lanham, MD: Hamilton Books, 2018.

———. *The Question of the Sanjak of Alexandretta: A Study in Turkish-French-Syrian Relations*. Ankara: Türk Tarih Kurumu, 2001.

———. Review of *Talaat Pasha: Father of Modern Turkey, Architect of Genocide*, by Hans-Lukas Kieser. *Journal of Muslim Minority Affairs* 38, no. 3 (2018):441–450.

Günaydin, Adem. "The Return and Resettlement of the Relocated Armenians (1918–1920)." Master's thesis in Middle East Studies, Graduate School of Social Sciences, Middle East Technical University, Ankara, 2007.

Gürbüzel, Aslıhan S. "Hamidian Policy in Eastern Anatolia (1878–1890)." Master's thesis, Department of History, Bilkent University, 2008.

Gürün, Kamuran. *The Armenian File: The Myth of Innocence Exposed*. London: Rustem, Weidenfeld and Nicolson, 1985.

Güven, Dilek. "Riots against the Non-Muslims of Turkey: 6/7 September 1955 in the Context of Demographic Engineering." *European Journal of Turkish Studies* 12 (2011):https://ejts.revues.org/4538.

Hadawi, Sami. "Sodomy, Locusts, and Cholera: A Jerusalem Witness." *Jerusalem Quarterly* 53 (Spring 2013):7–27.

Halim Pasha, Said. *L'empire Ottoman et la guerre mondiale*. Istanbul: Isis Press, 2000.

Hall, Richard C. *The Balkan Wars, 1912–1913: Prelude to the First World War*. London: Routledge, 2000.

Hanioğlu, Şükrü M. *A Brief History of the Late Ottoman Empire*. Princeton: Princeton University Press, 2008.

Harbord, James G. *Conditions in the Near East: Report of the American Military Mission to Armenia*. Washington, D.C.: United States Government Printing Office, 1920.

Hasanli, Jamil. "Armenian Volunteers on the Caucasian Front, 1914–1916." *The Caucasus and Globalization* 8, nos. 3–4 (2014):183–201.

Hassanpour, Amir. "Ferment and Fetters in the Study of Kurdish Nationalism." Review of *Kurdish Notables and the Ottoman State: Evolving Identities, Competing Loyalties and Shifting Boundaries*, by Hakan Özoğlu. H-Turk, September 2007. http://www.h-net.org/reviews/showrev.php?id=13540.

Hellenic Army General Staff, Army History Directorate. *A Concise History of the Balkan Wars, 1912–1913*. Athens, 1998.

Heller, Joseph. *British Policy Towards the Ottoman Empire, 1908–1914*. London: Frank Cass, 1983.

Herbert, Aubrey, and Desmond MacCarthy, eds. *Ben Kendim: A Record of Eastern Travel*. London: Hutchinson, 1924.

Herrmann, David G. "The Paralysis of Italian Strategy in the Italian-Turkish War, 1911–1912." *English Historical Review* 104, no.411 (April 1989):332–356.

Houshmatyan of the Armenian Revolutionary Federation Album-Atlas, vol. 1, *Epic Battles, 1890–1914*. Los Angeles: Western United States Control Committee of the Armenian Revolutionary Federation, 2006.

Hovannisian, Richard G. *The Republic of Armenia*. 4 vols. Berkeley: University of California Press, 1971–1996.

Inalcık, Halil. *From Empire to Republic: Essays on Ottoman and Turkish Social History*. Istanbul: Isis Press, 1995.

"In Tripoli after Zanzur, Tanks of Wine for Soldiers at the Front, Cafés Gay as Paris." *New York Times*, October 2, 1912.

Jelavich, Barbara. *History of the Balkans: Twentieth Century,* vol. 2. Cambridge: Cambridge University Press, 1983.

Jessup, Henry W. "The Future of the Ottoman Empire." *Annals of the American Academy of Political and Social Sciences* 84 (July 1919):6–29.

"The Joris Affair." Macquarie University Law School. www.law.mq.edu.au /research/colonial_case_law/colonial_cases/less_developed/constantinople /joris_affair_1906/.

Jwaideh, Wadie. *The Kurdish National Movement: Its Origins and Development*. Syracuse, NY: Syracuse University Press, 2006.

Kaisar, Hilmar. *The Extermination of the Armenians in Diyarbakir*. Istanbul: Bilgi University Press, 2014.

Kansu, Aykut. *Politics in Post-Revolutionary Turkey, 1908–1913*. Leiden: Brill, 2000.

———. *The Revolution of 1908 in Turkey*. Leiden: Brill, 1997.

Karakişla, Yavuz Selim. *Women, War, and Work in the Ottoman Empire: Society for the Employment of Ottoman Muslim Women, 1916–1923*. Istanbul: Ottoman Bank Archives and Research Centre, 2005.

Karpat, Kemal H. *Ottoman Population, 1830–1914: Demographic and Social Characteristics*. Madison, WI: University of Wisconsin Press, 1985.

———. *The Politicization of Islam: Reconstructing Identity, State, Faith, and Community in the Late Ottoman State*. Oxford: Oxford University Press, 2001.

Kasaba, Reşat. *A Moveable Empire: Ottoman Nomads, Migrants, and Refugees*. Seattle: University of Washington Press, 2009.

Kayahan, Ayşe Betül. "My Father Abdülhamit II." *Daily Sabah*, February 26, 2014.

Kayali, Hasan. "Elections and the Electoral Process in the Ottoman Empire, 1876–1919." *International Journal of Middle East Studies* 27, no. 3 (1995):265–286.

Kent, Marian. "Great Britain and the End of the Ottoman Empire, 1900–23." In *The Great Powers and the End of the Ottoman Empire*, edited by Marian Kent, 172–205. London: Allen and Unwin, 1984.

———, ed. *The Great Powers and the End of the Ottoman Empire*. London: Allen and Unwin, 1984.

Kévorkian, Raymond H. *The Armenian Genocide: A Complete History*. London: I. B. Tauris, 2011.

———. *La Cilicie (1909–1921): des massacres d'Adana au mandat Français*. Paris: Revue d'Histoire Arménienne Contemporaine, Bibliothèque Nubar de l'UGAB, 1999.

———. "The Extermination of Ottoman Armenians by the Young Turk Regime (1915–1916)." *SciencesPo. Violence de masse et résistance—réseau de recherche*. https://www.sciencespo.fr/mass-violence-war-massacre-resistance/fr/node/2646.

Khlebof, Twerdo. "War Journal of the Second Russian Fortress Artillery Regiment of Erzeroum from Its Formation until the Recapture of Erzeroum by the Ottoman Army, March 12th, 1918. Translated from the Original Russian Manuscript, 1919." http://louisville.edu/a-s/history/turks/Khlebof%20War%20Journal.pdf.

Kiernan, Ben. *Blood and Soil: A World History of Genocide and Extermination from Sparta to Darfur*. New Haven, CT: Yale University Press, 2007.

Kieser, Hans-Lukas. *A Quest for Belonging: Anatolia Beyond Empire and Nation (19th–20th Centuries)*. Istanbul: Isis Press, 2007.

———. *Talaat Pasha: Father of Modern Turkey, Architect of Genocide*. Princeton, NJ: Princeton University Press, 2018.

Kiliç, Engin. "The Balkan War (1912–1913) and Visions of the Future in Ottoman Turkish Literature." PhD diss., Department of Turkish Studies, University of Leiden, 2015.

Kiliç, Mehmet Firat. "Sheikh Ubaydullah's Movement." Master's thesis, Department of History, Bilkent University, 2003.

Kizilkaya, Emre. "How Did the Ottomans Really Enter World War I?" *Hurriyet Daily News*, August 10, 2015. www.hurriyetdailynews.com/how-did-the -ottomans-really-enter-wwi.aspx?pageID=517&nID=86679&NewsCatID= 550.

Klein, Janet. "Conflict and Collaboration: Rethinking Kurdish-Armenian Relations in the Hamidian Period, 1876–1909." *International Journal of Turkish Studies* 13, nos. 1–2 (July 2007):153–166.

Knaplund, Paul. *Gladstone's Foreign Policy*. New York: Harper, 1935.

Knapp, Grace Higley. *The American Mission at Van: Narrative Printed Privately in the United States by Miss Grace Higley Knapp* (1915).

Kolev, Valery, and Christina Koulouri, eds. *The Balkan Wars*. Thessaloniki: Centre for Democracy and Reconciliation in Southeast Europe, 2000.

Kozelsky, Mara. "Casualties of Conflict: Crimean Tatars during the Crimean War." *Slavic Review* 67, no. 4 (Winter 2008):866–891.

Kundil, Pınar. "The Armenian Question According to *Takvim i-Vekayi*, 1914–1918." Master's thesis, Middle East Technical University, Ankara, September 2003.

Kuneralp, Sinan, ed. *Ottoman Diplomatic Documents on the Origins of World War One: The Final Stage of the Cretan Question, 1899–1913*. Istanbul: Isis Press, 2009.

———, ed. *The Queen's Ambassador to the Sultan: Memoirs of Sir Henry A. Layard's [sic] Constantinople Embassy, 1877–1878*. Istanbul: Isis Press, 2009.

Kuneralp, Sinan, and Gül Tokay, eds. *Ottoman Diplomatic Documents on the Origins of World War One: The Bosnian Annexation Crisis, September 1908–May 1909*. Istanbul: Isis Press, 2009.

———. *Ottoman Diplomatic Documents on the Origins of World War One: The Road to Bulgarian Independence, September 1908–May 1909*. Istanbul: Isis Press, 2008.

"The Landing of Wilhelm II in Tangier, March 31, 1905. Report of Councillor von Schoen, Envoy in the Imperial Suite, to the German Foreign Office." http://wwi.lib.byu.edu/index.php/The_First_Moroccan_Crisis.

Langer, William L. "The 1908 Prelude to the World War." *Foreign Affairs* 7 (July 1929):635–649.

Larcher, M. *La guerre Turque dans la guerre mondiale*. Paris: Etienne Chiron/ Berger Levrault, 1926.

Lemon, Edward J. "Dunsterforce or Dunsterfarce? Re-evaluating the British Mission to Baku, 1918." *First World War Studies* 6, no. 2 (2015):133–149.

Lewy, Guenter. *The Armenian Massacres in Ottoman Turkey: A Disputed Genocide*. Salt Lake City: University of Utah Press, 2005.

————. "Revisiting the Armenian Genocide." *Middle East Quarterly* 12, no. 4 (Fall 2005):3–12.

Libaridian, Gerard J. "What Was Revolutionary about Armenian Revolutionary Parties in the Ottoman Empire?" In *A Question of Genocide: Armenians and Turks at the End of the Ottoman Empire*, edited by Ronald Grigor Suny, Fatma Müge Göçek, and Norman M. Naimark, 82–112. New York: Oxford University Press, 2011.

Lowry, Heath W. *The Story Behind Ambassador Morgenthau's Story*. Istanbul: Isis Press, 1990.

Lütem, Ömer Engin, and Alpogan Yiğit. "Review of *Killing Orders: Talat Pasha's Telegrams and the Armenian Genocide*, by Taner Akçam." *Review of Armenian Studies* 37 (2018):45–82.

Lyall, Sir Alfred. *The Life of the Marquis of Dufferin and Ava*. London: Thomas Nelson, 1905.

Lynch, H. F. B. *Armenia: Travels and Studies*. 2 vols. Beirut: Khayats, 1965.

Mason, Major Kenneth. "Central Kurdistan." *Geographical Journal* 54, no. 6 (December 1919):329–342.

MacGahan, J. A. "The Turkish Atrocities in Bulgaria: Horrible Scenes at Batak." *Daily News*, August 22, 1876.

————. *The Turkish Atrocities in Bulgaria: Letters of the Special Commissioner of the "Daily News" J. A. MacGahan Esq., with an Introduction and Mr. Schuyler's Preliminary Report*. London: Bradbury, Agnew, 1876.

MacMillan, Margaret. *Peacemakers: Six Months that Changed the World*. London: John Murray, 2003.

Mango, Andrew. *Atatürk*. London: John Murray, 2004.

Ma'oz, Moshe. *Ottoman Reform in Syria and Palestine, 1840–1861*. Oxford: Oxford University Press, 1968.

Marsot, Afaf Lutfi al-Sayyid. *Egypt in the Reign of Muhammad Ali*. Cambridge: Cambridge University Press, 1984.

Matossian, Bedross Der. "From Bloodless Revolution to Bloody Counterrevolution: The Adana Massacres of 1909." *Genocide Studies and Prevention* 6, no. 2, 2011:152–173.

Mazower, Mark. *Salonica, City of Ghosts: Christians, Muslims and Jews, 1430–1950*. London: HarperCollins, 2004.

McCarthy, Justin. *Death and Exile: The Ethnic Cleansing of Ottoman Muslims, 1821–1922*. Princeton, NJ: Darwin Press, 1995.

————. *Muslims and Minorities: The Population of Ottoman Anatolia and the End of the Empire*. New York: New York University Press, 1983.

————. "Muslims in Ottoman Europe: Population from 1800 to 1912." In *Population History of the Middle East and the Balkans*, edited by Justin McCarthy, 137–154. Istanbul: Isis Press, 2002.

————. *1912–13 Balkan Wars: Death and Forced Exile of Ottoman Muslims, an Annotated Map*. Washington, D.C.: Turkish Coalition of America, n.d.

www.tc-america.org/issues-information/turkish/history/1912-1913-balkan-wars
-death-and-forced-exile-of-ottoman-muslims-an-annotated-map-755.htm.

———. *Population History of the Middle East and the Balkans.* Istanbul: Isis
Press, 2002.

———. "The Population of the Ottoman Armenians." In *The Armenians in the
Late Ottoman Period,* edited by Türkayya Ataöv, 65–85. Ankara: Turkish
Historical Society, 2001.

———. "The Report of Niles and Sutherland: An American Investigation of
Eastern Anatolia after World War I." In 11 Türk Tarih Kongresi, Ankara, September 5–9, 1990, 1809–1853. Ankara: Türk Tarih Kurumu, 1994: Also
http://louisville.edu/a-s/history/turks/Niles_and_Sutherland.pdf.

———. *Turks and Armenians: Nationalism and Conflict in the Ottoman Empire.*
Madison, WI: Turko-Tatar Press, 2015.

McCarthy, Justin, Esat Arslan, Cemalettin Taşkiran, and Ömer Turan. *The Armenian Rebellion at Van.* Salt Lake City: University of Utah Press, 2006.

McCarthy, Justin, Ömer Turan, and Cemalettin Taşkiran. *Sasun: The History of
an 1890s Armenian Revolt.* Salt Lake City: University of Utah Press, 2014.

McDowall, David. *A Modern History of the Kurds.* London: I. B. Tauris, 2004.

McGilvary, Margaret. *The Dawn of a New Era in Syria.* New York: Fleming H.
Revell, 1920. Reprint, Reading, UK: Garnet Publishing, 2001.

McMeekin, Sean. *The Russian Origins of the First World War.* Cambridge, MA:
Belknap Press of Harvard University Press, 2011.

Meiselas, Susan. *Kurdistan in the Shadow of History.* 2nd ed., with historical
introductions and a new postscript by Martin van Bruinessen. Chicago: University of Chicago Press, 2008.

Melson, Robert. *Revolution and Genocide: On the Origins of the Armenian Genocide and the Holocaust.* Chicago: University of Chicago Press, 1992.

Metinsoy, Elif Mahir. *Ottoman Women during World War I: Everyday Experiences, Politics, and Conflict.* Cambridge: Cambridge University Press, 2017.

"Military Revises Death Toll of 1914 Caucasus Operation." *Hurriyet Daily News,*
December 28, 2007. www.hurriyetdailynews.com/military-revises-death-toll
-of-1914-caucasus-operation-2007-12.

Mojzes, Paul. *Balkan Genocides: Holocaust and Ethnic Cleansing in the Twentieth
Century.* Lanham, MD: Rowman and Littlefield, 2011.

———. *Ethnic Cleansing in the Balkans: Why Did It Happen and Could It Happen Again?* Cicero Foundation, Great Debate Papers 13/04. Rosemont, PA:
Rosemont College, 2013.

Molyneux-Seel. "A Journey in Dersim." *Geographical Journal* 44, no. 1 (July
1914):49–68.

Moumdjian, Garabet K. "Cilicia under French Mandate, 1918–1921. Armenian
Aspirations, Turkish Intrigues, and French Double Standards." www
.armenianlegacy.eu/en/historical-lcontribution/256-cilicia-under-french
-mandate-1918-1921.html.

———. "Rebels with a Cause: Armenian-Macedonian Relations and Their Bulgarian Connection, 1895–1913." In *War and Nationalism: The Balkan Wars*, edited by M. Hakan Yavuz and Isa Blumi, 132–175. Salt Lake City: University of Utah Press, 2012.

Murgul, Yalçin. "Baku Expedition of 1917–1918: A Study of the Ottoman Policy Towards the Caucasus." Master's thesis, Department of History, Bilkent University, 2007.

Mutlu, Servet. "Late Ottoman Population and Its Ethnic Distribution." *Nüfüsbilim Dergisi/Turkish Journal of Population Studies* 25 (2003):3–38.

Nalbandian, Louise. *The Armenian Revolutionary Movement: The Development of Armenian Political Parties through the Nineteenth Century*. Berkeley: University of California Press, 1963.

Nielsen, Fred K. *American-Turkish Claims Settlement: Under the Agreement of December 24, 1923, and Supplemental Agreements between the United States and Turkey, Opinions and Reports*. Washington, D.C.: United States Government Printing Office, 1937.

Oğuz, Çiğdem. "Prostitution (Ottoman Empire)." International Encyclopedia of the First World War. https://encyclopedia.1914-1918online.net/article/prostitution_ottoman_empire.

Önal, Sami. *Tuğgeneral Ziya Yergök'un Anıları—Sarıkamış'tan Esarete (1915–1920)* [Brigadier General Ziya Yergök's Memoirs—from Sarikamiş to Captivity (1915–1920)]. Istanbul: Remzi Kitabevi, 2007.

Önol, Onur. "The Armenian National Movement in Tsarist Russia (1870–1906)." Master's thesis, Department of International Relations, Bilkent University, 2009.

Orel, Şinasi, and Süreyya Yuca. *The Talat Pasha Telegrams: Historical Fact or Armenian Fiction?* Lefkoşa, CY: Rustem, 1983.

O'Shea, Maria T. *Trapped Between the Map and Reality: Geography and Perceptions of Kurdistan*. New York: Routledge, 2004.

Ottoman Archives, Yildiz Collection, the Armenian Question. 3 vols. Istanbul: Historical Research Foundation, 1989.

Özdemir, Hikmet. *The Ottoman Army, 1914–1918: Disease and Death on the Battlefield*. Salt Lake City: University of Utah Press, 2008.

Özdemir, Hikmet, and Yusuf Sarınay, eds. *Türk-Ermeni Ihtilafı Belgeler/Turkish-Armenian Conflict Documents*, no. 126. Ankara: TBMM Kultur, Sanat ve Yayın Kurulu Yayınları, n.d.

Özil, Ayşe. *Orthodox Christians in the Late Ottoman Empire: A Study of Communal Relations in Anatolia*. New York: Routledge, 2013.

Pamuk, Şevket. *A Monetary History of the Ottoman Empire*. Cambridge: Cambridge University Press, 2000.

———. "Prices in the Ottoman Empire, 1469–1914." *International Journal of Middle East Studies* 36, no. 3 (2004):451–468.

Patterson, Lieut. Col. J. H. *With the Judeans in the Palestine Campaign*. New York: Macmillan, 1922.

Pears, Edwin. *Forty Years in Constantinople: The Recollections of Sir Edwin Pears, 1873–1915.* London: H. Jenkins, 1916.

Penrose, Stephen B. *That They May Have Life: The Story of the American University of Beirut, 1886–1941.* New York: American University of Beirut, 1941.

Perinçek, Mehmet. *150 Belgede Ermeni Meselesi: Rus Devlet Arşivlerinden.* Istanbul: Kırmızı Kedi Yayinevi, 2012.

Poincaré, Raymond. *The Origins of the War.* London: Cassell, 1922.

Polatel, Mehmet. "Turkish State Formation and the Distribution of the Armenian Abandoned Properties from the Ottoman Empire to the Republic of Turkey (1915–1930)." Master's thesis, Comparative Studies in History and Society, Koç University, 2009.

Presland, John. *Deedes Bey: A Study of Sir Wyndham Deedes, 1883–1923.* London: Macmillan, 1942.

Quataert, Donald. "Agricultural Trends and Government Policy in Ottoman Anatolia, 1800–1914." In *Workers, Peasants, and Economic Change in the Ottoman Empire, 1730–1914,* edited by Donald Quataert, 17–30. Istanbul: Isis Press, 1993.

———. *Manufacturing and Technology Transfer in the Ottoman Empire, 1800–1914.* Istanbul: Isis Press, 1992.

Ramsaur, Ernest Edmondson, Jr. *The Young Turks: Prelude to the Revolution of 1908.* Beirut: Khayats, 1965.

Rankin, Reginald. *The Inner History of the Balkan War.* London: Constable, 1914.

Reconstruction in Turkey: A Series of Reports Compiled for the American Committee for Armenian and Syrian Relief. New York, 1918.

"Report of Leslie A. Davis, American consul, formerly at Harput, Turkey, on the work of the American consulate at Harput since the beginning of the present war." London and Cleveland, OH: Gomidas Institute, Armenian Genocide Documentation Project. www.gomidas.org.

Report of the Near East Relief for the Year Ending December 31, 1921. Presented by Mr. Lodge. Washington, D.C.: United States Government Printing Office, 1922.

Reynolds, Michael A. "Buffers Not Brethren: Young Turk Military Policy in the First World War and the Myth of Panturanism." *Past and Present* 203 (May 2009):137–179.

———. "The Ends of Empire: Imperial Collapse and the Trajectory of Kurdish Nationalism." 31–48. http://src-h.slav.hokudai.ac.jp/rp/publications/no14/14-04_Reynolds.pdf.

———. "The Ottoman-Russian Struggle for Eastern Anatolia and the Caucasus, 1908–1918: Identity, Ideology, and the Geopolitics of World Order." PhD diss., Department of Near Eastern Studies, Princeton University, November 2003.

———. *Shattering Empires: The Clash and Collapse of the Ottoman and Russian Empires, 1908–1918.* Cambridge: Cambridge University Press, 2011.

Robertson, Geoffrey. *An Inconvenient Genocide: Who Now Remembers the Armenians?* London: Biteback, 2014.

Rodogno, Davide. *Against Massacre: Humanitarian Interventions in the Ottoman Empire, 1815–1914.* Princeton, NJ: Princeton University Press, 2012.

Roosevelt, Kermit. *War in the Garden of Eden.* New York: Scribner's, 1919.

Rustem Bey, Ahmed. *The World War and the Turco-Armenian Question.* Translated by Stephen Cambron. Berne: Staempfli, n.d.

Safi, Polat. "The Ottoman Special Organization—*Teşkilat-i Mahsusa*: A Historical Assessment with Particular Reference to Its Operations Against British Occupied Egypt (1914–1916)." Master's thesis, Department of History, Bilkent University, 2006.

Sahara, Tetsuya. *What Happened in Adana in 1909? Conflicting Armenian and Turkish Views.* Istanbul: Isis Press, 2013.

Şahin, Erman. Review Essay, "A Critical Scrutiny of Akçam's Version of History and the Armenian Genocide." *Muslim Minority Affairs* 28, no. 2 (August 2008):303–319.

Salibi, Kamal, and Yusuf K. Khoury, eds. *The Missionary Herald: Reports from Ottoman Syria, 1819–1870.* 5 vols. Amman: Royal Institute for Interfaith Studies, 1995.

Salt, Jeremy. *Imperialism, Evangelism and the Ottoman Armenians, 1878–1896.* London: Frank Cass, 1993.

———. "The Narrative Gap in Ottoman Armenian History." *Middle Eastern Studies* 39, no. 1 (2003):19–36.

Sanjian, Avedis K. *The Armenian Communities in Syria under Ottoman Dominion.* Cambridge, MA: Harvard University Press, 1965.

Sarafian, Ara. *Talaat Pasha's Report on the Armenian Genocide, 1917.* London: Gomidas Institute, 2011.

Sarınay, Yusuf. "Arşiv Belgelerine Göre 1909 Adana Ermeni Olaylari." In *1909 Adana Olaylari/Makaleler: The Adana Incidents of 1909 Revisited*, edited by Kemal Çicek, 79. Ankara: Türk Tarih Kurumu, 2011.

———. "The Relocation (*Tehcir*) of Armenians and the Trials of 1915–16." *Middle East Critique* 20, no. 3 (2011):299–315.

———. "What Happened on April 24, 1915? The Circular of April 24, 1915, and the Arrest of Armenian Committee Members in Istanbul." *International Journal of Turkish Studies* 14, nos. 1–2 (2008):75–101.

Şaşmaz, Musa. *British Policy and the Application of Reforms for the Armenians in Eastern Anatolia, 1877–1897.* Ankara: Türk Tarih Kurumu, 2000.

Schatkowski Schilcher, Linda. "The Famine of 1915–1918 in Greater Syria." In *Problems of the Middle East in Historical Perspective: Essays in Honor of Albert Hourani*, edited by J. P. Spagnolo, 229–250. Reading, UK: Ithaca, 1993.

Schreiner, George Abel. *From Berlin to Baghdad: Behind the Scenes in the Near East.* New York: Harper, 1918.

Schulze-Tanielian, Melanie. "Disease and Public Health (Ottoman Empire/ Middle East)." International Encyclopedia of the First World War. https:// encyclopedia.1914-1918-online.net/article/disease_and_public_health _ottoman_empiremiddle_east.

Serdar, Mehmet Törehan. *Istiklale Açilan Ilk Kapı: Bitlis (Işgali ve Kurtuluşu)* [The First Door Opening to Independence: Bitlis (Its Occupation and Liberation)]. Bitlis: Bitlis Valiliği Kültür Yayınları, 2017.

Sertçelik, Sayit. *The Emergence of the Armenian Question 1678–1914.* Ankara: Grand National Assembly Publications, 2010.

Seton-Watson, R. W. *Disraeli, Gladstone, and the Eastern Question: A Study in Diplomacy and Party Politics.* New York: Macmillan, 1935.

Şeyhun, Ahmet. *Said Halim Pasha: Ottoman Statesman. Islamist Thinker, 1865– 1921.* Istanbul: Isis Press, 2003.

Shaw, Stanford J. *From Empire to Republic: The Turkish War of National Liberation, 1918–1923: A Documentary Study.* 6 vols. Ankara: Türk Tarih Kurumu, 2000.

———. "The Nineteenth-Century Ottoman Tax Reforms and Revenue System." *International Journal of Middle East Studies* 6, no.4 (October 1975):421–459.

———. "The Origins of Representative Government in the Ottoman Empire: An Introduction to the Provincial Councils of 1839–1876." In *Studies in Ottoman and Turkish History: Life with the Ottomans,* by Stanford J. Shaw, 183–231. Istanbul: Isis Press, 2000.

———. *The Ottoman Empire in World War I.* 2 vols. Ankara: Türk Tarih Kurumu, 2006.

———. "A Promise of Reform: Two Complimentary [*sic*] Documents." *International Journal of Middle Eastern Studies* 4, no. 3 (1973):359–365.

———. *Studies in Ottoman and Turkish History: Life with the Ottomans.* Istanbul: Isis Press, 2000.

Şimşir, Bilal N., ed. *British Documents on Ottoman Armenians*; vol. 1, *1856–1880*; vol. 2, *1880–1890*; vol. 3, *1891–1895*; vol. 4, *1895.* Ankara: Türk Tarih Kurumu, 1989–2000.

———. *Ege Sorunu Belgeler, 1912–1913/Aegean Question Documents, 1912–1913.* 2 vols. Ankara: Türk Tarih Kurumu, 1989.

———. *Ingiliz Belgelerinde Atatürk, 1919–1938/British Documents on Atatürk, 1919–1938*; vol. 1, *April 1919–March 1920*; vol. 2, *April–December 1920*; vol. 3, *January–September 1921*; vol. 4, *October 1921–October 1922*; vol. 5, *October 1922–December 1925.* Ankara: Türk Tarih Kurumu, 1991–2005.

———, ed. *Rumeli'den Türk Göçleri/Turkish Emigrations from the Balkans.* 3 vols. Ankara: Türk Tarih Kurumu, 1989.

Smith, Michael Llewellyn. *Ionian Vision: Greece in Asia Minor, 1919–1922.* London: Hurst, 1973.

Smyth, Sean Patrick. "From Smoking Gun to Muddied Waters: The Alleged Telegraph of Bahaeddin Şakir." Ankara: AVIM (Avrasya İncelemeleri Merkezi)

Center for Eurasian Studies, June 5, 2017. www.avim.org.tr/en/Analiz/from
-smoking-gun-to-muddied-waters-the-alleged-telegraph-of-bahaeddin-sakir.

Solmaz, Gürsoy. *İkinci Kuşak Anılarında Erzurum ve Civarinda Ermeni Zulmü*
[Armenian Oppression in Erzurum and its Surroundings According to
Second-Generation Memoirs]. *Yeni Turkiye* 60 (2014):1–29.

Sonyel, Salahi Ramadan. *The Ottoman Armenians: Victims of Great Power Diplomacy.* London: Rustem, 1987.

———. *Minorities and the Destruction of the Ottoman Empire.* Ankara: Türk
Tarih Kurumu, 1993.

Stavrianos, L. S. *The Balkans since 1453.* New York: Holt, Rinehart, and Winston,
1966.

Stuermer, Harry. *Two War Years in Constantinople: Sketches of German and
Young Turkish Ethics and Politics.* New York: George H. Doran, 1917.

Tamari, Salim. *Year of the Locust: A Soldier's Diary and the Erasure of Palestine's
Ottoman Past.* Berkeley: University of California Press, 2011.

Tomaszewski, Katherine Fiona. "Triple Entente or Unholy Alliance? Official
Russian Attitudes Towards Britain and France 1906–1914." PhD diss.,
Department of History, McMaster University, 1992.

Tonguç, Faik. *Birinci Dünya Savaşı'nda Bir Yedeksubayın Anıları* [A Reserve
Officer's Memoirs of the First World War]. Istanbul: Türkiye İş Bankası
Kültür Yayınları, 2015.

Townshend, Charles Vere Ferrers. *My Campaign in Mesopotamia.* 2 vols. New
York: James A. McCann, 1920.

Toynbee, Arnold J. *The Western Question in Greece and Turkey: A Study in the
Contact of Civilisations.* London: Constable, 1922.

Trotsky, Leon. *The War Correspondence of Leon Trotsky: The Balkan Wars, 1912–
13.* Translated by Brian Pearce; edited by George Weissman and Duncan
Williams. New York: Pathfinder, 1991.

Trumpener, Ulrich. "Germany and the End of the Ottoman Empire." In
The Great Powers and the End of the Ottoman Empire, edited by Marian
Kent, 111–140. London: Allen and Unwin, 1984.

Tulun, Teoman Ertugrul. *The Pontus Narrative and Hate Speech.* Ankara: Centre
for Eurasian Studies, 2017.

Turan, Ömer. "Turkish Migration from Bulgaria." In *Forced Ethnic Migration on
[sic] the Balkans: Consequences and Rebuilding of Societies: Conference Proceedings, February 22–23.* Edited by Ekaterina Popov and Marko Hajdinjak,
77–93. Sofia: IMIR, and Tokyo: Meiji University, 2005

Turkyilmaz, Yektan, "Rethinking Genocide: Violence and Victimhood in Eastern Anatolia, 1913–1915." PhD diss., Department of Cultural Anthropology,
Duke University, 2011.

Türkdoğan Uysal, Berna. *The Displacement: Turkish-Armenian Relations Since
1915.* Istanbul: IQ Culture and Arts, 2009.

Türkeş, Mustafa. *The Centenary of the Balkan Wars (1912–1913): Contested
Stances.* 2 vols. Ankara: Türk Tarih Kurumu, 2014.

UK Parliamentary Papers (London).

———. Turkey No. 1 (1921), *Reports on Atrocities in the Districts of Yalova and Guemlik and in the Ismid Peninsula.* Cmd. 1478. London: His Majesty's Stationery Office.

———. Turkey No. 8 (1881), *Reports on the Administration of Justice in the Civil, Criminal and Commercial Courts in the Various Provinces of the Ottoman Empire.* Cmd. 3008. London: His Majesty's Stationery Office.

Ulrichsen, Kristin Coates. *The First World War in the Middle East.* London: Hurst, 2014.

United States National Archives (USNA). Despatches from United States Ministers to Turkey, 1808–1906.

Ussher, Clarence D. *An American Missionary in Turkey: A Narrative of Adventures in Peace and in War*; Grace H. Knapp collaborating. Boston: Houghton Mifflin, 1917.

Üngör, Uğur Umit. "Young Turk Social Engineering: Mass Violence and the Nation State in Eastern Turkey, 1913–1950." PhD diss., University of Amsterdam, 2009.

Üngör, Uğur Umit, and Mehmet Polatel. *Confiscation and Destruction: The Young Turk Seizure of Armenian Property.* London: Continuum, 2011.

Vambéry, Arminius. *The Story of My Struggles.* London: Thomas Nelson, n.d.

———. Vambéry Papers, 1889–1911 (FO 800/32–33). Public Record Office: Kew, UK.

van Bruinessen, Martin. See Bruinessen, Martin van.

Verheij, Jelle. "'Les frères de terre et d'eau': sur le rôle des Kurdes dans les massacres Arméniens de 1894–1896." In *Islam des Kurdes*, edited by Martin van Bruinessen and Joyce Blau, 225–276. *Les annales de l'autre Islam* 5, special issue. Paris: INALCO/ERISM, 1998.

Vogel, Robert. "Noel Buxton: The 'Trouble-Maker' and His Papers." *Fontanus* 3 (1990):131–150. www.Fontanus.mcgill.ca/article/viewFile/37/38.

Wagner, Lieutenant Hermenegild. *With the Victorious Bulgarians.* London: Constable, 1913.

Wasti, Syed Tanvir. "The 1912–13 Balkan Wars and the Siege of Edirne." *Middle Eastern Studies* 40, no. 4 (2004):59–78.

Waterfield, Gordon. *Layard of Nineveh.* London: John Murray, 1963.

Wichhart, Stefanie. "The 1915 Locust Plague in Palestine." *Jerusalem Quarterly* 56–57 (Winter 2013/Spring 2014):29–39.

Wilhelm II. *The Kaiser's Memoirs.* New York: Harper, 1922.

Wilson, Sir Arnold T. *Loyalties: Mesopotamia, a Personal and Historical Record*; vol. 2, *1917–1920.* London: Oxford University Press, 1931.

Woods, Randall B. "The Miss Stone Affair." *American Heritage* 32, issue 6 (October/November 1981). www.americanheritahe.com/content/miss-stone-affair.

Yanıkdağ, Yücel. *Healing the Nation: Prisoners of War, Nationalism and Medicine in Turkey, 1914–1939.* Edinburgh: Edinburgh University Press, 2013.

Yasamee, F. A. K. *Ottoman Diplomacy: Abdülhamid II and the Great Powers, 1878–1888.* Istanbul: Isis Press, 1996.

Yavuz, M. Hakan, and Isa Blumi, eds. *War and Nationalism: The Balkan Wars, 1912–1913, and Their Sociopolitical Implications*. Salt Lake City: University of Utah Press, 2013.

Yeats-Brown, F. *Golden Horn: Plot and Counterplot in Turkey, 1908–1918, as Seen "from the Inside" by a Prisoner of War*. London: Victor Gollancz, 1932.

Zayas, Alfred de. "The Istanbul Pogrom of 6–7 September 1955, in the Light of International Law." *Genocide Studies and Prevention* 2, no. 2 (2007):137–154.

Zeidner, Robert F. *The Tricolor over the Taurus: The French in Cilicia and Vicinity, 1918–1922*. Ankara: Türk Tarih Kurumu, 2005.

Zürcher, Erik-Jan. "Between Death and Desertion: The Experience of the Ottoman Soldier in World War I." *Turcica* 28 (1996):235–258.

———. "The Ottoman Conscription System in Theory and Practice 1844–1918." *International Review of Social History* 43, no. 3 (1998):437–449.

———. *Turkey: A Modern History*. London: I. B. Tauris, 2004.

Index

Aaronsohn, Alexander, 205
'Abd al-Qadir ibn Muhi al-Din Mustafa al-Hasani al-Jaza'iri, 38
Abdülaziz (sultan, 1861–1876), 72
Abdülhamit II (sultan, 1876–1909): after Bosnia-Herzegovina uprising, 89; and Armenian uprisings, 62–63, 67; and attack on Imperial Ottoman Bank, 68–69; attempted assassination of, 176–77; authority over empire, 28–29; and British interference, 56; context of empire at accession of, 37–38; disillusionment with the British, 71–72, 73; establishment of Public Debt Administration, 21; and European reforms, 43, 49, 67; and European threats to Ottoman identity, 54; exile of, 102–3; fears and suspicions of, 40, 73, 76; Lady Somerset's description of, 335n57; modernizing reforms of, 40, 76; and Mürzsteg agreement, 97–98; as negotiator, 75; personality characteristics of, 74–75; reception of Grand Duke Nicholas, 88; views on Armenians, 39, 67, 68, 332n10; relationship with Germany, 96; relationship with Kurds, 29–30, 41–42, 46; relationship with Tsar Alexander III, 70–71

Abdülmecid II (caliph), 313, 380n3
Abdul the Assassin. See Abdülhamit II
Abu al-Huda al-Sayyadi, 100
Adana: Armenian destruction in, 281; battle in, 103–6, 341n24, 341n30, 341n37
Aegean islands and coastal area: disposition of, 121, 147, 148, 149–51, 265, 312, 348n77; Greek atrocities on, 164; Greek capture of, 144–45; Greek-Turk relationships in, 378n55; Muslim backlash on, 164–66; naval control of, 173. See also Izmir
Aerhenthal, Alois von, 108
Afyonkarahisar-Kutahya, battle of, 297
agriculture: effect of blockades on, 206–7; effect of locust plague on, 205; war's effects on, 199–200, 213
Ahmet Izzet Paşa, 145
air power in war, 117, 136
Aivas Baba, capture of, 146
Ajay, Nicholas Z., 204
Akçam, Taner, 233, 242, 246, 367n22
Akın, Yiğit, 5, 200, 203, 320
Aksakal, Mustafa, 162–63
Albania after Balkan wars, *xiii*
Albanians: and faith in Ottoman Empire, 80, 83, 109; and

403

Empire, 2, 320, 325–26. *See also* atrocities; disease, spread of; famine of 1873–1874; massacres; refugees; relocation of Armenians
humanitarian prejudice, 38–40, 65
Hunchakian Revolutionary Movement, 57, 59–61
Hunchaks, 103, 235

Ibrahim Paşa, 36
Ileri on Greek and Armenian returnees, 316
Imperial Bank of Persia, 269
Imperial Ottoman Bank, 18, 19, 21, 66, 68–69, 118, 139, 329n34
IMRO. *See* Internal Macedonian Revolutionary Organization (IMRO)
Industrial Revolution, 14
Inönü, battles of (1921), 297, 305
Inter-Allied Commission of Inquiry, 299–300, 301–2, 303, 377–78n54
Internal Macedonian Revolutionary Organization (IMRO), 97, 137–38, 139, 346n42
Iran, 17, 41., 71, 96, 99, 111, 211–12
Iraq, 3, 263, 264, 312
Ishkhan (Nikoghayos Mikaelian), 229
al-Islam, Shaykh, 102, 121, 314
Islamophobia, 354n3
Ismail Kemal, 102
Ismet, Inönü, 316
Istanbul (Constantinople): compared to provinces, 23; influx and plight of refugees in, 86–87, 88–89, 153–54, 161, 162; modernization efforts in, 23; occupation of, 263, 297; persecution of Greeks in, 311–12; pollution in, 191; as prize beyond compare, 133; relief committees in, 87–88
Istanbul Treaty of (1913), 167
Italy: and Aegean islands, 150–51; agreement with Turks, 274; attack on Ottoman forts, 118; costs of

war, 117–18, 343n8; Ethiopian defeat of, 109–10; harassment and attacks off Yemen and on Beirut, 118; and Izmir, 291; rising power of, 95; and share of spoils, 264–65, 293–94, 371n1; territorial ambitions of, 110, 113, 149; war against Ottomans, 6, 120, 343n15. *See also* European powers; Libya
Ittidal (Moderation, newspaper), 104
Izmir: Britain's designation of Greek control of, 293; Greek administration of, 296; Greek landing at, 294, 375n35; Italian and Greek desires for, 291–92; modernization efforts in, 23–24; populations of, 291, 375n19; revolt of "Turks" in, 295; Turkish revenge against Greeks in, 298–99, 377n54
Izvolsky, Alexander, 108
Izzet Paşa, 100

Jackh, Ernest, 242
Jacobite Assyrians, 48
jandarma: accusations against, 247, 251; Armenian attacks on, 218, 225, 228; behavior toward citizens, 65; Christians recruited for, 97; collectors of primary source material, 255; conflict with Armenians, 67; defense of northeastern towns, 226; exploitation of civilians, 200–201; recruited for war, 179; in tax protests, 94–95; treatment of population by, 234
Japan, 71, 98, 110, 354n56
Jerusalem, 187–88, 353n35
Jews, 48, 101, 127, 258–59
John 8:32, 322
Joris, Charles Edouard, 176–77

Kamil Paşa, 31, 101–2, 125, 126, 145
Kanayan, Drastamat (Dro), 223, 230

taxation reforms, 27–28, 36

Tehlirian, Soghomon, 368n35

Ter-Harutyunyan, Garegin (Garegin Nzhdeh), 134, 345n22

Terzibashian, Avetis, 231

Teşkilat i-Mahsusa (Special Organization), 171, 188–89, 220, 245–46, 369n41, 369n46

Tewfiq Paşa, 313

Texas (American ship), sinking of, 120

Thomson, Basil, 368n35

Thrace: buffer state in, 379n80; division of, 144–45, 148; exodus from, 152, 154, 161–64; Muslim backlash in, 164, 165–66; in Ottoman military planning, 141; refugees from, 126; as target of Balkan states, 106; Turkish control over, 308

The Times on Joris's trial outcome, 177

Tolstoy, Alexandra, 230

Tonguç, Faik, 197–98

Townshend, Charles, 181, 186–87, 353n52

Toynbee, Arnold, 249, 253, 301, 303, 304, 379n70; "The War of Extermination," 304–5

Transcaucasian Democratic Federative Republic, 269

travel and transportation of goods in eastern provinces, 24

Triple Alliance (Germany, Austria-Hungary, and Italy), 96, 172

Triple Entente (Britain, France, and Russia), 96, 371n1

Trotsky, Leon, 134, 142

Troupes Françaises du Levant, 279

Trowbridge, T. C. (missionary), 106

truth in historical accounts, 322

Tunisia, 114

Turjman, Ihsan, 180, 208–9

Turkey: abolition of sultanate and caliphate, 313, 314–15; borders drawn for, 312–13; establishment of, 309; and ethnicity of population, 91; Greek communities in, 310–11; map of, *xvi*; modern population of Thrace and Istanbul area, 312; and Mosul, 264; property rights for returnees, 316–17; rejuvenation of population of, 317–18; resurrection of, 293; return of relocated populations authorized by, 315–16; victory over Greeks, 297. *See also* Kemal, Mustafa (Atatürk)

Turkification, 167

Turkish identity, 318

Turkish military archives (ATASE), 323

Turkish nationalist movement, 2–3, 266, 268, 275, 277, 280, 281, 313

Turkish (later Iraq) Petroleum Company, 313

Turkish voices in historical accounts, 322–23

Turkyilmaz, Yektan, 230, 231–32, 363n60

Ubaydullah, Shaykh, 36, 41, 43–44, 332n16

United States. *See* Wilson, Woodrow

uprisings. *See* Armenian uprisings; Bosnia-Herzegovina; Bulgaria; Greek uprising; Kurds; Macedonia; Syrian Christians, uprising of

Üsküb (Skopje), 109, 143, 157,

Ussher, Clarence D., 232–33, 234, 363n74

Vaham, Midiciyan, 323–24

Vahdeti, Derviş, 102, 103

vali (governors) in governmental hierarchy, 31

Vambéry, Arminius, 28, 75, 337n93

Van, battle for: abandonment of city of Van after, 233–34, 362n55; conflicting accounts of, 232–34;